REWRITING THE JEW

Nostalgia Jewishness is a lullaby for old men

gumming soaked white bread.

J. GLADSTEIN, *modernist Yiddish poet*

CONTRAVERSIONS

JEWS AND OTHER DIFFERENCES

DANIEL BOYARIN,

CHANA KRONFELD, AND

NAOMI SEIDMAN, EDITORS

The task of "The Science of Judaism"

is to give Judaism a decent burial.

MORITZ STEINSCHNEIDER,

founder of nineteenth-century

philological Jewish Studies

REWRITING THE JEW

ASSIMILATION NARRATIVES IN
THE RUSSIAN EMPIRE

GABRIELLA SAFRAN

Stanford University Press • *Stanford, California*

Stanford University Press
Stanford, California

© 2000 by the Board of Trustees of the Leland Stanford Junior University

Printed in the United States of America

Library of Congress Cataloging-in-Publication Data

Safran, Gabriella
    Rewriting the Jew : assimilation narratives in the Russian empire /
Gabriella Safran.
        p.   cm.
    Based on the doctoral dissertation: Narratives of Jewish acculturation
in the Russian empire, 1998.
    Includes bibliographical references (p.) and index.
    ISBN 0-8047-3830-0 (alk. paper)
        1. Jews—Cultural assimilation—Russia.   2. Jews—Russia—Identity.
3. Acculturation—Russia.   4. Russia—Ethnic relations.   5. Jews—Russia—
Public opinion.   6. Public opinion—Russia.   I. Title.
DS148 .S34   2000
305.892'4047—dc21   00-057322
                                                                        Rev.

Original printing 2000
Last figure below indicates year of this printing:
09   08   07   06   05   04   03   02   01   00

Typeset by James P. Brommer in 10/14.5 Minion and Copperplate

For Michael and Eva

and for my parents

ACKNOWLEDGMENTS

I WOULD HAVE BEEN unable to write this book without help from many quarters. My first debt is to the Princeton University Slavic Department for my training in Russian literature. In particular, my adviser, Caryl Emerson, has inspired me—along with many others—by her example as a scholar and a teacher. I gratefully acknowledge the hours she put into reading the endless drafts of my "fat" chapters. Michael Wachtel, Ellen Chances, and Laura Engelstein, after reading my entire dissertation, asked me the questions that provoked my revisions. My fellow graduate students at Princeton created a collegial atmosphere, and Nicole Monnier helped me understand the critical debates of the 1860s. The unfailing generosity of my Princeton colleagues taught me to send out chapter drafts, believing that other Slavists would be equally generous with their advice: indeed, I received significant help from Herbert Eagle, Judith Deutsch Kornblatt, Kenneth Lantz, Olga Maiorova, Hugh McLean, Inès Müller de Morogues, Kathleen Parthé, Gary Rosenshield, and the Delaware Valley Seminar of Russian Historians.

Princeton also gave me the resources to foray beyond Russian literature. I am grateful for the time that Charles Townsend spent teaching me Polish and for the enthusiasm that Katarzyna Jerzak brought to our discussions of Polish literature. My work on Orzeszkowa relies on the foundations they gave me, just as it has benefited from the suggestions of Monika Adamczyk-Garbowska, Jacqueline Glomski, Madeline Levine, Barbara Milewski, Eugenia Prokop-Janiec, and Michael Steinlauf. Professors within and outside of the Slavic department, especially Froma Zeitlin, encouraged my interest in Jewish studies. Discussions with Barbara Mann and the members of the Jewish Studies Graduate Reading Group at Princeton improved my Chekhov chapter. Other scholars—Carole Balin, Israel Bartal, Sidra Ezrahi, Kathryn Hellerstein, Olga Litvak, Shimon Markish, Benjamin Nathans, and Anita Norich—helped me first train myself in Russian Jewish history and literature and then formulate my thoughts on Bogrov. In addition, Adi Livnat read through some Hebrew sources with me, and Mia Rollman, Bogrov's great-great-granddaughter, shared recollections and pictures of her family.

Several institutions made my work possible. I am grateful for my Princeton graduate fellowship, two summer grants from the Princeton Council on Regional Studies, a Fellowship in the Humanities from the Mellon Foundation, and a dissertation fellowship from the Social Science Research Council. Librarians at the St. Petersburg Public Library, especially Nikita Eliseev, and archivists at Pushkin House and the St. Petersburg history archive were most helpful. In Philadelphia, the Center for Judaic Studies at the University of Pennsylvania offered a haven, and Sol Cohen shared his expertise in Yiddish and Talmud. I thank the people at Penn, Nicholas Breyfogle, Rebecca Kobrin, Abby Schrader, and especially Bonnie Gordon, who gave me their advice as well as their friendship.

Friends in St. Petersburg made my research there more fun and more productive. I am grateful to the "leskovedy," Irina Vladimirovna Stoliarova, Svetlana Ipatova, and especially Svetlana Zenkevich; to Dmitry Eliashevich and Valery Dymshits at the Jewish University; and to Marina and Alesha as well as Nikita Eliseev, Dmitry and Elena Panchenko, and my "family" on Liteinyi—Julia, Maya, and both Sashas.

Since coming to Stanford, I have enjoyed the warm support of new colleagues. Gregory Freidin, Joseph Frank, Monika Greenleaf, and Lazar Fleishman each read my work and gave me very different kinds of advice, all of it useful, and Steven Zipperstein helped me refine my presentation of Russian Jewish history. Helen Tartar at Stanford University Press welcomed my manuscript, Nathan MacBrien guided it (and me) patiently through the production process, and Andrew Frisardi edited it expertly. My assistant, Marian Bassett, helped me answer his questions. Andrew Wachtel, who read the manuscript for the Press, helped me improve it, and Daniel Boyarin gave it a place in the Contraversions series. At the end, Desne Border did a fantastic job proofreading it.

Finally, I need to thank my parents, William and Marian Safran, who encouraged me to follow them into professions whose primary rewards are other than monetary; my in-laws, who fed me wonderful meals; my husband, Michael Kahan, my most patient audience, who listened to all my ideas, read all my drafts, and even learned Russian during a semester in Petersburg; and our daughter, Eva Hannah, whose imminent arrival accelerated the writing process considerably. In countless ways, these last two have made it possible for me to finish this project, and they have made it worthwhile.

CONTENTS

ILLUSTRATIONS

A NOTE ON TRANSLITERATION

In the Notes and Bibliography, I use the Library of Congress transliteration system. In the text, I modify it slightly. For personal names ending in *ii* or *yi*, I use *y* instead; for example, "Dmitry Merezhkovsky." I give the names of famous people in the forms that will make them most recognizable to readers, such as Tynjanov (not Tynianov), Tolstoy (not Tolstoi), and Isaac Babel (not Isaak Babel'). The names of tsars are anglicized (Nicholas I, Alexander II); most others are not. Bogrov's narrator, Yisroel (Srul'), is spelled Srul.

"A well-designed story has no reason to be like real life; life tries as hard as it can to be like a well-designed story."

—ISAAC BABEL

INTRODUCTION

Portrait of a Jewish General

In 1893, the Russian Jewish artist Moisei Maimon painted *Marrany* [The Marranos] (Figure 1). The title refers to Iberian Jews who submitted to pressure to convert to Christianity in the fifteenth century but continued to observe Jewish rituals in secret. The large painting depicts a family of Marranos discovered by members of the Inquisition while celebrating Passover. Thirty years later, the artist wrote that he had been inspired to paint this scene by an event in his own life, when he was a young art student. He had seen the St. Petersburg police interrupt a Passover Seder where he was a guest, demand to see everyone's documents, determine that his hosts were lacking the necessary residence papers, and then expel the Jewish family from the city. Maimon reported that a short time after this happened, he saw the distinguished-looking, white-bearded, retired artillery general, Arnoldi, at a reception and convinced him to pose as the Marrano family's patriarch. Later, the general told the perceptive artist that he too was a kind of secret Jew: he had been a cantonist, a Jewish boy recruited into the tsarist army, and, like many cantonists, had been forcibly baptized.[1]

Maimon's anecdote reveals his preoccupation with the image of the assimilated and the converted Jew. The story about the retired general's past as a cantonist implicitly contrasts two literary genres, or two possibilities for narrating his life. In telling this tale, Maimon suggests that the story of the Jew as general (the rags-to-riches tale of successful assimilation) offers little more than irrelevant fiction when set against the story of centuries-old Jewish persecution (in which the same scenes of apprehension, torture, and expulsion are endlessly repeated in different settings), epitomized by the Inquisition and the fate of the Marranos. The prototype here is the biblical flight from Egypt commemorated in the Passover service. In a larger sense, Maimon's story questions the very possibility of Jewish assimilation, indicating that even while some individual Jews might believe that they have adapted to gentile culture and been accepted by non-Jewish society, their "true" identity will always be apparent to themselves, to their fellow Jews, and to the non-Jews who will never forgive them for it.

General Arnoldi—if we take Maimon's word that he existed—was probably born in the 1820s. He would have been between twelve and eighteen, therefore (the age at which boys were officially taken as cantonists, though some were taken even younger), in the 1830s or 1840s, when the policy of cantonism was in effect, and he would have been in his late sixties or seventies when he posed for Maimon's painting. Over his lifetime, the general might have heard the tsarist government and spokespeople for gentile society and the Russian Jewish intelligentsia argue for a wide and shifting array of attitudes toward Jewish assimilation. Historians once argued that by the early 1890s, when Arnoldi met Maimon, the regime, the non-Jewish intelligentsia (especially on the Right), and most Jews had abandoned their earlier certainty that adoption of non-Jewish culture was a feasible or an advisable goal for the Russian Empire's Jews. Today, some of these assertions are coming under attack, as scholars point out that Jews continued to acculturate throughout the imperial period.[2]

Then as now, discussion of Jewish assimilation has evoked a number of the dichotomies that have given rise to debates about national and individual identity over the last two centuries. Proponents of self-reform, including the acculturation of members of minority groups to majority cultures, have been guided by the ideas of the European Enlightenment, seeing humans as capable of improving themselves through education and thereby conforming with a universal ideal of culture. Opponents of assimilation have opposed the Enlightenment view with a Romantic one that values some authentic essence of individuals and nations—whether identified as "spirit" or "blood"—over education, folk culture over classical models, and

FIGURE 1. Moisei Maimon, *Marrany* [The Marranos]. This print was made from the original oil painting, completed in 1893, which was later lost. Reproduced from *Evreiskaia entsiklopediia* (St. Petersburg: Brokgauz-Efron, n.d. [c. 1910]; facs. ed., Moscow: Terra, 1991), vol. 10, pp. 657–58.

the particular national past over the vision of a transnational future. This argument has raged especially strongly in Eastern Europe, among Russians, Poles, Jews, and others, all simultaneously drawn to and suspicious of the cultural standards of Western Europe.

The wider conflict that Maimon reveals in narrating General Arnoldi's life and the fact that both kinds of stories are equally legitimate—and equally one-sided, fictional, and problematic—speak to the heterogeneity of Russian imperial and Jewish cultures and populations. In the 1890s, the anecdote suggests, it was not possible for a person in Arnoldi's position to be "simply Russian" any more than he could be "simply Jewish." His example reveals contentiousness and uncertainty surrounding national, religious, and personal identity, especially that of the Russian Empire's growing Jewish population. Similar conflicts are often evident in historical accounts, journalistic debates, legislation and policies concerning Jews, and in fiction and memoirs, whether by Jews, Russians, Poles, or others, that describe individual cases of Jewish acculturation or conversion to Christianity. Like Maimon's tale about his painting, such texts tend implicitly to juxtapose two or more narrative prototypes, each with its own explanations of the Jew's past, present, and likely future.

In this book, I focus on some especially interesting texts of this sort, written in the 1870s and 1880s, a period of accelerating Jewish acculturation and loud debate over the "Jewish question." The four authors—one Russian-speaking Jew, Grigory Bogrov; one Polish Catholic, Eliza Orzeszkowa; and two Eastern Orthodox Russians, Nikolai Leskov and Anton Chekhov—hesitate among a range of attitudes, some closer to Enlightenment ideals, some more Romantic, and some transcending this dichotomy. Their characters are neither the imagined perfect assimilator—the true convert, the self who has been rewritten to the complete satisfaction of all concerned—nor the imagined "original" self, resistant to all change. Each writer examines Jewish self-transformation while raising questions about the reformability of personality in general. Close readings of these texts against their historical and generic backgrounds will clarify, I hope, some of the relations between fictional plots and constructions of an individual's loyalties.

Narratives about Jewish acculturation in the nineteenth-century Russian Empire contain images and terms that are not easy for the modern reader to understand. They use concepts such as "Jew," "Pole," or "convert," which developed out of specific literary traditions and specific realities. In this analysis, I explain and then employ the words my subjects used to describe the world they knew. One crucial term from this book's title must be defined right away. "Assimilation" refers to learning Russian or Polish, wearing European clothes, and pursuing a secular education. For some, it even means converting to Christianity. This is self-consciously ideological behavior, arising from the belief that Jews can and should be accepted into Russian or Polish society, provided they meet certain criteria. I distinguish "assimilation" from "acculturation," by which I mean engaging in similar practices without an explicit ideological motivation.[3] As I define them, the assimilator explained, "I am behaving like a Russian because that is what we Jews need to do now," while the acculturator insisted, "I cut my beard and started reading Russian novels because I felt like it." In various ways, the texts I examine question the beliefs behind assimilation, even as they depict the reality of acculturation.

For the most part, these texts do not acknowledge that for some Jews in the Russian Empire, acculturation itself and its connection to a Jew's acceptance by gentiles may not have been a subject of enormous anxiety and doubt. Some Jews may well have converted to Russian Orthodoxy, Protestantism, or Catholicism, possibly married Russians or Poles, and felt themselves at home in gentile society, whether upper- or lower-class. Others, especially in the 1890s and later, may have retained their Jewish identity legally, but embraced Russian or Polish culture and harbored little if any sense of themselves as distinctively Jewish. Many more adopted certain elements of non-Jewish culture—dress, language, reading materials, educational and professional goals—without displaying a tremendous amount of concern about whether this behavior would make them into Russians or Poles. Well-known biographies present examples of all kinds. Among converts, while the university professor Daniel Khvol'son was widely known to Jews and non-Jews as an insincere convert and a passionate defender of Jews, the former cantonist Viktor Nikitin converted to Orthodoxy and made a successful career as a highly-placed government official, apparently accepted in spite of his origins.[4] Among the acculturated but unconverted, one might point out Sholem Aleikhem, who spoke Russian at home with his family but was famous precisely as a Jewish cultural figure and a Yiddish writer; in the 1890s and the first decade of the 1900s, even while he wrote his best-known depictions of Russian Jewish life, a cadre of highly acculturated Jewish liberals and radicals would waste few words on their Jewishness.[5] Keeping the complexity of this picture in mind, I make use of memoirs and historiography that touch on the actual experience of acculturating Jews in the Russian Empire. My primary concern, though, is the literary texts that represent (and misrepresent) that experience.

This book is intended as an introduction to and preliminary reading of works that Western critics have largely ignored. The long books by Bogrov and Orzeszkowa were widely read in their own day, but they, like their writers, are little known today to English readers. The stories and the play by Leskov and Chekhov, more canonical writers, have been seen as minor pieces on obscure topics. The breadth of my scope—encompassing writers of three ethnicities and religions, who lived in four parts of the Russian Empire and wrote in two languages—has, of course, limited the depth to which I could examine each one. My hope is that the novelty of my juxtaposition, as well as that of the material itself, justifies its limitations, and that other scholars will be inspired to pick up where I have left off.

Jews in the Russian Empire

In each of the partitions of Poland (in 1772, 1793, and 1795), the Russian Empire absorbed portions of land on Poland's eastern borders, along with the resident Poles, Jews, and people who might be identified today as Belorussians, Lithuanians, or Ukrainians. After the final partition, the European part of the empire contained at least three hundred thousand Jews, and by the end of the nineteenth century (according to the 1897 census) they numbered over five million. Laws prohibiting most Jews from moving east into historically Russian lands ensured that over 90 percent of the Jewish population lived in the empire's fifteen westernmost provinces [*gubernii*] and in the Kingdom of Poland.[6] The Jews in this "Pale of Settlement" differed religiously, linguistically, and culturally from their Christian neighbors: their native language was Yiddish rather than Polish, Ukrainian, Lithuanian, or Belorussian, and they ate different food and had different occupations; also, custom and imperial law guaranteed that Jews and non-Jews did not intermarry (except after the conversion of the Jewish partner to Christianity; Christians were not permitted to convert to Judaism).

During the first eighty years of the nineteenth century, the Russian imperial government made occasional efforts to encourage these Jews to abandon their distinctive language, dress, and lifestyle, rewarding those who converted to Christianity. Tsar Nicholas I (r. 1825–55) pursued these goals most consistently, notoriously by enforcing cantonism on Jews (as on other groups that the government wished to reform, such as Old Believers and the children of exiled criminals). Enlisting Jewish boys in the army not only ensured that they would learn Russian but also, as in the case of Maimon's story of his model Arnoldi, could lead to their baptism. The next tsar, Alexander II (r. 1855–81), ended cantonism in 1856 and then promulgated laws permitting Jewish merchants of the first guild and those with higher education to leave the pale. Thus, by 1870, although the majority of Jews in the empire retained their traditions in the pale, a significant Jewish population, often wealthier, more acculturated, and fluent in Russian, appeared in some central Russian cities. At the same time, a class of Polonized Jews emerged in Warsaw, in the Polish Kingdom. Jews in some cities within the pale, such as Odessa, adopted certain elements of European culture. The growth of the Jewish population in the pale and the arrival of acculturated Jews in the cities contributed to an interest in the popular press in the status and the future of the empire's Jews, the "Jewish question" or "Jewish problem." Meanwhile, acculturated Jewish characters appeared in fiction by non-Jewish Russian and Polish writers, and a number of Jews began to write works in Russian and Polish.

The reign of Alexander II ended with his assassination in 1881 and the accession of Alexander III. The involvement of a Jewish woman in the assassination plot was seemingly one of the factors that triggered a wave of pogroms in 1881 and 1882. Historians have often seen 1881, the midpoint in the period I consider, as a natural division in Russian Jewish history; they have argued that Alexander III abandoned his predecessor's interest in encouraging Jewish acculturation in favor of policies aimed at reducing both the physical Jewish presence in Russia and Jewish participation in the imperial culture and economy. Indeed, he and his advisors blamed the Jews themselves for the pogroms, accusing them of exploiting the peasantry and thereby provoking resentment that "naturally" erupted in violence. After the pogroms, regulations forbidding most Jews from living outside the pale were enforced more strictly, and the infamous Temporary Laws, passed in 1882 and in effect until the 1917 revolution, further restricted Jewish residence and economic activity even within the pale. Nicholas Ignatiev, minister of the interior under Alexander III, reportedly announced that his brutal policies were intended to encourage the Jews to emigrate: "The Western frontier is open for the Jews."[7]

The decades following the pogroms saw the acceleration of the process of change already under way among the Jews of the Russian Empire. An average of 15,500 Jews per year emigrated to the United States (the most popular destination) in 1881–90 (and by 1903–7, the numbers would reach an average of 96,400 per year).[8] Others responded to the repressive legislation of the 1880s and 1890s by changing their legal status: while an average of 441 Jews per year had converted to Russian Orthodoxy in the 1860s, by the period from 1891 to 1897 the figure was 1,020 per year.[9] At the same time, the opinion (which some Jewish intellectuals had already expressed in the 1870s) that assimilation could never lead to an improved life for Jews under the current government became more widespread; it would serve as an axiom for the rising Zionist and Jewish socialist movements. Nonetheless, a growing number of the Jews in the Russian Empire continued to acculturate (but not convert), as evidenced by the efforts they made from the early 1880s to make sure that their children learned Russian.[10]

The attitudes of the Russian intelligentsia toward the Jews during the 1880s and later reveal similar contradictions. Government spokespeople and most intellectuals agreed that the pogroms expressed the legitimate wrath of the peasants against the Jewish tavern keepers, shopkeepers, and money-lenders who impoverished them and turned them into alcoholics [spaivali]. Some Russians went further, to imagine the Jewish danger in occult or racializing terms.[11] A few freethinkers, though, disagreed, and by the 1890s a number of Russian intellectuals would criticize the government's approach to the pogroms and the entire Jewish question as inconsistent, unfair, and deeply counterproductive.[12]

Regulating Acculturation

Throughout the imperial period, legislation regulating Jews, Jewish communities, and converts from Judaism illustrated and enacted the tsars' changing and contradictory policies and conceptions. Jews were defined as adherents to the Jewish religion; a notation on their passports under "religion" revealed their status. After the 1772 partition, Jews were initially recognized as Russian subjects. However, in 1835 they were reassigned to the category of aliens [inorodtsy], which, except in the case of the Jews, was a race-based category that could not be changed through conversion.[13] Jews, though, by converting, took on a new legal identity as Russian Orthodox [pravoslavnyi] and were eventually subsumed into the estate [soslovie] they selected (probably the merchantry [*kupechestvo*] or the townspeople [*mechshanstvo*]).[14] They would then enjoy the rights and fulfill the obligations of all other members of that estate.

Legal disabilities imposed on the Jews throughout the nineteenth century, and those eventually imposed specifically on assimilated Jews, converts, and persons "of Jewish descent," reflect the government's conflicting motivations. On the one hand, as we know, the government wished to encourage Jews not only to convert to Russian Orthodoxy but also to abandon their "barbaric" language and lifestyle. An 1899 handbook to laws affecting Jews mentions fines imposed on Jews who wore traditional Jewish clothes and on women who followed the custom of shaving their heads after marriage.[15] On the other hand, imperial legislation reflected an attempt to create and sustain an order that reinforced traditional power structures within groups, allowed for clear distinctions between different estates, and discouraged individuals from transgressing these boundaries, which were not just categorical, but geographical. A notation on the passport indicated whether or not a Jew belonged to one of the categories allowed to leave the pale. The authorities were aware that sufficient acculturation, while it might be laudable in itself, could also make it easier for a Jew to break the law, as evidenced by a specific paragraph in the Digest of Laws [Svod zakonov], published in 1832, that condemned Jews who tried to disguise themselves as non-Jews in order to circumvent residence restrictions. In a state that made changing one's name difficult for anyone, a specific statute insisted that Jews "living under Christian names in territories where they are not allowed to reside" were to be sent back to the pale "immediately."[16]

Laws passed at different times, whether meant to restrict or encourage acculturation, tended to remain on the books throughout the nineteenth century. Even the 1903 Criminal Code [Ugolovnoe ulozhenie] (approved but never enacted), which represented an effort to modernize and reform the imperial legal system, criminalized the efforts of Jews trying to appear to be non-Jews.[17] It reaffirmed the validity of older laws, including a punishment (a fine of up to three hundred rubles) for any person who gave the authorities a false name, and as a separate point indicated that this applied to a Jew "guilty of without authorization [*samovol'no*] changing the first or last name according to which he is listed in the record of births."[18] Singling it out in this way indicates a disapproval of the common practice among Jews in the Russian cities of abandoning their Yiddish names in favor of similar-sounding

Russian ones: Velvel (the nickname for Wolf) for Vladimir, Sora (or Sarah) for Sophia. Jews who did this were not necessarily attempting to hide a criminal past behind a false name, or even residing illegally outside the pale. They might merely have wanted to appear less Jewish to the non-Jews whom they met professionally or socially. By defining as illegal not only Jews' attempts to evade residence restrictions but also their efforts not to stand out, the law betrays the urge to make certain that Jews were identifiable as Jews.[19]

Other laws worked to create greater distance between converts to Christianity and unconverted Jews. Police regulations required a Russian Orthodox cleric who baptized a Jew immediately to inform the local authorities of the convert's new name and status.[20] The law not only created clear distinctions between converts and unconverted Jews but also proposed reinforcing these distinctions by geographical separation. Should there be a number of new converts to Orthodoxy living among non-Christians, and should the converts appear threatened by "temptations related to the conduct of religious services"—meaning, presumably, should they appear likely to backslide into the practices of their former religion—then the authorities should encourage them to move elsewhere.[21] The desire to physically separate Jews and Jewish converts led, by the 1880s, to absurd situations. As quotas were imposed on the number of Jewish students in institutes of higher education, some Jewish youths began to convert to Orthodoxy in order to study (although conversion for this reason appears to have been rarer in the Russian than in the Austro-Hungarian empire, and much less common in the 1880s than it would become after 1906).[22] A journalist reported in 1889 that due to laws preventing Christian students from living with Jews, one such converted Jewish student in Kiev was no longer allowed to live with his own parents.[23] Based on this affair, the journalist argued that Jews should be given equal rights to enroll in schools. Such a change, he implied, would threaten the stability of the state less than official denial of the authority of parents over children, a precedent that could be adopted based on the Kiev case.

By the final decades of the nineteenth century, the simultaneous encouragement of Jewish acculturation and conversion on the one hand and reinforcement of state security and stability on the other seemed more and more difficult. As Hans Rogger details, suspicion arose in many quarters that not only Russian-speaking Jews but even converts from Judaism to Russian Orthodoxy should not be allowed to occupy key positions in the government apparatus and the army.[24] Pointing out that most conservatives nonetheless favored Russification policies for the Jews and noting the numbers of converts from Judaism who were accepted by Russian society, another historian denies that this hostility stemmed from racism, that is, from the belief that a single "drop of Jewish blood" was enough to define a person as unreliable. Rather, he argues, it resulted from the widespread conviction that Jews were converting to Orthodoxy for reasons of convenience and profit, and that therefore they should not be seen as loyal Christians or loyal citizens of the Russian Empire.[25]

Popular culture mirrored official suspicions of Jewish acculturation. Throughout the nineteenth century, terms for converts in Russian [*vykrest*] and Polish [*meches*] sounded just as derogatory as the Yiddish word for an apostate [*meshumed*].[26] Russian folk sayings expressed a specific hostility toward converts: "A baptized Jew [is like an] enemy who's been subdued, a wolf who's been fed" [*Zhid kreshchenyi, nedrug pomirenyi, da volk kormlenyi*].[27] Clearly, the implication is that the transformation is only temporary. In addition, images of Jews in cheap popular literature during the period showed them to be less likely than other non-Russians to convert to Orthodoxy and be assimilated among the loyal subjects of the empire.[28] The evidence of such sources as well as an increasing number of legal distinctions between "born" Russian Orthodox and converts from Judaism indicate that some people were imagining Russian Orthodoxy—and the legal identity that it marked—as an inherited rather than a voluntarily adoptable status. Their doubts suggest that they reacted to the actual increase in Jewish acculturation and conversion with an attempt to reinforce traditional ethnic-religious identities more firmly.

Indeed, even while the Russian Orthodox Church continued to welcome converts, skepticism about invalid or "false" conversions arose among intellectuals in relation to a number of religious minorities, not only the Jews. A well-known jurist, the author of the commentary to a 1901 nongovernmental edition of the 1885 Criminal Code, defined a category of invalid converts that would include many formerly Jewish cantonists. Because they had been forced to accept baptism as children, he observed, they should be considered never to have been baptized at all and should be allowed to return to their former legal status as Jews[29] (they were permitted to do so in 1905). His caveat and the 1905 legislation show that by the beginning of the twentieth century, state administrators and members of the legal profession, like many in the public, doubted that the law and the church could provide a mechanism by which a person could move from one religious-ethnic category to another.[30]

Nationality, Citizenship, Empire

The contradictions in official and civilian, ecclesiastical and lay attitudes toward Jews, Jewish assimilation, and Jewish conversion were instances of larger ideological conflicts. Waves of social, economic, and legal reform and reaction in the Russian Empire in the nineteenth century took Western European nations as models to be either emulated or avoided. The situation of the Jews highlighted differences between Russian and Western European legal categories and conceptions of citizenship. The Western press, especially in the United States and England, frequently criticized the empire's Jewish policies, citing them as evidence of Russian backwardness.[31] Of course, the Russian press noted that the British authorities were no less guilty of abusing their own minority populations. Nonetheless, the Jewish case invited the most comparison and contrast, since the Jews—unlike the Hindus or the Irish, the Doukhobors or the Georgians—were a kind of universal minority, existing in both the Russian and the British empires. Their treatment could thus appear to be a kind of litmus test, measuring the degree to which a given state upheld Enlightenment ideals, and the difference between the legal status of the Jew in England and Russia, for some, marked the former country as modern and the latter as retrograde.

The last four decades of the nineteenth century, and especially the decades when the works I read were written, saw much debate about the "Jewish question." Though it had once been off-limits to journalists, Alexander II solicited the opinion of the public to help in its resolution.[32] The disputing parties used their arguments to articulate their principles of Russian citizenship and nationality. Reformers within and outside of the government envisioned an alternative to the estate system, in which subjects [*poddanye*] would be transformed into citizens [*grazhdane*], equal in the eyes of the law. They imagined a Russian state in which acculturated non-Russians (which for some meant only converts to Orthodoxy, but for others could include Russified Catholics, Lutherans, or even non-Christians) could participate on an equal basis.[33]

Thus, a reference to an assimilated Jew as a "Russian citizen" [*russkii grazh-*

danin] might invoke the complex of ideas associated with citizenship in general. The poet Nikolai Nekrasov, in his controversial 1856 poem "Poet i grazhdanin" [The Poet and the Citizen], defined the citizen as a patriot prepared to defend his country from any evil:

> A chto takoe grazhdanin?
> Otechestva dostoinyi syn.[34]
>
> And what is a citizen?
> A worthy son of the fatherland.

Censors and the public alike read Nekrasov as calling for the destruction of the current social system and its radical restructuring. Those who favored Jewish acculturation could have had Nekrasov's images in mind. They needed to believe that Russia was developing a civil society in which the acculturated Jew would be granted an equal place. The legal scholar Il'ia Orshansky based an essay encouraging acculturation on this idea of citizenship:

> Now there is a class of Jews, already quite numerous, who stubbornly defend the honor and the right to think themselves Russian people and citizens of Russia [*russkimi liud'mi i grazhdanami Rossii*]; and Russian society itself is becoming more and more used to the idea that Jews must bear all the obligations and enjoy all the rights of Russian citizenship [*grazhdanstvo*].[35]

However, as the historian Benjamin Nathans notes, the vision of citizenship that Orshansky and other Jewish lawyers of the period expressed rested on a "tenuous . . . juridical framework."[36] In another essay, Orshansky himself acknowledged that "it is impossible to consider [Jews] Russian citizens in the legal sense."[37]

Developments in the final decades of the Russian Empire would test the faith Orshansky had expressed in the eventual victory of a civil society that could include acculturated but not converted Jews. In 1863, the Polish uprising had brought the question of national loyalty to the fore. This revolt, perceived as a demonstration of a non-Russian group's hostility to the state, provoked a Russification campaign intended to weaken the economic power of the Polish gentry and strengthen the loyalty of non-Russians to the tsar. This campaign was not a single unified action, but rather an assortment of policies motivated by varying conceptions of faithful subjects and how they could be created;[38] scholars debate whether it was ever deliberately directed at the Jews.[39] Some Russifying officials at some times demanded only loyalty to the ruling dynasty or to the state; others attempted to foster Russian culture and to encourage non-Russians to convert to Russian Orthodoxy. The campaign intensified as the nineteenth century wore on. Members of nationalities in the empire's western, southern, and eastern borderlands were ever more persuasively convinced to convert to Russian Orthodoxy.[40] At the same time, a group of "exclusive nationalists" questioned the use of state resources for the Russification of minorities and argued that such efforts worked to the detriment of Russians.[41] It may have been under the influence of this opinion that the tsarist government eventually seemed to suggest that some minorities were unassimilable when it permitted members of certain groups, such as the Jews, to emigrate. The expansion of the term "aliens" in legal and everyday writing to include many nationalities, including the Jews, may support the contention that assimilation of minorities in the nineteenth century seemed less and less feasible.[42]

Because disagreements over the cultural and legal place of the Jews made reference to larger disputes about whether Russian citizenship should be redesigned according to Western models, examination of the changing treatment of the Jews opens a window on the interplay between changing notions of imperial subjecthood and citizenship as well as of the individual's possible personal, religious, and political affiliations. That is not to argue that the tsars' policy toward all nationalities can be equated with their policy toward Jews. It is, rather, to take into account that each attitude toward Jews and Jewish assimilation—whether expressed in a newspaper article or a work of fiction—implied a specific set of ideas about imperial citizenship and national identity. Belief in the possibility of Jewish assimilation, especially among liberals, can be connected with the idea that Russian civil society should be brought into conformity with the civil society of Western European countries such as France, where, by the late nineteenth century, the Jews were emancipated citizens (even though they still suffered from social disabilities). Skepticism about the advisability or the feasibility of Jewish assimilation, especially on the Right, can indicate a rejection of Western models of statehood. This seems to have been the case, for example, for the father of the poet Aleksandr Blok; his son equated his disillusionment with liberalism with his (presumably negative) attitude toward Jews:

Sei Faust, kogda-to radikal'nyi,
"pravel," slabel . . . i *vse* zabyl;
Ved' zhizn' uzhe ne zhgla—chadila,
I odnozvuchny stali v nei
Slova "svoboda" i "evrei."[43]

This Faust, once a radical
turned to the right, weakened . . . and forgot it *all*;
his life no longer burned, but sputtered
and the words "freedom" and "Jew"
began to sound the same.

Literature and the Jews

Regardless of the general skepticism, writers of fiction could and did depict a permeable boundary between Jewish and Christian societies in the Russian Empire in the late nineteenth century. In novels, stories, and plays, Jews take on Russian or Polish cultural attributes, at least to some degree, and their tales show that the line separating Jews and Christians can be crossed, at least in one direction. Both Jews and non-Jews wrote about Jewish assimilation; their works emerge primarily from three literary traditions: the Jewish Haskalah, the "Positivist" movement that developed among Polish intellectuals after the 1863 revolt, and the Russian Realism of the second half of the nineteenth century.

The Haskalah, or Jewish Enlightenment movement, is classically described as beginning in the late eighteenth century in Berlin and then spreading to Jewish communities in Eastern Europe (though recent historians see this account as too simplistic).[44] As I will explain in more detail in Chapter 1, in both East and West, the movement encouraged Jews to reform themselves by becoming literate in gentile languages, mastering secular knowledge, and often changing their way of life. It inspired an assortment of literary works in Hebrew, German, Polish, Russian, and Yiddish, which tended to tell the story of a male Jew's quest for learning, his physical departure from home and family as well as his intellectual journey from the Jewish religious canon into the literature of the European Enlightenment. Jews in the Russian Empire wrote novels of education, or *Bildungsromane*, in this tradition in various languages —Abraham Mapu and Moses Leib Lilienblum in Hebrew, Mendele Moykher

Sforim and Yisroel Aksenfeld in Yiddish, Judah Leib Nevakhovich and Lev Levanda in Russian—from the beginning of the nineteenth century through the 1870s.

The Polish Positivist movement, addressed in Chapter 2, described some similar figures. A number of acculturated Jewish characters began to figure in Polish literature in the 1850s, reflecting the emergence of a Jewish bourgeoisie in Poland. While some depictions were welcoming, others betrayed Polish uneasiness about Jewish success in the newly capitalist economy. The Polish uprising of 1863, though, fostered an atmosphere of Jewish-Christian brotherhood: Positivist writers imagined the evolution of a new kind of broadly based Polish nationalism, which would unite men and women, peasants and aristocrats, Jews and Christians. They showed Jewish characters who read Polish literature, identified themselves as Polish, and demonstrated loyalty to the Polish cause. Although Eliza Orzeszkowa distinguished herself by her dedication to learning about Judaism and Jewish culture, she was only one of many liberal Polish writers of this era to depict Jewish characters: others included Maria Konopnicka, Józef Ignacy Kraszewski, and Aleksandr Świętochowski. Although depictions of Jews in Polish literature grew more negative as memories of the uprising faded, some of the best-known sympathetic depictions of assimilated Jews appear in Bolesław Prus's famous novel *Lalka* [The Doll], written in 1890, long after the revolt.

Through the 1870s, Russian Realism was on the whole less sympathetic to the acculturating Jew. Even while paying lip service to the idea that Jews should embrace Western education and European ways, liberal Russian writers in the 1860s and 1870s usually portrayed assimilated Jews unattractively. They often relied on a stock character: a Jewish man driven to acquire wealth and the outward marks of Russian culture, willing to reject his traditions and even his religion in pursuit of this goal. As I will illustrate, this figure could take on aspects of many older Jewish stereotypes: the Jew as criminal, traitor, Judas, miser, or pimp. Realist writers wanted to depict the downtrodden elements of Russian society, such as peasants, the urban working class, and the lowest-level clerks. In this schema, the assimilated Jew, like his unassimilated cousins, was a foreign element in the world of the peasants, an oppressor, and an ugly, absurd figure. For example, Nekrasov, in the poem "Sovremenniki" [My Contemporaries; 1875], mocks Jewish bankers who have acquired wealth, jewels, a fondness for ballet, and even noble titles, but have not managed to shed their Jewish accents, and in "Tiazhelyi god" [A Hard Year; 1874],

Mikhail Saltykov-Shchedrin portrays a baptized Jew as a hypocritical patriot.[45] In the late 1880s and 1890s, liberal Russian writers such as Vladimir Korolenko and Maxim Gorky began to portray Jews more sympathetically, while remaining within the same schema: rather than being only oppressors, Jews began to be seen as victims of capitalism and autocracy.

The acculturated Jewish characters in these three literary traditions served patently ideological purposes. For the people described by Haskalah writers, it was easy to acquire gentile languages and immediate acceptance in gentile society without rejecting Judaism—a situation that illustrated the accessibility of secular learning and the folly of hidebound traditionalism. The Polish Positivists, meanwhile, idealized the patriotism of the assimilated Jewish characters and devoted tremendous attention to the example of Michał Landy, a young Jew who, having fallen fighting the Russians at the side of his Polish comrades, was baptized before death with the blood of Polish martyrs.[46] And in the Russian Realism of the 1860s and 1870s, the acculturated Jewish literary characters are foils for virtuous but vulnerable Russian peasants whom they abuse and exploit. Most of these authors use such characters didactically, rather than for analyzing the widespread Jewish acculturation of the time or the motivations of acculturating Jews. Before the 1870s, there were very few acculturating Jewish characters in Russian or Polish literature—or, for that matter, in the embryonic Hebrew and Yiddish secular literatures—who rose above the level of hackneyed stereotypes.

In the twentieth century, by contrast, Jewish themes and Jews themselves were more organically integrated into the secular literature and culture of Eastern Europe, and some Jewish characters, in life as in literature, might both identify themselves and be identified by others as primarily "radical" or "intelligentsia" rather than as primarily Jewish. In the 1920s and 1930s, the now canonical Russian Jewish writers Isaac Babel and Osip Mandelstam, like the Polish Bruno Schulz, engaged in complex efforts to define themselves, their Jewishness, and their creativity in relation to Jewish and Slavic literary traditions—efforts that have inspired a significant critical literature.

By looking at some underexamined but complex texts, I hope to shed light on the transition between the 1860s and the twentieth century, from Nekrasov's to Babel's Jews. My authors, one Jewish enlightener who wrote in Russian, one Polish Positivist, and two Russian inheritors of the Realist tradition, pause at length on the image of the acculturating Jew and, in so doing, begin to escape the ideological constraints of their various literary

legacies. In spite of their differing literary heritages, they face similar para-
doxes and display similar ambivalences. Their texts show that the subject
of Jewish acculturation itself justifies breaking with the literary-critical
norm by including Jewish and non-Jewish writers in a single study that
sees these authors not only as inheritors of particular national and linguistic traditions but also as parts of the shared literary and political contexts
of the Russian Empire.[47]

Identities and Transformations

Nationality

Since the nineteenth century, philosophers have pondered the origins of
national or ethnic identity. For Romantic thinkers, every people inherits and
creates an authentic, original "national" culture. Members of an educated
elite have often taken it on themselves to narrate a national history linked to
"folk" culture. Since the 1980s, theorists have conducted a lively debate about
the degree to which this group identity is arbitrarily formed, that is, whether
nationalism "invents" the nation or whether at least some aspects of the cultural identity of modern nations have archaic origins.[48] Those scholars involved in this debate have begun to examine nationalist rhetoric through literary lenses, considering the function of specific images, vocabulary, and
narrative techniques.

The image of the Jew has played a key role in the stories that define European national identities, perhaps in part because the biblical definition of
the Jews as "the Chosen People" lent them a precocious nationalism. Meanwhile, the isolation of European Jewish communities made the Jews a visible
minority against which the majority ethnicity might situate its own identity:
the symbolic exclusion of Jews has been able to define national communities
consisting of the dominant group and all other minorities.[49] Paradoxically,
then, widespread Jewish assimilation in the nineteenth century seems only
to have heightened European perceptions of Jewish difference.[50]

Although so many theorists of nationalism have focused their attention on
Western Europe, the nineteenth-century Russian Empire is a particularly appropriate test case for paradigms relating national-identity formation to attitudes toward Jews and Jewish assimilation. Not only did the empire contain a

Jewish population bigger than that of Western European nations, but the image of the Jew was especially complex there. Whereas Jews in Western Europe and the United States in the nineteenth century tended to be seen as "Eastern" (and indeed many Jews immigrated to these places from points east), Russians and Poles, perhaps more like Germans, associated Jews with both West and East, progress and backwardness, radicalism and conservatism.

The fluidity of the image of the Jew parallels that of Russian national identity. Russian identity since the eighteenth century has been formed against the model of Western nations, which has been alternately embraced and rejected as intellectuals and bureaucrats have worked to understand to what degree they want to be European and to what degree Asian. (A similar process has occurred among the Polish intelligentsia, for whom Russia or the Slavic nations in general have stood in for "Asia" or the East.)[51] The influential twentieth-century Russian religious figure Nikolai Berdiaev, in his synthesis of Russian nationalist thought, used geographic terms:

> The inconsistency and complexity of the Russian soul may be due to the fact that in Russia two streams of world history—East and West—jostle and influence one another. The Russian people is not purely European and it is not purely Asiatic. Russia is a complete section of the world—a colossal East-West. It united two worlds, and within the Russian soul two principles are always engaged in strife—the Eastern and the Western.[52]

Berdiaev himself noted the similarity between the Russian idea that he described as now European, now Asian, and his perception of the Jews: "Its polarized nature gives the Russian nation something in common with the Jewish nation."[53] Jewish and Russian intellectuals could imagine themselves and each other as equally backwards, "Eastern," in need of Westernization and modernization.[54]

What Berdiaev expressed in positive terms when he wrote in the 1940s echoed the use of the image of the Jew in Russian nationalist rhetoric for the previous century. The Jews have represented both of the extremes between which Slavic peoples hoped to find themselves. On the one hand, they were described as "Asians" who spoke an incomprehensible language, adhered to outdated, ridiculous customs, and demonstrated a fanatic loyalty to each other; on the other, they were identified with negative "European" qualities such as competitiveness, huckstering, and excessive cleverness. By using such stereotypes, both Russians and Poles have been able to construct their own identity in contrast to Jewishness, which was capable of embodying everything they feared to become.

The presence of a Jewish character in a narrative, then, could signal the author's—and the culture's—concern with Russian or Polish identity. Most frequently, of course, Jews in late-nineteenth-century Russian or Polish stories simply stood for stereotypical "Jewish" faults and thus offered the opportunity to admire "non-Jewish" virtues in other characters. Jewish cowardice demonstrated the bravery of Christian soldiers, and Jewish deviousness highlighted the peasants' innocence and simplicity. The assimilating Jew, though, who deliberately sets about to take on "non-Jewish" characteristics, can provide the occasion for a more complex narrative of non-Jewish national identity. While this character might be revealed as a "false assimilator" who in fact retains all the possible negative "Jewish" traits, the darkness that silhouettes the merits of Christians, he or she could also provide a writer or reader with the chance to step back from the nationalist narrative and notice its arbitrary, constructed quality.[55]

Literary Type

Just like national identity, individual identity tends to be articulated in narrative form. The relationship between narrative and personality particularly intrigued the Russian literary critics of the 1850s and 1860s. In their essays on literature, the "radical" or "progressive" critics Nikolai Chernyshevsky, Nikolai Dobroliubov, and Dmitry Pisarev conducted a debate with liberals such as Pavel Annenkov, Ivan Turgenev, and Aleksandr Herzen about what educated Russians were like and how (and whether) they could reform themselves. Their arguments centered on the contrast between the "weak" or "superfluous" man—that is, the many dithering, ineffective, weak characters who recur in texts by Turgenev, Aleksandr Pushkin, Ivan Goncharov, and others—and a "new man," a tough, decisive reformer who eventually came to be identified with Bazarov in Turgenev's 1862 novel *Fathers and Children* and with Vera Pavlovna and Lopukhov or, in a more extreme form, Rakhmetov, in Chernyshevsky's 1863 utopia *What Is to Be Done?* These critics defined the superfluous man and the new man as types: fictional characters who stood for real people, who contained the essential characteristics that united seemingly diverse individuals, and whose stories revealed the possible biographies of a generation of Russian intellectuals.[56]

The concept of type is fundamental for any understanding of portrayals of human change in the literature of the late-nineteenth-century Russian Empire. Annenkov, in his response to Chernyshevsky's review of Turgenev's story "Asya," supported the use of type as a category: "Taken as a whole, a society that has a literature even thinks in terms of literary types, not in terms of articles or lectures. Any image beloved by the public may act as a barometer to indicate the moods and thoughts of many thousands of people who would never express them out loud."[57] When a society "thinks in terms of literary types," then, every ideology, every theory about how people should or should not behave, is embodied and given a name. For example, Chernyshevsky saw the indecisiveness of the "Romeo" in Turgenev's "Asya" as a "symptom of an illness that—in exactly the same vulgar way—spoils all our endeavors."[58] The liberal Annenkov and the radical Chernyshevsky agreed that the stories of fictional heroes can explain the lives of real people more effectively than any other medium. Although they wrote in the critical style of the nineteenth century, their insight about the ways the narrative types associated with fictional heroes shape our thought has been echoed more than once in twentieth-century criticism. Within the Russian tradition, the Soviet critics Mikhail Bakhtin and Pavel Medvedev argue that we cannot help but think in terms of stories that fall into specific categories: "human consciousness possesses a series of inner genres for seeing and conceptualizing reality."[59]

For the radical critics, though, type influenced readers' real actions, not just their view of reality; they believed that a person who had learned to read literature and life through the prism of type would be able to change for the better. For Pisarev, the type of any hero was perfectly clear, as was the hero's standing in an almost Darwinian hierarchy of types. In "Pushkin and Belinsky," Pisarev's famous essay dealing with *Eugene Onegin*, he explained it by comparing the hero to familiar types from other works of literature: "Onegin is nothing more than a Mitrofan Prostakov. . . . The day of the Beltovs, the Chatskys, and the Rudins was over the moment the Bazarovs, the Lopukhovs, and the Rakhmetovs came on the scene."[60] The function of a literary work, in Pisarev's mind, is to contrast the flawed present with some ideal of the future: "The hero must be either the kind of person who typifies the status quo or the kind of person who bears within himself the seeds of the future. . . . The hero must be either a knight of the past or a knight of the future."[61] The stories that interested Pisarev, then, were essentially stories of human reform, and their characters were the pre-reform and the post-reform self. Using this vocabulary, we might say that Chernyshevsky saw the weak-willed hero of "Asya" as an effective knight of the past and a warning to all educated Russians: he summoned them to mend their ways and force themselves to take action before it was too late. Chernyshevsky implied that by recognizing in "Romeo" the deadly weakness of the Russian educated elite, the reader could bring himself and Russia closer to European culture, which Chernyshevsky periodically mentions in admiring terms; he thus reveals the parallels between his project for the reform of the individual and the debates over a Europeanizing reform of the Russian state.

The radical critics' belief in the transformative power of literature undoubtedly contributed to their appeal to the young Jews in the Russian Empire who were most dedicated to reforming themselves along Russian lines. Semyon An-sky, in his 1905 novella *The Pioneers* [Pionery], satirizes this phenomenon: fresh from his experience in yeshiva absorbing the Talmud, the young Uler decides literally to memorize Pisarev's "Pushkin and Belinsky." He is undaunted by his limited Russian:

> "So far I know only one article, 'Puskn and Blynski' [Puskn i Blynski]. But I know it! Ask me about any part you want!"
> "What could I ask you? Do you understand the individual words?"
> "Nah," Uler said with a scornful gesture. "The words—who cares about the words?" [*Slova! Chto slova!*].[62]

The memoirs of Russifying Jewish intellectuals attest to the possibility of this scene; they felt that they had bettered themselves precisely in accordance with the model they had found in Pisarev's and Chernyshevsky's writings. Eliezer Ben-Yehuda, an early Zionist who helped revive Hebrew as a spoken language, agreed on Chernyshevsky's *What Is to Be Done?* as a model for the new Jewish literature. He found "every single line" of a critique of a Hebrew novel by Mapu to be "a crude imitation of Pisarev's criticism of *Eugene Onegin*"—and he responded to this discovery with delight that "modern things like these were being written in Hebrew."[63] When An-sky's friend, the Yiddishist Chaim Zhitlovsky, said of his generation of Jews that "Russian literature had made us Russian," he was referring to the radical critics' own texts and to their interpretations of the classics.[64]

Non-Jewish writers too described the transformation of the Jew by means of literature, as exemplified by Raisa/Rebecca, the heroine of Rostislav Sementkovsky's 1889 novella *Evrei i zhidy* [Jews and Yids].

> She fell in love with the Russia that she found in its writers [*ona poliubila Rossiiu v litse ee pisatelei*]. . . . She took on the features [*srodnilas'*] of the heroines of the Russian poets; she began to feel their feelings; she was moved by their joys and sorrows. She often thought of the strong impression that the image of Tatiana made on her. . . . She remembered how she would muse on woman's calling, how the figure of Turgenev's Elena suffused her with a radiant light. . . . Social ideals [*obshchestvennye idealy*] appeared in her soul.[65]

Raisa accomplishes her transformation under the influence of the positive literary types she finds in Tatiana and Elena, the heroines, respectively, of Pushkin's "novel in verse" from the 1820s, *Eugene Onegin*, and Turgenev's 1859 novel, *Na kanune* [On the Eve]. Sementovsky's fictional description of Raisa's education echoes Zhitlovsky's comment. Both examples of a self-transformation by means of text recall Chernyshevsky's own detailed descriptions of his self-conscious efforts to reform his personality, to model himself after a better type of person.[66]

Although the liberal critics agreed with the radicals about the centrality of type, they were less certain that literary texts must contain positive types that could lead the reader straight toward a desirable transformation. Annenkov's article on "Asya" is a defense of what Chernyshevsky had called the weak man. If the literature of 1858 offers few positive examples of "bold men" and instead presents a host of vacillating "weak men," that, he writes, is because at the moment, seemingly "weak" men are the best that Russian society has to offer. Although these people seem paralyzed by doubts and incapable of taking necessary actions, their indecision signals their virtue. Because the weak men have learned to question their instincts, rein in their desires, and adopt a "European" attitude to knowledge, they can no longer make snap judgments and act on them.[67] Their present self-doubt indicates that at some point they will be able to attain a level of moral maturity that will make them far more useful to Russia than any number of decisive "strong men."

Annenkov's essay invokes and then explodes the literary types that his opponent uses. Rather than accepting the inferiority and obsolescence of the weak man and the superiority and modernity of the strong man, he turns these types around. In fact, he says, the strong man is so archaic that he belongs properly to the pre-Petrine era, and the weak man (who is not nearly as weak as he seems) stands for Russia's future.[68] When Annenkov defends literary "superfluous men" by considering the real people on whom the prototype is based, he engages the fundamental question raised by the radicals' literary theory: how can the literary type be simultaneously descriptive and prescriptive? That is, if literature shows us what we look like, how can it also inspire us to change?[69] For Annenkov and the other liberal critics, the type functioned not as an ideal that could inspire conversion, but instead as an illustration that might further a gradual, therapeutic self-recognition. The radicals' insistence that literature ought to lead to a dramatic change may account for the urgency of their writings on art and their genuine fear of "bad" art and "dangerous" types that might produce the wrong kind of conversion. The liberals' more limited account of art's power, by contrast, lies behind their tolerance for transitional, ambiguous figures, in literature as in life.

Annenkov's reading of Turgenev's story evokes a twentieth-century critical approach that redefines nineteenth-century Realism. The seminal Russian critic Vissarion Belinsky had seen Realism as the creation of convincing, true, and motivational types; Annenkov portrayed it instead as governed more by parody of older literary models and genres.[70] In Annenkov's analysis, Turgenev's "Romeo" is interesting precisely in the way he extends and challenges the concept of the "weak man." The Russian Formalists agreed that Realist writers, and indeed all good writers, after signaling that their work might belong to a given genre, then play with the readers' expectations of that genre, sometimes conforming to them, sometimes challenging them. The original choice of genre, or in Annenkov's terms, the human types at issue, provides a kind of canvas for experimentation, and differences from type mark a work as new and catch the reader's attention.[71]

Both the connections that Pisarev and Chernyshevsky make between the concept of type and a re-creation of the self, and Annenkov's transformation of the meaning of older types in order to complicate the picture of self-reform, can shed light on the narratives of Jewish acculturation considered here. Looking at the "Jewish question" through the lens of type allows us to see late-nineteenth-century literature, as its readers did, as closely bound up with the real world, mirroring and predicting the movements of real lives. In describing acculturating Jews, writers borrow Jewish literary types from multiple sources, including the Haskalah novel of education, the Christian Bible, Shakespeare, Slavic folk beliefs, and the newspaper polemics of their own time. As Realists and as artists, though, these writers not only reproduce older types but also parody them and reveal their limitations. Like the Turgenev whom Annenkov describes, even while drawing on an arsenal of static figures and an ideology of complete transformation, by manipulating these elements, they draw a more nuanced picture. In so doing, they bring the Jewish experience of acculturation to bear on one of the fundamental questions of aesthetics: does art change us?

The following chapters consider the images of Jewish acculturation in an array of literary texts, considered roughly chronologically. I begin with my only Jewish writer, Grigory Bogrov, whose six-hundred-page autobiographical novel introduced the theme to the Russian reading public. My analysis responds to a number of questions: Who was Bogrov, and what accounts for his reputation among Russians and Jews? How did he rework the story of the Jewish man drawn to non-Jewish culture—did he retain a Haskalah faith in the transformative power of reading, or did he imagine the assimilator as a Romantic hero, an unregenerate outlaw, cast out by all? In the following three chapters, I look at texts by non-Jews who modify Bogrov's tale of Jewish acculturation. While Eliza Orzeszkowa, Nikolai Leskov, and Anton Chekhov all refer to the story of the Jewish autodidact, familiar from Haskalah literature and its non-Jewish parallels, they also echo older, more static literary types. What can explain these Christians' obsession with the metamorphosis of Jews? Which terms and prototypes do they use to describe it, and why? In resolving these problems, I try to account for the connections that these writers drew among the peculiar historical and legal position of the Jews in the Russian Empire, the kinds of stories that people told about them, and the eternal dilemmas of human identity and mutability.

1 AN UNPRECEDENTED TYPE OF HUMAN BEING: GRIGORY BOGROV

In such novels . . . human emergence . . . is no longer man's private affair. He emerges along with the world and he reflects the historic emergence of the world itself. He is no longer within an epoch, but on the border between two epochs, at the transition point from one to the other. This transition is accomplished in him and through him. He is forced to become a new, unprecedented type of human being.

—MIKHAIL BAKHTIN

THE FRONTISPIECE to the first volume of Grigory Isaakovich Bogrov's *Collected Works* [Sobranie sochinenii] might give the reader certain ideas about the author.[1] It shows a well-dressed middle-aged man with a high forehead, a curly mustache, and sideburns (Figure 2). The capsule biography on the subsequent pages states that Bogrov was born on March 1, 1825, to a religious family in Poltava (today in Ukraine), and his father was a famous Jewish scholar. However, nothing about the picture would suggest that Bogrov is Jewish: he has no beard, *peyes* [sidelocks], or yarmulke, and his high white collar, soft shiny tie, and tailored jacket give him an elegant and thoroughly European air. The facing page contains two Russian words, "Zapiski evreia" [Notes of a Jew], the title of the six-hundred-page autobiographical novel that made Bogrov famous in the 1870s and later. Taken together, the words

FIGURE 2. Anon., portrait of Grigory Isaakovich Bogrov. Published as the frontispiece to his *Collected Works*. Reproduced from G. I. Bogrov, *Sobranie sochinenii* (Odessa: Sherman, 1912–13).

and the picture suggest that this work can be categorized as an example of the Russian Realist genre of "notes" [*zapiski*] about one person's impressions of a somewhat exotic milieu. The most famous representatives of this group are Ivan Turgenev's *Notes of a Hunter* [Zapiski okhotnika] (1852) and Fedor Dostoevsky's *Notes from the House of the Dead* [Zapiski iz mertvogo doma] (1861–62). Turgenev had given the Russian reader a glimpse into the life of the serfs, unprecedented in its detail and in the author's sympathy and respect for his subject, narrated by an upper-class "hunter" who seems just a bit more naive than the author himself could have been. Dostoevsky, after he spent ten years in Siberia as punishment for his youthful participation in a clandestine discussion group, produced a compelling description of the prisoners' regimen, behavior, and culture, purportedly written by a murderer named Gorianchikov. Given this tradition, Bogrov's work, published between 1871 and 1873, would seem to be precisely another ethnographic account of an obscure segment of the empire's diverse population. Just as Turgenev and Dostoevsky had broken new thematic ground in their "notes," so Bogrov was the first to publish such a detailed account of Jewish life. The urbane figure in the picture, then, might take his place as one more sophisticated and well-spoken researcher, drawing on his unusual personal experiences to enlighten the reading public.

The second word in the book's title, though, complicates this categorization. In the Russian Empire, "Jew" was clearly a term of an entirely different sort than "hunter" or "house of the dead." Turgenev and Dostoevsky wrote their stories from the perspective of a temporary denizen in an exotic location, a sort of visitor. Even while the word "notes" creates the fiction that their works were collections of impressions jotted down on the spot, their readers knew that the writers had actually left the place described, gathered their thoughts, and deliberately created a narrative. Bogrov could do nothing of the kind, because he could not, without converting, abandon the legal status of Jew. Thus, he could not align himself completely with Turgenev and Dostoevsky as an outsider to the world he described, albeit one possessing a privileged access to it.

The difference between Bogrov and the famous non-Jewish notetakers emerges most clearly in their varying treatments of education and change. Turgenev's hunter carefully records which of the peasants he meets can read, which ones have begun to imitate the manners of the gentry, which ones are making themselves over into wealthy men in their own right. His subjects are people at least potentially in transition, anticipating—like all of Russia at the time—their coming emancipation. (Reportedly, Alexander II said that his reading of Turgenev's stories even contributed to his decision in 1861 to free the serfs.) The prisoners in Dostoevsky's *Notes* similarly await liberation; questions of how their prison term is changing them, and whether it might ever lead to their moral rebirth, fascinate the narrator. Bogrov's narrator Srul, by contrast, concentrates on his own education rather than on the changes that might occur in the mass of Jews whom he describes. While the lessons that Turgenev's and Dostoevsky's narrators learn are kept to the background of the story, Bogrov keeps his narrator's transformation in the foreground. This focus, even more than the title, points to a gulf between the elegant figure in the picture and his non-Jewish predecessors. In the following discussion, I will explore that gulf, seeking other predecessors for Bogrov's *Notes* within and beyond the Russian canon. This will require some understanding of the publication history of *Notes of a Jew*, the life of its author, and the critical tradition that developed around them.

Bogrov and His Biography: The Jewish Writer as Notetaker

Notes of a Jew was unprecedented because it was the first book-length belletristic work written by a Jew in Russian to appear in a mainstream rather than a specialty Jewish publication. It came out in the respected "thick journal" of the Petersburg liberals, *Otechestvennye zapiski* [Fatherland Notes]. Bogrov had written the first half of the book in the early 1860s but at first could not find a publisher. Finally, the well-known poet and publicist Nikolai Nekrasov, then editor-in-chief of the journal, accepted the manuscript, encouraged the author to complete it, and paid what Bogrov called "flattering attention" to him.[2] In the words of a contemporary publisher: "Bogrov became Bogrov because *Otechestvennye zapiski* legitimated his talent by printing *Notes of a Jew*."[3] According to one source, the writer Mikhail Saltykov-Shchedrin, also associated with *Otechestvennye zapiski*, helped Bogrov edit his book.[4] In 1885, writers of Bogrov's obituaries (in non-Jewish publications) noted that this work, rather than any of his stories, his journalistic pieces, or his historical novel *Evreiskii manuskript: Pered dramoi* [The Jewish Manuscript: Before the Drama] (written in 1876 about Chmelnitsky's invasions of Galicia), "attracted the attention of the reading public and the critics."[5] Turgenev himself confirmed this when he wrote to Bogrov in 1882 that "two years ago or so I read [*Notes of a Jew*] . . . with the most lively interest."[6]

Among Jews and non-Jews, whether Judeophobe or Judeophile (to use the terms of the period), the work apparently achieved the status of a kind of travelogue for the empire's western borderlands, a handbook to the life of the Jews in the Pale of Settlement.[7] A reviewer in a Jewish publication, *Vestnik russkikh evreev* [Herald of the Russian Jews], addressed Bogrov's criticism of Jewish practices hesitantly but was quick to praise him for being among the first writers to undertake the task of informing the Russian public about the Jews.[8] The Hebrew poet Saul Tchernikhovsky, in an encyclopedia article on Russian Jewish literature, agreed that the first half of *Notes of a Jew* was valuable for its ethnographic content.[9] Sofia Lur'e, a young Jewish woman in Minsk who carried on a correspondence with Dostoevsky in the late 1870s, sent him a copy of the book that Bogrov (who spent his last years near Minsk) had given to her family; apparently she hoped that the book would make Dostoevsky more sympathetic to the Jews.[10] Long after the book was published, the non-Jewish wife of Bogrov's grandson explained that she too read *Notes of a Jew*, "well-known in its time," in part to learn about the traditional Jewish way of life.[11]

Sholem Aleikhem, in his autobiography, confirms that *Notes of a Jew* was required reading for young Russian Jews in the 1870s who fancied themselves enlightened. When given the chance to show off his knowledge of secular literature, his protagonist indicates that he has read the works of Berthold Auerbach, a spokesman for Jewish emancipation in Germany, and he is familiar with Chernyshevsky's radical classic, *What Is to Be Done?*, but as for *Notes of a Jew*, he says, "That I know by heart!"[12] In 1880, according to another memoirist, Mordechai Ha-Cohen, Bogrov's name was known to the Jews in all the small towns of the pale. Ha-Cohen describes the delight of a group of young Jewish students in St. Petersburg when the famous author, by then in his fifties, turned up unexpectedly at their celebration of the holiday of Purim and played the violin for them.[13]

Insofar as Bogrov has had any reputation in recent times, it is as a confirmed assimilationist, highly critical of Jewish traditions and religion. Such views were already prevalent in Bogrov's lifetime. One Jewish critic, writing for the Odessa Jewish newspaper *Den'* [The Day], accused him in 1871 of fostering Russian belief in the blood libel and attacking the Jews as ruthlessly as Yakov Brafman, a convert to Russian Orthodoxy, had in his infamous 1869 book *Kniga kagala* [The Book of the Kahal] (a screed claiming that Jews form a separate state within the country where they live and for that reason can never be good citizens).[14] Because Bogrov was willing to criticize Jewish traditions in the Russian language, this critic saw him as a self-hating Jew.

Bogrov indignantly denied such accusations. He responded to *Den'* in a postscript to his autobiography with a formulation that implies his rejection of any nationalism, calling the reviewer a "kugel [*kugel'nyi*] patriot" (p. 589).[15] Kugel, a baked noodle or potato pudding, is a characteristic Eastern European Jewish food.[16] Bogrov coined his expression as a play on the Russian "kvasnoi patriot" [kvas patriot]. Kvas is a mildly alcoholic, typically Russian drink, and the phrase refers to a jingoist, one whose patriotism is no more reasoned or sophisticated than his fondness for an intoxicating national drink. By dismissing his critic as a Jewish version of a Russian chauvinist, Bogrov evinced an equal distaste for Russian and Jewish nationalisms and insisted that his criticism of Jewish behavior did not make him a self-hating Jew.[17]

Nonetheless, many other Russian Jewish readers agreed with the reviewer from *Den'*. Lur'e warned Dostoevsky, "Don't believe everything he [Bogrov] says [in *Notes of a Jew*]; he exaggerates terribly."[18] One critic for *Voskhod* [Sunrise], a Russian-language Jewish publication, wrote in 1885 that Russian Jewish literature so far had been marred by the authors' sympathy for their Jewish characters, their urge to defend them, which prevented these writers from focusing their powers on "the artistic depiction of a true, real life."[19] He criticized Bogrov specifically, though, for the opposite reason: Bogrov's hostility toward his subject. "It is not at all that objective calm that is one of the most important virtues of every artistic work; it is, precisely, a kind of coldness, as though the author . . . is terribly bored with his characters."[20]

Until recently, the few references to Bogrov—who appears only in the most exhaustive surveys of Jewish and Russian literatures—have reiterated this critic's conclusions. The *Evreiskaia entsiklopediia* [Jewish Encyclopedia], published in the early twentieth century, dismisses his talent and emphasizes his criticism of traditional Judaism:

In spite of the wealth of Bogrov's knowledge of life and his powers of precise observation, the picture he draws is too one-sided: on the one hand, his negative attitude toward traditional Judaism and its spiritual concepts is too strong; on the other, so is his insistence that the spiritual rebirth of the people and its radical reeducation are possible only given the transformation of traditional religion into a moral-rational teaching.[21]

Similarly, other critics objected to Bogrov's tone, the "bitterness" and "anger" that distinguished him from his more optimistic and unambiguously ideological Russian Jewish literary peers.[22]

The force of this criticism could reflect not only Bogrov's apparently trying personality and his genuine hostility to Jewish traditions, but also his politics. He became estranged from some of the Russian Jewish intelligentsia (in particular, from the editors of the journal *Rassvet* [The Dawn]) as a result of his support for a Christianizing Jewish sect, and his conversion late in life to Christianity undoubtedly damaged his reputation further in the eyes of his erstwhile colleagues.[23] He was also involved in a painful dispute regarding the funding of some Russian Jewish publications.[24] What really damned him in the eyes of the Jewish historians of the twentieth century, though, was his 1884 story "Man'iak" [Maniac],[25] in which he offers a series of ugly predictions for a Jewish state that some were already talking about establishing in Palestine. (There will, he said, be fierce disputes between the religious and the secular; problems will arise because Jews will not want to work in certain occupations; and the meetings of the parliament will be extremely unruly.) Even Ha-Cohen, who had so admired Bogrov in his youth, was appalled by "Maniac," seeing it as proof that Bogrov had the lowest opinion of Jews and wished only not to have been born a Jew.[26] The negative evaluation of Bogrov among the founders of Russian Jewish historiography, people like the men and women who produced the *Evreiskaia entsiklopediia* in the first decades of the twentieth century, may reflect both the force of a thirty-year-old antagonism and their urge to distinguish between their own endeavor and the more extreme assimilationism (and in this case even anti-Zionism) of their forebears, Bogrov included. In any case, their judgment has become canonical. Even a Soviet critic who set about in the 1920s to defend Bogrov agreed that he "must be recognized as representing the extremist wing of our assimilationist movement," and a late-twentieth-century American reference work notes that he "sharply criticized Jewish leadership and advocated radical reforms. . . . [He] tended toward assimilation."[27]

Nonetheless, a few scholars have pointed out that Bogrov's assimilationism was tempered by sympathy for the Jewish masses and cynicism toward the tsarist government. One historian of Jewish literature observes sententiously that while the depiction of Jewish life in *Notes of a Jew* is "entirely vitiated by the author's antagonistic spirit . . . his negative attitude to Judaism and to Jewish values was partly redeemed by his pity for the fate of his brethren and his strong hatred of their persecutors."[28] The literary critic Shimon Markish notes that though the writer's negative descriptions of Jewish life provided fodder for Russian anti-Semites, he also inveighed against a society and a legal system that criminalized Jewish identity itself: in some ways, he questioned the entire assimilationist enterprise.[29] A Jewish historian also challenges the image of Bogrov as an uncompromising assimilationist, seeing *Notes of a Jew* as staging the narrator's confrontation with the ideology of Jewish enlighteners in the Nikolaevan era in his attempt to create a new way of imagining the modernizing Jewish personality.[30]

Bogrov's contemporaries were not all blind to his cynicism toward the future of the Jews in Russia. They found evidence of it in *Notes of a Jew*, and they could have noticed it elsewhere as well. An 1873 reviewer for a non-Jewish journal, *Syn otechestva* [Son of the Fatherland], discussed Bogrov's "revelations" or negative comments about Jews at some length, but pointed out that Bogrov also described an episode of anti-Semitism and corruption among Russian officials, showing that "the writer is no longer tweaking only the Jews!" [*avtor shchelkaet uzhe ne odnikh evreev!*].[31] Another journalist alleged that Bogrov's willingness to stray from his criticisms of Jews caused controversy with his publisher: "As we definitely know, the editors of this journal [*Otechestvennye zapiski*] agreed to publish [*Notes of a Jew*] only because the first chapters have a denunciatory character, and in the later chapters, when the tone changed, many pages, even with significant editing, were printed only after a fight."[32]

The irony arising from the similarities and differences between the actual biography of Bogrov and his family and his fictionalized autobiography highlights the tension between assimilationism and rebellion. Bogrov's narrator, a Jewish man, falls in love with a non-Jewish woman whom he describes as inaccessible to him. In fact, a few years before his death (but long after he had finished his book), Bogrov married a non-Jew.[33] In order to do so, he was legally required to convert to Christianity, even though he had earlier dismissed such an act as dishonorable even by a Jew like himself who felt drawn to Russian culture: "If the Jews in Russia were not subject to such oppression and systematic persecution, then perhaps I would cross to that other shore [that is, convert to Russian Orthodoxy]. . . . But my fellow Jews, about four million people, are suffering innocently; could a decent person turn his back on such injustice?"[34] Throughout his autobiography, the author portrays access to higher education and assimilation into the Russian professional classes as a goal that, were it only attainable, would make him—and every other reasonable Jew—completely happy. Bogrov's children achieved the ideal of his narrator in *Notes of a Jew*. His oldest son, Grigory Grigor'evich Bogrov, was a wealthy lawyer and the only Jew to belong to Kiev's prestigious Dvorianskii klub [Aristocratic Club]; his family was acknowledged as one of the "best" in the city. His brothers, Bogrov's three younger sons, all became doctors.[35] Nonetheless, it was the writer's grandson, Dmitry Grigor'evich Bogrov, in his early twenties in 1911, who gave the family name a permanent place in Russian history textbooks when he assassinated the prime minister, Peter Stolypin. The Bogrovs' family history, like Grigory's "autobiography," could be seen as shifting from one cultural pattern to another, from an assimilationist, bourgeois, rationalistic conformism to a dramatic, revolutionary anarchism. The contradiction between the sons' success and the grandson's rebellion parallels the one between the two terms in Bogrov's title, the gap between the notetaker, a disinterested observer, and the Jewish writer, legally —and most unhappily—bound to the underprivileged masses he describes and thus perhaps inevitably drawn into an adversarial stance toward the state that constrained them.

Bogrov and Solomon Maimon: The Jewish Writer as Educator

If Bogrov did not entirely share the perspective of the non-Jewish writers Turgenev and Dostoevsky in their *Notes*, it is not difficult to locate him within a Jewish literary genre (for my purposes, "Jewish literature" means works written by Jews about Jews): Srul has much in common with the well-known literary type of the *maskil*, or adherent of the Haskalah (the plural is *maskilim*), the movement for Jewish emancipation and education spurred by the eighteenth-century European Enlightenment.

There has been some debate in the twentieth century about the uniformity of the creators of this literary type. For a long time, Jewish historians described the Haskalah as beginning among German Jews, especially in Berlin, in the second half of the eighteenth century, and reaching the Russian Empire in the early nineteenth century. There, they once said, its ideals went unquestioned until the 1881–82 pogroms, at which point the evident hostility of the tsarist government showed the maskilim that their assimilationism was unrealistic and ignoble.[36] In fact, movements for enlightenment did arise among Jews to the east of Berlin: some urged that secular knowledge be allowed to inform the study of canonical Jewish texts, others that it guide a thoroughgoing communal reform.[37] However, Russian maskilim may not simply have recycled German Jewish ideas.[38] The differences between the political systems and cultures of eighteenth-century Berlin and the nineteenth-century Russian Empire made it impossible for Eastern maskilim to apply all the analyses and policies of their Western forebears.[39] Furthermore, in spite of the stereotype, the maskilim in the East had never blindly promoted assimilation (if that is taken to mean what the Zionist essayist Ahad ha-Am called the "effacement" of Jewish culture).[40] Although the Russian Empire's maskilim criticized some traditional Jewish practices, urging Jews to learn gentile languages and learn to act like the gentiles, to acculturate, if only selectively—in the Hebrew poet Judah Leib Gordon's famous words, to "Be a man on the street and a Jew at home"—they did not speak for wholesale rejection of Judaism, and still less for conversion to Christianity, the essential final step for release from the legal disabilities imposed on Jews.[41]

Not only did the Eastern maskilim differ ideologically from those in Berlin, they also produced texts in a wider variety of languages: Hebrew, Yiddish, Russian, and Polish. It would be misleading to gloss over the differences among literary projects in different languages. The maskilim tended to see Yiddish as a lowly vernacular, useful only as a tool to teach the ignorant masses; Hebrew as a more noble and elegant vehicle, albeit one that presented the author with enormous technical difficulties; and Russian and Polish as legitimate and fully functioning literary languages, the mastery of which represented the first step on the road toward a Western education.

Regardless of their hesitation at identifying the Eastern European Haskalah with the Western one or with an uncompromising assimilationism, scholars agree that the central image of the successfully acculturated, usually male Jew recurs in the literary works of maskilim from disparate eras and locations and writing in various languages. The heroes of Haskalah fiction, in the model of the first famous maskil, the Berlin philosopher Moses Mendelssohn, were, as Gordon prescribed, "'men' at home in European culture and also Jews."[42] At the basis of this figure is its duality, its ability to intercede, to filter, and to represent both the Jewish community to the gentile authorities and educated classes, and gentile culture to the Jews. Rather than declaring their loyalty to a single national culture, these figures and the authors who described them often imagined themselves as belonging to "a sort of pan-European community" that transcended state borders and that had room for Jews along with other enlightened people.[43]

A number of Hebrew and Yiddish writers in Bogrov's time and earlier centered their stories around such a maskilic hero who mediates between cultures. For instance, in the 1860s, Abraham Mapu wrote *The Hypocrite*, a Hebrew novel about Jewish life in Lithuania, in which he depicts a few enlightened Jews who are equally at home in their own and in European culture.[44] In the Yiddish novella *Dos Shterntikhl* [The Headband], published in 1867 (though it was written in the 1840s), Yisroel Aksenfeld lauds the young hero, Oksman, who learns to speak Russian and associate with gentiles. In his mockery of traditional ways and especially of Hasidism, Oksman voices the author's reformist views.[45] Aksenfeld imagined Jews who purposefully recreate themselves and their lives according to a Western model: he felt that the fictional stories of such individuals could do a better job than unconcealed polemics at provoking imitation and thus reform. Oksman's friend explains: "Not everyone wants to listen to a preacher, and even if you do listen to him you'll forget his sermon and his good words an hour later. But at a play, the audience pays strict attention and listens carefully to each word, so that it sticks in their minds."[46] The story of an attractive maskilic hero who mocked the traditional Jewish world that he came from might, Aksenfeld believed, induce it to improve.

The works of Jews who wrote in Russian before Bogrov also testify to the enduring attraction of the dualistic maskilic hero. The character of the assimilating Jew was introduced to Russian literature in the first years of the nineteenth century by Judah Leib Nevakhovich, author of *Vopl' dshcheri iudeiskoi* [The Lament of the Daughter of Judah].[47] A disciple of Moses Mendelssohn, Nevakhovich simultaneously displayed his own patriotism and love of Russian culture and argued against Russian hostility toward Jews. Others like him appeared in Russian literature in the 1860s and early 1870s, roughly the time when many Jews first emerged on the Russian cultural and economic scene. Their emergence coincided with the establishment of regular Jewish publications in Russian featuring fiction as well as journalism:

three short-lived Russian Jewish periodicals in Odessa in the 1860s preceded longer-lived ones in St. Petersburg in the 1870s.[48] The best-known Russian Jewish writers then were Osip Rabinovich (1817–69), who began writing stories in Russian in the late 1840s, and Lev Levanda (1835–88), who began to write in the early 1860s.[49] Like Nevakhovich, Rabinovich and Levanda defended the Jews against the criticism of non-Jews even while they pushed them to reform.[50]

Everything about works of this genre, whether written in Hebrew, Yiddish, or other languages, reinforces the ideal that the self-conscious acculturation of the Jewish hero to gentile society is both possible and a good idea. Alan Mintz observes: "Behind all the satirical indictments of superstitious beliefs and corrupt communal practices, there lies a confident implicit model of an ideal society based on reason, science, and justice."[51] The forces that could hinder the hero's acculturation are almost all located in the traditional Jewish community; he fights ignorance, sanctimoniousness, greed, and injustice, all of which have Jewish faces. His story corresponds to an Enlightenment teleology; he emerges from a traditional world he perceives as frozen in time into the historic current he sees as sweeping Europe swiftly forward. He rejects a Jewish religious conception of time, which is fundamentally cyclical and apocalyptic, marked by a cycle of festivals throughout the year and repeating episodes of persecution, guided by an unwavering hope for redemption. In its place he puts the dream of progress, attainable by deliberate steps along a clearly marked path. In the tale of a Jew's deliberate acculturation space is divided into the Jewish world and the outside world; the hero flees the Jewish town, which he associates with unwanted wives and children, dirt, poverty, and every sort of petty evil. He strives to enter the outside world, characterized by freedom, the fellowship of intellectual equals, and wealth untainted by greed or corruption. Time is similarly split into the past and the future, the former equated with traditional Jews who, in the hero's opinion, are literally living in the past by refusing to interact with the secular world, and the latter identified with the world of secular learning. This model permits a single path to the hero: he must struggle to leave the Jewish world of the past for the future and the outside world.

In considering Bogrov's adaptation of the maskilic type, I will briefly compare *Notes of a Jew* to an early Haskalah mastertext. The autobiography of Solomon Maimon, published in German in 1793, details a Jewish man's search for enlightenment and his struggle against Jewish obscurantism and conservatism.[52] Inspired by Rousseau's *Confessions*, Maimon writes in detail of his life and his thoughts, criticizing the society that had misunderstood him and the limitations that Jewish traditions imposed on his lifestyle and his learning.[53] Even as a child, he yearns for secular knowledge, mastering astronomy with a Hebrew text. Eventually, he gains access to German books, reading first philosophical and then belletristic literature. He leaves his wife and child in Poland to live in Germany, where he meets Jews and non-Jews who are equally interested in ideas. Bogrov and his Russian Jewish contemporaries read Maimon's autobiography in German or, after 1871, in Russian. The work's status as a standard-bearer for the Berlin Haskalah presumably inspired Adolf Landau, the editor of *Evreiskaia biblioteka*, the first literary-historical "thick journal" published in Russian on Jewish topics, to include a section of it in his first volume.[54] It appeared the same year as the first section of *Notes of a Jew* in *Otechestvennye zapiski*.

Maimon's famous work shares a host of formal devices with Bogrov's. Most obvious are the autobiographical features: first-person narration; frequent appeals to the reader (explanations, exhortations); the central role of a single character who moves from one place and time to another, frequently pauses to analyze his own actions and motivations, and reads voraciously.[55] Equally striking is the choice of language; both writers used a non-Jewish second language (literally, a third language, following Hebrew)—German for Maimon, Russian for Bogrov—rather than their native Yiddish, which would have made their works more accessible to Jewish readers.[56] Linguistic form and content combine in the project of encouraging Jewish readers to expand their knowledge. Both books describe the circumstances under which the narrator learned his second language, and both frequently refer to the power of this newfound learning. Bogrov's narrator, Srul, like Maimon's narrator, turns early in the story from study of the Talmud to secular literature in Jewish and non-Jewish languages (p. 69). The neighbors teach him Russian, then he reads "forbidden Yiddish books" (p. 309), undoubtedly by maskilim. Eventually, he learns German (the language that could have given him access to Maimon's book): "I acquired a familiarity with the German language and its belletristic and popular-scientific literature and I was suffused in bliss, immersed in that living source of ideas" (p. 426).

Srul leads through positive and negative examples, exemplifying the benefits of acculturation and mocking the traditions he despises. In the first paragraph of his autobiography, he addresses himself to the "Jewish reading public" with the assertion that he considers his book only "the first . . . step on the path toward the awakening of a consciousness that must lead the Jews toward a new life, one in accordance with the rational nature of man" (p. 1). Like Maimon, he opposes this "new life" specifically to Hasidism, corruption, poor education, and a lifestyle that condemned most Jews to poverty and unhappiness.[57] He and Maimon endorsed the same positive models: secular, especially German, culture, and the liberated Jew, at home among gentiles, dependent on no one.

Step by step, Srul remakes his attitudes according to the dictates of "the rational nature of man." In one incident, the young narrator and his Russian friend Olga insult each other's customs and national cuisine. He begins by pointing out that her meat fried in butter is not kosher:

> "It's disgusting and nasty. It's treyf. Yuck, how treyf!" I said.
> "And kugel, and onions, and garlic—what, they're not disgusting and nasty? They really stink!" Olga stated with no less aversion.
> "No, that's kosher, so it tastes good." (p. 62)

Before Olga's mother can intervene to stop the quarrel, Olga's brother Mitya, who had been reading a book of proverbs and ignoring the other children, observes, "Every sandpiper praises his own swamp" [*Vsiak kulik svoe boloto khvalit*] (ibid.)—that is, we admire only what we know. Bogrov's reader can extrapolate from the children's example to understand the point: understanding of general truths about human behavior will give the lie to old-fashioned prejudice.

The choice of a Russian folk saying to summarize a general truth signals Srul's interest in his own mastery of Russian culture. Later, he quarrels with his wife about his fondness for these sayings:

> "God helps those who help themselves [*Na Boga nadeisia, a sam ne ploshai*]. Do you know this wise Russian saying?"
> "I don't know anything Russian, and I don't want to. I've said this to you a hundred times already." (p. 572)

The wife, in rejecting "anything Russian," recalls Maimon's wife (pp. 141–42): both women symbolize backward Jews who avoid contact with Russian culture, and contrast to those Jews who are able to acculturate fully to Russian norms.

Prototypically, acculturation is bound up with reading. Whereas the maskilic hero gains enlightenment through his reading of secular literature in European languages, the ignorant Jews whom he criticizes have only an inadequate knowledge of any language, even the one they purport to know best, Hebrew. The maskilim lambasted the teaching method in traditional Jewish schools, where pupils were taught to read Hebrew without the benefit of grammars or dictionaries. Aksenfeld, like his more popular contemporary the Yiddish author Y. Y. Linetski, concentrated on exposing the absurdity of ignorant and ill-read Hasidim. One contemporaneous critic noted that Bogrov, more than other Jews writing in Russian, revealed his debt to Yiddish writers such as Aksenfeld and Linetski in his ironic descriptions of these comical types.[58] For instance, Srul realizes that his despotic boss Tugalov is appallingly ignorant of even the most basic Hebrew texts. Tugalov calls him in to ask him a question:

> "I've heard, smarty-pants [*shchegol'*], that you're a terrible bookworm. Please tell me if this book is telling the truth."
> "Please inform me what book you mean."
> "The Devil knows what book it is. But it tells a horrible story about some forefather of ours, Abraham . . . that apparently he wanted to kill his own son, Isaac." (p. 313)

Srul explains that the story is not only biblical, but even part of the daily prayer service: "After all, you yourself, every morning during your prayers, tell this story, which in Hebrew is called the *Akedah*." Once he is out of his boss's presence, Srul joins the reader in laughter. However, he does not blame Tugalov alone for his ignorance: "Though Tugalov read Hebrew, he did not understand a single word of it, like the majority of the Jews, who pray meaninglessly."

Unlike Tugalov, Srul reads carefully, and he learns from his texts and his experiences. Bogrov signals his debt to Maimon by borrowing an entire episode from him illustrating the process of his education. Maimon's narrator learns from a rabbi about the kabbalistic secret of becoming invisible. He fasts three days and recites the necessary prayers, then tests his invisibility by hitting another student, who demonstrates that the spell has failed when he immediately returns the blow (pp. 75–76). Eighty years later, Bogrov's adolescent narrator and a friend dip into works of the kabbalah and also learn of a method for becoming invisible. Inspired by thoughts of the miracles they will work once no one can see them, they attempt to go through the procedure. After fasting, taking a ritual bath, and reciting the prescribed prayers, they are discovered by a passerby who informs them that he can see them perfectly well and then laughs at their confusion (pp. 179–84). For both authors, the failed invisibility spell marks the beginning of the path toward enlightenment. The narrators attempt the spell when they still believe in Jewish mystical learning, then go on to reject those aspects of Judaism that they see as "superstition." Their tests of the invisibility spell oppose the mysticism of the kabbalah to knowledge that results from gathering information and forming testable hypotheses.

Although Bogrov recycles Maimon's depictions of education, he recognizes that all new knowledge is not of the same uniformly high quality. The first secular book that Srul attempts to read on his own—after he has lost the guidance of his Christian neighbors—represents an aspect of secular culture that both attracts and repulses him. His father's coworker lends him a book called *Angliiskii milord* [The English Milord], with a frontispiece featuring two scantily clad ladies and a man in a helmet and armor. This immensely popular story, published over and over from the seventeenth through the nineteenth century, was a Russian version of a European romance in verse, *Sir Beves of Hamtoun.*[59] It tells of a knight who falls in love with a beautiful lady but must undergo countless trials before being reunited with her.[60] It is usually classified as a *lubok*, a cheaply printed popular work of pulp fiction. (The plural is *lubki*.) Bogrov's young narrator reads with fascination and delight about the adventures of this hero, "completely forgetting the entire world" (p. 175). After he is married, Srul finds books of the same type in a library belonging to his wife's relative: "I swallowed up all sorts of literary rot [*gnil'*], which heated up my young imagination without enriching my mind" (p. 258). (He could have been reading works of romance and adventure not only in Russian, but also in Yiddish—and Srul admits that he reads a great deal in Yiddish as well as Russian when he compliments himself on the fluency and wit of his spoken Yiddish, the result, he notes, of a certain "well-readness" [*nachitannost'*] [p. 268]).

Srul's wife, Khaika, mocks his favorite reading material: "Someone might think that he's gathering money from the pages, but he's reading about how Vas'ka fell in love with Tan'ka" (p. 259). Although he defends himself against his wife's recriminations, Srul is yet unkinder in his own evaluation of these books:

> I was reading one of those pointless, mindless old-fashioned novels, that had no direction or any developed ideas and which, it seemed, were created solely to tickle the lazy imagination of a sleepy public. My imagination, already fairly active, was stirred up to a grotesque degree by this fanciful novel. It told of some kind of specter that appeared in the form of a woman to the hero of the novel at deepest midnight. (p. 27)

From a literary-historical perspective, the frequent disparaging references to *The English Milord* and other pulp novels show that Bogrov shared the concerns of both his Jewish and non-Jewish intellectual contemporaries. Yiddish writers such as Mendele Moikher Sforim and Aksenfeld were unified in their scorn for "mindless old-fashioned novels," Yiddish adventure stories, popular adaptations of chivalric romances—including the "Bovo-bukh," the Yiddish version of the story of Sir Beves—and contemporary potboilers.[61] The highbrow Yiddish writers called these stories *shund*, a term linked to the many Yiddish translations of European works of romance and adventure that were published during the second half of the nineteenth century and to writers such as Shomer (N. M. Shaykevich) and his disciples, who produced literally hundreds of blatantly derivative Yiddish adventure stories.[62]

Simultaneously, for educated Russian critics, *The English Milord* exemplified the problems with the literature of the *lubok*.[63] Indeed, in Nekrasov's *Komu na Rusi zhit' khorosho?* [Who Is Happy in Russia?], a catalogue of Russian life in the 1860s and 1870s (written from 1863 through 1878), the "stupid milord" exemplifies the trash that peasants foolishly choose over works by the more socially relevant authors Vissarion Belinsky and Nikolai Gogol:

Ekh! ekh! pridet li vremechko,
[. . .] kogda muzhik ne Bliukhera
i ne milorda glupogo—
Belinskogo i Gogolia
s bazara prineset?[64]

Well, well, will the time ever come
[...] when the peasant will bring not Bliukher
and not the stupid milord
but Belinsky and Gogol
home from the market?

So by the 1860s, when writers like Turgenev and Chernyshevsky were depicting high-minded youths and their efforts to reform society, Srul was not alone in disdaining (in public, if not in private) the socially irrelevant *lubki*.

Within *Notes of a Jew*, the references to pulp fiction participate in an essential phase of the novel of education: locating the texts whose reading can guide an adequate self-reform. Just as Srul first learned to reject kabbalistic treatises in favor of scientific textbooks, so he now details his attraction to and then his disillusionment with adventure stories. Those who read only Russian pop literature, it appears, will not reform themselves as successfully as those who absorb more serious works. Pantiel Berkovich, or, as he calls himself in Russian, Kondrat Borisovich, the clerk who lends the young narrator *The English Milord*, exemplifies the unsuccessful, incomplete assimilator. Kondrat first appears to Srul as a paragon of style, learning, and manners:

One young blond fellow stood out among them. He was a young man of about twenty-two, fairly handsome, with an extremely well-groomed face and with blue, damp, calflike eyes. . . . His shoes squeaked in the most melodic way when he stepped on the ground, and he stepped very confidently, proudly raising up his pomaded and perfumed head. . . . "Now that really is a good-looking man!" [*Vot krasavets, tak krasavets!*], I thought and inadvertently began to primp. (p. 168)

Over the next few pages, it becomes clear that Kondrat is a dandy who doesn't even know enough Russian to understand his own lowbrow books (p. 177). Srul brings Kondrat to meet Khaikel, a hunchback and professional *badkhen* [wedding jester] who mocks everyone and everything. Khaikel poses Kondrat a series of questions and finds out that he believes in God and believes that God forbids him to shave his beard, but that he shaves nonetheless because "it looks nicer." Khaikel concludes that Kondrat belongs to a class of "people with no character, people who act not on conviction, but on the spur of the moment. These are the most dangerous kind of people" (p. 200).

After thinking over Khaikel's words, Srul concludes that Kondrat offers a poor model for a modern Jew, although Khaikel himself can do little better:

> These are two transitional Jewish types, the combination of which should produce a third type, a perfect, reasonable Jew [*tip sover-shennogo, poriadochnogo evreia*]. Empty, elegant good-for-nothings [*svishchi*] like Kondrat Borisovich, and cynical Khaikels, though with their businesslike and sober minds, are still, unfortunately, all too plentiful among the Jews. May God grant that they evolve and change into a third, more complete type as soon as possible. (p. 201)

By defining Kondrat as a "transitional Jewish type," Bogrov's narrator employs the logic of the Russian literary critics of the 1850s and 1860s. He steps back from the text and, following Pisarev, defines it as populated by figures who stand in various relationships to the project of self-re-creation, "knights of the past" who incarnate the old values, and "knights of the future" who can inspire a beneficial reform. In this schema, Kondrat becomes a "knight of the past," a "weak man," a transitional type who is not suitable as a model for self-transformation. In dismissing Kondrat along with his library, Bogrov seems to acquiesce with the beliefs of the intellectuals of his era about the transformative power of literature, just as he reiterates their prejudices about adventure stories.

The lure of pulp fiction for Srul as well as Kondrat, though, may indicate something more complex than the ideology that acculturating Jews, like peasants, really ought to read "serious" books. One might interpret it instead—especially given the evident warmth and energy that the writer brings to the topic—as an indicator that Bogrov differed in some way from all the Russian and Jewish intellectuals who believed in the efficacy of novels of education. Perhaps Srul's susceptibility to the charms of love stories, ghost stories, and other "literary rot" points to the possibility that Bogrov had some hesitation about the idea of remaking oneself by means of a new reading list. Although pulp fiction might have made Kondrat into a ridiculous "transitional type," Srul still acknowledges his debt to it. He sees his reading, whether serious or trivial, as a window into a better world; even after losing his livelihood, when he is overwhelmed by the work necessary to pay off his debts and support his wife and children, his "irrepressible imagination, which developed in the soil of fanciful novels . . . sang another, sweet song" (p. 408).

By Nekrasov's standards, Srul's literary tastes improve little through the course of the book. The poet had called on the peasant reader to replace *The English Milord* with Nikolai Gogol's stories (oddly, held at the time to be the height of a denunciatory Realism) and Vissarion Belinsky's fiery literary-critical essays. Srul, seemingly, reads neither. The only Russian writer he cites explicitly in *Notes of a Jew* comes in the context of encountering his child-hood sweetheart, Olga, after many years; throughout their love affair, he compares her to the heroines of novels: "That lovely image seemed familiar to me, entirely taken from some novel I had read (p. 455). . . . For the first time in my life, I had come face to face with one of those charming creatures whom I had believed to be a myth, the fruit of poets' and novelists' imagina-tion" (p. 465). Finally, he feels compelled to ask Olga if she realizes her own similarity to a fictional character:

> "Have you read Vonliarliarsky's *The Great Lady* [Bol'shaia bary-nia]?" burst from my lips, almost against my own will. I sensed the in-congruity of the question, but it was already too late.
> "No." . . .
> "You . . . Madame Przyn'skaia . . . are a *Great Lady*. Farewell!" (pp. 472–73)

The Great Lady, the novella Srul cites, was written in 1852 by Vasily Von-liarliarsky. An author whose fame outlived him only briefly, Vonliarliarsky produced a few stories and travel sketches between 1850 and 1852, when he died at the age of thirty-eight. He was born in 1814, the same year as his close friend Lermontov, and the two were products of the same milieu; Vonliar-liarsky similarly claimed descent from an old, aristocratic family with exotic non-Russian roots (Lermontov's were Scottish, Vonliarliarsky's German). He and Lermontov were educated in the same officers' institute, served in the Guards, and sported similar moustaches. Vonliarliarsky was apparently ac-knowledged to be the better looking of the two, Lermontov the better writer.[65]

Vonliarliarsky's novel describes the sad fate of Petr Avdeevich Miunaby-Polevolov, a military man who retires at age twenty-eight in order to live in the provinces and manage his small estate. Petr Avdeevich is brave, handsome, and endowed with a fine mustache himself. He rescues Pelagaia Vlasevna, an attractive local damsel, when her carriage nearly rolls into a ravine. Their engagement is about to be announced when Petr Avdeevich meets the visiting widow Natal'ia Aleksandrovna, a wealthy countess. He falls in love with this "great lady," through a misunderstanding comes to the conclusion that she will marry him, and follows her back to St. Petersburg. When he realizes that she has no intention of the kind, his heart breaks. On the last pages, reduced to a ragged, penniless wanderer, Petr Avdeevich freezes to death on Natal'ia Aleksandrovna's land. His final thought is of her.

Based on this plot summary, if nothing else, it seems fair to assume that Vonliarliarsky was not one of the progressive critics' favorite writers. His novel has much more in common with *The English Milord* than with the works of Belinsky. It neither exposes the evils of society as it was then, nor suggests ways in which things might improve. In a larger sense, *The Great Lady* and the novel of education are centered around contrasting types, which grow out of contrasting understandings of the logic of human life. Where Maimon described a hero who wants to seize power over his own life and move it in a new direction, Vonliarliarsky's hero, like all "superfluous" men, fears that he can do nothing of the sort. In *The Great Lady*, chance plays a far greater role than the hero's will, and random meetings determine his fate. If Petr Avdeevich had not taken his servant's suggestion to participate in the Christmastide fortune-telling by going out on a clear night and asking the name of the first passing stranger, he would never have met Natal'ia Aleksandrovna.[66] Petr Avdeevich abandons all his life plans after he meets the countess and actually knows full well that she would never marry him: "That's a bird of a different feather, it's out of my range [*ne nashego polia iagoda, ne po nas zverek*]," he tells his neighbor.[67] Nonetheless, his obsession with her makes him believe that she might love him.

Characters in such a romance cannot plan their actions rationally, because, as Bakhtin notes, "all initiative and power belong to chance."[68] Romantic types such as Petr Avdeevich make it clear to the reader that they have relinquished control over their fate. The best-known example of this attitude in the Russian canon appears in Lermontov's *Hero of Our Time*, whose main character, Pechorin, constantly muses about the power of chance in determining the course of his life. Even while he thought he was pursuing his own pleasures, he realizes, he only "played the axe in the hands of fate."[69] At the same time, he denies that fate creates human lives in accordance with any kind of pattern: "Once wise people thought that the heavenly spheres cared about our picayune fights for a patch of ground or some kind of made-up rights! . . . Unlike them, we have neither hope nor the pleasure awaiting one who defies men or destiny."[70]

Even though Srul repeats the common criticism of adventure stories, and even though he begins his book by warning that his life is not "filled with the kind of romantic surprises that make the reader go all hot and cold" (p. 1), the world of his own hero, like Vonliarliarsky's world, obeys many of the rules of a romance. When he touches on love, honor, and fate, his narrative recalls *The English Milord*. The event most clearly drawn from the romance is his affair with Olga, with whom he has three fateful meetings. First, she and her family live next door to him when they are both children. Olga, who inspires him with childish love, knows her power over him and occasionally abuses it. Her decision to call him by a Russian name, Grisha (the nickname for Grigory), instead of the Yiddish Srul (p. 61) (the nickname for Yisroel, the Yiddish for Israel), symbolizes the beginning of the re-creation of the Jew according to Western standards: the quintessentially Jewish moniker is replaced by the name of popes and saints. Second, Olga appears at Srul's wedding. Intrigued by the colorful celebration, she has no idea that her long-lost childhood friend is involved (p. 249). On recognizing Olga's voice, Srul is overcome by despair, presumably because he identifies her with a better world, which his new wife can only prevent him from reaching. Third, Olga turns up as the estranged wife of a retired officer who worked as a clerk under Srul. Predictably, Olga and Srul fall in love, but she soon dies of tuberculosis. These three meetings, so important and so unanticipated, turn Srul's life into a romance. Like Vonliarliarsky's Petr Avdeevich, he encounters the heroine accidentally and promptly becomes obsessed by her, even though he realizes that she is "a bird of a different feather."

When the characters realize that they had known each other in childhood, they both acknowledge that Bogrov's plot device is a novelistic cliché:

"Well, well, I beg your pardon, my poor little Yidling [*bednyi zhidenok*]! From now on I am a fatalist [*fatalistkoi*]. Yes, that's why when I read your name in Przhin'sky's letter, I was so interested. . . . Yes. Life is more romantic than a novel [*Zhizn' romantichnee romana*]."

"And some novels are more banal than life itself [*Inoi roman—poshlee samoi zhizni*]."

"In the future you must not dare to insult life, don't dare to call it banal."

"No. Now I have no right to do that, but before . . . " (p. 487)

Olga begins by reversing her and Srul's roles: though he has just helped her, she recalls the time when her family had helped him, a "poor Yidling." She then evokes the final chapter of *Hero of Our Time*, "The Fatalist." Both "Yidling" and "fatalist" suggest that Olga sees the two of them as playing parts in a familiar story; she then goes on to pun about the predictable turn the novel has taken. Srul's answer recalls his earlier dismissal of such boilerplate romances: they are *poshlyi*, that is, vulgar, banal, low class. When Olga chides him, though, he agrees that "he has no right" to level such criticism. Both characters' lines are heavy with irony, especially following the criticisms of Srul's reading tastes throughout the book. Practically every detail of the love affair echoes the "novelistic" tone at its onset—indeed, Olga herself seems to have been created piecemeal out of familiar literary motifs. Although as a child she speaks Russian at home, she marries a man with a Polish last name, Przyn'sky, and is later herself described as Polish (p. 496). (The image of beautiful Polish women like Olga appears often in Russian fiction.)[71] She earns her living as a painter, but she is also a pianist—artistic leanings that similarly fit a literary pattern. When she accompanies Srul as he plays his violin, he realizes that she is "an artist in her soul" who knows that her favorite melody is "a cry, a sob," created not by "cold science" but by "the heart" (p. 476). Even Olga's death from tuberculosis is a literary cliché.

In this context, Srul's affair with Olga shows not so much that true fellowship between Jew and gentile is conceivable as that, as Vonliarliarsky showed, the world is not kind to lovers.[72] Olga herself has no prejudice. When Srul points out that his Jewishness might be a barrier to their love, she asserts that she does not believe in such differences, because her mother had imbued her with tolerance: "Since childhood I was taught to see in a person a human, and not a Russian, a Frenchman, or a Turk; a human, and not a Christian, a Muslim, or a heathen; a human, and not a general, a merchant, or a bourgeois. As a child I was even in love with one of Cooper's heroes, an Indian, ha ha ha!" (p. 461).

However, others' unwillingness to accept the love affair makes Srul realize that her broad-mindedness is an unworldly ideal, doomed, like her, to what a Romantic might see as a beautiful death. The imagined childish love affair with an exotic—and fictional—Indian prefigures Olga's adult attachment to an equally exotic Jew. In addition, it further unsettles the novel of education by creating a link between Bogrov's hero and James Fenimore Cooper's, between a Russian Jewish autodidact and a quintessentially Romantic figure, an American Indian such as the hero of Cooper's *Pathfinder* (popular in Russia in the 1840s), imagined as noble precisely in his ignorance and savagery.

One historian reads Olga's love for Cooper's Indian as an indication that her affair with the Jew is similarly ridiculously literary; it serves to highlight the naturalism of the story of the cantonist Yerukhim that follows it. Olga's death thus becomes a necessary step in Srul's maturation, his abandonment of the "bookish sentimentality" that constrains his development of a truly modern consciousness.[73] One might also interpret the episode as making it easier for Srul to assume the stance of Lermontov's Pechorin, isolated from society, disappointed in love as in all other human interactions, convinced that the individual is powerless against the pitiless fate that controls human lives. After Olga's death, when he is not allowed to attend her funeral in a church, Srul speaks to a friend who agrees with this understanding of life: "Two forces battle eternally. Evil is stronger . . . it will win. Evil fate has done you an ill turn" [*medvezh'iu uslugu okazala tebe . . . zlaia sud'ba*] (p. 494). The emphasis on the power of merciless fate over the individual brings the narrative closer to Lermontov's fatalism and further away from Maimon's rationalism.

Whereas Olga had defined herself as a "fatalist," the hero of a romance, Srul clearly wants that role for himself. His actions as well as his words show that he understands himself in terms of the behavioral code by which Lermontov's and Vonliarliarsky's heroes lived. Hearing gentile friends tell anecdotes demonstrating that Jews are cowards, he responds with a tale in which a Jew takes advantage of his reputation for cowardice to defeat an attacker. He then tells a story from his own life, in which he rescues a traveling Russian aristocrat who has encountered difficulties. The aristocrat, not realizing that his companion is Jewish, exhibits his prejudices about the Jews, then exposes his own cowardice when he hesitates to try a dangerous river crossing in bad weather. During the difficult passage, the aristocrat faints from fear (p. 151). When the two part, Srul's revelation that he is Jewish elicits a shocked apology.

The story of a Jewish traveler rescuing a gentile who takes him for a non-

Jew is not original to Bogrov. It appeared, for example, in a work typical of the Enlightenment, Gotthold Ephraim Lessing's 1749 play, *Die Juden* [The Jews].[74] Lessing, a friend of Moses Mendelssohn, based on him his famous portrayal of a generous and judicious Jew in *Nathan der Weise* [Nathan the Wise]. In the eyes of the maskilim, Lessing represented gentile tolerance and the best European values. However, by setting a tale like Lessing's in the context of a discussion of the Jews' bravery, Bogrov underscores the difference between his priorities and those of the Berlin Haskalah. Lessing tells of a Jew who rescues a wealthy Christian, who then attempts to reward the Jew with money and offers him his daughter's hand in marriage. When the traveler, declining the match, reveals his Jewishness, the Christian is embarrassed to remember the disparaging remarks he had made about Jews earlier. All the action of Lessing's play reinforces the moral that one must judge others in a "less sweeping way."[75] Bogrov's hero, in contrast, is concerned less about judgment as such and more about bravery, cowardice, and what constitutes them. He justifies his risky behavior with a credo reminiscent of Pechorin's: "Life is not worth trembling over; in any case, it's already lost, or we'll soon lose it" (p. 152).

Whereas the viewer of Lessing's play sees that sufficient care in judgment will disclose the world's logical underpinnings, Bogrov's reader might come to Pechorin's realization that the universe is ironically ordered and that the assumption of a brave stance (even one associated with an obviously foolhardy action) is more aesthetically valid than a reasoned decision. The episode shows that Srul cares not only about acquiring a Western education but also about showing that he is as fearless as any nobleman, ready and willing to endanger his life for his honor. The change in focus between Lessing's original and Bogrov's imitation is linked to the differing denouements of the love story: while Srul goes on to love the Christian Olga, Lessing's traveler renounces the possibility of romance with a non-Jew.

What does it matter that even while Bogrov makes fun of thrillers and romances, he writes some chapters of his story of Jewish acculturation according to the model of a thriller and a romance? He was certainly not alone in his ambivalence. Many writers in Russian (and undoubtedly every other language) have attempted to distinguish themselves from the majority of scribblers by defining within their texts a category of "pop fiction" or "trash." Their own work, they imply, must be better than the stories that the maturing hero learns to put aside (no matter how hard it might be for the reader to see the difference). The combination of philosophical musings in a serious tone with what one scholar calls "wildly improbably melodrama" is especially characteristic of the Hebrew fiction that the maskilim produced in the nineteenth century.[76] The ideological position of the Haskalah writers, who urged their readers, like their heroes, to take control over their lives and to seek out enlightenment, did not prevent them from depicting a world governed by coincidence and chance rather than the decisions of individuals. The motif of a beautiful love affair doomed by an unfeeling world is especially common in Hebrew Haskalah fiction, whose heroes tended to divorce the wives whom their parents had chosen for them in adolescence, without going on to find any satisfying mature erotic attachment.[77]

Thus, I do not want to argue that the reliance of Bogrov's narrative not only on the model of Maimon but also on those of *The English Milord* and *The Great Lady* makes it stand out among the literature of the nineteenth-century Eastern Haskalah. Rather, his draw toward romances and his casting of episodes from the hero's life in romanticizing terms point toward some of the differences between his view of the possibility of self-reform and the depictions of reformers that he found in sources such as Maimon's autobiography. Although Bogrov and Maimon are united by their pathbreaking decisions to write their autobiographical tales of Jewish assimilation in the languages of their respective target cultures, and although their works share formal features and an intense focus on the process of education, it seems that Bogrov could not imagine the narrative of acculturation entirely in Maimon's terms. In the language of nineteenth-century Russian literary criticism, he could not entirely reaffirm Pisarev's faith in the transformative power of the literary "knight of the future." His narrator, though he undoubtedly reads Maimon, cannot go on successfully to reeducate himself and thus turn himself into a new type of person. Nor can he, in his own text, model such a new man, one whose story should lead his readers to remake themselves in his image. By putting himself in the place of Vonliarliarsky's hero, his narrator assumes the role of the superfluous man or, by his own definition, the bad assimilator. When contrasted with Maimon's autobiography, *Notes of a Jew* appears closer to Annenkov's liberal vision than Chernyshevsky's radical one. Bogrov depicts the process of education and change as gradual and contingent, and the inspirational type of the unquestionably new man as terribly elusive.

Bogrov and Pinkus: The Jewish Writer as Criminal

Bogrov's hesitations about the effectiveness of self-reeducation emerge most strongly in his later works: the second half of *Notes of a Jew* and other texts of the 1870s. Most striking are Srul's musings after he has lost his house and all his possessions to arson.

> However I tried to look at my life—whether I remembered the bitter past, faced the unsuccessful present, or imagined the probable future—on all sides I was struck by an unanswerable question: Who is to blame?
> Of course, first of all, I am to blame: I am a Jew!
> To be a Jew—that is the most serious crime; it is a sin that cannot be redeemed; it is a blot that cannot be erased; it is a brand that Fate impresses at the moment of birth; it is a mustering call for all accusations; it is the mark of Cain on the forehead of an innocent person whom everyone has already judged.
> The Jew's groan does not evoke pity in anyone. It serves you right: don't be a Jew. No, even that's not enough! Don't be *born* a Jew. (p. 407)

The rich allusions in this passage undermine the story of the Jew as successful autodidact. The first sentence concludes with a question familiar to the Russian readers of Bogrov's time, "Who Is to blame?" [*Kto vinovat?*], the title of a novel that Alexandr Herzen wrote in 1847. A favorite of the progressive critics, the book depicts the efforts of some noble young people to free themselves from an unhappy marriage and from the stultifying atmosphere of the Russian provinces. In Herzen's formulation, the answer to the title's question is clear: a conservative society, a reactionary government, and the heroes' own weaknesses are to blame for their continuing unhappiness and for the suffocation of everything in Russia that could be virtuous, intelligent, or productive. When Srul answers the question by blaming not society and not his own actions but what he defines as his unalterable essence, his bitterness strengthens his implied rejection of Herzen's progressive ideals.

In the following paragraph, Bogrov presents a series of six metaphors for the condition of the Jew. He argues against the mutability of that condition when he compares it to a sin "that cannot be redeemed" and a blot "that cannot be erased." Borrowing the language of a legal system that condemned criminals to branding in order to mark their exclusion from society and their deprivation of rights, he compares the Jew to a branded person—but though the state's branding of the criminal was undergoing challenges from liberal activists, the Jew, in his formulation, is branded by an inexorable fate. In mentioning the mark of Cain, Bogrov uses a potent biblical image. In Genesis 4:8–16, after Cain kills his brother Abel, God punishes him but then puts a sign on his forehead in order to prevent others from attacking him. The sign serves just as brands did in the Russian Empire: it marks Cain as a criminal and it prevents him from seeking the comfort of society. To be a Jew in Russia, Bogrov suggests, is to be forced to play a degrading and inappropriate biblical role: to be treated as Cain in spite of one's innocence.

The speaker's voice changes in the final lines. At first, as throughout the book, Bogrov had used the first person ("I tried to look. . . . I am to blame"). Here, switching to the second person, the narrator assumes the perspective of a non-Jew, who repeats and justifies the opinions of a hostile gentile society: "It serves you right: don't be a Jew." The poisonous irony of the tone is heightened by all the attention that the narrator had paid in the first half of the book to his acquisition of a second language, and his longing to take on that very Russian perspective from which he now stands condemned. No education, the narrator asserts here, could remedy his problem. The only solution is impossible: "Don't be *born* a Jew."

Merely by being born Jewish, the narrator asserts, he has broken a law and committed "the most serious crime." By employing the metaphor of the Jew as criminal, Bogrov gestures toward a literary type with a lengthy pedigree in Russian literature and folklore. Jews in the Pale of Settlement often worked as merchants, the grain of truth inside Russian (and Polish) stereotypes of them as wheeler-dealers, unscrupulous profiteers who cheat their customers right and left.[78] Russian literature had developed various types of the shifty Jew, from Yankel, the trader and informer in Gogol's "Taras Bulba," to the Jewish moneylender in Pushkin's "Covetous Knight" [Skupoi rytsar'] who offers to help his client poison his wealthy father. "The Criminal" [Prestupnik], a poem by Lermontov, even features two Jewish highwaymen.[79] By evoking the type of the Jewish criminal, so familiar in depictions of Jews by non-Jews,

Bogrov measures his distance from the Haskalah effort to reform not only the Jew but also the Jew's image among the gentiles.

Bogrov would go even further in that direction in the late 1870s. His own novel had been published in a non-Jewish journal at the beginning of the 1870s, but toward the decade's end his mood seems to have soured. He warned Levanda that it would not even be worth it to submit such a work to a mainstream journal: "A long novel, with *Jewish* heroes to boot, will not be accepted. . . . Jewish goods, as we can see, are not in style."[80] He was not entirely right in this, since stories on Jewish topics continued to be written and published—at least by non-Jews. For instance, in 1878, a few months before Bogrov's letter to Levanda, the Russian writer Nikolai Leskov had published a story with a particularly foreign-sounding title—"Rakushanskii melamed" [The Melamed of Österreich]—in Mikhail Katkov's *Russkii Vestnik* [The Russian Herald].[81] In it, he repeats all the clichés, spread by Bogrov, Levanda, and other Russian Jewish writers, about the *melamed* [Talmud teacher for children], the *heder* [the school where the melamed teaches], and the inefficiency and backwardness of the entire traditional Jewish system of education. Bogrov, evidently annoyed by this story, responded in 1879 with a four-part series in the journal *Russkii evrei* [The Russian Jew] entitled "Talmud i Kabbala po 'Russkomu Vestniku'" [The Talmud and Kabbalah according to *Russkii Vestnik*].[82] In his parodic review, as in *Notes of a Jew*, Bogrov uses the type of the Jew as criminal to challenge the ideology associated with the Jew as maskil. As in the longer work, by manipulating old literary types, he creates new, hybrid forms, perhaps more adequate to describe his experiences and his attitudes.

Leskov's frame narrator in "The Melamed of Österreich," Major Nikanor Ivanych Pleskunov, had spent years as a customs official among the Galician Jews, on the border between the Russian and the Austro-Hungarian empires. This experience, he boasts, has given him the opportunity to study Jews and to understand them, their customs, their religion, and their weaknesses. The soldiers in his battalion voice their fears (common in the late 1870s) of a worldwide Jewish conspiracy, led by the British Empire in the hands of Disraeli, that threatens to crush the Slavs. Pleskunov uses his anecdote—one that, like many of Leskov's stories, is reminiscent of a folktale—to demonstrate that

Jews are really not that frightening. In his story, a drunken Cossack enters the home of the melamed Skharia and demands food and vodka. Skharia, in fear of the Cossack's whip, produces them. However, Skharia's slow-witted Ukrainian maid Oksana shames the melamed by appropriating the whip and using it to drive the Cossack out of town. The moral: Jews are cowardly, imprisoned by their own superstitions, and certainly not to be feared.

Bogrov accepts Leskov's signature claim that he did not invent the story — he just wrote down what he heard from Major Pleskunov. Bogrov therefore describes the circumstances under which Major Pleskunov could have heard the story from Pinkus, his Jewish servant, or factor. In Bogrov's retelling, Pinkus simultaneously acts as Pleskunov's agent and works with a band of the very smugglers who are Pleskunov's adversaries. One snowy night, the smugglers order Pinkus to distract Pleskunov while they sneak some valuable goods across the border. So Pinkus visits the major and his wife and spends the evening telling them the story of the Austrian melamed, embroidering it with as many ridiculous details about Jewish customs as he can remember or invent, until his co-conspirators' operation is over.

Bogrov's reaction to Leskov's story has three somewhat contradictory goals, which demonstrate that, like *Notes of a Jew*, the review falls among several attitudes toward the possibility of revising the self. First and most obviously, as he did in *Notes of a Jew*, Bogrov is defending Jews—here including melameds—from an assault on their honor and their courage. Second, Bogrov is returning to his interest in education, attacking Pleskunov's—that is, Leskov's—credentials for telling this story. He does not go so far as to argue that Leskov's conclusions about the backwardness of the traditional Jewish way of life and system of education are incorrect because he is not Jewish, but he insists that Leskov does not have the expertise to make this claim authoritatively—that Leskov is an inadequate intermediary between Jewish and Russian cultures. Third, Bogrov's choice not just to review "The Melamed of Österreich," but to parody it, reveals that his purpose is not only rejection of Leskov's critique of Jewish traditionalism but also, as in *Notes of a Jew*, experimentation with and a kind of commentary on some of the types in canonical Russian literature.

In *Notes of a Jew*, Bogrov had assailed all the aspects of Jewish life that Leskov criticizes in his story, and had even complained that other Jews had attacked him for his willingness to disparage Jewish traditions in Russian, to wash the Jews' dirty linen in front of non-Jews (pp. 587–88). But regardless of the fundamental similarity of their views, Bogrov's primary concern in his review seems to be to denounce Leskov for his criticism of Jews and Jewish traditions. His playful description of the cheerful Cossack merrily terrorizing the backward Jews evidently struck a nerve with Bogrov, who takes issue with the author's light tone, his effort to "present his favorite as a bold and clever chap" when "for the Jews these victorious warriors were a real scourge of God" who stole from them and abused them physically.[83] Not only, he points out, were the Jews oppressed by the government and harassed by Cossacks, they were also very poor. Leskov's narrator had described the fear of the devil that made Skharia get dressed under the covers: "Skharia never put on his shirt while standing or sitting, but did all that only while lying under the bedcover, so that the devil who spies on every Jew wouldn't see his wondrous body" (p. 415).

Bogrov, in his retelling, simultaneously defends the Jews from the charge of superstition, exhibits their poverty, and accuses all Russians—presumably including Leskov and his narrator—of a lack of delicacy:

If Pleskunov only knew that the pious Jew observes this custom not from the stupid fear of some demon but from delicacy and modesty, in his cramped quarters, where several unrelated families often crowd together . . . then he would see such an act of modesty as less blameworthy than the custom . . . by which our [Russian] public baths are open at the same time to clients of both sexes.[84]

Bogrov put even more time and energy into an attack on Leskov—masked, of course, as an attack on Pleskunov—for pretending to be what he was not: an expert on Jewish matters with privileged knowledge of Jewish culture. At the story's beginning, Pleskunov claims to know the Jews well, telling his audience, "If you really knew the Jew . . . " (p. 414). Leskov himself had made similar claims in a letter he wrote to the Judeophobic publisher Aleksei Suvorin, advertising "The Melamed of Österreich":

Keeping your anti-Yid [kontro-zhidovskie] articles in mind, I wrote you a story of the same type. . . . I don't know Yiddish and don't work with it, but based my story on the Yids' temperament, which arises out of the Yids' Talmudic morals and superstitious prejudices, which are stronger in that tribe than in any other. Usually fiction writers don't talk about them, because they don't know about them—because it's harder to study them than it is to make fun of Yiddish.[85]

Leskov presents himself in the letter and Pleskunov in the story as ethnographers who have studied the Jews in detail and can relay their knowledge to the Russian public.[86] Bogrov challenged precisely Leskov's credentials as an ethnographer. He began his review with a quote from Ivan Krylov: "It's trouble when the shoemaker starts to make pies and the pastry-chef to fix shoes [*Beda kol' pirogi nachnet pechi sapozhnik, /A sapogi tachat' pirozhnik*]."[87] Bogrov asserts—none too subtly—that Pleskunov and by extension Leskov are incompetent cooks who don't belong in the kitchen when they try to pass themselves off as ethnographers.

Bogrov presents himself here, as he does in much of *Notes of a Jew*, as a more professional mediator, an expert on Jewish life who is truly competent to describe it for outsiders. He backs up this assertion with numerous examples of Leskov's inaccuracies and exaggerations. In maskilic fashion, Bogrov relies on sarcasm to attack the attitudes of which he disapproves. He reserves his most withering scorn for Pleskunov's most obvious blunder: Skharia, the melamed in the story, is described as a wealthy man who has grown rich from teaching. However, in every description of shtetl life, melameds are inevitably, famously, eternally poor. Bogrov goes on at some length about this "melamed who has grown rich from teaching":

And how could he not have grown rich! Please! Melameds receive ten to fifteen rubles per semester. Multiply the number of students by the amount they pay, and you get a figure that Rothschild himself would envy. True, you have to subtract the amount you would need to feed the melamed's wife and a crew of ragamuffin kids, but when you consider that Yids eat only onions and garlic, you'll see that these expenses will be quite insignificant.[88]

Although Bogrov's use of humor to reveal ignorance places him securely in the maskilic tradition, it might seem that he is indulging, in his review, in a kind of in-group politics, asserting that only Jewish writers have the authority to describe and especially to criticize Jews. Such a belief would contradict the Enlightenment principle that all knowledge is accessible to everyone, in favor of a more Romantic faith in the authenticity and uniqueness of each artist, as well as of the nation that artist represents. Explicitly, though, Bogrov does not condemn the entire project of Russian ethnographic writing on the Jews; he simply finds Leskov incompetent in this matter. As a member of the ethnic group described, he can tell that Leskov, like most other non-Jewish writers who described Jews at the time, hasn't done his homework: "They know just as much about the religious, communal, and personal life of the Jew as a redskin knows about life in our ladies' institutions."[89] Bogrov accuses these particular writers of being too lazy to do their job right, but he does not explicitly renounce his faith in education, indicating that some non-Jewish writer may eventually put enough work into learning about the Jews and produce a worthwhile piece.

Once Bogrov dismisses Leskov's credentials as a writer "on the Jews," he can explain how to recognize the kind of writer who is truly competent to address this topic: in his words, "a person who knows and has studied the Jew, his external and internal forms, his character and qualities," a person who is in addition "unbiased and objective."[90] One might even conclude from this description that Bogrov has himself in mind. If Leskov's story is "a pointless waste of writing paper," then Bogrov hints that his own writings on the Jews and the Jewish question, in contrast, are worth the paper and the reader's time.[91]

Even while he distances himself from Leskov, though, Bogrov identifies with him by reusing his appropriation of Russian Romantic literature. "The Melamed of Österreich" is subtitled "rasskaz na bivuake," a story told around the fire at an army camp. This subtitle situates Leskov's work in the Romantic genre of the soldier's tale, some of whose most famous practitioners were Lermontov, Alexandr Bestuzhev (author of "Vecher na bivuake" [Evening at the Campfire] and "Vtoroi vecher na bivuake" [Second Evening at the Campfire]), and Pushkin (e.g., "Vystrel" [The Shot]). Military service—most frequently in the Caucasus—was a rite of passage for aristocratic men in the early-nineteenth-century Russian Empire and, especially, for Romantic writers. Thus, the *rasskaz na bivuake* became a genre particularly closely associated with the honor of a Russian officer. Leskov follows up on this association in the story's first paragraph, where he describes his narrator, Major Pleskunov, as "an amiable, calm, and brave officer of the vanishing breed of Lermontov's Maxim Maximych" (p. 409). If Pleskunov is cousin to one of Lermontov's narrators in *Hero of Our Time*, then Leskov's story aligns itself with Lermontov's tradition. Like Lermontov's novel, Leskov's story has elements of the joke [*anekdot*]; like Bestuzhev, Leskov chooses this genre to show off his knowledge about an exotic non-Russian group.

Bogrov, in his review, makes the most of Leskov's references to Lermontov. He too, in his first paragraph, notes Pleskunov's descent from the "vanishing (alas!) breed of Lermontov's Maxim Maximych."[92] In the next paragraph, he calls Pleskunov a "fatalist," another obvious reference to the final chapter in *Hero of Our Time*. Later, he calls the drunken Cossack a "hero of his own time" and a "Lermontovian hero."[93] In an atmosphere so redolent of Lermontov, the reader cannot fail to notice that Bogrov, just like Leskov, has set his tale in the Romantic genre of the story at an army encampment.[94] Like Leskov in "The Melamed of Österreich," Bogrov, in his story about Pinkus, the double-dealing Jewish agent and part-time Scheherazade, exploits the genre's possibilities for telling a joke and for displaying the writer's ethnographic prowess.

Bogrov's reversal of Leskov's original, in which he assigns the narrative voice to the smuggler Pinkus, recalls another *rasskaz na bivuake* that forms a chapter of *Hero of Our Time*. In "Taman'," Pechorin is almost drowned by a band of smugglers, but at the end of the episode, he seems to regret having "disturbed the peace" of some "honest contrabandists" [*chestnye kontrabandisty*].[95] The literary genealogy of Pinkus the smuggler, though, includes more than Lermontov's honorable criminals. The Jewish smuggler is a common type in Russian literature. In story after story (and perhaps in reality as well), the Jews in the western borderlands of the empire took advantage of their linguistic and familial ties to Jews on the other side of the border in order to import and export all manner of goods without paying taxes. To cite only two examples, Movsha in Faddei Bulgarin's picaresque novel *Ivan Ivanovich Vyzhigin* (1828) smuggles luxury goods concealed in barrels of tar and potash, and Yankel in Gogol's novella "Taras Bulba" (1842) agrees to smuggle the hero to Warsaw under a load of bricks (after explaining how experience has taught him it would be a mistake to conceal him instead in a barrel of fish or *gorelka* [Ukrainian vodka]).

In giving the narrator's role to a Jewish smuggler, Bogrov continued the juxtaposition of conflicting types and conflicting ideologies that he had begun in *Notes of a Jew*. As in the novel, he places some emphasis on education, on the process by which the hero acquires knowledge (even if, as in the case of Major Pleskunov, he learns only to repeat tall tales). Bogrov was the heir to a maskilic tradition that urged Jews to work to attain an education in order to convince the state to grant them emancipation. The goal was to show one-self worthy of certain rights, such as residence outside the Pale of Settlement. The narrative of such an education contrasts with the criminal's tale, which celebrates strength in adversity and the ability to make do. Of course, the review is not in itself an acculturation narrative, but in its development of the two literary types of the Jew as educated person and the Jew as criminal, it picks up the themes of *Notes of a Jew*, casting light on it and thus on the way in which the story of the Jew's self-reform entered Russian literature. In *Notes of a Jew* and even more in his review of "The Melamed of Österreich," Bogrov gives a figure standing in for the Russian Jewish writer the face of a criminal who recognizes that he is outside the state's legal system from the start. That the literary type of the Jewish criminal represented everything that the maskilim strove to refute in non-Jewish perceptions of the Jews makes Bogrov's use of it more shocking and more potently ironic.

What does Bogrov, a pioneering Russian Jewish writer, accomplish by adopting and adapting a stereotypical figure that would have offended other Russified Jewish intellectuals? By complicating the education narrative, he worked to question the ideal of quick and easy self-reform. The introduction of the metaphor of the Jew as criminal two-thirds of the way through *Notes of a Jew* suggests that the hero may be a recidivist rather than a real reformer. The persistence of the narrator's "bad," lowbrow literary taste could do the same thing. While a generation of Russian intellectuals, including the acculturating Jewish youth, read Belinsky, Chernyshevsky, and Pisarev, Bogrov's narrator's self-conscious irony could do little to conceal his preference for ghost stories, *lubki*, and Vonliarliarsky's derivative romance. The conclusion of *Notes of a Jew* speaks to the same ambivalence. In the broadest outline of the plot, Srul appears to be a positive hero. Unlike the characters of Herzen's *Who Is to Blame?* he succeeds in extricating himself from a hateful social tie when he divorces his wife. That accomplishment suggests a return to the prototypical plot of the Jewish autobiography and an indication that one can, in fact, remake one's own life. However, Srul's final words concern not the divorce but his own midlife crisis, his loneliness, and his realization that he will never attain the dreams of his youth.

In emphasizing these gloomy musings rather than the successful divorce, and in focusing on Srul's reading tastes, the episode at the river crossing, the metaphor of the criminal, and its further development in Bogrov's review, I am consciously reading against genre and prototype, against the expectations associated with the Haskalah narrative. However, I suspect that the elements I stress may have contributed to the work's mixed reception. While rebellious Jewish youths, such as the character Sholem Aleikhem depicts in his memoirs, apparently found the book inspiring, Jewish critics hesitated to praise it, and the next generation of Russian Jewish historians was happy to let it be forgotten. They may have been put off because rather than concentrating on a fictional "strong man," a "knight of the future" whose story might lead him toward a positive self-transformation, Bogrov instead wallowed in the moral mire of the unreformed and unreformable superfluous man.

While the Jewish historians may have been justified in their hostility by Bogrov's challenge to the ideals of self-reform, they ignored the many ways in which he anticipated the themes and concerns of a later generation of Jewish writers. The comment of the critic from *Syn otechestva* in 1873 points out one of the most striking similarities: in *Notes of a Jew*, Bogrov criticizes not just Jews but Russian officials as well, portraying them as corrupt extortionists who take even bigger bribes from Jews than from everyone else (p. 556). In so doing, he not only upset the Russian critic's expectations for a Russian Jewish writer but also sounded for a moment less like Maimon and more like one of his era's best-known Yiddish writers, Mendele Moikher Sforim (S. Y. Abramovich). In the early 1870s, Mendele grew skeptical about the maskilic ideal that an individual's rational pursuit of an education can improve things for that individual or for people in general. While his work of the early 1860s elevates Russians and Russian culture above all else, by the 1873 work *Di kliatshe* [The Mare], he presents the Russian authorities as a force entirely hostile to the Jews, and he lambastes Jews who cooperate with them.[96] The novella reveals Mendele's growing doubt that by reforming themselves according to Russian standards, Jewish communities could win emancipation or better themselves or their lot in any significant way.[97] Even though Bogrov did not urge Jews openly to rebel against the tsarist system, he also was entirely willing to point out the flaws in imperial law and logic.[98] In the wake of the pogroms, Bogrov spoke out in favor of emigration and, in the words of one historian, agreed that "there was no solution in the strictly Russian context for the enormous economic problems of the Jewish people."[99] Although he expressed doubt about the feasibility of the Zionist dream, he also urged Jews to stop hoping for succor from "European civilization" but instead to rely on themselves and to cultivate their own abilities and strengths.[100]

Even Bogrov's use of the metaphor of the Jew—and especially the Jewish writer—as criminal anticipates the attitudes of later Jewish writers. In 1881 and later, several Jewish writers in St. Petersburg published semiautobiographical pieces whose titles as well as their themes drew on the notion that merely by living in the Russian capital, a Jew was a kind of criminal. Benjamin Nathans, in his analysis of this tendency, cites a novella by Gershon Lifshits called *Confessions of a Criminal* [Ispoved' prestupnika] and a poem by Iakov Shteinberg called "The Criminals" [Prestupniki].[101] Neither these Jewish criminals nor Bogrov's serve the functions that such figures would in twentieth-century Russian Jewish literature. Unlike the Jewish swindlers in the work of Semyon Yushkevich, they do not illustrate a Marxist criticism of the capitalist system that allows some to take advantage of others. They bear little resemblance to the exuberant Jewish criminals who populate the Moldovanka district in Isaac Babel's Odessa stories. By no means do I want to argue that Bogrov's was an early narrative of the return of the alienated Jewish intellectual to the Jewish folk, idealized even in its criminal elements—but his work does shed light on the creative problems associated with reimagining and rewriting the self in accordance to a specific textual model.

Through Bogrov's work, the narrative of Jewish acculturation entered mainstream Russian literature. The contradiction in his texts between various methods for imagining the Russifying Jew—as notetaker, as educator, as criminal—poses a challenge to the radical literary-critical consensus that the right text can inspire effective self-reform, that art can make superfluous men strong, decisive, and ready to lead society toward a bright future. The narrator of *Notes of a Jew*, with his affection for the stories of superfluous men, recalls Annenkov's liberal reading of type and his insistence that self-reform is gradual, unpredictable, and contingent on outer as well as inner factors. As we will see in the following chapters, when some non-Jewish writers—both Polish and Russian—took on the story of Jewish acculturation they reproduced Bogrov's ambivalence, casting about widely for appropriate literary types, themselves uncertain if it was feasible to remake the Jew.

2   THE NATION AND THE WIDE WORLD: ELIZA ORZESZKOWA

THE REVIEWERS of Bogrov's *Notes of a Jew*, like Bogrov in his own review of "The Melamed of Österreich," debate who has the right and the ability to describe the Jews. Bogrov insists that Leskov, a non-Jew, reveals the ignorance that makes him an inadequate choice for the task; at the same time, Bogrov's critics assert that even though he has sufficient knowledge, he lacks the sympathy for his subject that would make him a truly satisfactory writer on the Jews. Reading their polemics, one might wonder if any writers on the Jews could ever meet with everyone's approval.

In fact, one did: Jewish and non-Jewish critics alike praised the prolific non-Jewish Polish writer Eliza Orzeszkowa, the author of the most influential nineteenth-century Eastern European depiction of a Jew's education, for what everyone saw as informative and sympathetic depictions of Jews. Bogrov's rival Lev Levanda, in a commentary to a Russian translation of one of Orzeszkowa's articles published in *Russkii evrei*, calls her work "sober" and "unbiased" and asserts that the article "stands almost alone in both Polish and Russian literature." He reiterates his respect for her knowledge of Jewish matters, even while voicing some doubts about her conclusions in this article.[1] Polish Jewish critics as well defended her as an advocate of Jewish causes even when they criticized specific points in her writings; for instance, Adolf Cohn lists the ethnographic mistakes she made in describing Jews but asserts that they are not significant.[2] Orzeszkowa's reputation among Jews lasted long past the 1880s: Sofia Dubnova-Erlikh (a Russian poet and the daughter of the historian Semyon Dubnov) observes in Orzeszkowa's 1910 obituary that even while a younger generation of Jewish activists was put off by the author's assimilationism, they remained charmed by her attractive images of Jewish life.[3] Even the Zionist theorist Vladimir Jabotinsky, in his brutal exposé of the hostility to Jews apparent in the Russian literary canon, cited Orzeszkowa as a humanitarian counterexample.[4]

Non-Jews found these images equally compelling. The Russian writer Mikhail Saltykov-Shchedrin, who had created some ugly Jewish characters in his own work in the 1870s, admits the superiority of Orzeszkowa's depictions in an essay he wrote in 1882 in response to the pogroms:

> History has never sketched on its pages a more painful question . . . than the Jewish question. . . . There is nothing less human and more foolish than the beliefs . . . [that] from one century to another pass on the brand of shame, alienation, and hatred. . . . Only recently has a light been cast in our literature on that suffering world. And even now one can barely point out anything worthwhile, with the exception of Mme. Orzeszkowa's marvelous story, "Strong Samson." So those who want to know the sympathetic side of the suffering Jews . . . should turn to this story, every word of which breathes the truth. What we need first of all is to know; knowledge inevitably produces humanitarian feelings.[5]

Even Leskov himself, in what may be a concession to Bogrov's criticisms of "The Melamed of Österreich," agreed in 1881 that Orzeszkowa's work offers a better picture of Jewish life than anything written in Russian:

> What we [Russian literature] have so far in the form of little sketches, stories, and plays with puppets who have Jewish names, is primarily *caricature*, sometimes very funny and well-aimed, but still caricature and not artistic truth. It will not help anyone attain what is most important: through caricature it is impossible to come to understand reality. Russian belletrists of Jewish origin have appeared among us only very recently, but unfortunately they too are barely able to treat the subject as it demands, since on the one hand, none of them displays any special talent, and on the other, they suffer from bias. We must con-

sider the most artistic depiction of the Jewish way of life [*byt*] to be the work of the Polish author Mme. Orzeszkowa, *Meir Ezofowicz* (Russian translation in the Moscow newspaper of Gattsuk), although it too has considerable bias, which threatens its artistic truth. The Jewish way of life, rich in diverse types, awaits a talented artist, who would be able to acquire fame and serve humanity. But this person would have to be not only intelligent and talented, but also free from enslavement to any prejudices, unbigoted, and absolutely *good* [*dobryi*].[6]

Meir Ezofowicz, the novel Leskov cites, remains Orzeszkowa's best-known fiction on a Jewish topic. She wrote it in Polish in 1877 and published it in 1878, first in the journal *Kłosy* [Ears of Grain], and then as a book. Within the next four years, it appeared in three different Russian translations: an incomplete first translation appeared in 1879 and 1880 in a short-lived journal, *Biblioteka Zapadnoi polosy Rossii*; the second translation, substantially shortened and edited, was published in 1880 in *Gazeta A. Gattsuka*; and two years later, the third translation—the first complete one—was issued as a supplement to the newspaper *Svet*.[7]

One might wonder why an author would allow several translators simultaneous access to her work. In fact, virtually no copyright law governed translation in the Russian Empire, so that except in a very limited number of circumstances, any person who wanted to translate a book into Russian from any language had full rights to do so and to receive the resulting profits.[8] Orzeszkowa's lack of control over her translations undoubtedly accounts as well for their widely varying ideological slants. The editor of *Biblioteka Zapadnoi polosy Rossii*, who declared that he intended his publication to "take on itself the great mission of an intermediary between the Russian and the Jewish peoples," seemingly agreed with the consensus that Orzeszkowa's fiction was sympathetic to the Jews, and the editors of *Svet* provided no indication of their Jewish politics.[9] The translation published in *Gazeta A. Gattsuka*, though, included a translator's introduction describing the terrible danger that Jews pose for Christians and praising the novel as a useful tool for the study of this "powerful hidden enemy" in order to find its "Achilles heel."[10]

This evaluation contrasts strikingly with all the others available: its writer (whom I will call the "Gattsuk translator" and refer to for convenience as "he," though this person might well have been a woman) was alone in interpreting the work of the famous Judeophile Orzeszkowa as a proof of a Jewish threat. In translating the book, how did this translator deliberately shift its ideological orientation? Did his changes extend a subtle Judeophobia that he had located in Orzeszkowa's novel? In order to answer these questions, I will compare and contrast the literary and political prototypes of both original and translation, as well as the texts themselves.

How Non-Jews Wrote About Jews

Orzeszkowa's novel describes a young Jew, Meir Ezofowicz, a typically mas-kilic figure who rebels by rejecting certain Jewish texts in favor of others. By constructing her critique of Judaism and Jewish culture as a critique of its canon, Orzeszkowa took part in a European project, ongoing since the six-teenth century, of describing the Jew and Judaism and considering how Jews and non-Jews should coexist and how the state should administer the Jews. A host of individuals with widely varying ideologies took part in this proj-ect. In his classic history of non-Jews' attitudes toward Jews, Jacob Katz de-scribes many of these ideologies and explains how they each justify hostility to Jews, whom they define variously as members of a religiously, politically, culturally, or racially foreign group.[11] Most of these philosophies can also be associated with a brand of philo-Semitism, that is, an assertion that a given thinker is motivated by a self-consciously benign interest in Jews and wishes to solve the "Jewish problem" in a way satisfactory to all parties. In each case, a single logical schema describes the Jew and the Jewish religion and pro-vides for a way to distinguish between "good Jews" whose behavior con-tributes to the resolution of the "Jewish question," and "bad Jews" whose be-havior constitutes the problem. Anti-Semitism and philo-Semitism can be two manifestations of a single philosophy and can happily coexist in a single person or text.

Katz describes four European approaches to the Jews: the Christian He-braic, the rationalist, the Romantic nationalist, and the modern or racializ-ing. The work of the seventeenth-century scholar Johann Andreas Eisen-menger epitomizes the Christian Hebraic treatment of the Jew. His magnum opus, *Endecktes Judentum* [Judaism Uncovered], is a compendium of cita-tions and interpretations of Jewish writings, all of which, he argues, show the inferiority of Jewish to Christian ethics and demonstrate that Jews should convert to Christianity. The eighteenth century produced a new attitude toward Jews. Rationalist philosophers like Voltaire examined both Christianity and the Judaism from which it had sprung with a skeptical eye, concluding that much in Jewish (as in Christian) beliefs reflected illogic and superstition and should be abandoned. By the early nineteenth century, Romantic thinkers were examining the role of the Jew not vis-à-vis the moral fellowship of Christianity or the community of reasonable people, but in terms of individual European nations. Political theorists tend to link the rise of nationalism to a decline in religious faith, seeing the nation as reproducing the functions and many of the forms of worship associated with the church.[12] Benedict Anderson specifically associates the rise of nations and nationalism in the nineteenth century with the disappearance of the "great sacral cultures," with their unifying languages, religions, and bureaucracies. He distinguishes religion from nationalism by its permeability toward outsiders: the great religions (meaning Christianity, Islam, and Buddhism) are "imbued with an impulse largely foreign to nationalism, the impulse towards conversion."[13] However, the religious habits of nineteenth-century nationalists included the possibility of proselytism. Nationalist philosophers, influenced by both Christian Hebraic and rationalist teachings, asserted that the solution to the "Jewish problem" involved a kind of "conversion" to a specific national culture. Some of them believed that the political loyalties of an acculturated Jew required legitimation through formal conversion to Christianity; others disagreed. Finally, the late nineteenth century saw the rise of a different kind of nationalism, one predicated on the developing idea of race. Its adherents argued that Jews were Semites, members of a degenerate race, condemned from birth to an inferior status in relation to the Aryans, their racial superiors, and incapable of loyalty to an Aryan people or an Aryan state.[14]

As Katz points out, Eisenmenger's "uncovering" of Judaism consists of an examination of hundreds of Jewish writings—the Bible, the Talmud, other legal works, sermons, kabbalistic and philosophical sources, and so on—produced over many centuries, in various countries, by different writers. This multivoiced tradition contains not only much that is fantastic and obscure, but also many contradictory elements, reflecting the differences among writers and their times. Many aspects of Jewish tradition, not surprisingly, recall Christian doctrine and Christian texts; many others conflict with Christian ideas. As Katz explains, traditional Jewish scholars interpreted (and continue to interpret) these polyphonic texts so as to find the single meaning that seems moral to them, while Eisenmenger, citing the same texts in his book, does the opposite: "The Jewish scholar of the seventeenth century accepted the opinions prevalent among the Jews regarding right and wrong, true and false, the permitted and the prohibited—and sought to justify those opinions in the sources; Eisenmenger accepted the opinions about Jews prevalent in the hostile Christian society and was guided by them in his study of the same sources."[15] Thus, Jews could conclude that their sacred texts required them to respect the life, property, and religion of Christians and to live among them peacefully and inoffensively, while Eisenmenger could find "proof" in the same documents that Jews are legally obligated to rob and murder Christians and to desecrate their holy places. His solution: Jews should replace this flawed canon with another book, the New Testament.

Both rationalist and Romantic nationalists, in distinguishing between the "good Jew" and the "bad Jew," focused on the Jew's reading material. Even while Voltaire's ideas about religion differed dramatically from Eisenmenger's, the rationalist, like the Christian Hebraist, based his criticism of Jewish belief on extensive but selective analysis and quotation of Jewish texts—specifically, the Bible—that created an image of Jewish ethics as far as possible removed from his own convictions. And again like Eisenmenger, Voltaire saw the solution to the "Jewish problem" as the Jew's rejection of this problematic reading material in favor of different works—for him, those of the Enlightenment. To the degree that they were influenced by Christian Hebraic or rationalist models for thinking about Jews, Romantic nationalists mimicked the text-based approach. They similarly identified Judaism with a simplified redaction of its canon, which they then argued that Jews must reject in order to adopt one proper to a new national identity.

Non-Jews were not the only ones to attack Jewish texts. The maskilim used many of the methods of the rationalists to question their own religious canon. Like non-Jewish observers of the Jews, they wrote fiction whose heroes sifted through the Talmud, Bible, and other Jewish writings in search of a usable intellectual heritage. Even though they approached this tradition from the Jewish "inside" rather than the gentile "outside," they did not hesitate to quote selectively from the texts they disliked, distorting and simplifying them. While their critique may have been more informed than that of most non-Jews, it was equally harsh and, especially when it came to attacks on Hasidism, they were equally willing to cite out of context and exaggerate objectionable elements.[16]

However, the maskilim differed from gentile writers on the Jews in their lack of specific recommendations for new reading to replace the rejected Jewish texts. They opposed Jewish conversion to Christianity, rejecting Eisenmenger's contention that the New Testament was the only adequate supplement and corrective to the Old. Many individual maskilim identified with and became literate in the culture of the country where they lived; nonetheless, the classical texts of the Haskalah, unlike the works of Romantic nationalists, rarely stress the Jews' duty to replace their outmoded textual tradition with a single national literature. The maskilim and their descendants were criticized for being Germanophiles in Poland, Russophiles in Lithuania, and Francophiles in Germany. Meanwhile, the Haskalah gave rise to a movement promoting modern literature in Hebrew, rather than (or, usually, along with) European languages. Thus, when anti-Semites used "cosmopolitan" as a code for assimilated Jews, their invective had a basis in the maskilic unwillingness to define the "Western culture" it admired as the patrimony of any single Western nation.[17]

Like the Haskalah, the fourth approach to the Jews differs from the others in its recommendations to the Jewish assimilator. As Katz notes, "modern" or racializing anti-Semites, following Christian Hebraic and rationalist models, often criticized the Jewish textual tradition. However, they did not propose that by reading different texts in its place, Jews could solve the "Jewish problem." Whereas the maskilim were reluctant to place limitations on the secular texts they recommended, modern anti-Semites were unwilling to believe that any new text could accomplish the reform of the Jews. The modern development reveals a striking difference from the earlier ones, in that where the key factor was once conceptualized as text, it later became blood. According to this ideology, a Jew's conversion to Christianity can never be other than superficial and insincere, and a Jew's assimilation to a gentile culture can only be interpreted as an attempt to penetrate enemy ranks, to take on protective coloring in order better to attain a destructive goal. The change in focus from text to blood and its implications for the possibility of assimilation can create a different kind of story about Jewish acculturation. The notion of identity that is carried in one's blood evokes an assortment of biological metaphors for cultural changes in an individual: assimilation can be seen as dilution of blood, the retention of aspects of an older culture can be described as the sway of a "dominant" blood type, and the entire project of acculturation can be made to appear as impossible as the denial of one's own blood.

Jews in Poland

While the first evidence of a Jewish presence in Poland dates from the tenth century, a large and for the most part unacculturated population of Jews lived there from the sixteenth century, typically working as merchants, artisans, and administrators on the estates of the *szlachta* [the Polish gentry] and living their lives according to strict religious guidelines. After the Partitions, the land the Jews inhabited became the Russian Empire's western provinces and what was now referred to as the "Polish Kingdom" (or, after the 1815 Congress of Vienna, which defined its borders, the "Congress Kingdom").[18] Until the 1863 uprising, the tsars administered the western provinces and the Polish Kingdom differently. The western provinces were assimilated directly into the empire and its inhabitants subjected to some Russification, while the Polish Kingdom was allowed a greater measure of cultural and administrative autonomy. After 1863, the Polish Kingdom, renamed "Vistulaland," also became simply part of the empire, subjected to stricter Russification and granted no self-government.[19]

The status of the Jews in the two areas was correspondingly different. Catherine the Great had decreed at the end of the eighteenth century that the partitioned area would become a "Pale of Settlement," outside of which Jews were not permitted to move. During the second half of the nineteenth century and the beginning of the twentieth, some Russian Jews agitated for emancipation. The idea of emancipation was represented for them most vividly by the abrogation of the pale and permission to move into the Russian cities.[20] These Jews resented their confinement to an economically underdeveloped area in which opportunities for investment—or simply for making a living—were strictly limited and competition among Jewish merchants and artisans, fueled by high population growth, drove down their standard of living. In the Polish Kingdom, in contrast, Jews were more free to move from the overcrowded shtetlach to the cities and, from 1862 through the revolution, they were subjected to fewer limitations on their right to acquire property.[21]

Jewish status in the Polish Kingdom was affected by the area's political instability. Both Polish rebels and tsarist authorities perceived the Jews as potential allies. Thus, the imperial government was prepared to make concessions to the Jews in the Polish Kingdom that it never considered extending to those in the western provinces. Most significantly, an 1862 law, introduced by the imperial administrator Count Aleksandr Wielopolski, eliminated many of the restrictions on Jews' rights to participate in the Polish economy. Meanwhile, Poles who were trying to cast off the Russian yoke sometimes saw Jews as possible fellow freedom fighters. The support of some Jews, especially assimilated ones in Warsaw, for the abortive 1863 uprising contributed to the image of the Jew as Polish patriot. Meanwhile, in early 1863 the insurrectionists apparently felt compelled to match Wielopolski's terms with a call for equality of "all the sons of Poland, irrespective of their faith, race, origin and estate."[22]

The initial Polish optimism, based on a false understanding of the Jews' situation and expectations, was unsustainable. The famous demonstrations of Polish patriotism by Jews during the uprising (such as the speeches by Rabbi Dov Meisels and the martyrdom of Michał Landy, the Jewish student who took a cross from a fallen protester moments before he too was shot) occurred in Warsaw, in the heart of the Polish Kingdom. In the western provinces, in contrast, the Jews, like the peasants, often saw no reason to participate in the struggle of their erstwhile Polish masters against their new Russian ones. Orzeszkowa lived in the western provinces, near Grodno, in a region with an especially large and economically influential Jewish population.[23] As a young woman, she had heard Meisels speak in a Warsaw synagogue and had been impressed by his Polish patriotism.[24] However, she complained in a letter to a Jewish correspondent in Warsaw that the Jews she encountered frequently felt more loyalty to Russian than to Polish culture:

> The Jews in the Polish Kingdom, and especially in Warsaw, differ distinctly and significantly from their Lithuanian brethren [parts of what is today Belarus were then called Lithuania]; moreover, the former are superior in every way. . . . As for the Russians, the Jews have taken up a position in relation to them that upsets and cannot fail to upset even those among the local Poles who—believe me—have the very best attitude toward Jews.[25]

Orzeszkowa's words hint at a problem that would, in various forms, put an end to the dream of Poles and Jews united against Russians. While many in both groups agreed that the Jews needed to become open to new influences, to change their reading in some way, they disagreed about specifically what new influences were necessary. By the last decades of the nineteenth century, the competition between Polish and Russian cultures as models for Jewish assimilation would be complicated by the attractions of new kinds of Jewish identity, associated with Zionism, Yiddishism, and socialism; Orzeszkowa disapproved heartily of these developments.[26]

Positivism

While the imperial government reacted to the 1863 Polish uprising by eliminating the autonomy of the Polish Kingdom and intensifying efforts at Russification both there and in the western provinces, a new generation of Polish intellectuals responded by questioning the ideals that had led to the series of disastrous uprisings. These "Positivists" rejected the rebels' Romantic nationalism along with their urge to defy the Russians in brave, albeit doomed, military stands. In its place they proposed a new kind of nationalism, based on the modern ideals of economic and scientific progress. Taking their cue from Auguste Comte, the French originator of Positivist philosophy, they placed science above religion, believing that a methodical search for knowledge would produce a superior secular morality. They based their philosophy on what they saw as the real, meaning "that which really exists and can be observed, as opposed to the dubious fancies of theology and metaphysics."[27] Thus, rather than taking their inspiration from the Romantic idealization of the Poland of the past, a "paradise for noblemen," they dreamed of a future in which, by developing industry, promoting education, and benefiting from the energies of newly emancipated peasants, women, and Jews, the Poles could surpass the Russians. Their willingness to question the central image of the Polish patriarchy—the knight wielding sword and *liberum veto*[28]—signals the radicalism of the Positivist vision.

Censorship of journalism encouraged writers in Polish as in the other languages of the Russian Empire to conceal their political messages in fiction. The Positivist writers, in contrast to the Romantics, preferred prose to poetry. They embraced the ideal of art as an illustration of scientific truths, literature as lessons in psychology, sociology, and a rational morality. Rather than troubling themselves over possible contradictions between scientific truth and artistic beauty, they were convinced that the two were indistinguishable, that good art was always and only that which could educate readers and set them more securely on the path toward progress.[29] For example, one of the best-written and best-known Positivist novels is the 1890 work *Lalka* [The Doll] by Bolesław Prus [pseudonym of Aleksander Głowacki]. Its figures represent many of the economic levels and ethnic groups that participated in Warsaw society in the late 1870s. Prus shows the impoverishment of those in the *szlachta* who disdain the "dirty work" of industrial development, the rise of the Polish hero and of Jews who make the most of economic opportunity, and the hero's fatal preference for an empty-headed aristocratic woman over a hardworking widow. The readers can see the inevitability of the rise of capitalism and the folly of opposing it.

A push for the emancipation and assimilation of the Jews was consistent with the Positivist program. A certain skepticism about the Church, implied by the rejection of the "dubious fancies of theology," led to the reevaluation of that Christian hostility to Jews typified by Eisenmenger. Rather than insisting that Jews would have to convert to Christianity in order to become part of Polish society, the Positivists, following Voltaire and the rationalists, wanted them to give up their religious "superstitions" for the secular ideals of progress and education. In addition, Jews had long acted as an essential link in the Polish economy, the agents or administrators of the landowners and the merchants who supplied both aristocrats and peasants. Thus, the Positivists' impulse to abandon the entire social and economic system associated with the Poland of the past led them to question the traditional role of the Jew.

The combination of the liberation of the peasants and the heavy taxes the imperial government imposed on Polish landowners ensured that by the 1870s the rural economy based on large aristocratic estates could not last much longer. Insofar as they acknowledged this reality, the Positivists sought a new role for the Jews, one less tied to the institutions of the past. They found that role in the economic model of industrial capitalism, which made its way from Western Europe to Poland in the final third of the nineteenth century. Given the prevalence of the stereotype associating Jews with money and financial transactions, it was logical for the Positivists to picture Jews as providing the know-how and the capital needed to turn Poland into an industrial power, using the skills that had defined them in the past to guide the country into the future.[30] Indeed, as Prus emphasizes in *The Doll*, in a society that had traditionally disdained trade as such, it was not surprising that Jews and other ethnic non-Poles (such as Germans) in fact came to dominate the new economy.

The Positivists' writings on the Jews were characteristic of their political and economic philosophy.[31] They divided their subject into "good Jews" and "bad Jews," the former characterized by a striving for education and emancipation and a rejecting of the exclusivity of the traditional Jewish community, accepting the fellowship of non-Jews. Their behavior was seen as leading to the intellectual and material enrichment of both parties. The "bad Jews" stood for the past, exploiting non-Jews, especially peasants, but avoiding further contact with them, preferring their own language, dress, textual tradition, and company.

The literary tradition associated with Polish Positivist philo-Semitism predated Positivism itself. It stemmed from a series of texts intended to encourage the reform of the Jews. The first and most influential Polish work to feature an assimilated Jew was Julian Ursyn Niemcewicz's 1820 epistolary novel, *Lejbe i Sióra*, which describes the eponymous pair of enlightened Jewish lovers and their efforts both to free themselves from the constrictions of Jewish traditionalism and to reform their community as a whole.[32] In Niemcewicz's words, he had the purest Enlightenment ideals:

> To direct the Jews toward the true light, to heal them of their prejudices, to point out to them that in maintaining the inhuman laws of their elders, they sink into degradation and want, they block their own way toward all the advantages in human society—that is the entire object of this work. I will be happy if I attain my desire, even if only in part.[33]

Niemcewicz's rationalist perspective made him attractive to the Positivists. For the most part, later fictional works on the Jews recycled Niemcewicz's ideas. The literary historian Magdalena Opalski has studied a representative sample of these works, including *Lejbe i Sióra* (1820), I. T. Mosalski's *Pan Podstolicz* (1830–33), Józef Ignacy Kraszewski's *Żyd* (1866), Zygmunt Sarecki's *Słonecznik* (1882), Ignacy Maciejowski's *Zyzma* (1884), Jan Kasprowicz's *Lejbele* (1888), M. Gawalewicz's *Mehesy* (1894), and Gabriela Zapolska's *Jojne Firulkes* (1899). They all distinguish between the "degenerate" Judaism of the present and the "pure" religion of the past; they criticize Yiddish, the educational system of the shtetlach, and the authority of religious leaders, epitomized by their privilege to excommunicate heretics (by an institution called *herem*, which in fact was unenforceable and used rarely); they blame

Jews rather than Poles for problems in Polish-Jewish relations; and they star the familiar type of an attractive male Jew who strives to guide his community toward correct assimilation.[34] This modern Jewish type battles endlessly with an opposing type, the traditional Jew, here aligned with all the unattractive figures available in Polish folklore and literature: the Jew as smuggler or con man, the Jew bent on outwitting and exploiting Christians.[35]

Thus, *Meir Ezofowicz* came out of a literary tradition that began during the Enlightenment and flowered under Positivism and that provided a detailed formula for depicting Jewish assimilation. Orzeszkowa distinguished herself from the initiators of this tradition by her dedication to learning about Judaism and Jewish history and by the degree to which she relied for her information on sources by Jews in European languages. Her novel remains the best-known exemplar of the Polish narrative of Jewish reform.

Eliza Orzeszkowa

Eliza Orzeszkowa was a Positivist and a model Polish patriot whose residence in the western provinces exposed her to all the excesses of the Russification campaign. The tsarist administrators "targeted for repression" precisely the Polish intelligentsia and the *szlachta*, the two classes to which Orzeszkowa belonged.[36] Orzeszkowa was consistently loyal to Polish culture rather than Russian. Although she read and wrote Russian, she refused to speak it, a particularly political move after 1863, when the imperial government was doing its best to outlaw the Polish language as well as Polish culture in the western provinces. In an 1879 letter to Teodor Tomasz Jeż [the pseudonym of the writer Zygmunt Miłkowski], Orzeszkowa described the formal opening of a Polish-language bookstore she had founded. The attending dignitaries were forbidden to speak in Polish, as it was a public event, but Orzeszkowa would not speak Russian. A compromise was reached when the authorities "condescended" to allow them to speak French. In another letter to Jeż, Orzeszkowa told of an incident in which her interlocutor truly could not speak Polish: she spoke to him in Polish but was willing to listen to him speak Russian.[37]

The writer felt that her convictions had been formed by the events of 1863. Born in 1841 on her family's estate near Grodno, she had a typical childhood for a provincial noblewoman, though it was marred by the death of her father and siblings. She was tutored at home, then taught by nuns at a girls' boarding school in Warsaw. At sixteen she married Piotr Orzeszko, also a petty aristocrat and small landowner, and moved to his estate. She was in her early twenties when the uprising occurred. When Polish rebel forces passed by the estate, she offered shelter to one of the leaders, Romuald Traugutt, and then provided camouflage by escorting him to his next destination. Ironically, it was her husband, by most reports less of a patriot than she, who suffered from her bold action: in 1864 he was exiled to Siberia, where he remained for three years (after an amnesty he was allowed to settle in the Polish Kingdom, where he died in 1874). Biographers have speculated at length about why Orzeszkowa, unlike other patriotic Polish women in her position, did not follow her husband east. The reasons may include a flaw in the marriage, rather than in her patriotic feelings.[38] However, it would in addition have been in accord with the ideals of Positivism for her to reject the beautiful but ultimately useless romantic gesture of accompanying her unloved husband to Siberia.

Orzeszkowa credited the uprising of 1863 for not just ending her meaningless marriage, but for making her a writer[39]—a statement that reflects her economic as well as personal motivations. When her husband was exiled, his estate was confiscated. The heavy taxes the tsars imposed on Polish landowners in the western provinces were one of the factors that forced Orzeszkowa to sell her own estate a few years after 1863, although she remained in the Grodno area. Even while suffering from eye problems and other illnesses, she supported herself into her late sixties with her voluminous writing, producing lengthy stories, novels, and articles on many topics, and a copious correspondence, only some of which has been published. She concentrated her energies on writing in Polish and attempting to improve the lives of her countrymen through her fiction and her journalism, and she even made efforts to found small businesses that would support Polish culture and industry, including a glove factory that never got off the ground, as well as the Polish-language bookstore in Vilnius.[40]

Like her interest in commerce, the author's views on other aspects of society were typical of the Positivists. She had a skeptical attitude toward the Church, verging on anticlericalism. She admitted in a letter that "a long time ago I lost all *childish* faith and I have the right to call myself a Positivist."[41] Her hostility to Catholicism had several probable causes, including the length and expense of the annulment proceedings that she undertook to free herself from Piotr Orzeszko. Tied to her insistence on the legalization of divorce was her approach to women's rights. She felt that she had been married off too young and unwisely, and she called for women to seek education and claim control over their own lives.

An interest in Jews and their situation was common in Orzeszkowa's milieu. In the two decades after 1863, liberal Polish patriots, especially in Warsaw, associated freely with the most assimilated among the Jewish intelligentsia and declared their sympathy for them. Even while she remained in the western provinces, Orzeszkowa was in constant contact with Warsaw liberals. Her lawyer, Leopold Méyet, was a Warsaw Jew who maintained a popular salon.[42] The author's letters reveal her attachment to and reliance on him.[43] Franciszek Salezy Lewental, the editor of *Kłosy* [Ears of Grain], the journal in which she published *Meir Ezofowicz*, was a respected figure in Warsaw literary life who participated in a number of Jewish community organizations until he converted to Christianity late in life. Orzeszkowa maintained a friendly correspondence with him until a disagreement over a publication caused a break.[44] She corresponded with a number of similar figures, such as Henryk Nusbaum, a prominent doctor and the son of an assimilationist, who converted to Catholicism but continued to identify with Jews and take an interest in Jewish problems.[45]

Orzeszkowa's contacts with Jewish assimilators were not limited to social or legal matters; like a number of Positivists who wrote about Jews, she faithfully read *Izraelita*, the organ of the Warsaw assimilationists. According to the historian Alina Cała, "the majority of the Positivists saw the Jews through the eyes of that publication's editors. It provided a (and frequently the only) source of information."[46] From 1866 until 1915, this newspaper was published in Polish for an audience of Poles and those Polish-speaking Jews who referred to themselves not as *Żydzi* [Jews] but as *Polacy wyznania mojżeszowego* [Poles of the Mosaic persuasion]. With their vocabulary as well as their choice of Polish over Hebrew or Yiddish, the editors defined themselves as the most Polonophile of the heirs to the maskilim. Their stated goal was to help the Jews of Poland improve themselves intellectually and materially, ideally with the help of sympathetic non-Jewish Poles. An unstated goal was undoubtedly the urge to show the Polish reading public that some Jews were literate in Polish and prepared to demonstrate in print their loyalty to Polish culture.

Unlike most of the other Polish writers who addressed the Jewish question, Orzeszkowa read more than *Izraelita*. Particularly during the seven years before writing *Meir Ezofowicz,* she sought out more detailed sources on Judaism and Jewish history. In order to find them, she initiated correspondences with some of *Izraelita*'s editors, including Samuel Peltyn and Adolf Cohn.[47] In 1870, she admitted to Peltyn that she would like to write a novel on the Jews and asked him to suggest works "with whose help I could find out what I want and need to know."[48] Six years later, she told Cohn that she had found no useful information in works by her fellow Poles, with the exception of Niemcewicz's *Lejbe i Sióra* and a few works of historical fiction by Kraszewski.[49] She had read a monumental work by a German Jew, Heinrich Graetz's multivolume *Geschichte der Juden* [History of the Jews].[50] She also read Aleksander Kraushar's *Historia Żydów w Polsce* [History of the Jews in Poland], essays by the French scholar Joseph Salvador, and "an enormous mass of brochures, prayer books, and so on." Despite her hostility to Russian, she delved into Russian-language works on Jews, including several volumes of *Evreiskaia biblioteka* (an annual published by St. Petersburg Jews with views similar to those found in *Izraelita*). When she told Cohn that she had read *Żydzi i Kahały* [Jews and Kahals], a Polish translation of Brafman's *Book of the Kahal,* he sent her I. I. Shershevsky's Russian refutation of Brafman as well as a three-volume collection of excerpts from the Talmud and rabbinic works translated into Russian.[51]

This education in Jewish studies inspired Orzeszkowa to produce a number of works, including two novels in addition to *Meir Ezofowicz*—*Eli Makower* (1874–75), which describes the relationship between an impoverished Polish nobleman and a Jewish merchant, and *Mirtala* (1882/1886), on Jews, Christians, and pagans in ancient Rome. She published five stories about Jewish life in Poland: "Silny Samson" [Strong Samson] (1877); "Daj kwiatek" [Give Me a Flower] (1877); "Gedali" (1884); "Rotszyldówna" [Rothschild's Daughter] (1890); and "Ogniwa" [Links (in a Chain)] (1895). "Silny Samson," her best-known and most frequently anthologized Jewish story and the one Mikhail Saltykov-Shchedrin had so admired, is about a poor Jewish scholar named Szymszel [a Yiddish nickname for Samson] who suddenly understands his own spiritual and material poverty after playing Samson in a *purimspiel* [a play performed on the holiday of Purim]. Finally, Orzeszkowa wrote two essays on the Jewish question, "O Żydach i kwestii żydowskiej" [On the Jews and the Jewish Question] (1882), in response to the pogroms of 1881–82, and "O nacjonaliźmie żydowskim" [On Jewish Nationalism], which was published posthumously in 1911.

In all these works, Orzeszkowa was guided by a consistent understanding of the "Jewish problem." She felt that Polish Jews needed to abandon their traditional lifestyle, the Yiddish language, distinctive Jewish dress, and their isolation from non-Jews. Throughout her work, Orzeszkowa emphasized language as the key to assimilation; she scorned Yiddish, which she blamed for reinforcing the Jews' isolationism.[52] In Orzeszkowa's view, Jews did not need to convert to Catholicism; instead, they should adhere to a more modern version of Judaism, without "superstitions" and more open to interactions with non-Jews. This reform would be an essential first step allowing Jews to learn Polish and become Poles—that is, "Poles of the Mosaic persuasion." Orzeszkowa insisted that such a transformation would be in the best interest of both Jews and Poles.

From the perspective of the early twenty-first century, Orzeszkowa's ideals may seem less than tolerant. Cała observes that "the Positivist attitude toward separatism and difference was xenophobic," but she concedes that Orzeszkowa made more serious efforts than the other Positivists to study and to understand the Jews. Orzeszkowa herself and her Jewish and non-Jewish contemporaries thought of her as a philo-Semite.[53] In one of her first letters to Peltyn she explained, "I cherish a warm sympathy [for the Jews, and they] simultaneously inspire in me an equally strong intellectual interest."[54] In her mind and the minds of most Polish intellectuals of the period, Orzeszkowa's insistence on the feasibility and necessity of Jewish assimilation was a sign not of her intolerance for Jewish difference or her inability to accept the validity of other cultures, but rather an indication of an impressive broadmindedness that made her think that Jews were potentially equal to Poles.

While some critics accepted her message unquestioningly, or ignored it to concentrate on the artistry of her depictions of the exotic Jewish setting, others were troubled by what they saw as her excessive liberalism or at least her unwary optimism. In 1879, J. Kotarbiński was willing to accept that even while no Jews as virtuous as Meir yet existed, they might some day:

> Although Meir, with his love for every person in distress, with his penetrating thirst for spiritual enlightenment, with his passionate hatred for those who bind minds with the fetters of fanatical darkness, seems to be a theoretical ideal in the Jewish world, nonetheless we willingly believe in the possibility of such a type, just as we believe in the victory and the endurance of the most noble instincts of human nature.[55]

A decade later, though, this critic had given up his belief, at least in reference to Jews. He asserted that Orzeszkowa's liberalism was founded on humanitarian ideals that "in the real conditions of the development of the Jewish problem would be difficult to achieve."[56]

In the six decades after the publication of *Meir Ezofowicz*, the conviction grew among many Jews and non-Jews, in Poland as elsewhere in Europe, that ideals such as Orzeszkowa's were unrealistic because Jews could not and should not assimilate into non-Jewish cultures. By the late 1930s, during an especially strong wave of anti-Semitism in Poland, one scholar turned precisely to Orzeszkowa as an example of interracial tolerance. She concludes her earnest study of the novelist's Jewish-themed works with a paean to liberal ideas:

> The author united all the forces of an unusual intellect and talent so that, in accordance with the passion of the time and her own conviction, she could propagate the idea of brotherhood and assimilation throughout society. Her works reveal a healthy public mind and the warm current of a heart that was able, better than others, to understand the suffering and the distress of other people.[57]

The Polish *Meir Ezofowicz*

Meir Ezofowicz offers an enthusiastic and detailed portrait of the main character and his struggles to educate himself. Meir, a young Jewish man who lives in the shtetl of Szybów, is tall, attractive, intelligent, and warmhearted. Rejecting the bride his family chooses, he falls in love with another positive Jewish character: Golda, a Karaite girl, member of a sect that, in Poland in the nineteenth century, had poor relations with other Jews.[58] His relationship with Golda, his challenges to the authority of the rabbi and the melamed, and his attempts to prevent a crime planned by a Jew against a local Polish landowner, all defy the religious and social norms of the community. The shtetl's authorities therefore subject him to a herem. Orzeszkowa based the story on a newspaper article about a herem in the Belorussian city of Shklov.[59] She ends the book with the hero's departure from the shtetl, as required by the herem.

An orphan, Meir lives in the house of his grandfather, Saul Ezofowicz, the wealthiest man in town and the head of an ancient family of merchants who have always had relatively good relations with Poles. Orzeszkowa endows the Ezofowiczes with two ancestors, both representing points in the past at which greater Polish-Jewish brotherhood seemed possible. The sixteenth-century Michał Ezofowicz, founder of the family, was a historical figure who received a title ("Senior") from the Polish king Zygmunt.[60] His era stands out in Polish and Jewish memory as a time of tolerance and prosperity, when Jews fled to Poland from persecutions in Western Europe. Orzeszkowa describes Senior's descendant, Hersz Ezofowicz, who lives in the late eighteenth century and participates in the effort of the Four Years Diet [Sejm czteroletni] to reorganize the Polish government on the revolutionary French model, which could have included the equality of religious minorities. (This process ended with the second and third partitions of Poland in 1793 and 1795.)[61]

Each of these Ezofowicz ancestors faces opposition from the town's other leading family, the Todroses, who fled to Poland from Spain after the Inquisition and who retain a deep suspicion of non-Jews. Orzeszkowa apparently based the Todros family on another historical figure, Meir ben Todros Halevi Abulafia, a thirteenth-century Toledan opponent of Maimonides. She probably read in Graetz's *History of the Jews* about that first Todros's "hostility to science and his tendency towards an ossified Judaism," making him the "chief of the obscurantists."[62] It is a descendant of the Todros family who pronounces the herem on Meir, maintaining his family's traditional opposition to innovation and enlightenment.

Competing Canons

Throughout the book, the conflicts between characters mirror oppositions between texts. Orzeszkowa divides the Jewish textual tradition into four strains, represented by the Old Testament, the Talmud, the texts of the kabbalah, and the writings of Maimonides. In the face of multiple Jewish texts that might indicate either the presence of many identities or the difficulty of establishing any identity as simple and singular, she imposes a taxonomy that creates neat correspondences between texts and types of people.

Orzeszkowa associates the Karaites with the Bible, which she sees as unquestionably good. Like other non-Jewish writers of her day, she assumes (mistakenly) that the Karaites had no interpretive tradition of their own, instead maintaining a "pure," unmediated relationship with the text itself. The Ezofowiczes are linked to the Talmud, a collection of Jewish law and interpretations, which Orzeszkowa describes as a mixture of good and bad elements, requiring careful sifting and evaluation: "The book of your faith is like that pomegranate, which a foolish person ate with the peel . . . but when Rabbi Meir saw that foolish person, he picked a fruit from the tree, threw away the hard and bitter peel, and ate the sweet juicy core" (p. 347).[63]

The Todros rabbis prefer the books of the kabbalah to all other texts. In Orzeszkowa's depiction, the kabbalah, a mystical doctrine concerned with understanding and approaching the nature of God, becomes a justification for abusing unorthodox Jews and hating non-Jews. For example, when Meir defends the home of Golda and her grandfather from the melamed's pupils, who throw stones at it on a Friday night, Todros's supporter criticizes him. In a speech filled with incomprehensible references to kabbalistic ideas, he accuses Meir of having broken the Sabbath. As Meir points out, Todros does not admit that the children who threw stones were also breaking the Sabbath, nor does he mention the Talmudic injunction that one is permitted to break the Sabbath in order to save a life (pp. 60–61). Finally, Meir and some of the other young men in the shtetl gather together to read their precious copy of Moses Maimonides' philosophical work *A Guide to the Perplexed* [More nebuchim], until the community discovers them and they are compelled to give it up to be burned. This text, for Orzeszkowa as for the maskilim, symbolizes the possibility of rationalism within the Jewish canon.

Orzeszkowa's analysis of Jewish texts is not limited to the traditional ones. She adds to Meir's reading with a text of her own invention, a testament, apparently in Polish, left by the sixteenth-century Senior Ezofowicz. After the Jewish community, incited by the Rabbi Todros of that time, had turned against him, Senior wrote down his thoughts and plans. He intended the document not for his children or grandchildren, but for distant descendants, who would want "to save the Jews from imprisonment to the Todroses and lead them to that sun in whose light other nations warm themselves" (pp. 26–27). Senior's great-grandson, Hersz, was the first to study the old papers, and he found in them inspiration for his dream of emancipating the Jews of Poland, in accordance with the plans of the Four Years Diet. In Orzeszkowa's rendition, this would involve the Polonization of the Jews, their adoption of the same language, dress, and schooling system as other Poles.

After the partitions put an end to the Four Years Diet, Hersz returned the document to its hiding place. The next person to read it is Hersz's great-grandson Meir, who searches for it after his rebelliousness has put him in danger of excommunication. Meir realizes that Rabbi Todros will want to take the manuscript away, so he gives it to Golda, asking her to protect it. In the penultimate scene, just before Meir leaves the town, he discovers that the rabbi's minions, in a vain attempt to steal the manuscript, have killed Golda and her grandfather. With her insertion of Senior's manuscript into the Jewish textual tradition, Orzeszkowa advances her project of Polish-Jewish fellowship in the future by pointing out incidences of such fellowship in the past. Just as her depictions of the first Ezofowiczes symbolically include Jews in Poland's history, so her invention of Senior's papers interpolates friendship with Poles into the Jewish literary past.

One more text entered into stories of Jews like Meir. Orzeszkowa's novel itself became a favorite work of young Polish Jews who, like him, scorned Jewish traditionalism and yearned for access to Polish culture. Cała notes that Orzeszkowa, unlike the other Positivists, could boast that her works truly served the cause of Jewish enlightenment: "With her work [she] helped the activists of the movement [for assimilation]. Her stories and novels, for many young Jewish men and women, tearing themselves out of the Orthodox environment, were a first, fascinating, and greatly promising contact with Polish language and culture."[64] The addition of *Meir Ezofowicz* to the canon discussed in the book points to the logical conclusion of the literary reevaluation the author describes. Once young Jews come to understand that they must read the Old Testament, ignore the kabbalah, sift through the Talmud, and study Maimonides, their newfound intellectual bravery will allow them to approach another type of text altogether: Polish literature, including the novels of Orzeszkowa.

With the exception of the Ezofowicz manuscript, the texts Orzeszkowa mentions are commonly cited in other works on the Jews, written by gentiles or by Jews themselves. Given the effort that Orzeszkowa put into reading works by maskilim in various European languages before beginning her novel, it is not surprising that it contains numerous references to their ideas and a plot that recalls Maimon's autobiography.[65] Also influential was Graetz's *History of the Jews*, about which Orzeszkowa said she had "swallowed all eleven volumes."[66] She echoes Graetz's negative attitude toward the kabbalah (an attitude that, as we saw, Maimon and Bogrov shared), and she borrows from Graetz not only the character of Rabbi Todros but also the story of Akiva ben Joseph, a first-century scholar whose wife encouraged him to leave her in order to acquire learning.[67] Golda assures Meir that if he follows his desire for knowledge out of the shtetl, she will wait for him just as Akiva's wife did (p. 369). Orzeszkowa's descriptions of Karaites appear to rely on Graetz, rather than on her own observations or contemporary Polish accounts of the Karaites then living in what is today Lithuania and Belarus. Graetz insisted that while this sect had an interesting and noble history, by the eighteenth century it "became more and more boorish, and sank into profound lethargy."[68] Although he was referring to the state of scholarship among the Karaites, Orzeszkowa applied his words to their economic condition. Described as the remnant of what was once a thriving community, the Karaites in the novel, Golda and her grandfather, live on the edge of the shtetl in a poor hut. (In fact, the Karaite community in the western provinces in Orzeszkowa's time was economically well-off but lived primarily in isolated communities, avoiding contact with the other Jews, whose language and customs were foreign to them.)[69]

Orzeszkowa's reading of maskilic material prevented her from making the absurd allegations about Jewish behavior favored by some of her Polish and Russian contemporaries. Her account of the life of her Karaite characters is unconvincing, but she does not repeat clichés about their "innocence" in the Crucifixion, versus the "guilt" of the Rabbinites [non-Karaite Jews]. Though she probably read Brafman's attack on Jewish community leadership, most of her descriptions do not strain probability, perhaps because she also read Shershevsky's refutation of Brafman.

Orzeszkowa's novel typifies the Polish narrative on the reform of the Jews in more than its approach to the Jewish textual tradition. Like other Polish narratives of Jewish acculturation, it delineates a struggle between two "types," that is, two generations or camps of Jews, the younger ones striving for education and open to fellowship with non-Jews, the older ones intent on limiting their mental and social horizons. In *Meir Ezofowicz*, as in similar Polish works, the hero associates enlightenment specifically with Polish culture, feeling compelled to master Polish before going on to other European languages. All these elements could have been familiar to Orzeszkowa's readers from *Lejbe i Sióra*.

Like earlier Polish writers on the Jews, Orzeszkowa knew that her readers would be attracted by a detailed depiction of the Jews' exotic qualities. Several of her critics noted the artistry of her portrayal of what many Poles might never have seen before. Józef Ignacy Kraszewski, a highly prolific writer and by 1879 the éminence grise of the Positivists, praised her for completing the ethnographic work of recording all the human types to be found among the Jews. "Among this exceptional population, Pani [Madame] Orzeszkowa managed to find such a variety of types and to illustrate them with such truth that not only does one's interest not wane before the end of the story, but it grows and intensifies. . . . As a work of art and as an intellectual labor this is a thing of great value."[70] Another critic lauded Orzeszkowa for "photographing unique types, a social order that is different from ours, that is, that Jewish world that so faithfully retained its individual originality and, for centuries dispersed and exiled, neither merged nor joined with the elements that surrounded it."[71]

Indeed, Orzeszkowa appears aware of her ethnographic mission: she devotes lengthy passages to physical descriptions of her characters and their setting, emphasizing their foreignness. She pauses for a number of paragraphs on the town itself and particularly the "tall, dark house of prayers, with its peculiar shape" (p. 9). She describes in even greater detail her favorite aspect of Jewish life, the male characters' love and respect for their mothers, demonstrated most clearly in the image of Frejda, the matriarch of the Ezofowicz family, wearing expensive jewelry and surrounded by her offspring (p. 168). Orzeszkowa's fascination with exotica is most apparent in this portrayal of Jewish social structure as practically matriarchal—a model she clearly finds both aesthetically and ethically appealing.

The text's abundance of physical descriptions is enhanced by the illustrations that accompanied the original edition and have appeared in most translations and reprintings. Lewental hired the artist Michał Elwiro Andriolli, who had already created other images of Jews, to produce a series of twenty-eight lithographs (see Figure 3).[72] These works, with their accurate detail and graceful human figures, contributed to Orzeszkowa's project of displaying the unknown Jewish world. One reviewer gushed that "her pen and Andriolli's pencil, acting in an equal alliance, expose for us the interiors of the houses, and, what is more, the secrets of the Israelite soul."[73]

The emphasis on the interiors of buildings—as well as souls—in both this review and the novel reflects a difference between *Meir Ezofowicz* and the stories of the maskilim. The Haskalah, as we know, produced narratives of acculturation whose heroes followed a simple trajectory: from ignorance

FIGURE 3. Michał Elwiro Andriolli, *The Sabbath*. Illustration to Eliza Orzeszkowa, *Meir Ezofowicz*, as published in the journal *Kłosy* [Ears of Grain] in 1878. Reproduced from Eliza Orzeszkowa, *Meir Ezofowicz* (Warsaw: Spółdzielna Wydawnicza "Czytelnik," 1988), p. 235.

to knowledge, piety to secularism, the shtetl to Western civilization. Meir sets out on this same path; he also dreams of abandoning a narrow tradition for the "wide world." But the author's focus on the confined spaces from which he comes steals some of his momentum. Ironically, even while Orzeszkowa wanted Jews to abandon their cultural distinctiveness, it was her portrayal of that distinctive culture that appealed to her readers most. Indeed, Dubnova-Erlikh wrote in 1910 that Orzeszkowa, in spite of her assimilationism, continued to appeal to an anti-assimilationist generation of Jewish intellectuals precisely because of her fascination with ethnographic detail.[74] Her attractiveness for such Jewish nationalist thinkers may reflect her own pull, rationalist Positivist though she was, to a nationalist worldview that values the details of a culture over the ideal of progress.[75]

Bad Assimilators

Orzeszkowa's attraction to particularism over universalism may account for the dichotomy she sets up between what her contemporaries would have recognized as two Jewish types: "good" and "bad" assimilators. The Witebski family has committed what Orzeszkowa considered the mistake of incorrect assimilation. A few years before the novel begins, the Witebskis had moved to Szybów from Vilnius, where they had abandoned most of the regulations governing traditional Jewish life and enjoyed all the benefits of what they saw as Western civilization. Upon moving to the shtetl, Eli Witebski, a canny businessman, realizes that the Orthodox Jews around him suspect him of being a freethinker:

> But those suspicions disappeared quickly, and the force that drove them away was Eli's extraordinary gentleness, pleasantness, and pliability. . . . He had been lucky in life, he felt happy and content, so he liked all people and most thoroughly and sincerely did not care if the person he was dealing with was a talmudist, a kabbalist, a Hasid, observant, a renegade, or even an Edomite [a Christian],[76] so long as the person did not harm him personally. (pp. 154–55)

Eli's pliability allows him to take on protective coloring in Szybów by reassuming the Jewish customs he had ignored and attending synagogue regularly. His wife, however, refuses to change her habits, shocking the townspeople with her dress, behavior, and speech. She flouts conventions forbidding physical contact between unrelated men and women, greeting men with an "English shake-hand [sic]" (p. 143), and she refuses to wear the wig that symbolizes a religious Jewish woman's married status. The narrator explains her behavior thus: "She was in love with civilization, represented for her by beautiful dresses, one's own hair on one's head, prettily furnished rooms, very polite dealings with people, the French language, and music" (p. 156). She and her daughter, educated in Vilnius, speak French between themselves (p. 162). Her visiting nephew, Leopold (occasionally referred to as her son), smokes on the street on the Sabbath, although he knows the townspeople will see it as a sin and an affront, and he lights up again in the home of the observant Ezofowiczes, with no concern for the feelings of his pious host.

It is clear from Orzeszkowa's letters that she tailored the image of incorrect assimilators such as Leopold to deceive the imperial censors. She told one correspondent that she had copied the image of Leopold "straight from nature," then explained her theories for his behavior: "I attribute it . . . to the influence of that civilization under which educational institutions become ruling bodies and thus from which the Israelite youth obtains its learning. It is a distorted civilization, a superficial one. . . . Those concepts and customs that are the actual root of civilization are foreign to our schools."[77] Her concern was really not so much Jews who smoked on the Sabbath as it was those who spoke Russian rather than Polish, acculturated to Russian norms, and educated their children in schools where, by imperial edict, instruction was in Russian only. The French and English phrases in the Witebskis' speech stand in for Russian ones. Saul Ezofowicz, the host who chastises his guest Leopold for breaking the Sabbath in his home, represents Polish landowners, offended at Jews who display their knowledge of Russian culture on what Orzeszkowa considered Polish land, where Jews were inevitably guests. The behavior Orzeszkowa disliked was common in the western provinces, where the Jewish population was large, the Polish landowning population small, and the imperial authorities' Russification efforts particularly intense. St. Petersburg seemed administratively, if not geographically, closer than Warsaw, and many Jews deliberately chose Russian culture, which they frequently saw as more "universal" than Polish, and which was more likely to help them gain political rights.[78]

Orzeszkowa's description in another letter of what she saw as the perfidy of these Russifying Jews struck a biblical note:

> But the more or less wealthy and influential Jews all, without exception, unconditionally, have denied us, as Peter denied Christ, in our hour of grief. In all the [Jewish] homes you hear only the Russian language; children wear the Russian national dress and have names like Volodya, Ivan, etc. We are compelled to accept the fact that they speak with us in our own homes in a foreign language.[79]

Rather than analyzing the Jews' decision to embrace Russian culture as a practical response to imperial policy, the writer defines it as the abandonment of a Poland cast in its Romantic role of "Christ among nations." The dichotomy between Polishness and Russianness, the former Christlike, the latter petty and worldly, appears explicitly in Orzeszkowa's letters and implicitly in her novel.

Despite her Positivist rejection of some Romantic ideas, Orzeszkowa's definitions of Jewish Russification and Polonization imply a Romantic conception of Polish culture and nationhood. Rather than noting that the acculturating Jews of the western provinces have simply chosen a Russian over a Polish standard, she reduces the Russian culture propagated by the tsarist government to a "distorted civilization," suggesting that a "real" national culture is something completely different, which cannot be attained by following a clearly defined path, learning a language, adopting a style of dress, and accepting certain social codes. National identity becomes an ineffable, intangible, and deeply moral allegiance.

In contrasting Meir Ezofowicz, the good assimilator, to Eli Witebski, the bad one, Orzeszkowa follows the tradition of Polish novels about reform of the Jews. While the maskilim urged the acculturating Jew to read secular texts in general, Orzeszkowa insisted that only specific texts are adequate for sincere acculturation—and that an incorrect choice would doom the Jewish assimilator to turn into Eli instead of Meir. This assertion recalls Niemcewicz. Although the assimilators in *Lejbe i Sióra* appear sincere, he presents images of insincere, indeed hostile Jewish assimilation in another, shorter work, "The Year 3333; or, An Incredible Dream" [Rok 3333 czyli sen niesłychany].[80] The dreamer sees a terrible vision of a future Warsaw, after Jews, granted the right to hold public office and buy rural land, have taken over the Polish capital. The entire city is dirty, smelly, and corrupt; its new inhabitants have imposed a barbaric order on the country and its few remaining Polish Christians. Like the Witebskis, these Jews have given up some of their traditions for Western customs, but their understanding of civilization is equally superficial. They give balls, but behave rudely at them; they attend operas, but bad ones; they have no appreciation for the city's ancient treasures of art and architecture or for the famous magnate families. The Zamojskis are now their coachmen, the Czartoryskis gardeners, the Radziwiłłs bricklayers, and the Potockis horse dealers. Like the Witebskis, Niemcewicz's nightmarish future Jews speak French, which may well, for him as for Orzeszkowa, mean Russian. Niemcewicz indicates that Jewish assumption of Western mores is not always a good thing, and that true Polonization may be more complicated than his Lejbe had assumed. Orzeszkowa would seem to agree that a Jew might seem on first glance to belong to one type—the virtuous, forward-looking assimilator—but then turn out to have more in common with an older type—the Jew as an excessively adaptable trader, unreliable as an ally because he is interested only in his own profit.

The Russian *Meir Ezofowicz*

For readers in central Russia, Poles such as Orzeszkowa were seen as experts on the Jews. Thus, that she was one of the best-known Polish writers in Russia both in her own time and since is a result of her Jewish thematics as well as the peculiar history of Polish literature in the Russian Empire. Although Polish men of letters were extremely influential in the formation of Russian literature in the seventeenth and early eighteenth centuries, by the second half of the nineteenth, even educated Russians tended to be unfamiliar with Polish writers. In 1862, Leskov chided his countrymen for this ignorance: "Among [Poles] everyone knows a little bit about Russian literature, but among us hardly one person in ten knows two lines of Mickiewicz or has heard of the existence of Korzeniowski, Kraszewski, Odyniec, or Syrokomla."[81] After 1863, rather than encouraging Russians to expand their knowledge of Polish culture, imperial authorities worked toward the opposite goal.

In the late 1870s and the 1880s, though, some individuals attempted to introduce the Polish canon to the Russian public. Shigarin, the editor of *Biblioteka Zapadnoi polosy Rossii*, who dreamed of creating a bridge between Russians and Jews, strove at the same time to mend relations between Poles and Russians by publishing translations of Polish fiction into Russian;[82] in 1882, Rostislav Sementkovsky published a collection of Polish stories.[83] Both of these editors appeared particularly interested in giving the Russian reader access to works by Orzeszkowa and other Poles on Jewish themes. It is not surprising that these Russians, with their liberalism regarding the "Polish question" (the debate over the status of Polish culture and the Polish gentry within the Russian Empire), promoted Polish fiction such as Orzeszkowa's, which they saw as offering the possibility of a tolerant solution to the "Jewish question."

However, the person who translated *Meir Ezofowicz* for *Gazeta A. Gattsuka* used Orzeszkowa's work to support less liberal views. He stated in his introduction that proposals to eliminate the Pale of Settlement and permit the Jews to settle throughout the Russian hinterland were especially valuable because this general exposure to Jews would convince the imperial government of the danger these "terrible societal locusts [*strashnaia grazhdanskaia sarancha*]" pose, a danger that consists in the Jews' "*status in statu*," the "state within a state," a shadow government that competes with the tsarist state.[84] This secret administration, he warns, links all Jews in all countries, from the inhabitants of the shtetlach in the Russian pale to British prime minister Benjamin Disraeli, a Christian convert from Judaism. Like Fedor Dostoevsky in his 1877 essay "The Jewish Question" [Evreiskii vopros], the translator connects the Jews to Russia's external enemies by asserting that an international Jewish conspiracy, with Disraeli at its head, had supported the Turks in the Russo-Turkish War (1877–78).

Following Brafman's lead in *The Book of the Kahal*, the translator connects this international Jewish conspiracy to the kahals, Jewish community organizations that regulated some legal matters until they were outlawed in the Russian Empire in the nineteenth century. (This occurred in different places within the empire at different times; for most of the pale it happened in 1844.) In the decades before their elimination, the kahals were transformed by the the tsarist administration into imperial agents, whose most important functions were tax collection and the rounding up of military recruits. Although by 1881 the kahals existed officially only in a few parts of the empire, the translator insists that they continue to function secretly throughout the empire and indeed the world, and he calls for resolving the Jewish problem by eradicating them completely.[85] (His paranoia had some basis in fact: even after the juridical elimination of the kahal, Jewish communities in the Russian Empire retained a certain administrative autonomy.)

While the translator suggests that outlawing the kahals would coincide with the desires of one camp within the Jewish community (as indeed it did when it happened), he frankly admits having edited out all calls for non-Jews to help such Jewish reformers: "We offer [the novel] to our readers in a significantly shortened form, since the author, clearly, writes it primarily for civilized Yids, and thus often digresses into details and humanitarian discourses that are not very interesting to an outsider."[86] Here he summarizes what he sees as the similarities and the differences between the original and the translation. He and Orzeszkowa, he argues, agree on the basic significance of the novel: to demonstrate the danger posed by the Jews it describes in their current state, and to argue for their reform. However, while Orzesz-kowa addresses her appeal to "civilized Yids" (presumably, assimilated Jews) in an attempt to bolster their fight against forces of Jewish obscurantism, the translation is aimed instead at arousing the hostility of non-Jewish Russians toward traditional Judaism.

The definition of the audience underscores the difference between original and translation. The translator's elision of Orzeszkowa's two audiences, Poles and "civilized Yids," suggests that he understands her goal of bringing Jews and Poles closer. By distinguishing between that dual readership and his own singular one, he reveals his cynicism about her unifying project. For him, it seems, Jews and non-Jews are separated by their reading material as by all else. At some points, the translator's emendations of the original coincide with the program he outlines in the preface. At others, he goes beyond not only Orzeszkowa's ideology but also his own, as he states it here. Rather than arguing for the necessity and possibility of reform, he suggests that it is impossible because the Jews are essentially unreformable. Some of his omissions change the locus of the "Jewish problem" from Judaism, its traditional texts, and its ossified communal-religious structures, to the Jews themselves, defined according to terms that go beyond reading and beliefs and thus hint at race. Where Orzeszkowa focuses on texts, the translator seems to believe in the power of blood.

The translator's redaction of *Meir Ezofowicz* reflects aesthetic as well as ideological biases. The translation is indeed "significantly shortened," approximately 70,000 words to the original 128,000. The 45 percent reduction in word count comes largely at the expense of descriptive passages about the inhabitants of Szybów, its buildings and interiors, the surrounding countryside, and the weather. Such changes have little effect on the plot; nonetheless, they indicate that the descriptive goal for which Polish critics praised the writer— the combination of her pen and Andriolli's pencil that revealed not only the Jews' way of life, but also the secrets of their souls—was of less concern to the translator. Although the Gattsuk translation, printed in an illustrated newspaper, included faithful reproductions of Andriolli's illustrations, the translator eliminated many of Orzeszkowa's physical descriptions of the Jews.

The most telling change in the translation may be in the terms used most frequently for "Jew." Orzeszkowa primarily alternates between two Polish words: "Żyd" and "Izraelita" (I translate both as "Jew"). The former, although it was not an entirely positive term for "Jew" in Orzeszkowa's time, was not primarily an insult and was used not only by Orzeszkowa, but by other Polish intellectuals who were seen as pro-Jewish.[87] (The most common Polish derogatory term for Jews, in both the nineteenth and the twentieth centuries, is *parch* [scab] or *parszywy Żyd* [scabby Jew].)[88] However, just as assimilated Jews in English- and French-speaking countries in the late nineteenth century began to reject "Jew" and *juif* in favor of "Hebrew" and *d'origine Israélite*—terms that, perhaps due to their biblical or historic associations, sounded more positive and more dignified—so assimilated Polish Jews began looking for alternatives to "Żyd." The term "Izraelita" was favored by Orzeszkowa's acquaintances, the editors of the eponymous journal, along with *Polacy wyznania mojżeszowego* [Poles of the Mosaic persuasion] and *starozakonni* [people of the Old Testament]. Orzeszkowa's preference for "Izraelita" to describe laudable Jewish persons or actions is probably a bow to this fashion among Jews.

The polite Russian speaker had—and has—fewer choices. After the Jews of the Pale of Settlement were absorbed into the Russian Empire, Catherine the Great agreed to adopt as the official Russian term for Jews not the Polish-sounding *zhid* (which I translate "Yid") but instead *evrei* (here I use "Jew"), a word that some of her new subjects assured her was more dignified.[89] Perhaps as a result, though fairly neutral in Pushkin's time, the term *zhid* has had unpleasant associations and been used as an insult in Russia since the 1870s.[90] Since that time, the only polite term commonly used for Jews in Russian is *evrei*. It is ironic that the stylistic weights attached to the various terms for "Jew" in Russian have little if anything to do with their etymologies. Both *zhid* and *evrei* are words of Semitic origin that entered Russian and other Slavic languages from Greek or Latin. *Zhid*, like "Jew," stems from the geographical and tribal name "Judah" [in Hebrew, "Yehudah"]; *evrei*, like "Hebrew," from the Aramaic "Ebrej."[91] Even while words derived from "Judah" in other European languages remained more or less acceptable, as did another Russian term of the same origin, *iudei* (referring to an adherent of the Jewish religion rather than a person whose ethnicity is Jewish), the Russian word *zhid* became unacceptable in polite society by the time of Orzeszkowa.

Where Orzeszkowa uses the Polish words "Żyd" and "Izraelita," the Gattsuk translator, unlike the novelist's other contemporaneous translators, seems to follow her as closely as possible by using similar-sounding Russian words, *zhid* and *izraelit*.[92] However, given the associations of the various terms for Jews in the Russian language at the time, his decision in fact constitutes an editorial change. By calling Orzeszkowa's characters *zhidy*, he links them, in Dostoevsky's words, to an ideological image of the Jew: in "On the Jewish Question," he wrote, "I have always used the word 'Yid' to denote a certain idea: 'Yid, the Yiddish scourge, reign of the Yid' [*zhid, zhidovshchina, zhidovskoe tsarstvo*], etc. This refers to a certain concept, an orientation, a characteristic of the age."[93] For the translator as for Dostoevsky, the Jews—or the "Yids"—are the enemies of the Russians and the organizers of a worldwide shadow government in competition with the Russian Empire. The two writers' use of the word *zhid* reaffirms this shared belief. Meanwhile, the Russian word *izraelit*, unlike the Polish "Izraelita," was not recognized as a positive term for Jews; rarely used in nineteenth-century Russian, it probably had little meaning for the translation's readers. Therefore, what appears to be his faithfulness to the original in his terminology for Jews in fact is an indication of the translator's effort to misrepresent Orzeszkowa's Judeophile ideology as well as her text itself.

An equally strong indication of the translator's hostility is his systematic deletion of Orzeszkowa's references to the Jewish community of Szybów as composed of positive as well as negative Jewish types, that is, reformers or potential reformers as well as conservatives. When Orzeszkowa describes the arrival of the first Todros rabbis in the shtetl, she notes that there was opposition to their conservatism even in the sixteenth century:

> The Todroses were respected since time immemorial by the entire Israelite population inhabiting Belarus and Lithuania as a perfect example and an unshakable ark of religious orthodoxy. Was it truly so? Learned talmudists could be found here and there who, at a mention of the talmudic orthodoxy of the Todroses, smiled in a somewhat strange way and, once they had gone out together, whispered about something sadly. The famous talmudic orthodoxy of the Todroses gave the learned talmudists a great, great deal to think about. (p. 12)

In the Gattsuk translation, this passage is truncated after the first sentence (p. 13). Where Orzeszkowa imagines the Jewry of the past and of the present as composed of different individuals with varying viewpoints, some of which she clearly prefers to others, the translator represents it as eternally monolithic, united "since time immemorial" by an unquestioning allegiance to a pernicious "orthodoxy."

The translator also deletes a passage where Orzeszkowa describes Saul Ezofowicz's internal struggle when he is compelled to take Rabbi Todros's advice concerning his grandson. It begins, "The spiritual process that was taking place in Saul's old, but still stalwart breast was very interesting. In the depths of his soul he did not like Isaac Todros" (p. 134). Saul's ability to experience two conflicting emotions and urges simultaneously mirrors the communal tension that Orzeszkowa points out throughout the history of Szybów. The translator eliminates lines that ascribe this dualism to human nature as a whole:

A person who carefully observes human affairs sees many mysteries of this kind, many of these riddles. In the human bosom a kind word intertwines strangely with a vengeful one, a friendly one with a hostile one. The world has often seen men mercifully binding human wounds with one hand, and with the other lighting the fires at the stake and turning the torture wheels. (p. 334)

The lengthiest section that the translator omits concerns the reaction of the Szybów populace to Meir's excommunication (pp. 379–88). Meir's friend Eliezer, the synagogue cantor, defies Rabbi Todros and his cruel decree by chanting a blessing for Meir. The congregation indicates that it too disapproves of the rabbi's severity by responding, "Amen." With this scene, Orzeszkowa displays what her contemporaries saw as her humanitarian ideals, her belief that Jews were capable of enlightenment and of membership in a renewed Polish national community. By omitting this segment, the translator demonstrates the distance separating his and Orzeszkowa's ideas, indicating that he only pays lip service in his preface to the possibility of Jewish "reform" or assimilation.

The translator's changes reflect an understanding of the Jews as a static people. Not only do his deletions suggest doubt that the "Jewish character" will change in the future, they also indicate that it could not have changed in the past. He eliminates all the sentences in which Orzeszkowa explains characteristics of the Jewish community or any Jewish individuals in the present by referring to past events or influences, and he deletes most of the history of the community of Szybów (pp. 12–19), shortens the descriptions of Yenta and Frejda's difficult lives (pp. 81, 168), and eliminates references to the Inquisition, the cause of the Todroses' ingrained hostility to non-Jews (p. 103). The changes disrupt Orzeszkowa's narrative, which leads smoothly from the evolution of Jews in the past to the changes she hopes they will undergo in the future. Rather than allowing Jews to participate in such a dynamic plot, the translator situates them in a static universe where change cannot happen.

The translator disapproves of and deletes any revision of Christian stereotypes about Jews, such as a passage in which Orzeszkowa reverses the traditional Christian description of the Jews as blind (because blind to the message of the New Testament) when she describes those who do not understand the Jews as equally blind: "Israel! Blind from birth or blinded by the pepper of spite is the eye of anyone who, looking at your visage, does not see your ancient dignity! Dry from birth or dried out by a wind blowing from Hell is the pupil that, seeing the great torments you have endured, does not shed a tear!" (p. 337). This passage creates an unbroken connection between the Hebrews of the Old Testament and the nineteenth-century Jews of Szybów. While Christians of the time insisted on a disjunction in Jewish history, dividing the "pure" Jews who were Jesus' ancestors from the "degenerate" and "blind" ones of the present, Orzeszkowa asserts that the two groups are linked. Her mention of "great torments," in the context of her descriptions of the Todros clan, evokes the Christian persecutions of the Jews during the Inquisition. She thus hints that Christians must blame themselves not only for their ignorance about the Jews, but also for having contributed to the Jews' present isolationism.

Although Orzeszkowa hints that in the past the actions of Christians have proven detrimental to Jews, she insists that future interactions may be beneficial. She frequently depicts Jews as innocent, childlike, and in need of help and guidance that would likely profoundly influence them. Her image of the child Lejbele plays into this ideology of the Jew as tabula rasa:

> He [Meir] kept his hand on the head of little Lejbele and gazed into his face, with its pretty features and enormous black eyes, as though in that pale, ill, dulled, and trembling child, he saw a personification of that entire large number of the Israelite people who, suffering from poverty and diseases, still believed and worshipped blindly, peacefully, timidly and untiringly. (p. 130)

By the end of the novel, Lejbele has found the courage to run away from his parents and the harsh melamed and to join Meir on his journey into the "wide world." By identifying this child with the Jews as a whole, Orzeszkowa indicates that just as Meir's kindness to Lejbele helped him transcend his environment, so Poles' kindness to Jews could prove equally effective. The translator indicates his disagreement by eliminating the passage about Lejbele as well as Orzeszkowa's concluding appeal to her reader, as she sends her hero out of the shtetl: "If someday in your path you meet Meir Ezofowicz, offer him a sincere, swift, brotherly hand of friendship and help!" (p. 394).

The version of *Meir Ezofowicz* published in *Gazeta A. Gattsuka* is a virtual reinterpretation of Orzeszkowa's novel. While the plot, the characters, and 55 percent of the original prose are retained in the translation, the translator's selective changes retrofit the story into a different kind of narrative about the nation and the Jew's role in it. Orzeszkowa, given her political views, told a story in which, by seeking enlightenment and working together for progress, the Polish people could proceed toward a better, brighter future. The Gattsuk translator saw the nation as fully formed not in the future, but in the past; rather than envisioning a way for education and industrialization to create a modern nation out of ethnically disparate elements, he denied the malleability of different groups and of the future itself. The depiction of the Jew that appears in his version of the novel indicates that for him, the future promises not the unification of nations but their confrontation. Rather than imagining the reign of a beneficial capitalism, he saw a Jewish conspiracy to dominate innocent non-Jews. Rather than proceeding purposefully into such a future, he would urge the Russian reader to "return" to the premodern idealized "home" of the nation.

Gattsuk, Brafman, and Krestovsky

The Gattsuk translation belongs to a late-nineteenth-century tradition of Russian anti-Semitic literature, whose mastertext is the *Book of the Kahal*, in which Yakov Brafman accused kahal leaders of creating and reinforcing the aspects of Jewish life that upset Russians: isolationism, the economic exploitation of Christians, and adherence to a confusing assortment of complex regulations governing daily life. He depicted Jewish communities as strictly hierarchical, with the poor masses deliberately kept ignorant and subjugated to the kahal, which, he said, could excommunicate or even kill its critics. Brafman and his allies saw the kahal as continuing to exist underground, acting through an array of front organizations, including all the national Jewish groups that developed in the late nineteenth century. (Often cited were the Russian OPE [Obshchestvo dlia rasprostraneniia prosveshcheniia mezhdu evreiami v Rossii (Society for the Spread of Education Among Jews in Russia)] and the Alliance Israélite Universelle in France.) This web of organizations created, according to Brafman, a kind of international shadow state that threatened all legitimate states. Brafman was skeptical about any Jewish "reform" that did not first eliminate all communal organizations; he was hostile to Russian Jewish intellectuals and to assimilated but not converted Jews.[94] His theories spawned more explicit attacks such as Sergei Nilus's *Protocols of the Elders of Zion* (c. 1902), an account of the Jews' purported plan to rule the world.

A number of works of fiction drew on Brafman's ideas. Rejecting the notion that Russian Judeophobia is a variant of the "modern" anti-Semitism imported from Germany in the 1880s, one literary scholar cites a number of stories that depict a world secretly controlled by an international Jewish conspiracy: an 1872 Russian translation of Herman Goedsche's "Jewish Cemetery in Prague";[95] Vsevolod Krestovsky's 1881–1888 *T'ma egipetskaia* [Egyptian Darkness] (the first volume of his trilogy, *Zhid idet* [The Yid Is Coming]); N. P. Wagner's 1890 *Temnyi put'* [Dark Path]; V. I. Kryzhanovskaia's 1907 *Mertvaia petlia* [The Loop]; and E. A. Shabel'skaia's 1912 *Satanisty XX veka* [Twentieth-Century Satanists]. The historian Savelii Dudakov, looking at these same texts, argues that *The Protocols of the Elders of Zion* emerged from an intellectual tradition that appeared in the political context of the nineteenth-century Russian Empire, with its painful sense of impossible competition with the West.[96] He says that although some pseudoscientific works may have contributed to the rise of Russian anti-Semitism, fiction was "not only its midwife, but also its wet-nurse."[97] Fiction such as Krestovsky's *The Yid Is Coming* persuasively presented Russian history as proceeding toward a confrontation between Russia, seen as the last bulwark of Christendom, and the rest of the world, under the control of the Jews. Regardless of surface differences among them, all Jews in these texts turn out to belong to a single type: the fierce enemies of Christians.

Published in 1881, the same year as the Gattsuk translation of *Meir Ezofowicz*, Krestovsky's first volume, *Egyptian Darkness*, exemplifies contemporaneous anti-Semitic fiction. (Krestovsky's biological definition of the Jew makes it fair to label him an anti-Semite, rather than a Judeophobe.)[98] Krestovsky himself (1840–95) was a popular, talented, and often contentious writer. His first and best-known novel, *Peterburgskie trushchoby* [The Petersburg Slums] (1864), is a naturalistic exposé of the lives of poor and rich in the capital. Like its model, Eugène Sue's *The Mysteries of Paris*, it focuses on the injustice of the capitalist system and the sufferings of the disenfranchised. However, both Krestovsky and his writing soon took a turn to the right. He renounced his youthful attraction to nihilism and, by 1874, produced a pair of novels on the Polish uprising of 1863 that depicted it as a threat to Russian sovereignty and the Russian people. The views of Jews that he expresses in *The Yid Is Coming* are consistent with his opinions of Poles and Germans: Russians and non-Russians are natural enemies.[99]

Given Krestovsky's hostility to Jews, the plot of *The Yid Is Coming* is not entirely predictable. The heroine is the sincere, intelligent, and attractive Tamara Ben-David, who starts the story as a Jew and the heiress to the considerable fortunes of her father and grandfather. The narrator warmly describes her relations with her pious grandparents. A visitor to their home, though, incarnates the danger that Krestovsky believes Jews pose to Christians. Rabbi Ionafan, the Ben-Davids' honored guest on Friday night, the beginning of the Jewish Sabbath, gives a sermon at dinner that resembles a battle speech. He calls on all Jews to attack Christians, to exploit them and undermine their civilization in every possible way. When Tamara decides to convert to Christianity from this aggressive version of Judaism, the reader cannot help but sympathize.

However, just as he avoids representing all Jews as evil, so Krestovsky refrains from depicting all Russians as good. The unscrupulous Count Karzhol', a Russian fortune hunter, persuades Tamara to convert. Refusing to believe what Tamara tells him—that if she converts, her family will disinherit her—he convinces her to run away from her grandparents. While awaiting conversion, she takes refuge in a convent led by the only entirely positive Russian character, Mother Serafima. Some of the young Jewish men in town, learning of her actions, attack the convent's walls. In retaliation, the peasants who have gathered for market launch a pogrom, destroying all the Jews' possessions. (Krestovsky probably based this episode on a much publicized incident in 1867: a crowd of Jews threatened to riot outside a monastery in order to prevent the baptism of a Jewish woman.[100] However, from a strictly historical point of view, the events described are not realistic. Krestovsky's pogrom, perpetrated by a mixed crowd of men and women of various ages who studiously avoid violence against people, has little to do with real pogroms, which were carried out mainly by young men and included assault, rape, and murder.)

In the second volume, Tamara converts; in the third, she becomes a country schoolteacher. Most of the Russians she meets are weak, corrupt, and unable to help her in her valiant attempt to leave her origins behind. In the final scenes of the unfinished third book, she renews contact with her grandfather. Her words to herself as she does so phrase identity in biological terms: "This is a matter of a kindred heart, my own blood [*Tut delo rodnogo serdtsa, delo krovnoe*]."[101] Krestovsky depicts Tamara's effort to escape the evil environment of Jews like Rabbi Ionafan as brave but doomed, both by the spinelessness of the Russian characters and by the tribal loyalty that persists in her blood after she eradicates it from her mind. In a letter describing the novel, he stressed precisely the strength of blood: "We [Russians] have grown flabby [*odriableli*] and undisciplined [*raspustilis'*], we have turned into some kind of milksops [*razmazniu*], but the Yid stands strong. He is strong first because of the power of his faith, and second because of the physiological potency of his blood."[102]

This writer differs from other Judeophobes in centering his story around a positive Jewish figure and in harshly criticizing non-Jews. His narrative is more complex than Brafman's, and his portrayals of Jews and Russians more nuanced. Like Orzeszkowa, he devoted some time to studying Judaism and to learning something about Jewish culture from the Russian Jewish writers of his time, and he even displays his research, footnoting Bogrov's *Notes of a Jew* repeatedly.[103] He also read Orzeszkowa herself, apparently admiring her even while he disagreed with her. In a letter to a young writer, he cited *Meir Ezofowicz* as a work that reveals the author's sincerity:

> Take, for instance, Eliza Orzeszkowa, who takes the Jewish way of life [*byt*] in the Western borderlands as her subject and who treats it most sympathetically. You can disagree with her personal sympathy for the Jews, but you will nonetheless be engrossed in this work, seeing before you living images [*obrazy*] and a living world, in all its colors. And why is this? Because the author is first of all deeply sincere. On the other side, take myself. I too, in my trilogy, *The Yid Is Coming*, chose the Jews as my subject, and especially the Jews of the Western borderlands, but my sympathies as regards this world are diametrically opposed to Eliza Orzeszkowa's. Nonetheless you write to me that you are engrossed in *Egyptian Darkness* and *Tamara*.[104]

Even while he mined Orzeszkowa's and Bogrov's books for information about Jews, Krestovsky preserved a far more one-sidedly negative picture than they did. He was a prototypical Russian anti-Semite in his depiction of a Jewish conspiracy and in his pessimism about Jewish assimilation, which is inevitably undermined by Jewish group loyalty.

Krestovsky and the translator of the Gattsuk edition express the same opinion of the Jewish present and future. Through careful editing of *Meir Ezofowicz*, the translator emphasizes precisely those elements that then stand out in Krestovsky's novel. He depicts the Jewish community as unchanging and unchangeable, not divided against itself but rather bound together by its members' unquestioning loyalty. He omits passages that imply that an individual Jew might ever learn and "improve." Where Krestovsky assumes that Christians cannot help Tamara, the Gattsuk translator omits Orzeszkowa's call for Christians to "extend a hand" to Meir. His ideology differs starkly from that of the Polish Positivists who believed that the "reform" of a Jew was possible and desirable, that is, that Meir's story would turn out well. The translator is far closer to Russian anti-Semites such as Krestovsky, who felt that Jewish reform was neither possible nor desirable, and that Tamara's tale could only be a tragedy for all concerned. These two attitudes toward the outcome of the story of Jewish assimilation resulted from two different understandings of national and imperial identity. In both the Polish and the Russian cases, narratives of Jewish assimilation provide a window onto prevailing anxieties and hopes about the cultural model toward which the Jewish hero strives.

The Limits of Education

Even though Orzeszkowa always explicitly rejected a racial view of the nation,[105] *Meir Ezofowicz* functions in some similar ways for Polish and Russian nationalism, making it possible to theorize connections between Orzeszkowa's and Krestovsky's nationalist ideologies. Orzeszkowa, in the tradition of Voltairian rationalism and the Haskalah, criticizes that in Judaism which appears illogical to her. She offers an analysis of texts that she divides into the reasonable and the unreasonable, the Old Testament and the *Guide to the Perplexed* versus the Talmud and the Zohar [a kabbalistic text]. Her attitude toward sacred Jewish texts is so coldly analytic that one of her contemporaries suggested that she, like Voltaire, might inspire readers to turn an equally skeptical eye onto Christian texts.[106] Krestovsky, seemingly more indebted to

Eisenmenger and the Christian Hebraic tradition, stresses the aspects of Judaism that appear unchristian to him; emphasizing the enmity between Jews and Christians and describing Jews who interpret their own texts to justify exploiting non-Jews and who long to attack Christian holy things. Krestovsky's Jews are inspired by preachers such as his Rabbi Ionafan, who tell them that in their dealings with non-Jews they must "destroy their sacrificial altars, and tear down their columns, and cut down their sacred trees, and burn their idols, because you are a holy people for our God."[107]

In spite of ideological differences, though, the two authors and their schools are united by their method of critiquing Judaism. Both base their vision of the Jewish religion on a selective reading of Jewish texts. Both Orzeszkowa and Krestovsky follow the technique of Eisenmenger, as Katz describes it: they offer the reader edited selections from the Old Testament and the Talmud. Their goals are different, however: Orzeszkowa presents Jewish history, as reflected in Jewish texts, as motivated by a continual struggle between forces of obscurantism and enlightenment, metaphorical darkness and light; Krestovsky depicts that same history and literature as unchangingly focused on reinforcing hostility toward other groups. But both accomplish these goals by creating their own versions of Judaism and the Jewish canon, replacing the original's complex multivoicedness with a more straightforward image of an ethical and social system opposed to the one the author endorses.

The two authors also demonstrate a common impulse first to suggest a solution to the "Jewish problem," a plan for the Jews' assimilation into a non-Jewish culture, and then to note the limitations of that solution. Orzeszkowa's hero strives to escape the intellectual confinement of the shtetl for the "wide world" of secular European culture, but upon meeting the Witebskis realizes that a Jew can adopt non-Jewish culture incorrectly and superficially. The author represents resentment of the Russification of Jews in the western provinces by countering Meir with Leopold Witebski, the bad assimilator. The ideology circumscribing Orzeszkowa's call for Poles to "extend a hand" to assimilating Jews, then, is clear: rather than approving the efforts of all acculturating Jews, she confines her sympathy to those who choose a Polish cultural model. Instead of arguing, as Maimon would, that Jews should acquaint themselves with European culture broadly defined, she wants Meir to choose Polish culture in particular, which she thereby opposes to non-Polish —specifically Russian or imperial—culture.

Krestovsky presents a similar image of the insincere assimilator when his Rabbi Ionafan preaches that, in order to further the Jewish plot to take over the world, a Jew may become an apostate, pretending to abandon Jewish tradition or to seemingly convert to another religion:

> For this, if it is necessary, we can, I suppose, forgo our outward peculiarities, even (though this is horrible to say!) superficially take another religion (pfui!). And this is even permitted to us in an extreme case, but we must then religiously preserve the secret source of our internal essence, not for a second ceasing to be a Jew and a faithful slave to Jewry in our soul.[108]

The author opposes this image of religiously condoned insincere conversion to that of Tamara Ben-David, who exemplifies both the sincere convert and the sincere assimilator—speaking Russian with no accent, loving Russian culture, and getting higher grades in Russian literature than the non-Jewish girls at her school. Tamara decides to convert not by calculating what she will gain, but by reading the New Testament. Indeed, she recognizes that conversion, which will lead to her disinheritance, will actually hurt her financially. Her sincerity so impresses the mother superior at the local convent that she agrees against her own better judgment to grant Tamara shelter. Despite Tamara's sincerity, by the end of the trilogy her effort to assimilate away from Judaism is doomed: she must respond to the "call of her blood."

Krestovsky, like Orzeszkowa, thus suggests the restrictions of his model for assimilation. For both authors, these restrictions stem from a definition of the culture toward which the assimilating Jew strives. By defining Polish culture in opposition to Russian, and by envisaging the former as "real" and the latter as "false civilization," Orzeszkowa sets up a dichotomy within which the Jew, by deciding to learn Russian instead of Polish, can easily make the wrong choice and be revealed as a false assimilator. For Krestovsky, the enmity between cultures results not from the legitimacy of one culture and the illegitimacy of another, but from some quality of blood itself. His fascination with blood signals his skepticism about the possibility of assimilation, which would, for him, imply that one could tamper with one's own "racial" identity. His definition of Russianness leads him to suggest that false conversion and false assimilation are not only a danger, as Orzeszkowa suggests, but the inevitable result of any Jewish attempt to acculturate, as indicated by Tamara's change of heart. While for Orzeszkowa false assimilation is a threat that can be resisted by sincere Jews and their non-Jewish supporters, for Krestovsky no effort can make the Jew's conversion "stick," despite the convert's sincerity. The fear of ineffective conversion in its various forms unites the two writers.

What is the relationship between Orzeszkowa's concern about improper assimilation and Krestovsky's doubts that assimilation is at all possible? Her ideology is based on a definition of the Polish nation as something that a Jew—or another outsider—could voluntarily join, while he relies on a pro-toracial idea of both Russians and Jews as defined not by choices but by blood. Both of them, though, evoke the fear of the assimilated Jew, not as a loyal citizen of a single nation-state but as a creature of undefinable loyalties. The accusation that the assimilated Jew is "cosmopolitan" implies that Jews, having abandoned their outmoded religious textual tradition, will replace it not with the sacred texts of a modern nationalism but with some non-national literature that reveals their frightening lack of national allegiance.

An obsessive concern in nationalist ideology about Jews can function as a mirror for other anxieties, and an attempt to "solve" the "Jewish problem" can compensate for an inability to solve other, more substantive problems. In Sartre's formulation, the anti-Semite's stance reflects "a basic fear of one-self and of truth."[109] For both Orzeszkowa and Krestovsky, as for many Poles and Russians in the 1880s, these fears concerned the fragility of national identity. In the annexed Polish Kingdom and even more so in the western provinces, the future domination of Polish culture over what Orzeszkowa perceived as historically Polish lands was in doubt.[110] The threat that the Russian language and culture, backed by imperial policy, would gain adherents not only among Jews, Lithuanians, and Belorussians but also, eventually, among ethnic Poles must have seemed very real. In that context, perhaps Orzeszkowa's depiction of incorrect Jewish assimilation is connected to a fear of incorrect Polish assimilation, that is, to the anxiety that Polish identity might someday dissipate and vanish, especially in her region, just as the tsar's administrators hoped it would.[111] The Russification of Lithuanian Jewry could be both a manifestation and a symbol of a terrifying process of cultural destruction.

Even while Orzeszkowa argued for Jewish assimilation, she frequently wrote about Jews and Jewish nationalism in order to convey her opinions about Poles and Polish nationalism. As several scholars note, her depictions of Jewish group loyalty and Jewish resistance in the face of domination by a larger nation sometimes conceal arguments for Polish group loyalty and resistance against the Russians: images of Jews could simultaneously represent Orzeszkowa's hopes for the Polish nation's rise and fears about its decline.[112] In criticizing the Witebski family's superficial culture, the author may have been expressing not only her fear that in a culturally weakened Poland, Jews with their unclear loyalties could further threaten Polish culture, but also her worry that Polish culture and Polish identity were not strong enough to withstand assault.

From the Russian perspective, the threat to identity was less clearly defined. Rather than fearing an attack from an outside power, the Russians had to contend with the potentially centrifugal forces latent in their vast multinational empire. Their role as the "leading" ethnicity in a hugely diverse country has always both defined and threatened the Russian self-understanding.[113] As we know, during the second half of the nineteenth century, the imperial administration and local governing bodies shifted constantly among an assortment of approaches to the various minority nationalities, including the Jews.[114] As the actual incidence of Jewish assimilation rose, so, seemingly, did resistance to the notion that a non-Russian could simply choose to take on a Russian identity. Krestovsky's skepticism about Jewish assimilation, then, may stand for the urge to redefine Russian identity as innate rather than choosable. If so, then just as Orzeszkowa's depiction of incorrectly assimilating Jews may stem from her own fears of Polish assimilation to Russian culture, so Krestovsky's description of Jewish false assimilation may reflect his own fears that Russification campaigns would harm Russians by diluting Russian identity. At least one of his own readers found his picture of Russian weakness more central to the story than his illustration of Jewish strength. Mikhail Katkov, his editor at *Russkii vestnik*, who had reservations about the work, pointed out after reading an early draft of *The Yid Is Coming*, "The Yid isn't coming—the Christian is leaving."[115]

In a multinational empire or a multiethnic modern state, assertions about any unitary national identity present both logical and narrative difficulties. Perhaps it is for this reason that Krestovsky could not write directly about the problem of maintaining and reinforcing a pure Russianness. Instead, he could express both the fear of the loss of Russian identity and the hope that it would prove as inalienable as blood by describing, on the one hand, Jewish cosmopolitanism, and on the other, Jewish group loyalty. Rabbi

Ionafan, in his sermon, tells Jews that they are free to pretend to take on other identities, to assume the mask of the cosmopolitan, but that they must —and will—always retain their Jewish identity. Krestovsky's Russian readers—and the readers of the Gattsuk translation of *Meir Ezofowicz*—might deduce that even though they may be attracted to other cultures, whether within the empire or outside its borders, they must not pay the price of successful empire-building by forfeiting their provincial values. Unlike Meir Ezofowicz, they must not give in to the pull of new texts. Instead, like Krestovsky's Tamara, they should heed the "call of their blood" and remember their "true identity."

The creation of the Gattsuk version of Orzeszkowa's *Meir Ezofowicz* illustrates the power of the translator to change the text; it also points to a paradox in the theory of literary types. The author's Russian and Polish critics had agreed that Jewish communities contained "diverse types," "a variety of types," "unique types," and that the task of the talented author was to describe them in fiction.[116] Meir, the reformer, is the novel's central "type." Like Bogrov's Srul, he would seem to exemplify the positive hero and the new man, a stark contrast to the negative type represented by Rabbi Todros. The character of Meir was designed to represent the reform tendency that already existed among young Jews, and simultaneously to reinforce that tendency by inspiring readers to imitate the example they found in literature. The Gattsuk translator seems to have ignored this message and misread Meir, transforming him into a different, more static, and older type, resident of a world in which self-transformation through text appears impossible. Extending Orzeszkowa's fear of the Russifying Jews in the western provinces as false assimilators, he hints that all acculturating Jews may be false—or at least ineffectual—allies for Christians. Krestovsky's *The Yid Is Coming*, the ideological parallel to the Gattsuk translation, makes the impossibility of such change yet clearer; both men thus challenge the progressive conception of literary type along with the ideology of human permutability that lay behind it.

Ironically, conservative Russian nationalists such as Krestovsky and the Gattsuk translator were not the only ones to demonstrate the difficulty of finding a consistent and reliable message in a Jewish literary type that was meant to be positive. Dubnova-Erlikh wrote that one part of Orzeszkowa's appeal for the Jewish reader of the early twentieth century was her enthusiasm for "the heroic" in Jewish life.[117] Even young Jewish intellectuals of Dubnova's generation and circle, who were, she suggests, skeptical of the idea that they should re-create themselves entirely according to the standard of one or another European culture, found something to admire in Orzeszkowa's Meir—not, surely, his willingness to question Jewish traditions, but rather, it would seem, some kind of archaic glory that adhered to the world he rejected, and perhaps even to the most obviously negative type, Rabbi Todros. Readers such as Dubnova might have read Meir's story as Annenkov had read Turgenev's "Asya," finding it absorbing regardless of the hero's strength or weakness. The readers Dubnova describes, just like the Gattsuk translator, refused to categorize Meir conclusively as a knight of the future (and his enemy Todros as a knight of the past). They may have found his tale more compelling because it was closer to their own experience of living in neither the corrupt past nor the hoped-for future, but instead the uncategorizable present.

3 JEW AS TEXT, JEW AS READER: NIKOLAI LESKOV

IF THE STATE REWARDS converts to Christianity with money and privileges, should we attempt to distinguish a conversion based on conviction from a hypocritical one? When the government treats religious belief as a public service to be officially compensated, should any citizen imagine it instead as a personal relationship between an individual and God? While Bogrov's work spoke to a philosophical dilemma posed by the project of Jewish acculturation, and Orzeszkowa and her Russian translator considered political issues associated with it, two of Nikolai Leskov's stories reflect on some religious questions raised by the specter of Jewish conversion in the late-nineteenth-century Russian Empire. In his depictions of converts from Judaism, he touches on larger questions about the faith and the identity of the Russian Orthodox.

The many works that Leskov wrote about Jews reveal his fascination with the "Jewish question." From 1877 through 1886, he published six stories whose main characters were Jewish: "Vladychnyi sud" [Episcopal Justice] (1877), "Rakushanskii melamed" [The Melamed of Österreich] (1878), "Zhidovskaia kuvyrkollegiia" [Yid Somersault] (1882), "Novozavetnye evrei" [New Testament Jews] (1884), "Ukha bez ryby" [Fish Soup Without Fish] (1886), and "Skazanie o Fedore-khristianine i o druge ego Abrame-zhidovine" [The Tale of Fedor the Christian and His Friend Abraham the Jew] (1886).[1] During the 1880s, he produced a series of twenty articles on Jewish rituals, as well as several pieces on other topics related to Jews.[2] Finally, the St. Petersburg Jewish community commissioned him to write the book *Evrei v Rossii* [Jews in Russia] (1884), a refutation of certain accusations made against Jews, which was published anonymously and submitted to the Pahlen Commission, a body created to deliberate on the legal status of the empire's Jews.[3]

Those scholars who have addressed these texts are primarily interested in the question of Leskov's general attitude toward Jews. From Iulii Gessen and V. Vodovozov at the beginning of the twentieth century to William Edgerton and Hugh McLean near its end, critics observed that while the writer used ugly stereotypes to portray the Jewish characters in some of his earlier pieces, his later ones depicted Jews more positively, suggesting that he repented from or rethought his intolerance.[4] Indeed, especially in his later years, he seemed to have been self-conscious about his reflexive hostility to Jews, which he opposed to an ideal Christian morality. In a letter written in 1888, he first admitted that "I would rather order work from a German or a Russian than a Jew," then asserted that "a human being deserves our sympathy primarily because he is human."[5] His biographer A. I. Faresov quotes him on the difficulty of finding a single clear answer to the Jewish question: "I believe that one must live in a brotherly way with all nations, and I express that view, but personally, I am afraid of Jews, and I avoid them. I am for equality [*ravnopravnost'*], but [I am] not for Jews."[6]

For Leskov's biographers since Faresov, analysis of this Russian writer's feelings about Jews and the empire's other nationalities poses a fascinating psychological problem. In my study of depictions of the mutability of the acculturating Jew, I am most interested in Leskov's invocation of varying archetypes in his description of his own attitudes toward the Jews. If we accept the accuracy of Faresov's transcription, Leskov describes himself as "for equality," aligning himself with the liberals who believed that the future would and should contain a Russian state in which Jews could enjoy the same privileges as Christians, as well as Jews who would appreciate these rights. At the same time, Leskov admits that he is "not for Jews" and that, just like the ignorant soldiers who learn from Major Pleskunov's story in his own "Melamed of Österreich," he is even afraid of them. In the vocabulary of his time, Leskov identifies alternately with the types of the sophisticated Judeophile and the primitive Judeophobe, that is, both the liberal, philosophizing Westernizer whose sympathy extends to everything human, and the conservative nationalist who refuses to patronize a Jewish business.

Leskov recognized his own inconsistency on this issue. In connection with his equivocations on the "Jewish question" and a few other matters, Faresov cites Leskov's musings on human inconsistency in general: "Varied people sometimes inhabit a single body. . . . It's not even always possible to sense what gorilla might be resurrected [*voskresnut'*] in each of us. That's why dissimilar children, Cain and Abel, can be born to a single family."[7] The debates about the status of the Jews, which focused on their loyalty to the Russian state and the Russian people, and the discussions of converts from Judaism, which centered on their loyalty to the Church, all forced Leskov to recognize the insubstantiality of some of his own loyalties. Even while he participated in the argument in his fictional and nonfictional texts, it would seem, Leskov acknowledged the logical flaw at the heart of the "Jewish question"—that is, the impossibility of reliably and permanently defining any person's allegiances.

Leskov identifies the irreconcilable human types in a single family or individual with Cain and Abel, the two sons of Adam and Eve whose story culminates in Cain's murder of his brother. The reference to Genesis in this context reveals the tendency that Leskov shared with many of his contemporaries to imagine the Jews of the Russian Empire in the framework of biblical archetypes. By using biblical terms, he signals that he sees Jews first of all as playing a role in Christian history. If the posited unreliability of the Jew compels the writer to admit his own inconsistency, then the problem of Jewish mutability inevitably forces him to confront questions about Christian faith and the Orthodox believer. After considering some of the ramifications of these questions for this writer, I will address Leskov's most complex "Jewish" story, "Episcopal Justice," and the shorter "New Testament Jews," before comparing his treatment of Jews and Russian identity to a few of Fedor Dostoevsky's famous pronouncements on the topic.

Leskov, Russian Jewry, and the Christian Question

Although Russian law had always made conversion to Christianity legally and economically advantageous, a perceived increase in Jewish baptisms in the late nineteenth century disturbed members of the Russian intelligentsia in various political camps and even some thinkers within the Orthodox Church.[8] On one end of the spectrum, some believed that baptized Jews were without exception hypocrites who posed a danger to Christianity, and that the Church should forbid their conversion rather than allow them to enjoy its benefits.[9] On the opposite end, others saw the phenomenon as a reason to change the law, to introduce equality and religious tolerance, rather than force people into religious hypocrisy.[10]

Doubt about Jewish conversions produced writings that worked to distinguish between "true" and "false" converts. Fictional and nonfictional images of these two kinds of converts relied on mastertexts from the Gospels. The paradigmatic conversion narrative about the transformation of a Jew into a Christian begins when a light from heaven strikes Saul, who had persecuted the Christians, while he is on a journey to Damascus. Saul hears the voice of Jesus, loses consciousness, then, after baptism, comes to with a new faith and a mission to propagate it (Acts 9). His new name—Paul—signifies the completeness of his transformation. Similarly, Augustine, who had sinned, converts after hearing a voice that tells him to read the Bible, which brings "a peaceful light streaming into [his] heart."[11] The classic conversion tale recounts the path toward baptism, from crisis toward rebirth, featuring the sequence of guilt, retribution, redemption, and then blessedness, and the association with illumination and a journey or a road.[12] This conversion narrative coexists with a kind of double: the tale of a false or insincere conversion. Again, the New Testament furnishes the archetype: Judas Iscariot, one of Jesus' disciples, proves disloyal to him when he betrays him. This scene equates Judas with the Pharisee priests who bribe him, creating a story in which a Jew who has been baptized is revealed as no Christian but a Pharisee. In the lexicon of Leskov's era, in Russian and other European languages, "Pharisee" could mean "Jew," "religious hypocrite," or "hypocrite" more broadly defined.

The European tradition of writing on Jews and Jewish conversion tended to assign the biographies of all Jews—including assimilated and even baptized Jews—to one of these two categories. It defined Jews as either Pharisees—"blind" fools whose stories are frozen in the stasis of their eternal rejection and persecution of Jesus—or potential converts who can move forward to "see" the truth of Christianity.[13] In this system, Jews and Pharisees were associated with law instead of grace or mercy, and with formalistic approaches to texts and life. Unbaptized and unassimilated Jews could only be

Pharisees, but those who reached out toward gentiles and gentile culture were liminal figures, who immediately brought up the question of categorization. They could fit the model of either Paul, the sincere convert, or Judas, the false convert and secret Pharisee.

The attraction of these opposing biblical stories as archetypes for Christian narratives about contemporary Jews stems from the tradition of figural reading; in Christian exegesis, the events in the Hebrew Bible portend those that appear in the Greek Bible. As Erich Auerbach explains, "*figura* is something real and historical which announces something else that is also real and historical."[14] That is, biblical events are seen as no less real for their placement in a symbolic system that defines them as leading toward a First and then a Second Coming. Postbiblical history, for the Christian exegete, always demands interpretation: "history, with all its concrete force, remains forever a figure, cloaked and needful of interpretation."[15] Thus just as Dostoevsky's characters in *The Idiot* read and reread Revelation, trying to fit their own experience into a biblical model of apocalypse and redemption, so their nonfictional late-nineteenth-century Russian counterparts wrote and rewrote the Jewish acculturation and conversion they witnessed, using the genres they had inherited from the Christian Bible.

In Russian journalistic polemics as in literature, the stories of Paul and Judas were clearly differentiated, the image of the sincere convert distinguished from that of the hypocrite who accepted Christianity for profit. Stories of "good" converts—whether cast as nonfiction, autobiography, or fiction—stress not the advantage that Russian laws gave to converts but instead the persecution of converts by the Jewish community (recalling the persecution of Jesus, as well as Paul).[16] Leskov wrote newspaper articles as well as fiction that worked with this model. For instance, in an 1885 piece he praised a group of Jews who espoused Christian beliefs without converting officially. The members of the "New Israel" "synagogue" in Kishinev believed in Jesus as the Messiah and rejected the Talmud. Leskov praised their movement: "this is a most important, free and sincere step toward spiritual rapprochement [*sblizhenie*]."[17] His enthusiasm reveals a catch-22 dilemma: by accepting the legal benefits of baptism, converts were in danger of appearing "false"; only those who somehow rejected the material advantages of conversion—like the "New Israel" congregation in Kishinev, whose members advertised their sympathy for Christianity, but did not convert—had the potential to be "true" Christians.

Even while some writers worked to imagine a "true" conversion, others described the "false" instance of it. In Aleksey Pisemsky's 1873 play *Baal*, the virtuous Russian characters are disgusted by a Jew who converts to Orthodoxy in order to marry a Russian woman, then happily accepts a fifty-ruble government payoff.[18] Mikhail Saltykov-Shchedrin, in a section of *Sovremennaia idilliia* [A Contemporary Idyll] published in 1883, refers to a Jew's plans to convert in order to obtain a residence permit for himself and his relatives as "blasphemous double-dealing" [*koshchunstvennyi gesheft*].[19] Leskov, too, in his newspaper articles, criticized both Jews who convert for the sake of material gain and the policy that encouraged them to do so. In an 1883 piece about government policy in the Baltics, he draws attention to a high-level administrator's distress at having to carry out a law according to which Jewish converts to Christianity received thirty rubles:

> The law did not please him [Governor-General Suvorov in Riga]. There's nothing wrong with that—that law didn't please a great many people, who much more broadly and truly than the prince understood the multifaceted danger that such an honorarium posed both to faith and to morals. This law, nicknamed the "Law about the thirty pieces of silver," led to many of the very worst instances of "commerce in faith," and we can be sincerely happy that it has been eliminated.[20]

Suvorov's—and Leskov's—discomfort with this image is understandable. The law itself created a scenario that casted the Jewish convert as Judas, the person who received thirty pieces of silver in exchange for a betrayal of a worthy cause, making him by definition unlikely to be a good Christian, and it gave the role of the Pharisees to the tsarist government and its unwilling administrators. Leskov's commentary on the "law about the thirty pieces of silver" places him in unexpected company, evoking a fear similar to the one that Karl Marx articulated in the 1840s in his obscure essay "*On the Jewish Question*." In Marx's formulation, Jewish assimilation and emancipation occur in tandem with the growth of capitalism and the concomitant involvement of Christians in unethical transactions: "The Jew has emancipated himself in a Jewish manner. . . . money has become a world power and the Jew has become the practical spirit of the Christian people. The Jews have emancipated themselves in so far as the Christians have become Jews."[21] The liminality and the moral ambiguity of assimilating Jews for Marx and of Jewish converts for Leskov seem to taint the Christians who interact with them.

While many depictions of Jewish converts defined them either as "true" Christians or "false" Pharisees, cantonists who had converted to Russian Orthodoxy as children could not necessarily be assimilated into this binary system. By emblematizing the categoric dilemma posed by forced conversion, they could challenge the ancient archetypes. The decision to draft Jewish children was explicitly motivated by tsarist policy aimed at conversion of the Jews to Orthodoxy. One member of Nicholas's secret police even wrote a memorandum urging that the Jews be required to furnish only child recruits, since children were less likely than adults to refuse conversion.[22] Leskov's fictional narrator in "Episcopal Justice" confirms this when he observes that the government preferred child recruits, since "there was a conviction that small children adapted more quickly and could be more easily baptized [*legche krestilis'*]" (p. 90).[23] Indeed, to judge by the autobiographical accounts of surviving cantonists, army officials used force as well as persuasion to convince Jewish recruits to convert. Ultimately, half of the Jewish child recruits and significant numbers of adult soldiers were baptized.[24]

It is important to remember that regardless of this official preference for child recruits, the Jewish communities under Nicholas had the option of offering men ages eighteen to twenty-five. Nonetheless, a large percentage of the recruits whom communities turned in were boys, some even younger than twelve. Their decisions were influenced by several factors: first, Jewish boys eighteen and over were often already the heads of families, whose elimination would create a more severe economic impact on the community than would the drafting of young children; second, tsarist regulations permitted community officials to draft selectively rather than exacting the same number of boys from each family. Thus, the poor and unemployed and those who had no influence with community leadership or had offended it in some way were more likely than others to be drafted themselves or have their children given to the army. Not surprisingly, this policy exacerbated rifts within Jewish communities.[25]

Few non-Jewish Russian writers aside from Leskov took up the grim theme of cantonism. Aleksandr Herzen, while being sent on exile for political crimes, was shocked and "wanted to sob" when he ran across a detachment of child soldiers. For him, the fate of Jewish cantonists epitomized the "monstrous crimes . . . buried in the archives from the criminal, immoral reign of Nicholas."[26] By the 1870s, the story of the cantonists was no longer buried. Subscribers to *Otechestvennye zapiski* could read not only Bogrov's tear-soaked accounts of the cantonists' sufferings in the chapter "The Wanderings of Erukhim," near the end of *Notes of a Jew*, but also a story by the former cantonist Viktor Nikitin on the same topic, "Mnogostradal'nye" [The Suffering Ones], published in 1871.[27]

Like these writers who breached the topic of cantonism in the mainstream Russian press, Leskov was apparently inspired to write about it after witnessing it himself. He worked in Kiev on the "production of recruits" [*proizvodstvo nabora*] in the early 1850s, at a time when the government demanded ever increasing quotas of recruits from Jewish communities,[28] and his experience as a government official clearly conditioned his approach to the topic. Bogrov and Nikitin wrote of cantonism from the perspective of the child recruit or his Jewish friends; Leskov wrote from that of the administrator who processed recruits.

While Leskov's fiction, as we will see, deals ambiguously and figuratively with the responsibility of military administrators for the sufferings of child recruits, he addresses this topic explicitly in his journalism. In an article on the enforcement of Nicholas's decrees in the empire's Baltic borderlands, Leskov comes close to analyzing his own work in Kiev. He often wrote about a community in Riga of Old Believers, schismatics seen by the Orthodox Church as heretics.[29] In 1849, Riga General Governor Suvorov decided that Old Believer orphans should be enrolled into cantonist units. City policemen were required to pursue the defenseless boys, arrest them, and take them to another city, where, like the Jewish cantonists, they faced a probable forced conversion to Orthodoxy. The situation in Riga mirrored that in the Kiev story, because in both cities the officials who enforced the rules of recruitment and the cantonist boys represented different ethnic groups (most often the Riga policemen were not ethnic Russians, but from the Baltic German middle class).

Leskov's signal that he saw cantonism in Riga, as in Kiev, as a slaughter of the innocents is his frequent repetition in both contexts of a biblical citation about "lamentation in Ramah" ("Rachel weeping for her children . . . would not be comforted" [Matt. 2:18, quoted from Jer. 31:15]).[30] He appears intrigued by the officials who created this "lamentation" in Riga. In one article in 1869, Leskov cites a letter by Count Sologub, a local administrator who disagrees with the general governor. Sologub describes the behavior of the German policemen: "The more the local militia . . . feel an internal revulsion for their duties, the more severely they carry them out." In 1869, Leskov expresses the opinion that such repulsive duties provoke in the Germans an ever greater hatred for Russians. Thus, they carry out their duties more severely, hoping that the Old Believers will come to hate the tsarist authorities more strongly. In Leskov's retelling, the German policemen think, "So don't blame us, but your own kind—those who forced us into this chase, which is *repulsive* to us!"[31]

Nonetheless, Leskov does not limit himself to a single explanation of the phenomenon. Thirteen years later, in another article on Riga, he again cites that same sentence from Sologub's letter. This time he rejects the opinion that he himself had earlier proposed:

> Some people say that the Germans "had their own political motivations," that they wanted to show these settled people of the Russian breed [the Old Believers] that they are being crowded out and tormented not by Germans, but by Russians. Thus, as these people would have it, the Germans wanted to set them [the Old Believers] against the Russian government. But I think that is unlikely, empty speculation.

Leskov proffers a more subtle psychological analysis of the German militia's actions:

> A person who is compelled to do a repulsive thing tries to finish with it *as quickly as humanly possible*. It's the same as drowning cats. It's better to drown them right away and at such a depth that they can't climb out, than to torment them at length and to hear how they meow in the agonies of death.[32]

In the articles about the Riga Old Believers, Leskov offers two explanations for the militia's cruelty: either the German policemen hated the Russian Old Believers because they represented a different nationality, in which case their behavior reflects an ingrained racial or cultural hatred, or the Germans in fact sympathized with the Russians, and acted harshly because they did not want to prolong the agony of the child cantonists. The parallel between the German militia in Riga and Leskov's own employment in Kiev indicates that these answers might describe Leskov's ambivalence about his behavior as a military administrator. Given his experience when he came to Riga, he probably identified with the militia even while he doubted the wisdom and the theological justification for the capture and likely forced conversion of Old Believer children.

The situation of the Jewish cantonists Leskov encountered in Kiev may have troubled him because it produced a sort of cognitive dissonance. The New Testament, as well as the patristic literature that is so important in Eastern Orthodoxy, presents sincere Christians, in the model of Jesus, as the victims of sanctimonious Jews. Leskov, as he so often boasted, was far more literate in Church traditions than the average Russian writer of his time: he knew the Gospels and the Church Fathers well. The disjunction between the stereotype of the Christian victim in sacred literature and the reality of Jewish victims of what Leskov clearly saw as Christian religious hypocrisy could lie behind his fascination with Jews and Jewish converts to Christianity and his association of them with a reevaluation of Orthodox piety.

In questioning Orthodox practices, Leskov took part in a discussion that engrossed the intellectuals of his time: others too decried what they saw as hypocrisy and pharisaism in the state church and were attracted to what were identified as Protestant practices (Bible reading, lay preaching, spontaneous individual prayer, a pastoral focus for the work of priests, and a certain skepticism about ritual, miracles, and the Church hierarchy).[33] The most vocal critic of the Church was a friend of Leskov, Father Ioann Belliustin, whose scathing description of the inadequate education and ridiculous obligations of rural priests in his 1859 book (published abroad without his knowledge) provoked a scandal and loud cries for reform.[34] While the state did impose significant reforms on the Church and the priestly estate, it put up great resistance to "Protestant-style" innovations.[35] The state grouped the many Protestant movements among the peasantry under the title "Shtunda" and repressed them energetically. Meanwhile, the echoes of the debate are clearly audible in the Russian fiction of the period, from the Bible-reading prostitute in Dostoevsky's *Crime and Punishment* to Lydiia Ivanovna's patronage of foreign mystics in Tolstoy's *Anna Karenina*. In most of his writings, Leskov, rather like Belliustin himself, supported the criticism of Church practices (implicit in his 1870s work, but increasingly explicit later on) with examples drawn from his own provincial experience; at the same time, he emphasized his respect for certain aspects of Russian religious culture (icon painting, church architecture, etc.). In 1877, though, Leskov published a book dealing with a more urban issue, a religious trend among the St. Petersburg aristocracy: an English Protestant, Baron Radstock, had decided to preach in Russia and attracted a host of followers.[36] In *Velikosvetskii raskol* [Schism in High Society], Leskov alternated between mocking Radstock and delicately pointing to the problems that might account for educated Russians preferring this exotic Protestant to their own Orthodox priests. As he would in the Jewish stories, Leskov took advantage of a seemingly peripheral topic to comment on the state of the Orthodox Church.

At the same time, in establishing a connection between Christian treatment of Jews and reform of Orthodox practices, Leskov took a stance similar to that of Vladimir Solov'ev, a contemporaneous religious philosopher whose critique of Orthodoxy owed nothing to Protestantism. In the 1884 essay "Evreistvo i khristianskii vopros" [Jewry and the Christian Question], Solov'ev explicitly defined negative attitudes toward Jews as a denial of the Christian doctrine laid out in the Bible: "If the commandment of the Gospels is feasible, if we can deal in a Christian way with everyone, not excluding even the Hebrews [*iudeev*], then we are completely to blame when we do not do this."[37] As Judith Kornblatt notes, the Jews constitute a key element of his Christian theology: "Solov'ev's interest in the Jews goes well beyond the 'Jewish question' and anti-Semitism. It in fact corresponded to his most central philosophical categories."[38] Critics have often used Leskov's writings on the Jews, like Solov'ev's, primarily as a litmus test measuring the writer's liberalism. Following Kornblatt's lead in her writings on Solov'ev, I want to set Leskov's depictions of Jews against the broader canvas of his understanding of the future of Russian Orthodoxy itself.

"Episcopal Justice"

The Jewish cantonist first appeared in Leskov's fiction in 1863, in the story "Ovtsebyk" [The Musk-Ox], where an encounter with a group of child recruits, some sick, provokes a crisis in the hero. Fourteen years later, in 1877, Leskov returned to the theme to address it at length. In "Vladychnyi sud" [Episcopal Justice], he weaves commentary on Judaism and Christianity into a characteristically complex plot. This story combines biblical and historical themes, describing an underage Jewish recruit like the ones whom Leskov might have processed when he worked in Kiev—and the narrator, like Leskov, works as an administrator at the recruitment office. The boy's father, a bookbinder, is a freethinker who has dipped into Christian works. To punish him for his heterodoxy, the Jewish community has selected his son as a recruit. In order to save his son, the bookbinder hires another Jew— paying him in advance—to take his place, but problems arise when this substitute recruit decides to convert to Russian Orthodoxy before his army service begins, in order to make himself ineligible (since only a Jew could substitute for another Jew). The substitute recruit is clearly motivated by the urge to avoid army service, rather than by any true change in faith. The bookbinder, with the help of the narrator and a string of other people, eventually succeeds in convincing the metropolitan of Kiev to declare the substitute recruit "unworthy" of conversion, thus forcing him to enter the army as a Jew. In spite of this victory, we learn in the final chapters that the bookbinder's son had been so abused by the soldiers who held him pending his recruitment that he died soon after his father had him freed. The narrator encounters the bookbinder many years later, long after the death of his son and his wife, and finds out that the bookbinder himself has converted to Orthodoxy. In assigning responsibility for the bookbinder's problem, the narrator criticizes tsarist law and excoriates the Jewish community, but glosses over his own role and that of the other Russian officials who processed the cantonists.

It is easy to situate this story in the tradition of Christian writing about the Jew and to focus on the distinction between the bookbinder, the real convert, whose story resembles Paul's, and the substitute recruit, the false convert, who evokes Judas. Within that context, the work becomes a lightly concealed attack on the hypocritical attitude toward the sacrament of baptism enforced under Nicholas I, which fails to distinguish between faith and profit.

Such a conclusion would follow a trail of clues that Leskov himself laid. He began "Episcopal Justice" with a digression about a story he had written two years before, "Na kraiu sveta" [On the Edge of the World] (1875). Critics have often analyzed Leskov's "Episcopal Justice" in the context of that better-known work, which also describes conversion to Christianity in Russia's borderlands.[39] Its hero, Father Kiriak, an Orthodox missionary to the Far East, teaches the native peoples about Christianity but refuses to participate in a campaign to baptize masses of them as quickly as possible. In "Episcopal Justice," Leskov coyly notes that some had criticized that earlier story, accusing the priest of "indulgence of unbelief and even a careless attitude toward the salvation of souls through holy baptism" (p. 88). He then introduces his new story as proof that "Na kraiu sveta" was not the only incident of its type. This introduction makes it clear that Leskov saw both stories as revealing the hypocrisy of missionary efforts that promoted "baptism either from fear, or for material gain." Thus, the encounter with the baptized bookbinder at the end of "Episcopal Justice" mirrors the note at the end of "On the Edge of the World" that a "whole crowd" of pagans had converted to Christianity, represented for them by the vision of Kiriak's God. Given the dichotomy of Paul and Judas, both works show that voluntary baptism, inspired by the association of Christianity with mercy and virtue, is better than forced, bribed, or bought conversion. Only voluntary converts, like Paul, can become "real" Christians.[40]

Ever-present references to the New Testament reinforce the connections between Leskov's Jewish converts and their biblical prototypes. The story begins with two biblical epigraphs, the first introducing the conflict between true "Christian" mercy and a "pharisaical" or purely formal approach to law: "Judge not according to appearance, but judge righteous judgment" (John 7:24), Jesus' rebuke to the Pharisees who criticized his healing on the Sabbath. The second epigraph prefigures the metropolitan's rejection of the substitute recruit: "For he shall have judgment without mercy, that has shown no mercy" (James 2:13).

Biblical citations describe both the torment of the bookbinder's son and the Jews' responsibility for it. The recruitment of Jewish boys as cantonists, like the recruitment of Old Believer children in Riga, is compared to the Massacre of the Innocents in Bethlehem: "In all the Jewish towns and shtetls the 'lamentation in Ramah' was literally renewed: Rachel wept loudly for her children, and would not be comforted" (p. 90) (Matt. 2:18, from Jer. 31:15). The narrator uses strong language to emphasize the responsibility of Jews themselves for the situation: "Jewish entrappers [sdatchiki] tore the little Yids out of their mothers' embraces almost indiscriminately" (p. 90). The "severity" of Russian law, he says, is only furthered by "the limitless cruelty of the Yids' injustice [nepravda] and trickery [plutovstvo]" (p. 90). Biblical epithets reinforce this negative depiction of Russian Jews: the narrator speaks of "stiff-necked Jews [zhestokovyinoe evreistvo]" (p. 96) (Acts 7:51; see Exod. 33:3,

34:9; Deut. 9:13) and anachronistically criticizes their "Pharisaic talmudism" (p. 96). (Few of the non-Jews who participated in the nineteenth-century debates surrounding the Jewish question in Russia seemed to realize that the Talmud was written several centuries after the events described in the Christian Bible, by which time the Pharisees no longer existed.)

The web of biblical subtext prefigures the eventual conversion of the unhappy bookbinder, who invokes Jesus: "Oh, Yeshua! Yeshua ha-Notsri ['Jesus the Nazarene' in Hebrew]! He [the substitute recruit, who is seeking baptism so as to avoid army service] wants to deceive you" (p. 100). The narrator then compares the bookbinder to one of Jesus' patients, the possessed boy (p. 100) (Matt. 17:14–21; Mark 9:17–29; Luke 9:38–43), and imagines Jesus' sympathy for him: "isn't *He* coming to take up in His holy arm this unhappy sheep, perhaps by chance bleating out His name" (p. 113) (see Matt. 18:12–14). These references to Jesus' kindness and mercy make the bookbinder's sincere conversion seem inevitable.

The substitute recruit's false conversion is described in equally biblical terms. By converting in order to avoid the army, he would become the kind of Christian "due to whom 'the name of God is blasphemed among the Gentiles' [*imia bozhie khulitsia vo iazytsekh*]" (p. 138), the words Paul uses to accuse the Jews of disobeying religious laws: "For the name of God is blasphemed among the Gentiles through you, as it is written" (Rom. 2:24; see Isa. 52:5 and Ezek. 36:20). During the story's denouement, the metropolitan begins his refusal of baptism with another citation of Paul, heightening the contrast between sincere religious devotion and the actions of the substitute recruit. His words, "*Liuby nikoli ne oslabevaet*" (p. 141), are an archaic version of the first line of the verse, "Love never faileth, but whether there be prophecies, they shall be done away; whether there be tongues, they shall cease; whether there be knowledge, it shall vanish away" (1 Cor. 13:8).

After converting to Orthodoxy, the bookbinder offers one last reference to the New Testament. He asserts that although the Old Testament "about some things [*pro shcho*] is silent, like dumb Zachariah, and about others stutters [*gugnit*], like Moses . . . the evangelicum [Evangelium] is a simple, clear book" (p. 143). "Dumb Zachariah" is Zachariah, the father of John the Baptist, who didn't believe the angel who foretold the birth of his son and was punished for his doubt by temporary muteness (Luke 1:11–22). The bookbinder deems the Hebrew Bible an inadequate source of information and justifies his own conversion with reference to the text that inspired it, asserting that the Old Testament has been made irrelevant by the advent of Christianity and the New Testament.

The profusion of biblical citations reinforces the story's connection to the New Testament mastertext, identifying the substitute recruit with Judas and the bookbinder with Paul. The narrator makes this link between biblical and contemporary themes explicit: "Eighteen centuries have not altered this *ancient story*; but now I must return to my story" (p. 96).

In Search of the Pharisees

However, Leskov's tale and the New Testament story are not perfectly parallel. Although "Episcopal Justice" contains easily identifiable counterparts for Paul and Judas, the search for characters who correspond to the New Testament's other leading players, the Pharisees, is more difficult. It first appears that the narrator, in the tradition of Christian Hebraics, associates the Pharisees simply with the contemporary Jewish community, assigning the Jewish leaders full responsibility for the plight of the freethinking bookbinder and his son:

> A man with a good conscience by nature had shifted his mental horizon slightly and, without betraying the faith of his fathers, tried to have his own opinion about the spirit of the law, concealed by the letter . . . and the case against him was ready. He became a "dangerous freethinker"; pharisaical talmudism tries to destroy his kind, eliminate them, wipe them off the face of the earth. If he had . . . completely forgotten about Jehovah and never thought about His commandments, but never threatened the Pharisees' sanctimoniousness [*lzhepravednosti*], then it wouldn't matter. . . . But he demonstrated a kind of *breadth*, a kind of freedom of the spirit, and that's what these law-ridden [*podzakonnoe*] Yids cannot tolerate. (p. 96)

Given that he must have understood the rules concerning recruits, the narrator's assertions that Jews alone were to blame for the bookbinder's sad plight are intriguing. Of course, both the real Leskov and his narrator knew perfectly well that tsarist law encouraged the Jews to turn in underage boys as recruits. The paradoxicality of Leskov's description may in fact have been motivated by an attempt to provoke resistance in the reader. Dmitry Likhachev (after Viktor Shklovsky) calls this device in Leskov's work "false ethical evaluation."[41] Leskov's narrator offers an absurd opinion, what Likhachev calls a "provocative evaluation." The reader, of course, disagrees—but imagines that he or she is doing so against the will of the author. By 1877, several years after descriptions of the lives of the cantonists had been published in *Otechestvennye zapiski*, the readers of "Episcopal Justice" certainly could have understood the absurdity of the claim that the Jewish community was solely to blame for the excesses of the recruitment system.[42]

The force of the moral ambiguity surrounding the tsarist administrators draws the reader's attention to them and thus changes the center of the story's gravity, making it about them just as much as it is about the bookbinder and his redemption by the metropolitan. If the most important characters in the story are the bureaucrats, then the tale cannot fit as neatly as it seemed into the biblical genres inspired by Paul and Judas. However, the ever present references to the New Testament suggest that the life of Jesus must relate somehow to Leskov's tale. To follow Likhachev's logic, Leskov probably called those who abused the bookbinder and his son "Pharisees," then deliberately proposed inappropriate actors to fill their role, in order to urge the reader to seek out the real Pharisees. In this way he could lead the reader to read between the lines and discover his criticism of Nicholas's cantonism policy and those who carried it out.

We know that in Leskov's day, "Pharisees" meant hypocritical religious formalists. The definition best fits Aleksei Kirilovich Kliuchkarev, the narrator's boss, described at the beginning of the first chapter. Kliuchkarev is a "martinet" and "a bureaucrat from his head to his heels" (p. 89), a "severe and dry formalist"; he loves only his small dog and "precision in all things," but shows no mercy to human beings: "I never saw a time when a single muscle twitched in his dry, almost cruel face when he drove a civil servant with a large family from his job or sheared underage Jewish boys as cantonists" (p. 90).

"Pharisaical" epithets in this story apply not only to Kliuchkarev but also to other bureaucrats and to the system of cantonism in general. The division commanders who forcibly baptize child recruits are religious hypocrites, "in their own way carrying out Christian rites [*radevshii o khristianstve*] and, probably, understanding Christianity in their own way [*po-svoemu*]" (p. 91). In McLean's words, the sacrament of baptism is so "degraded" by their actions that the reader is led to question whether it "can . . . have any sacred content."[43] Baroness B., who helps and shelters the fleeing substitute recruit, has her own pharisaical trait, a "surface religiosity [*vneshnaia religioznost'*]" (p. 109). The narrator sees the law on cantonists itself as so unbendingly formal that it has no meaning: it allows for "no exceptions" (p. 128), regardless of circumstances. Such descriptions make it clear that the "truly pharisaical" business in the story and the real target of the author's criticism is not the Jews' wheeling and dealing, but rather the recruitment system itself. Thus, while Leskov at first seems to set his story within the traditions of Christian writings about Jews and to be prepared to focus on the distinction between Paul and Judas, "sincere" and "false" converts from Judaism, he steps over the boundaries of his genres by identifying not only Jews but also insincere Christians with the Pharisees.

The Jew as Good Reader

"Episcopal Justice" is not only a critique of cantonism and the forced baptism to which it led. What makes the bookbinder's conversion real is his own confrontation with and comprehension of Christian doctrine, as represented by his solitary reading of the New Testament. By stressing this moment, Leskov approaches a criticism of Orthodox practices that goes beyond the call not to abuse the sacrament of baptism. Not only does he modify the biblical tradition so as to identify Christians as well as Jews with the Pharisees, but he also expands the framework of the conversion story to examine the sincerity of other Christians. While for centuries Christian theologians had distinguished between "true" and "false" Jewish converts, Leskov extends the comparison to differentiate between "true" Christians and pharisaical hypocrites. This difference emerges in their contrasting approach to text and in the sincere Christian's ability to read metaphorically.

The believer's metaphorical approach to text—specifically, to parable—is fundamental to the Evangelists' teachings. Jesus explains his allegorical style as a means of distinguishing those who believe and understand from those who neither believe nor understand:

> And the disciples came, and said unto him, why speakest thou unto them in parables? He answered and said unto them, Because it is given unto you to know the mysteries of the kingdom of heaven, but to them it is not given. . . . Therefore speak I to them in parables, because

they seeing, see not; and hearing, hear not, neither do they understand. (Matt. 13:10–11, 13)

Here the disciples are metaphorical listeners, who do not limit themselves to
the letter of the story, but instead look for deeper meaning. Those who "seeing, see not, and hearing, hear not, neither do they understand" are pedantic listeners, who only see that which lies on the surface and can penetrate no
deeper. Christian theologians such as Aquinas have expanded on the epistemological concerns expressed in Matthew to distinguish among the various
levels—the literal, the metaphorical, the moral, and the anagogic—at which
a reader might understand the Bible.

The allegorical nature of the Gospels emerges on two levels; not only
does the primary hero, Jesus, speak in parables, but the Evangelists, like him,
create a code, borrowing words, expressions, sentences, and literary devices
from the Hebrew Bible, the text they know best. Their narrative style assumes a reader who knows that text equally well and who will be able to de-
cipher a secret language that links ancient biblical predictions about the
coming of a Messiah with events from the life of Jesus. The complex and
paradoxical traditional attitudes of the Christian churches toward Judaism,
the religion that gave rise to Christianity, and to the Jews themselves, arise
against this literary background. The conversion of the Jews has, for most
Christian denominations, seemed both more significant and more complicated than that of other non-Christians. As the "people of the Book," they
can simultaneously represent the most appropriate objects of proselytism,
the first and most logical potential converts, who know the Old Testament
better than anyone and for that reason are better able than anyone to understand its hints about the future victory of Jesus; and, should they refuse
conversion, they can appear to be Christianity's most stubborn enemies. In
other words, given these stereotypes, Jews face a choice between two strictly
defined roles: they can act either as the "best" readers of the Gospels, or the
"worst," most adamant pedants.

These views of Jews as potential readers of the New Testament have a direct bearing on their roles in Leskov's stories. The Jewish father in "Episcopal Justice" is nothing if not a reader, one who works as a bookbinder, literally preserving and repairing books. Absurd and pathetic, but well-read, in
his written appeal to the narrator he emphasizes that he has studied "the
wisdom of God's word [*premudrost' bozhego slova*]" (p. 95). In the last

scene, the bookbinder turns out to be not only a reader, but a "good"—that is, a metaphorical rather than a pedantic—reader. The narrator relays their conversation:

> "Who convinced you," I asked, "of the truth of Christianity?"
>
> "Well, that's clear in the Biblium [Bubel]: it's written there that the Messiah is supposed to come in the second Temple, and so that's what I saw, that he came. . . . What else can you seek [shukat'] or wait for, for he is already with us?"
>
> "But the Jews have all read that place, and they don't believe."
>
> "They don't believe because they've read too many talmuds and some other pointless [pustogo] things too, and came up with God alone knows what kinds of silly requirements, about what kind of Messiah he will be, and how he'll appear—who knows from where— and start to reign like a worldly power on earth, and they will begin to rule [ponuvat'; from Polish panować, "to reign"] the earth. . . . But that's all emptiness: he came in our form, a slave's form, and we need only hold to his teaching. (p. 143)

These statements recall Leskov's description of Baron Radstock's distribution of Bibles on the streets of St. Petersburg. According to the bookbinder, Bible reading is indeed the key to faith: in order to become a Christian one need only correctly read the New Testament and correctly interpret its references to the Old Testament, without insisting on the literal meaning of the descriptions of the coming of the Messiah. Saying disparagingly about other Jews that they have "come up with . . . silly requirements," the bookbinder agrees with the standard nineteenth-century Christian definition of Jews as those who rejected and continue to reject Christ; he criticizes their formalist approach to text. His own conversion, it is clear, results from his effort to be a good reader in spite of all resistance. By understanding biblical texts metaphorically rather than literally, he demonstrates that he is one of the Christian believers to whom "it is given . . . to know the mysteries of the kingdom of Heaven."

However, the bookbinder is not the only metaphorical reader in the story. The other characters, including the narrator, also confront a difficult "text" when they hear the bookbinder's tale. His very words pose an interpretive problem. Because Leskov is so well known for his ability to represent the accented or mannered speech of his characters, it is not surprising that his bookbinder's Russian is so peculiar, both in its phonetics and its vocabulary. Like many Russian writers at the time, Leskov conveyed a "Jewish accent" by making the bookbinder confuse *s* and *sh* sounds: he says *vase* for *vasha* [your] and *gashpadin* for *gospodin* [mister]. As Leskov told his publisher, he did not know Yiddish.[44] Thus, with the exception of a few examples, such as *gval't* [help!] (p. 99) and *meshiginer* [crazy person] (p. 100), the non-Russian words the bookbinder uses come not from Yiddish but from Polish and Ukrainian, two languages that Leskov knew well. Actually, it is not improbable that a character such as the bookbinder would have used such words: Jews in the Pale of Settlement, living among Ukrainians and Poles, sometimes picked up their languages and used this knowledge to make themselves understandable among Russians.

The imbedded narrators in Leskov's stories often speak in idiolects that distance them from the reader, highlighting their ignorance, their foreignness, or their innocence and authenticity. In "Episcopal Justice," the bookbinder's strange Russian creates a distance between himself and the narrator—a distance that the narrator traverses with some intellectual effort. When the narrator describes the process of his gradual comprehension of the bookbinder's problems, he begins with the bookbinder's letter, written in a combination of Russian, Polish, and Yiddish:

> It was impossible to understand what language it was in and even what alphabet. . . . Instead of rejecting the scrap of paper, given its incoherence [*neformennost'*], as "incorrectly submitted," I began to read it and "rebelled in my spirit—and then learned to read."[45] The absurdity [*nelepost'*] of the writing was nothing in comparison with that of the contents, but in that very absurdity desperation cried out yet more importunately. (pp. 94–95)

This attention to the difficult process of reading the bookbinder's strange prose reflects the story's central epistemological concern. Both the narrator, in reading the letter, and the bookbinder, in reading the Bible, like the original Christian disciples, overcome a pedantic need for complete and transparent clarity before they can locate a deeper and more complex meaning.

In a series of short chapters, the narrator recounts how, after he gets through the letter, his friend Drukart, then a higher official, and finally the archbishop of Kiev, slowly come to comprehend the bookbinder's tragedy. The bureaucrats who levy recruits cannot decide if they should mock the bookbinder or sympathize with him. Drukart, in contrast, grasps that although the substitute recruit's conversion would be in accordance with the policy of the Orthodox Church in Russia at the time, it would in fact be neither fair nor truly Christian. He demonstrates his ability to think allegorically by recognizing the bookbinder's cries about a "karkadyl" (presumably, a crocodile) as a description of his dog, and then referring to the bookbinder himself as a "karkadyl," saying, "Look what a vile thing they've done [*ish kakaia merzost' ustroena*] to this karkadyl" (p. 121).

The third audience of the story, Prince Illarion Illarionovich, can also see the position of the bookbinder metaphorically. His lack of pedantry is demonstrated in his sentences, themselves requiring interpretation: "Take that Yid too . . . in the sleigh . . . and go . . . with him . . . right away . . . to the metropolitan . . . (. . .) tell everything . . . and from me . . . bow to him . . . and say that I'm very sorry . . . and I can't do anything . . . since the law . . . Right-o . . . you understand" (p. 128). The prince hopes that the metropolitan will defy the law, but he does not say this directly. His evasive speech reveals his understanding of the complex situation.

The final and most influential person to hear the bookbinder's story is the metropolitan of Kiev, Filaret Amfiteatrov, to whom the narrator devotes seven of the story's fifty pages. Filaret's behavior in the story is often as surprising as that of the unpredictable Orthodox saints who were considered "fools for Christ" [*iurodivye*]. He has no respect for rank, and he insults practically all his suppliants, calling each of them "fool" and "stupid." He demonstrates his consistency by first calling the bookbinder these derogatory names (p. 140) and then saving his son by refusing baptism to the substitute recruit. The inanity of the metropolitan's answers testifies to his lack of formalism. He deals with aristocratic Russians and with poor Jews with the same absence of etiquette but, in the end, with mercy.

All of these characters demonstrate their ability to read a difficult situation metaphorically, and their struggles implicitly encourage the reader to adopt a similar interpretive strategy toward the story. The reader is in a privileged position, able not only to interpret the bookbinder's story, but also to evaluate all the characters' words and their reactions to the bookbinder and to one another. Thus, the reader can see "Episcopal Justice" not as a transparent text with a single meaning but as a complex, ambiguous "parable," whose deciphering might define a faith community, just as the interpretation of Jesus' stories unites Christians.

Bloody Sweat

One of the elements in the story that most urgently demands—and resists—interpretation is the Gothic image of the bookbinder's "bloody sweat." It is first mentioned in connection with the package of papers that the Jew brings out of his bosom, "soaked through with some kind of stinking brownish, somehow pus-like [*sukrovistoiu*] dampness—exceptionally nasty" (p. 102). Only after a few more pages, when the bookbinder tells his story to the bureaucrats, does the narrator elaborate on this "brownish" dampness:

> All of us, with all our unfortunate experience of grief and suffering of this kind, were, it seemed, struck by the frightful horror of these frenzied torments, which produced in this poor fellow *bloody sweat.*
>
> Yes, that . . . was nothing other than *bloody sweat,* which I saw with my own eyes on another human being only that one time in my life. . . .
>
> To anyone who has never seen this *bloody sweat . . .* I would say that I saw it myself and that it is inexpressibly *horrifying.*
>
> At least this dewy, cranberry-colored spot over the auricle still hovers before my eyes, and it seems to me that through it I see a gaping human heart, suffering from the most terrible torment—the torment of a father trying to save his child. . . . O, I will say it again: it was terrible! . . .
>
> I involuntarily remembered the bloody sweat of the one whose righteous blood, through the fateful decision [*obrokom*] of their forefathers, was cast down onto the offspring of an outcast breed, and my own blood rushed into my heart and then quickly flooded back and sounded in my ears.
>
> It was as though all my thoughts, all my feelings were swept away, underwent something both excruciating and sweet. It seemed that in front of me there stood not just a man, but some kind of bloody historical symbol. (pp. 111–12; emphases in original)

This description is exaggerated, even surreal. This "bloody sweat" startled not only the story's characters but also Leskov's contemporaries. The critic from *Otechestvennye zapiski,* who in principle opposed Leskov and his political views, noted that he touchingly depicted the distress of the Jewish father.[46] Another reviewer pointed out the ghastliness of certain images: "wherever the author describes how recruitment used to happen here, horror wafts from the story."[47] Leskov's biographer Il'ia Shliapkin located precisely the image of "bloody sweat" as the center and the motivation of the story: "he [Leskov] was shocked by a frightened Jewish recruit, who emitted, out of fear, bloody sweat."[48] Following Shliapkin's lead, the author's son Andrei Leskov insisted on the authenticity of this image and on its importance for the writer. "He . . . tells with sincere feeling of the torments of the 'introligator' ["bookbinder" in Polish], whose underage son was treacherously taken as a cantonist and who, praying for help and defense, became covered with 'bloody sweat.'"[49]

The image of bloody sweat may have so impressed the narrator and Leskov's critics not only because of its shock value but also because of its polyvalence. It evokes three scenes from the New Testament: first, the moment when Jesus refuses death, or "this cup," when "his sweat was, as it were, great drops of blood falling down to the ground" (Luke 22:44); second, the mixture of blood and water that dripped from Jesus' body after the Crucifixion, when "one of the soldiers, with a spear, pierced his side, and immediately came there out blood and water" (John 19:34); and, third, the Pharisees' assumption of guilt for the death of Jesus: "Pilate . . . took water, and washed his hands before the multitude, saying, I am innocent of the blood of this righteous person. See you to it. Then answered all the people, and said, His blood be on us, and on our children" (Matt. 27:24–25). Thus, the image can symbolize both the blood of Jesus, a suffering and innocent victim, and the guilt of the Pharisees in his death; it can be identified with both a perpetrator and a victim.

The strength of this vision of corporeal suffering challenges the millennia-old tradition of figural reading. Its resistance to formulaic interpretation may be what moved the critics, as well as the narrator and his coworkers. The bureaucrats' hearts have "become numb" due to their grim daily grind, since "even given the most obvious abuse of the weak, [we had] no time, means, or desire to judge, to lay down the law, or to stand up for him" (p. 92). Having seen so much horror, the officials who deal with the cantonists are no longer concerned with the justice of the rules that they are required to enforce. They probably seek comfort in a traditional Orthodox attitude toward the Jews as criminals, the inheritors of the Pharisees, who after their betrayal of Jesus merit any abuse. The bookbinder's bloody sweat can surprise and touch them because it calls Christian prototypes into question—within the context of canonical Christian text—by forcing them to see in the Jew a suffering human body with the "human heart" not of a criminal Pharisee, but of an innocent Jesus.

The image of bloody sweat functions in the story like a two-edged sword. On the one hand, it reinforces Christian stereotypes about Jews, defining the bookbinder as a Judas, a descendent of Pharisees, whom Christians are permitted to treat cruelly, and on the other hand, it shows that the bookbinder might be a victim rather than a criminal, in which case the Russian Christian administrators, including the narrator himself, become the Pharisees. The adjectives that describe the bloody sweat are yet more ambiguous: it is "horrible [strashno]" and it stinks, but also attracts the narrator, seeming in some way "both excruciating and sweet" (p. 112). Perhaps this sweetness reflects the deceptive, seductive simplicity of the story of a familiar literary type. If the bloody sweat symbolizes only Jewish guilt, then it is not criminal to recruit, baptize, or abuse the bookbinder's son, perhaps a "sweet" conclusion to the narrator. However, if the bloody sweat also symbolizes Jewish innocence, then its horror may lie in its incrimination of the narrator and his fellow functionaries as Pharisees.

The bloody sweat emblematizes the humanity of the bookbinder, which motivates Leskov's critique of Nicholas's cantonism. In conjunction with the many references to reading, it also exemplifies the kind of text that demands a metaphorical approach. This image spurs the story's characters to reconsider the ossified definitions regulating their Christianity. By situating this complex image of Jewish conversion at the center of his story, Leskov may have provoked his Christian readers to reexamine a number of concepts: their stereotypes about Jews, the way they were used to reading and interpreting the Bible so as to justify these stereotypes, and the narrative traditions within which they were used to telling stories not only about the Jews, but also about the Russian Orthodox.

"New Testament Jews"

"Novozavetnye evrei" [New Testament Jews] (1884), in a sense, picks up where "Episcopal Justice" (1877) leaves off. The earlier story undermines archetypes of Jewish converts, portrays a Jew as an ideal reader of biblical text, and includes a lightly camouflaged criticism of Russian Orthodox practices surrounding baptism and a more deeply concealed criticism of Orthodox understandings of Jews. The later story, in showing the Jew Bazin, who, after reading the Bible, decides to convert to Protestantism rather than Orthodoxy, implicitly extends these criticisms. In fact, many Jews in the Russian Empire did, like Bazin, convert to Protestantism—the poet Osip Mandelstam being probably the best-known example. Bazin's tale, though, reveals less about the motivations of people like Mandelstam than it does about Leskov's unwillingness to identify the religion described in the New Testament exclusively with Russian Orthodoxy. As James Muckle meticulously documents, both Leskov's dissatisfaction with some aspects of Orthodoxy and his fascination with and attraction to some of the Protestant movements active in Russia, specifically to their emphasis on Bible reading rather than ritual, grew during the mid-1880s.[50] In "New Testament Jews," as in "Episcopal Justice," the figure of the Jew becomes a kind of lens facilitating a critical gaze on Russian society and Russian Orthodoxy. In reducing Bazin—even more than the bookbinder—to a penetrating readerly eye, Leskov participates in Solov'ev's project of testing Orthodoxy by investigating its relations with the Jews.

The 1884 story describes three Jews, all purportedly Leskov's acquaintances, "with Christian inclinations." The writer summarizes the lives of the first two heroes: An engraver in Kiev attended meetings of a group of Jews who were interested in Christianity, but he himself refused baptism, since he felt "ashamed to turn his back on [*brosat'*] his little Yids [*zhidkov*] while they had it badly and they themselves were stuck in the rubbish [*izdrianilis'*]" (p. 72).[51] A retired Jewish soldier, the second hero, reads the New Testament and lives according to its principles but does not agree with the proselytizing of an Irvingite lady.[52]

The biographies of the first two heroes preface the tale of the story's main hero, Bazin, a young rabbi, wise and learned, who one day happens to read the Gospels and immediately decides to convert to Christianity. The Jewish community persecutes him for his "betrayal" of Judaism, trying to turn him in as an army recruit or even to kill him, but he continues to believe in Jesus and even to convert other Jews to Christianity. Bazin carefully researches various branches of Christianity. He reads first the Orthodox catechism, then

FIGURE 4. Anon., *The Jew Bazin*. Illustration to Nikolai Leskov, "Rasskazy kstati: Novozavetnye evrei," *Nov'*, vol. 1, no. 1 (November 1884), p. 79.

the Catholic one, but in neither does he find that which attracted him to Christianity when he read the New Testament. Finally he meets an English missionary, leaves for England, marries an Englishwoman, and himself becomes a Protestant missionary. Unlike the two other Jews described in the story, Bazin is an official convert.

Bazin's biography corresponds very neatly to the renditions of the tale of the Russian Jew as "true" Christian convert that appeared in evangelical literature.[53] The story seems to be based on a historical figure, a Jewish follower of Radstock, whom Leskov described in *Schism in High Society* as distinguished by a "phenomenal memory" and knowledge of the Bible.[54] However, Leskov's story seems to have owed something to his imagination. A contemporary reviewer in a Jewish newspaper notes that the picture printed along with Leskov's story above the caption "The Jew Bazin" actually showed not Bazin but Shapiro, a Jewish photographer from Petersburg, who had taken his own photo in the guise of a rabbi as a lark (see Figure 4).[55] Regardless of its accuracy, the story of Bazin shows that Leskov was intrigued by the story of a Jew reading the New Testament and then choosing Protestantism over Orthodoxy.

Like the bookbinder, the Jews in "New Testament Jews" not only read the Bible but are connected in other ways to images of written text. The first one, a carver of seals [*rezchik pechatei*] and an engraver, is involved with book production. And Bazin himself, like the Jewish Radstockite, resembles a book: "he knew the Old and New Testaments almost by heart in Russian, and he possessed a phenomenal memory; he was, one might say, a living concordance [*zhivoiu 'Simfonieiu'*], and had no need for printed references [*pechatnykh svodkakh*] or concordances ['*Konkordantsakh*']" (p. 81). The picture (of Shapiro) accompanying this story shows a Jew engaged in Bazin's favorite activity: reading a large tome. The link between these characters and text in general suggests that here, as in "Episcopal Justice," Jews figure precisely as readers—ideally, readers of the Bible.

Like the bookbinder, Bazin, who is so strongly linked to books, can personify the ideal reader of the Bible and therefore the ideal Christian. Bazin's choice of Protestantism thus testifies to Leskov's lifelong conviction that Bible reading is fundamental to Christianity; he appears to be suggesting that both Jews and excessively formalistic Orthodox Christians could find inspiration in the New Testament for a new, less ritualistic religiosity. Leskov's fascination both with Jews who reject traditional Judaism (even while, like the "New Israel" congregation and the first two characters in "New Testament Jews," they remain nominally Jewish) and with Russian Orthodox who are drawn to Protestant forms of Christianity is consistent with the utopian vision of a community united by the rejection of "empty," ritualistic religious traditions. This vision both draws on the imagery of the debate on church reform in the era and prefigures the Jewish-Christian friendship that Leskov would describe in 1886 in "Skazanie o Fedore-khristianine

i o druge ego Abrame-zhidovine" [The Tale of Fedor the Christian and
His Friend Abraham the Jew].

Leskov and Dostoevsky, Parable and Icon

Leskov was far more interested than Dostoevsky in Jews, whether they were
traditional, assimilated, or converting. However, although Leskov's numerous stories and articles on Jews and Judaism have been rarely read and only
partially addressed in scholarly literature, the many fewer mentions of Jews
in Dostoevsky's novels, journalism, and letters, which range from the comical (Isai Fomich in *Notes from the House of the Dead*) to the sinister (Al-
yosha's silent affirmation of the blood libel in *The Brothers Karamazov*),
have inspired substantial criticism. Rather than replicating the efforts of the
many scholars who have attempted to explain all of Dostoevsky's complex
and changing views of Jews, I will contrast Leskov's depictions of Jews and
Christians in "Episcopal Justice," "New Testament Jews," "The Tale of Fedor
the Christian," and a series of articles on Jewish ritual with Dostoevsky's
one piece envisioning Jewish-Christian coexistence, the final section of his
Diary of a Writer entry on "The Jewish Question."[56] I chose this one short
work as my "control sample" because it is the only piece of Dostoevsky's devoted solely to the Jewish question and because it has certain things in common with Leskov's texts. Dostoevsky's and Leskov's works on Jews are
united not only by their shared geographical and historical context but also
by polemical and literary devices. Both writers cite letters from Jewish readers who accuse them of attacking the Jews unjustly; both produce their
more Judeophilic pieces after writing some more Judeophobic ones, perhaps as part of an effort to appear more liberal; and both end with a picture
of harmony between Jew and Christian that is set, not in the present but in
(for Leskov, in "The Tale of Fedor the Christian") the past or (for Dostoevsky) the future.

In spite of these similarities, Leskov's and Dostoevsky's works, both
equally religious in tone and teleology, draw on different Christian media.
Specifically, Leskov's images of the shared future of Christians and Jews are
like a parable that demands interpretation, while Dostoevsky's view of the
same dream is more iconic. In thinking about the difference between icon
and parable, I have in mind a number of the ways Christian theologians

have defended icons, arguing that they convey a message to the viewer that words alone could not transmit. The Church in the eleventh century adopted the doctrine of the sixth-century Pope Gregory the Great, who justified the icon as an instructional tool by explaining that it can speak to an illiterate audience.[57] John of Damascus, a seventh-century Christian thinker, extended the argument to legitimate the worship of icons by the literate, asserting that the icon, by reproducing the appearance of Christ and the angels on earth in human form, can make the divine, which is invisible, visible. This visibility satisfies the human need to perceive in images and lets the icon mediate between humanity and the divine.[58] Pavel Florensky, an early-twentieth-century Russian theologian, used similar terms: "When we contemplate this holy countenance [on an icon], we thus behold the divine prototype. . . . countenances proclaim—without a word, and solely by their appearance to us—the mysteries of the invisible world. . . . The icon is a boundary between the visible and the invisible worlds. . . . An icon remembers its prototype."[59] Florensky, like John of Damascus, argues for icons because they give the viewer an understanding of God that words alone could not.

The arguments of the iconodules counter a bias against images that the early Christians had inherited from the Jews. The Evangelists at times reveal this bias in a preference of word to image, in Matthew, for instance, where Jesus explains his use of parables. Matthew's words about those who "seeing, see not, and hearing, hear not" recall some famous verses in the Psalms on the disadvantages of idol worship:

> Their idols are silver and gold, the work of men's hands.
> They have mouths, but they speak not; eyes have they, but they see not.
> They have ears, but they hear not; noses have they, but they smell not.
> (Ps. 115:4–6)

By using the language of this psalm, Jesus, as cited by Matthew, implicitly equates those who do not understand his parables with inert images and their deluded worshipers. His words set up a contrast between the interpreters of parables and the viewers of images. Somewhat ironically, some of the defenders of icons embrace that contrast, arguing that images are not only different from words but sometimes better.[60]

An iconic image is at the heart of Dostoevsky's essay "The Jewish Question," which appeared in *Diary of a Writer* in March 1877. The piece is divided into two chapters. The first begins with a reference to a letter from a Jewish journalist, Abraham Uri Kovner, but it soon degenerates into a litany of clichés that echo the complaints about Jews elsewhere in Dostoevsky's prose. The second chapter is more original, relaying a story told to the writer by Sofia Lur'e, the young Jewish woman who had sent Dostoevsky her copy of Bogrov's *Notes of a Jew*. In Minsk (Lur'e's native city), the elderly German doctor Hindenberg, famed for his charity and his willingness to help all, regardless of religion or ethnicity, had died. Huge numbers of Jews and Christians attended his funeral and mourned him sincerely. In the second part of this chapter, "A Singular Instance," the writer imagines a scene from this doctor's life, in which he attends a poor Jewish woman in childbirth. When the baby is born, the good doctor wraps him in his own shirt. This action, for Dostoevsky, could herald a new era of brotherhood between Christians and Jews:

> The solution to the Jewish question, gentlemen! The eighty-year-old torso of the doctor, naked and shivering in the morning damp, could occupy a prominent place in the picture; I won't even mention the face of the old man and that of the young, worn-out mother, looking at her new-born child and at the doctor's tricks [*prodelki*] with him. Christ sees all this from above, and the doctor knows this: "This poor little Yid will grow up and, perhaps, will himself take the shirt from his back and give it to a Christian, remembering the story about his birth," the old man thinks to himself with a naive and noble smile. Will this really happen? It is most likely that it won't, but, after all, it might, and it's better on this earth and there's hardly anything better to do than to believe that *this* might and will happen. (p. 91)

The author goes on to explain that the virtue of saintly individuals like the doctor can inspire virtue and eliminate prejudice in others.

Examining the Dr. Hindenberg scene in the context of Dostoevsky's other Jewish images, David Goldstein sees the writer as an anti-Semite whose brand of messianic Russian nationalism required him to denigrate Jews as another purportedly messianic nation, inspiring in him "profound hatred for a community whose very existence constituted in his eyes a formidable challenge to his nation and the 'God-bearing' mission he claimed for it." In accordance with this general understanding of the writer's views, he dismisses the final chapter of "The Jewish Question" as liberal posing, an "ineffectual . . . antidote against the redoubtable effects of the chapter that preceded it."[61] Joseph Frank, unwilling to condemn Dostoevsky so roundly, sees evidence in that final scene that the author recognized and regretted his own Judeophobia, that he was at least a "guilty anti-Semite" who "could never reconcile himself inwardly to his own violation of what he knew very well were the commands of the Christ in whom he believed."[62] Gary Saul Morson dismisses as self-serving Frank's attempt to "split" Dostoevsky into one moral, likable writer and another immoral, hateful one.[63] Felix Dreizin also disagrees with Goldstein and Frank: he sees Dostoevsky as not a "guilty" but rather a "compulsive" anti-Semite, who raged against Jews precisely because he identified his own father with them. For him, this "conciliatory conclusion of Dostoevsky's anti-Semitic manifesto" was inspired not by the writer's guilt for his sins against Christianity but by his need to maintain a "public" persona who, by paying lip service to humanitarian ideals, avoided violating social norms.[64]

However, Goldstein, Frank, Morson, and Dreizin all fail to point out the New Testament resonances of the scene Dostoevsky describes. The male child born to a Jewish woman and into great poverty is a familiar image and, as Dostoevsky hints, one that has often been painted. Gary Rosenshield calls it an *obraz*, an image with a hint of the sacred.[65] It cannot help but evoke the Nativity of Jesus. In this context, the writer's insistence that a single act of charity toward this child will inspire him toward charity that will lead to brotherhood among nations becomes more comprehensible. Although Dostoevsky's vision of this Jewish child's messianic role might contradict his association of the Russian nation with messianism, it is hardly innovative.

Comparison of Dostoevsky's vision of Jewish-Christian brotherhood in this essay with Leskov's images of Russian Jews illuminates the divide between the two writers' conceptions of the place of religious minorities in the Russian Empire, and the reasons why their political philosophies might inspire different kinds of art. Dostoevsky, it appears, sees the "Jewish problem" as located primarily in the Jews, in their exclusivity and their hostility to Russians. The solution: non-Jews, by heroic acts of kindness, will inspire kindness in the Jews. Dr. Hindenberg's donation of his shirt will lead the baby someday to acts of selfless generosity that will unite peoples. For Leskov, the issue is more complicated. Like Dostoevsky, he insists that Jewry is in need of reform, and he imagines that charitable deeds by Christians toward Jews might inspire that reform. His metropolitan, Filaret Amfiteatrov in Kiev, resembles Dostoevsky's Dr. Hindenberg. However, Leskov does not assume that once a single Jew is kind to a single Christian or vice versa, brotherhood will ensue. Rather, he portrays single Jews "of Christian inclinations," officially converted or not, like all of his Christian or pagan righteous people [*pravedniki*], as, from most people's point of view, cranks [*chudaki*]. Thus, the bookbinder in "Episcopal Justice," after his conversion, is not embraced by Christian society but rather condemned as a "superstitious person" [*suever*] and a "madman" [*pomeshan*] because he gives away all his money indiscriminately to Jews as well as Christians (p. 144).

Dostoevsky outlines a fairly xenophobic political philosophy in the part of the March 1877 *Diary of a Writer* that precedes "The Jewish Question." In the three sections of chapter 1, he reaffirms his earlier statement (and the title of the chapter) that "Constantinople, sooner or later, must be ours [Russian]." In his discussion of the empire's Turkish policy, he demonstrates a belief that history is driven by competition among nations for cultural as well as territorial dominance. He imagines that earlier contact between Greeks and Russians would have weakened Russian culture (p. 66), and he asserts that it is now time for Russia to expand geographically, "finally to leave that locked room in which it has grown to the ceiling" (p. 67). However, the writer knows that many enemies seek to prevent this emergence. He defines them as both the Turks and the British (p. 77), whose link to the Jews is symbolized by the person of Disraeli. The Russian people, he asserts, also suffer the attacks of internal enemies—not only "the German pastor who was fomenting the Shtunda or the visiting European, the correspondent for a political newspaper, or some kind of superior educated Jew, one of the ones who doesn't believe in God—so many of them have sprung up lately," but also Russian émigrés and even "an enormous portion of our Russians of the very highest society" (p. 69). This schema situates Dostoevsky's fear of Jews in the context of hatred and fear of most non-Russians, as well as Russians who are insufficiently loyal to their own people. It exhibits a conviction that all these other groups want nothing more than to oppose the "Russian idea" and to destroy the Russians.

In the first part of "The Jewish Question," centered around Kovner's letters to Dostoevsky, the writer narrows his focus to the Jews' hostility to Russians. He finds evidence of this hostility in Kovner's condescension ("he treated the poor Russian people a bit too condescendingly" [*neskol'ko slishkom uzh svysoka*]) (p. 76), Disraeli's Turkish policy (p. 77), and religious Jews' refusal to eat with non-Jews (p. 80). He summarizes what he believes to be the Jews' attitude toward non-Jews in a few sentences in archaic language, which he sets in quotation marks, thus suggesting that the words come from some ancient text such as the Old Testament or the Talmud:

> Separate yourselves from the other nations and form a separate body and know that from now on you are *God's only one*. Destroy the others, or enslave them, or exploit them. Abhor everyone and have no congress with anyone. And even when you lose your own land and your political identity, when you are scattered over the face of the earth, among all the other peoples, still you must believe in everything that was promised to you. Believe, once and for all, that it will come to pass, and until then you must live, abhor, unite, exploit, and await, await. (pp. 81–82)[66]

If, as these words suggest, Jews are commanded to hate and destroy all other peoples, then the "Jewish question" becomes entirely a Jewish problem, whose resolution would require the reform of the Jews themselves but no particular action by Russians or any other nation.

In the final section of "The Jewish Question," Dostoevsky, as he so often does, retreats somewhat from the extreme position he had just laid out, suddenly insisting that, earlier indications to the contrary, he believes Jews should be granted the same rights as Christians (p. 86). In the passage about Dr. Hindenberg, he proposes that the resolution of the Jewish problem, without involving any Russians, might nonetheless require the participation of some non-Jews—such as the German Lutheran doctor Hindenberg, whom the writer might have associated with the "German pastor who was fomenting the Shtunda" in an earlier section of the same chapter. This suggestion allows him to reconcile a competitive model of nationalism with a belief in the virtue of the Russian people and a Christian faith in conversion. To sum up the views Dostoevsky expresses here: the Russians are innocent victims in a nation-eat-nation world, where all the players, especially but not only the Jews, are driven to oppress and conquer one another. However, one should have faith that all these warring nations might conceivably perceive the error of their ways and suddenly become peaceful (the Russians, presumably, having no need for such a conversion). Thus, the image linking the German doctor and the Jewish child, so reminiscent of the Nativity, depicts a kind of miraculous new beginning for a world at war. The Russian role in the rebirth is not that of a participant but rather a prophet, a conveyer of religious meaning who paints a scene—whether in words or colors—and awaits the day when the world will see and understand it. Dostoevsky's vision of Russia partakes of both the Slavophile notion of a national unity unchanging over time and the Hegelian (or in a Russian context, perhaps the Danilevskian)[67] concept of each nation playing its own role in a historical schema where some nations are more important than others. In this context, the transformation of the Russian nation is impossible and abhorrent. Thus, the only "brotherhood" that can be imagined involves a change in the behavior of Jews, a limited rapprochement [*sblizhenie*] but no real merger [*sliianie*].

While Dostoevsky is fascinated by the historical missions of nations, Leskov is more interested in different national cultures. His notion of nation depends less on the Slavophile conception of the significance of the Russian people and more on the Herderian idea that national cultures are incommensurable and all valuable in their idiosyncrasies. Thus, Leskov's "Jewish" pieces dwell on individual quirks, accents, national dress, and legends. Rather than urging that one people adapt to the other, he presents a model for an imperial Realpolitik, arguing that the two peoples should each learn about the other, or at any rate that Russians, by reading his articles and stories, should learn about Jews, presumably so as to be able to live with them in their current, unreformed state.

In the articles that Leskov wrote on Jewish rituals between 1879 and 1884, his evaluations of Jewish practices change perceptibly between the first and the last article.[68] At first, he presents himself as a primitivist specializing in the exotic and barbaric Jews and describing their beliefs and practices for the edification of the Russian public. Later, the line separating ethnographer and subject becomes blurrier and blurrier. At some points, Leskov seemingly becomes distracted from his criticism of Jewish traditionalism by his own fascination with Jewish traditions. In a telling instance, he notices and apparently becomes embarrassed about his own attraction to a Jewish legend, then defends himself by pointing out a connection between Jewish and Slavic folk traditions. He suggests that Jews borrowed from the Ukrainians the belief that the dead are thirsty and drink from ponds in the evenings: "I must admit that of all the Jewish legends and beliefs, this must be nearly the warmest and most poetic. For all that, it is very close to beliefs that we know of in part in Little Russia."[69]

Leskov's ethnographic stance falters as well when he cites the voices of Jewish readers who challenge his conclusions about Jews. In a footnote, he reveals that Jewish readers had complained about his work, presumably pointing out the many errors that he had copied from his source: "Printing these sketches, which of course are not my own fantasy, but a selection from ancient works that the Jews have bought out of circulation, I not infrequently hear that something that I wrote is purportedly *not fair*."[70] Leskov then addresses these readers, engaging in a kind of dialogue with them. In parentheses, he attempts to anticipate their objections:

> Those who want to be offended by any stories about anything comic in Jewish rituals and superstitions—as though they alone had superstitions—perhaps will start to deny this; they should turn with their complaints to Pfefferkorn,[71] where they will find proof that all of this was not thought up by us to offend or belittle Jews, which the present author considers neither necessary nor productive. Jews, like other nations, have superstitions, and learning about them is interesting. That's all.[72]

While Dostoevsky responded to Kovner's critique of his attitudes by attacking Kovner as anti-Russian, Leskov responds to his Jewish readers by equating Jewish and Russian folk beliefs. As throughout his work, he betrays his attraction to the details of foreign cultures, and thus implicitly to cultural diversity, to manyness. His Jews are convincingly Jewish, with the appropriate accents, looks, and even their own approach to text. The Jewish child at the end of "The Jewish Question," though, the only Jewish character in Dostoevsky's works who is imagined as one day interacting happily with Christians, has been stripped of his cultural specificity. The child is born naked, then wrapped not in any markedly Jewish cloth, such as a prayer shawl, but in the doctor's torn-up shirt: he is literally clothed by Christian kindness. The later vision of him as an adult also avoids specific cultural details. This contrast might demonstrate the "emptiness" of Dostoevsky's image of the Jew, whom he can associate either with timidity, obsequiousness, and wealth, the horrifying violence of the blood libel, or, just as easily, Christian kindness. Indeed, Goldstein's emphasis on Dostoevsky's obsession with Russian messianism and his vision of the author's Judeophobia as the flip side of his Christianity makes Jews into the obligatory negative component, that which Christians are not, that thing whose denial gives Christians the right to claim the Bible as their own.[73]

One might also contrast Dostoevsky's and Leskov's "Jewish" works on the level of genre. Dostoevsky presents the ideal image of the Jew—the baby who will grow up to love Christians—in an iconic context. The picture of the Jew as Jesus during the Nativity is perfect and static—frozen in space, always being born, always capable of sincere conversion, not present, accented, and uncomfortably Jewish, like Leskov's bookbinder. This iconic image is like a congealed form of the biblical parable; it is a story that has already been solved, whose single, correct interpretation has already been revealed. The viewer cannot dispute its meaning or attempt to interpret it in different ways. It does not offer a framework in which an individual can, like the bookbinder, gradually come to understanding and thereby attain faith.

Leskov, in contrast, values the parable and imitates it in "Episcopal Justice" and elsewhere in his work where he makes use of Aesopian language, concealing a pointed criticism of his society under colorful verbal decorations. One might see Leskov's parables as allowing more freedom of reading than Dostoevsky's icon. For him, perhaps the parable shades into the folktales that inspired him. Walter Benjamin defines Leskov as the quintessential storyteller, then goes on to describe storytellers as those who offer advice for living but no ultimate answers about Life, who "arouse astonishment and thoughtfulness" by refusing to force "the psychological connection of the events" on the reader.[74] One scholar of pre-nineteenth-century Russian literary history argues that the parable has been linked precisely with this arousal of "thoughtfulness": "A single subject [of a parable] could be seen as purely didactic, entertaining, publicistic, and so on. Such freedom of reading, along with the awareness of overt fantasy as the basic contents of the literary creation, nurtured the reader's multifaceted understanding of any artistic work."[75] Leskov was always fascinated and compelled by Dostoevsky and his writing, even while he disagreed and quarreled with him on a number of issues. Similarly, one could argue that Leskov was intrigued by the iconic literary genre, with its clearly defined message, but that ultimately his art, and in some sense his complex politics, would not allow him to limit (or stretch) himself to such a form.

The contrast here between the parable or the story, as defined by Benjamin, and the icon delimits two philosophies, or perhaps two epistemologies. One of them requires an art form that has a single right answer, its correct reading revealing the one who bears grace. Leskov, as we saw in "Episcopal Justice," is attracted toward this model, and therefore used genres that permitted his readers to decode a simple political subtext concealed under what Hugh McLean calls "camouflage." But on a deeper level, following Benjamin's model, Leskov's parables may not be so easy to solve. They are closer to a form in which the story has many possible meanings, no single one of which entirely precludes the others. In the end, although he loved and collected icons and both wrote and acted in defense of the ancient Russian art of icon painting, Leskov was inspired less by the images on icons than by Jewish legends and by the Christian tales in the *Minei-Chetii* [a major collection of the lives of Russian saints for daily meditation and worship], by the wealth of exotic detail in stories whose traditional meaning he can ignore.

For instance, in "The Tale of Fedor the Christian," a story of a sincere friendship between a Christian and a Jew, set in fourth-century Byzantium, Leskov takes a subject from Christian folklore, embroiders it, makes the most of its exotic setting, alters many crucial plot details, and drives toward a moral that may have little to do with the original version. In this story of the friendship between a Christian and a Jew, Leskov strays from the original, in which the Jew converts at the end of the story to Christianity, concluding, instead, with the two friends' establishment of a nondenominational school that fosters tolerance in children, rather than inculcating loyalty to any individual religion. McLean calls this work Leskov's "last public pronouncement on the 'Jewish Question,'" one "in favor of tolerance and fraternity."[76] Given the connection between folkloric stylization and the Herderian notion of the incommensurability of national cultures, it seems appropriate for his message to appear in such a form.

～

The understanding of imperial identity that emerges in Leskov's work is both more nuanced and more hesitant than in Dostoevsky's essay "On the Jewish Question." While Dostoevsky apparently accepted the Hegelian notion of the historical missions of nations, imagining the "God-bearing" Russian nation as in competition with Jews and all other non-Russian ethnic groups, Leskov's vision of Russianness was more complex and more Herderian in its presentation of the multiplicity and the incommensurability of the values of different cultures.[77] Rather than imagining a single unified culture with a single mission, he saw the nation itself as divided and as engaged in complex negotiations with modernity, negotiations in which there could be no simple resolution. Rather than arguing, like Dostoevsky, for a denial of Western influence or, like the radical critics, for immediate Westernizing reform of Russia's cultural, educational, economic, and religious traditions, Leskov always insisted on moderation, on preserving folk cultural traditions even while eliminating the abuses to which they led. It is not surprising, then, that Faresov presents him as willing to accept his own personality and opinions, about Jews and other matters, as hopelessly inconsistent and not subject to reform along rational lines.

Scholars are often troubled by Leskov's apparent capriciousness, and especially by what seems to be his simultaneous allegiance to nationalist and internationalist ideals. Maxim Gorky provided the canonical Soviet view of Leskov as a writer who was "Russian through-and-through [*naskvoz' russkii*]" and had a privileged understanding of "that ungraspable thing called 'the soul of the people.'"[78] Although, in the 1980s, Leskov's virtuous and markedly Russian heroes, the righteous people [*pravedniki*], were associated with a resurgent literary nationalism,[79] researchers have accurately pointed out the writer's enduring belief in brotherhood among nations and his disdain for chauvinism.[80] Perhaps Inès Müller de Morogues, by distinguishing between the patriotism that Leskov admired and that of which he disapproved, most accurately describes the nationalism of this "Janus with two faces."[81]

Leskov's refusal to design Jewish characters entirely according to biblical prototypes, literary types whose stories allow for simple conclusions, reflects his views of his own nation and the other nations that constituted the Russian Empire. The tales of Jewish converts in "Episcopal Justice" and "New Testament Jews" demonstrate that the assimilation of an ethnic minority, in art as in life, can trace the fault lines that undermine any simplistic depiction of national identity or imperial superiority. These stories are not, in the end, about assimilating Jews so much as they are about the Christianity of the Orthodox Russians whom the Jews presumably imitate. The figure of the baptized Jew in Leskov's work provides the opportunity to reconsider and to question accepted definitions of the Orthodox Christian and thus the Russian.

4 MUTABLE, PERMUTABLE, APPROXIMATE, AND RELATIVE: ANTON CHEKHOV

WHILE NIKOLAI LESKOV'S interactions with Jews as an administrator at a center for processing recruits inspired him to write "Episcopal Justice," his protégé Anton Chekhov based a few texts on his own, much closer, interactions with Jews. He was good friends for a period with the assimilated Jewish painter Isaac Levitan, and he and some of his brothers had romances with the Golden sisters, who had converted to Russian Orthodoxy from Judaism. Most interestingly, in tones ranging from serious to joking, he discussed marrying Evdokiia Isaakovna Efros, a Jewish friend of his sister Maria, in his letters in the first half of 1886. His references to her through that year reveal anxiety and desire directed toward her and her wealth.[1] For instance, after their first breakup, he told the writer Viktor Bilibin that he "complained to her [Efros] about being short of funds and she told about how her brother-Yid drew a three-ruble note so perfectly that the illusion was complete: a cleaning-woman picked it up and put it in her pocket."[2] Later he wrote, "As for good-looking women. . . . Just now there was a whole bouquet [of them] visiting my sister, and I melted like a Yid by a gold coin [*chervonets*]."[3] In the fall, he told another correspondent, "There's no money at all [*deneg—kot naplakal*]. . . . In answer to the question you asked my sister about whether I have gotten married, I answer: no. . . . Ma-Pa [Maria] sees the long-nosed Efros."[4] Later, he reported an encounter with Efros: "There's no money. . . . My mother and my aunt plead with me to marry a merchant's daughter.

Efros was just here. I vexed her, saying that Jewish young people aren't worth a groschen [*grosh*]; she took offense and left."[5]

The constant association of Efros with money, and especially the dismissal of young Jews as not "worth a groschen," suggests that Chekhov was fascinated by the question of what his potential fiancée was "worth." His references to a three-ruble note, a chervonets, and a groschen recall the gold coins in Pushkin's play *Skupoi rytsar'* [The Covetous Knight] and other depictions of prototypical Jewish misers. Chekhov's images of Efros, with their conflation of money, a Jewish female body, and some kind of suspicious transaction, evoke a specific literary type: the daughter of a wealthy Jew, a woman who, like Shylock's daughter, Jessica, in Shakespeare's *Merchant of Venice* or Tamara in Krestovsky's *Egyptian Darkness*, has a romantic or sexual relationship with a Christian man.

During and after the affair with Efros, Chekhov wrote works that engage this archetype and some related ones. His pieces with Jewish characters include not only two of his best-known stories, "Step'" [The Steppe] (1888) and "Skripka Rotshil'da" [Rothschild's Fiddle] (1894), both of which describe traditional Jews, but also two stories, "Tina" [The Mire] (1886) and "Perekati-pole" [The Tumbleweed] (1887), and the play *Ivanov* (1887–89), that portray converts from Judaism to Russian Orthodoxy.[6] Against the background of the biographical scholarship on the reverberations of the Efros affair in Chekhov's work, I will first consider this literary type in more detail and the artist who engaged it, then turn to an analysis of his stories of Jewish converts.[7]

First, a definition: Chekhov's Jewish characters presented philosophical problems in their own time and place, and they also present a linguistic problem for a contemporary writer in English. For most Anglophones and especially for most Americans today, expressions such as "Jewish Christian," "Jewish convert," or "baptized Jew" are contradictions in terms: a Jew who converts to Christianity is usually perceived as ceasing at once to be a Jew (though such a person can be "of Jewish origin"). In Russian, these phrases were and are differently valenced. All the common terms for "Jew," both the neutral *evrei* and the derogatory *zhid*, refer to nationality, ethnicity, or race, rather than religion. (Lesser-known terms, *iudei* and *iudaist*, refer to Jews by religion and correspond better to the standard English usage of the word "Jew.") For a Russophone, a person can as easily be a "Jewish Christian," as a "Polish Catholic," or a "Black Baptist." In order to portray the world in which

Chekhov and his characters lived, I will call persons who have converted from Judaism to Christianity "Jewish converts," in opposition to "Russians" or "Russian Christians."

Fathers and Daughters, Pimps and Prostitutes

Literary depictions of the Jewish woman involved with a Christian man tend to make her father a wealthy Jewish miser who cheats and exploits Christians, especially through usury, that is, charging interest on loans. Shakespeare's Shylock provides the model that later writers followed. In a book on the "Jewish question" and English identity, Michael Ragussis investigates some ways in which "Shylock perennially holds the English imagination in thrall, perennially mediates, regulates, and displaces Jewish identity for the English mind."[8] Shylock's hold on the Russian mind was equally perennial. The small and highly assimilated community of English Jews had very little in common with the Jewish masses of the Russian Empire, a few wealthy and Russified, most impoverished and isolated. Nonetheless, Russian literature adopted and adapted the image of the Jew created in England by Shakespeare and Sir Walter Scott. A humorous piece in an 1828 Russian journal suggested that the authors of trendy historical romances include this kind of Jewish character: "These Jews are extremely fashionable; they derive their origin from Shakespeare's Shylock and Walter Scott's Isaac [the father of Rebecca in *Ivanhoe*]."[9] Joshua Kunitz details the direct borrowing from *The Merchant of Venice* in the plays of Nestor Kukolnik and asserts that similar examples abound in nineteenth-century Russian literature: "the eternal father-daughter theme is repeated *ad nauseum*. And the fathers are regulation fathers—inhuman fiends, Judases, magicians, usurers, murderers, poisoners, spies. And the daughters are regulation daughters—invariably beautiful, gentle, and, of course, in love with Christians."[10] The father seems to make little distinction between his family and his money: "My daughter! O my ducats!" Shylock cries after Jessica flees (act 2, scene 8). Through the first half of the nineteenth century, Romantic Russian writers who described Jews continued to borrow English and other European models. Only with the rise of ethnography and ethnographic naturalism in the second half of the nineteenth century did Russian writers begin to base their descriptions on the actual Jews living in the Russian Empire. Many of these naturalistic writers, however, continued to recycle the prototype of Jews as usurers: as miserly, exploitative Jewish men with rebellious but virtuous daughters.

Given these images of Jews as either money-hungry men, such as Judas and Shylock, or innocent young women who are potentially available to non-Jewish men, such as Jessica or Scott's Rebecca, it is not surprising that throughout nineteenth-century Europe, Jews were associated with prostitution.[11] The belief that most pimps, madams, and prostitutes were Jewish created a new version of the old model for telling the stories of Jews. Shylock, the Jewish victimizer, became the pimp or madam who exploited prostitutes or their clients. Meanwhile, the good, innocent Jew, the Jessica or the Rebecca, could be identified with the prostitute herself. In the 1847 story "Zhid" [The Yid], Ivan Turgenev offers an early fictional treatment of the theme in Russian. The elderly Jew Girshel' cajoles an army officer into paying for the services of his beautiful daughter Sarah but refuses to leave her alone with him. At the end of the story, the narrator lets the daughter's curse against all Russians pass without comment but notes that he found the father ugly as well as pathetic when he is hanged as a spy, in spite of all his efforts to buy a pardon. In Jabotinsky's sarcastic evaluation, the story is nothing but rehashed stereotypes:

> Reading it, you see clearly that the author never saw anything of this kind anywhere and could not have, but invented it, just as he invented ghost stories,—and what he invented is really something, he drew it and colored it in with such feeling! The old Yid is of course a spy, and in addition he sells his daughter to the officers. The daughter is of course beautiful. That makes sense. One mustn't deprive the poor tribe completely. One must at least leave them some goods to trade.[12]

The image of the Jew as a suspicious trader of some kind underlies stories such as Turgenev's. Narratives linking Jews to prostitution suggest that non-Jews might be drawn into and threatened by this disturbing trading. As I noted in my discussion of Leskov, Karl Marx, in "*On the Jewish Question*," asserted that the growth of capitalism would implicate non-Jews in what he saw as a "Jewish" money economy: he feared that the Christians would somehow become Jews. In this essay, Marx provides a useful nineteenth-century articulation of the much older idea that a "Jewish" economy turns people into victims and victimizers, or into prostitutes and pimps.[13] His formulations make the prostitute both the manifestation and the victim of the money economy. If that economy is controlled by Jews and represents a fundamentally Jewish set of attitudes toward money and commerce, then prostitution becomes an inherently Jewish industry, even in those cases when prostitute, pimp, and client are all Christians.

If Jews control money, then they can be identified with the substance that makes the capitalist economy function and that is inherently replaceable. The government decrees and the public accepts that one ruble note has exactly the same value as any other ruble note, regardless of who holds it and what is done with it. The link between Jews and money, then, suggests that Jews support a system in which any one person would have exactly the same value as any other. This logic indicates that prostitution and Jewish assimilation can symbolize both the rise of the money economy and the disintegration of old identities. Assimilated Jews can be equated with the pimps and madams who benefit from the capitalist system and with the prostitutes who embody it by themselves becoming as exchangeable as money.

What does Marx's reinterpretation of older stereotypes linking Jews, prostitutes, and money have to do with discourse concerning Jews in the Russian Empire? By the end of the nineteenth century, Jews were imagined to control and benefit from the recent changes in the economic system, and anti-Jewish policies and attitudes in Russia grew out of a hostility to modernization and the money economy.[14] Tsarist ministers argued that Jews were driven by the urge to exploit Russians, especially peasants; the emancipation of the peasants and the economic changes in the country, they believed, furthered the Jews' evil intentions.[15]

Starting in the 1880s, though, Jews were sometimes seen not as the powers behind but as the victims of the new system: literary representations of Jews in this period occasionally identified them with victims of capitalism.[16] Constructions of the Jew as either victim or oppressor within the capitalist system paralleled images of Jews as either pimps and madams or prostitutes. In Leo Tolstoy's 1889 novella, *Kreytserova sonata* [The Kreutzer Sonata], the tormented Pozdnyshev, explaining to a fellow train passenger what compelled him to murder his wife, outlines the intersections among Jews and seductresses, victims and oppressors, in a tone of terrified sympathy:

> On the one hand woman is reduced to the lowest stage of humiliation, while on the other she dominates. Just like the Jews: as they pay us

back for their oppression by a financial domination, so it is with women. "Ah, you want us to be traders [*torgovtsy*] only—all right, as traders we will dominate you," say the Jews. "Ah, you want us to be merely objects of sensuality [*predmet chuvstvennosti*]—all right, as objects of sensuality we will enslave you," say the women.[17]

The discursive equation between Jews and prostitution was not entirely a product of Pozdnyshev's fevered imagination: the economic changes of the late nineteenth century led to a real as well as a perceived growth in Jewish participation in prostitution. Statistics show that many Jews maintained brothels and worked in them.[18] When combined with traditional Russian prejudices about Jews, this reality reinforced the image of pimps and madams as "rapacious Jews who profited off the bodies of young Russian women."[19] This image was most fully developed in the myth of "white slavery," in which predominantly Jewish men seduce innocent Christian girls, then sell them to brothels in Latin America and Asia. In fact, while many European and especially Eastern European women worked in the sex industry in Latin America, they seem for the most part to have chosen their career willingly—and all the women listed as "Russians" and "Poles" working in Argentinean brothels were, in fact, Russian and Polish Jews.[20]

Late-nineteenth-century Russian literature and political debates tended to associate prostitutes—whether Jewish or not—with two literary types: the prostitute as opportunist and the prostitute as victim. That is, while some elided prostitutes with pimps and madams, seeing all of them as part of a nefarious underworld bent on entrapping and infecting innocent males and in need of state regulation and control, others drew a line between prostitutes and the administration of the brothels, portraying prostitutes themselves as the innocent prey of men in general, procurers and clients in specific, the governmental system of regulation, or the entirety of hypocritical bourgeois society. The first group told stories that concluded with mortal conflict between prostitutes and others, the result of an enmity predicated on the prostitutes' measurable distance from the rest of humanity and coded as genetic inferiority. The narratives of the second imagined the prostitutes' goal—whether or not any individual prostitute reached it—as progress toward reentry into the society of "honest" men and women.

The view of prostitutes as opportunists lay behind the state's system of regulating prostitution by issuing women official licenses, "yellow tickets," in place of their passports, and requiring them to report for regular medical checkups. Such nineteenth-century legislation perpetuated the image of prostitutes as threats to public order and public health.[21] Seemingly unaware that the venereal diseases they feared—particularly syphilis—were spread by men as well as women, tsarist administrators assumed that by instituting a system to separate infected women from male clients, they would protect the public at large. One of the most vocal advocates of regulated prostitution was Dr. Veniamin Tarnovsky, a criminologist and an expert on venereal diseases, who wrote widely on medical issues. More than others in the Russian medical community of his time, he agreed with and articulated the principles motivating state policy. In an 1888 tract in favor of regulation, he argued against the "sentimental view" that prostitutes are victims; instead, he asserted that prostitutes choose their profession deliberately and repeatedly, and thus should not be compared to slaves. Rather than suffering as the prey of men, the prostitute, in his view, happily preys on them. Not only, like any merchant, does she do whatever is required to increase the demand for her services, but she also "calmly, with no pricks of conscience," infects her clients with syphilis. Ironically, Tarnovsky's emphasis on prostitutes' responsibility for their actions does not prevent him from arguing that they constitute a measurably different, indeed "congenitally flawed" [*prirozhdenno-porochnyi*] subgroup of humanity.[22] His uncompromisingly negative image of the grasping, evil prostitute, which found little echo in Russian literature, resembles Emile Zola's depiction, in the immensely popular 1880 French novel, *Nana*, of a woman who, influenced by both her flawed heredity and faulty environment, cheerfully exposes and sells her body, thereby ruining countless men morally, financially, and physically.

The conviction that prostitutes, unlike Nana, were more victims than victimizers inspired the arguments of many of Tarnovsky's fellow doctors, as well as the early-twentieth-century Russian social reformers who sought to eliminate the yellow ticket.[23] The same view guided a Russian literary tradition identified with the saintly Sonia Marmeladova in Fedor Dostoevsky's *Crime and Punishment*, the prototypical prostitute with a heart of gold.[24] The most detailed Russian novel about prostitution is Aleksandr Kuprin's 1908–15 book *Iama* [The Pit]. Kuprin makes it clear that no matter how badly any individual prostitute behaves, other people are to blame for her situation; indeed, every prostitute in the brothel he describes tells her story of the male exploitation that brought her there. One of his heroines, the hardened prostitute Zhenya, voices the romantic notion that "a woman loves only once and forever," which lay behind the wide belief that if her first lover abandoned her, a girl would probably "fall" into prostitution.[25] Kuprin illustrates male exploitation and female innocence most vividly in the scenes involving a procurer, Semyon Iakovlevich Gorizont, who first appears in a train accompanied by his new bride and, unbeknownst to her, three young women expecting to find employment as seamstresses, as well as, in yet another compartment, a large group of experienced prostitutes from another city. Once they reach their destination, he sells the sexual services of all these women (including his wife). Gorizont's rapacity makes him the prototype of the males who benefit from prostitution, while his unsuspecting wife embodies its victim: the reader knows that he, and not she, is responsible for her fate.

In Kuprin's world, it appeared entirely logical for Gorizont and his bride, pimp and prostitute, to be Jews. Not only were both Jews and prostitutes (and even more so pimps and madams) conceived as benefiting from the capitalist economy by taking advantage of others, but the two groups shared other identifying marks. Particularly when portrayed as exploiters, Jews were described as identifiably non-Russian—with strong Jewish accents, features, and odors—and hostile to Russians. Similarly, in spite of evidence to the contrary, prostitutes were distinguished from peasants and identified instead with the urban proletariat, a group less linked to Romantic notions of Russian national identity.[26] Both Jews and prostitutes were imagined as looking or smelling unsanitary and repulsive.[27] Tarnovsky's views of the degeneracy of prostitutes indicate that heredity makes them susceptible to disease as well as vice: "Regular prostitutes are for the most part diseased or undeveloped creatures, burdened by a malignant heritage, presenting undeniable physical and psychological signs of degeneracy."[28] Although Tarnovsky was unusual among Russian thinkers for his emphasis on biological rather than environmental factors as responsible for the prostitutes' ill health, many observers agreed with the principle that they were very likely to be ill with syphilis and other diseases.[29] It was a commonplace that Jews too were often ill, though not necessarily with the same diseases.[30] One ethnographer saw this as a result of genetic and environmental factors, which he links in a Lamarckian schema:

As for the appearance of the Jews, one should note that their frailty and the weakness of their body strength result not only from historical causes, but also from many of the conditions of their lifestyle that depend on them alone. . . . Jews marry young. . . . mothers themselves nurse their infants. . . . Jewish boys begin to learn to read young. . . . As soon as a child reaches the age when he is capable of learning . . . he sits in school at his studies for days on end, so that finally bending over books becomes a habit for him. Various diseases stem from this, such as hemorrhoids, scrofula, consumption, and eye problems, which the Jews transmit by inheritance to their distant descendants.[31]

Perhaps most significant is the incorrigibility that some Russians attributed to both Jews and prostitutes. Scientists such as Tarnovsky argued that prostitutes were "congenitally flawed" and therefore unlikely to benefit from any effort to "liberate" or "reform" them. Vsevolod Krestovsky, as we saw, held similar views about Jews, asserting that regardless of any individual Jew's attempt to change his or her status, to abandon Jewish culture and characteristics for Russian ones, some congenital trait—carried in the Jew's "blood" —would make true, permanent assimilation impossible.[32]

The other side of the dichotomy offers just as many points of contact: the presentation of the Jew as victim has much in common with that of the prostitute as victim. Depictions of the prostitute in this light stress that a callous "system" controlled by men, bourgeois society, or the government's regulation of the sex industry is responsible for her plight. Similarly, the sympathetic depictions of Jews as victims that became more prevalent in Russian literature in the 1880s tended to focus on their abuse, not at the hands of individuals who perpetrated pogroms but at those of the authorities, perceived as permitting or even encouraging violence.[33] Writers who portrayed Jews and prostitutes sympathetically often stressed their poverty, which, these writers argued, drove them to act against their nature. Son'ka Rul', a Jewish prostitute in Kuprin's novel, exemplifies the victimization of both groups: the narrator reports that the woman's own mother was compelled to sell her to a brothel following a pogrom in their town. For such writers, both Jews and prostitutes were, at least in principle, reformable. Orzeszkowa depicted a Jew who, by striving to acquire an education, might become a full member of a Western nation; those who would reform the prostitute espoused the same agenda, arguing that education and a new set of attitudes were all that was required to make the former prostitute an "honest" member of society.[34] This is a story governed by the Enlightenment idea of progress toward a goal that is, at least in principle, attainable.

Chekhov's story "Pripadok" [A Nervous Breakdown] (1889), his best-known treatment of prostitution, describes a student's first visit to a brothel in the company of friends, and his ensuing mental collapse. This story rejects the typical victim/victimizer split; Vasil'ev is torn between the two conflicting positions of the day: either prostitutes are potentially his moral equals, victims of the madams and the johns, or they are congenitally flawed and somehow less human than he is: "One of two things must be true. Either it merely appears that prostitution is evil, and we are exaggerating it, or, if prostitution really is as evil as we conventionally believe, then my dear friends are the same kind of slave-owners, aggressors, and murderers that they illustrate in *Niva*" (p. 213).[35] The student concludes that both the prostitutes and his friends cannot be civilized; if prostitutes are fully human, then the clients, by paying to have sex with them, transform themselves from the cultured readers of the illustrated journal *Niva* to something more like the exotic barbarians pictured in it. Although the state saw the prostitute's client as initially healthy and attempted to protect him from a physical disease, syphilis, Vasil'ev fears a more moral contagion, which would reflect the clients' image of the prostitutes back onto themselves.[36] He proposes that a painful solution, the full acknowledgment of guilt, is the only way to rescue men from the horror of their exploitative role. This acknowledgment, though, cannot save the student. Even without having sex with a prostitute, he becomes terrified at his own potential guilt. His terror manifests as an illness, an attack of a stereotypically female disease, hysteria, prompting the student's friends to bring him to a psychiatrist.

Did Chekhov share Vasil'ev's obsession with the relative guilt of prostitutes and their clients? For his contemporaries, his depiction in "A Nervous Breakdown" of dissolution leading to self-destruction was reminiscent of the puritanism that Leo Tolstoy displayed in *The Kreutzer Sonata*. Although Chekhov was fascinated with Tolstoyan ideas until around 1891, his views of prostitution cannot be so easily aligned with those of other late-nineteenth-century Russians.[37] Rather than showing a client infected with syphilis by an evil prostitute, or a prostitute infected with syphilis by an exploitative man, he describes a case of hysteria, a less contagious disease. Meanwhile, Vasil'ev's friend, the medical student, suggests an alternative to the question of whether johns murder prostitutes, or prostitutes johns: "We human beings murder each other mutually [*ubivaem vzaimno drug druga*]. . . . This is, of course, immoral, but philosophy won't help here" (p. 214). While others described sexually transmitted diseases as infections passed either by women to men or by men to women, the medical student states that the seeds of destruction travel in both directions—and Vasil'ev's illness confirms his friend's logic.

In "A Nervous Breakdown," Chekhov spoke against the easy assumption that those on the fringes of society were necessarily infected and infecting, implicitly rejecting Tarnovsky's congenital model for criminality, "the tautology of the biological argument, as well as its sinister social implications."[38] One might assume that this physician was also willing to question the criminologist's linkage of physical diseases to moral flaws. He suggests as much with his statement that "S [syphilis] is not a vice, not a product of an evil will, but a disease [*S est' ne porok, ne produkt zloi voli, a bolezn'*]."[39] In "A Nervous Breakdown," rather than linking disease primarily with stereotypically diseased prostitutes, he shows a seemingly ideal type, a Russian university student admired by his peers and professors, as equally susceptible to illness. Thus he refuses to portray disease as a manifestation of moral rot.

Chekhov and Jews

Regardless of Chekhov's liberal views on illness and morality, he was associated with some conservative voices in Russia, especially with the avowed Judeophobe Aleksei Suvorin, the powerful publisher of the daily *Novoe vremia* [New Times]. Suvorin and his ilk saw assimilating Jews, like prostitutes, as fundamentally insincere, unreliable people who adapted their reactions to the demands of the market by being anything for anybody; as we might expect, these thinkers viewed all Jewish conversion to Orthodoxy as evidence of a dangerous pliability rather than of faith. In 1880, Suvorin published a letter to the editor by an anonymous author, alleging that the number of Jewish students in institutes of higher education was far out of proportion to their representation in the population as a whole. This letter appeared under the heading "Zhid idet" [The Yid Is Coming], the phrase that Vsevolod Krestovsky used to title his trilogy of anti-Semitic novels.[40] The letter writer, like the novelist, assumed that Jews are willing to engage in any tactics in their effort to exploit and conquer Russians. The campaign to impose quotas on Jewish students capitalized on the fear that Jews sought education not merely in order to better themselves and their economic prospects but also in order to make life worse for non-Jews; the Jews' seeming attraction to Russian culture, therefore, was portrayed as concealed hostility.

Chekhov's views on Jews sometimes seem similar to those of Suvorin's letter writer. He frequently used *zhid*, as well as another derogatory term for Jew, "shmul'," in letters to friends. His tone sounded especially hostile when he referred to Jewish literature and theater critics (he seemingly had in mind Akim Volynsky [Flekser] and A. R. Kugel'), for whom, he asserted, the "spirit, the form, the humor" of Russian life, as reflected in the works of writers such as Aleksandr Ostrovsky and Nikolai Leskov—and perhaps Chekhov too— were entirely foreign and incomprehensible.[41] Although these critics, who wrote in Russian, presumably thought of themselves as successfully assimilated, Chekhov here suggests that their understanding of Russian culture is superficial, their avowed love for it insincere. This hostile tone can be heard in certain of his stories as well. For instance, a very brief story from 1886, "Znakomyi muzhchina" [A Gentleman Friend], juxtaposes the themes of prostitution and Jewish assimilation in a particularly ominous way. A Russian dancing girl visits a client, a Jewish convert who is a dentist, to ask for a loan, but instead finds herself paying him her last ruble to have a tooth extracted needlessly. The encounter leaves her bleeding and newly aware of the pathos of her life. Here, the Russian seems to be the victim of the Jew as well as fate.

Critics have often seen Chekhov's letters and stories of this sort as proof of a fundamental distaste for Jews that made him unwilling to examine them closely enough to produce a convincing Jewish character.[42] Jabotinsky suggested that Chekhov might exemplify the "asemitic" Russian intellectual, who simply wants "to exist in his circle without an unloved element [i.e., the Jews]," and who thinks, "I write my play for my own people [*dlia svoikh*] and I have the right to prefer that my own people perform it on stage and write criticism about it."[43] (For Jabotinksy, this attitude was not wholly unreasonable: he concluded his article with a call for a fight against Russification of the Jews.[44]) One might extend this argument by finding in some of Chekhov's works not only distaste but actually fear of Jews, especially assimilating ones. Elena Tolstaia argues that stories such as "A Gentleman Friend" show that, for Chekhov, Jewish conversion and other examples of Jews' rejection of their traditions were disturbing for nontheological reasons: they made Jews more threatening by bringing them closer in every sense ("any minute now they will overtake us").[45] This Hegelian view of national identity, based on competition between groups, closely equates Chekhov's attitude toward Jews and Russians with that of conservatives who saw Jewish acculturation as part of a campaign to destroy Russians.

Chekhov's attitude toward Jews, however, did not consist only of hostility or fear. While Chekhov sometimes insulted specific Jews or Jews in general in his letters, he also defended them and, as his defenders point out, attacked anti-Semitism (though Karlinsky's assertion that Chekhov used *zhid* in his letters only because it was the standard term in his southern hometown sounds deliberately naive, given the awareness that the author would display in *Ivanov* of the term's implications).[46] At the same time, Chekhov's frequent joshing of his wife, Ol'ga Knipper, for her German background shows that he used ethnic slurs lightly and without hostility. The accumulated evidence of his letters shows a Chekhov who, much like Leskov (and unlike Orzesz-kowa), was not consistently on one side or the other of the "Jewish question." Unlike Leskov, Chekhov did not appear troubled by his own inconsistency and never attempted to come up with a "Jewish policy" and define it explicitly.

Even while Chekhov used stereotypes to dismiss Jewish theater critics, his literary works challenged those same stereotypes. His depictions of Jewish converts reveals an intense interest in the processes of human mutability. Julie de Sherbinin writes that he "defines religious identity as a cultural construct," a set of shared stories and attitudes rather than a powerfully experienced faith.[47] Thus, his interest in Jews who change their religion might stem from an urge to understand the roots of identity and the degree to which an individual's identity can evolve.

Chekhov portrayed himself, no less than his characters, as ever in flux, unable to define his opinions and his desires once and for all. Typically, in describing his personal life, he acknowledged not only the dangers of promiscuity but also its attendant pleasures. Even though, until his marriage with Ol'ga Knipper, his letters were full of self-mockery for avoiding matrimony, he admitted that he feared the "boredom" of life with a wife [*mne bylo by skuchno vozit'sia s zhenoi*], and he mentioned prostitutes and visits to brothels in letters to male friends.[48] While inconstancy may have symbolized the frightening moral decline of his age, it signified its delights as well. Chekhov's depiction of the attraction of mutability distinguished his works from contemporary genres telling of Jews and prostitutes. Rather than focusing on enmity between groups and disease as the punishment for transgression of social or moral boundaries, Chekhov defines a new kind of art—one in which inconstancy is not wholly negative.

"The Mire"

In 1886, the year when Chekhov wrote so much in his letters about Dunya Efros and her money, he published "The Mire" [Tina] in Suvorin's *Novoe vremia*. His story and *The Merchant of Venice*—both of which rely on the exchange of flesh for money—have similar but in some ways opposing plots. Shylock wants his debtor to pay his debt with a pound of his own flesh rather than money, but Chekhov's Jewish heroine, Susanna Moiseevna, offers her creditor her own flesh—that is, she has sex with him—rather than paying back the money she owes. Susanna, a sharp-featured, dark-haired woman, the daughter of a wealthy father, has recently inherited his vodka-distilling fortune, when Aleksandr Grigor'evich Sokol'sky, an army lieutenant on leave, comes to her to collect a debt her father owed his cousin, Aleksei Ivanovich Kriukov. Kriukov had promised to lend him the money, which Sokol'sky needs in order to get married. Susanna first agrees to give Sokol'sky the money, then suddenly destroys his IOU and refuses to pay it. After a tussle, he finds himself staying for breakfast and the next twenty-four hours, after which he returns to his cousin confused and embarrassed. The cousin berates him and proceeds to Susanna's house to reclaim the debt, but she seduces him in his turn. After his leave has ended, Sokol'sky leaves his cousin's house to return to duty. A few days later, Kriukov finds himself drawn to Susanna's home, where he is startled to see many of his acquaintances, local landowners, and—even more shocking to him—Sokol'sky, who apparently has abandoned his army career and his fiancée to take up residence with Susanna.

This story is propelled by the mystery of the Jewish woman's attractiveness to the two Russian men: is Susanna a Shylock out to do harm to Christians, a Jessica who would help them, or someone quite different from either of these? Susanna's words as well as her actions make her difficult to categorize. Explicitly and implicitly, she challenges the other characters' assumptions, embodying confusion about sexual, ethnic, and even species identities. When Sokol'sky explains that he needs his cousin's money in order to marry, she launches into a tirade about her dislike for women. She freely admits her inconsistency: "I love myself very much, but when I am reminded that I am a woman, I begin to hate myself" (p. 365).[49] She displays similar ambivalence about Jews and her own Jewishness. She asserts that she is a Jew "to the marrow of her bones" [*do mozga kostei*] (p. 367) and tells Sokol'sky that she knows her accent gives her away; then she says that she, unlike other Jews, speaks correctly (p. 368) and attends Orthodox mass regularly (p. 365). Adopting the "blood" language of modern anti-Semitism, she says that she abhors Jews who love money: "what I dislike in our Semitic blood is the passion for profit [*strast' k nazhive*]" (p. 367). Nonetheless, she shows no remorse for stealing Sokol'sky's cousin's money, explaining that "I have my own opinion about things" [*U menia svoi sobstvennyi vzgliad na veshchi*] (p. 370). During his struggle with her, Sokol'sky sees her as not exactly human but more "like a cat . . . like a captured fish . . . like an eel" (p. 369). His inability to assign her a single, stable definition makes her a symbol of mutation and assimilation in all its forms.

Although Susanna's words and her behavior link her to the negative Jewish stereotypes that Suvorin endorsed, the story's many biblical subtexts complicate any effort to see Susanna simply as a Jew who victimizes Russians. Chekhov hints at the uncertainty of Susanna's identity with his choice of her name. As Robert Louis Jackson demonstrates, this writer, more than others of his time, was able to integrate a real knowledge of the Bible into his depictions of contemporary Russian Jews.[50] The story of Susanna, which is not included in the Hebrew Bible, appears in the Protestant Bible as Apocrypha and in the Catholic and Eastern Orthodox Bibles as Daniel 13. It tells of a beautiful and virtuous woman, who, while washing in her garden, is surprised by two lecherous old men. They threaten that if she does not have sex with them, they will testify that they saw her meeting a young lover. Susanna repulses them, is brought to trial, and is about to be executed when Daniel, by cross-examining the witnesses, reveals their duplicity, thus saving Susanna's reputation and her life. The tale is a favorite topic of Christian iconography, and continued to inspire paintings through the eighteenth century, including some voluptuous nude Susannas, by the French artist Jean-François de Troy, that hang in the Hermitage in St. Petersburg and in the Pushkin Museum in Moscow.[51] Chekhov probably saw these paintings or other similar renditions of the theme.

Savelii Senderovich sees the Apocrypha of Susanna as the clue to Chekhov's story, focusing on the voyeurism of the elders, mimicked by that of viewers of the paintings: "The penetrating eye, the interested gaze, the act of seeing—these are the real heroes of the story." Comparing "The Mire" to other Chekhov stories illustrating the power and pleasure of the voyeur who censures the illicit behavior of others while vicariously indulging in it himself, Senderovich concludes that the writer described both the fictional Susanna Moiseevna and the real Dunya Efros so harshly because the Jewish "type" that they both represent attracted him so strongly, perhaps precisely because it was somehow off-limits.[52]

Senderovich is undoubtedly right that Chekhov was aware not only of the association of the name with a visual seduction. Chekhov may also have noticed the ambiguity of the biblical story—an ambiguity that Shakespeare also recognized. In *The Merchant of Venice*, "Daniel" can mean a defender of either Christians or Jews: when Portia, disguised as a lawyer, makes an argument in Shylock's favor, he calls her "A Daniel come to judgment"; when she then argues against the Jew, Gratiano makes the same comparison: "A Daniel . . . a second Daniel / I thank thee, Jew, for teaching me that word" (4. 1). In the Susanna story, Daniel's lawyerly skills freed her from the charge of adultery, but she might nonetheless qualify as a temptress whose beauty led the elders into crime. While Susanna Moiseevna has fewer pretensions to virtue, she is as confusing and compelling a figure as her biblical namesake, and equally capable of leading two men astray.

Susanna Moiseevna's name is only one of the elements of the story that complicate the culture's tendency to view nineteenth-century Jews through biblical and other lenses that make their stories predictable. One of the items in Susanna Moiseevna's waiting room catches Sokol'sky's attention: "There were almost no strictly Jewish things in the room, except perhaps for a large painting showing the meeting of Jacob and Esau" (p. 366). The scene depicted is presumably the twins' reconciliation (Gen. 33:1–16), many years after the rupture that followed Jacob's manipulation of his father, Isaac, into giving him the blessing that Isaac had meant for the older brother, Esau (Gen. 27). As Chekhov must have known, the story of Jacob and Esau evoked a division between Jews and Christians: Christian exegesis associates Jews with Esau, Christians with Jacob; in contrast, Jews traditionally trace their lineage from Jacob, while European Jews identified the Christians among whom they lived with the Edomites, the descendants of Esau.

Both Christian and Jewish traditions might motivate the painting in Susanna Moiseevna's house. Senderovich notes that Susanna's last name, Rot-shtein, includes the German for "red," linking her to the Edomites, whose name comes from a Semitic word for "red."[53] The equation aligns Chekhov's story with a Christian tradition making Christians the true heirs to the bib-lical patriarchs and associating Jews with those whom the patriarchs reject: thus, Sarah, Abel, and Jacob represent the Christians, and Hagar, Cain, and Esau the Jews. This reading of biblical text has justified a Christian hostility to Jews that could confirm an understanding of "The Mire" in the spirit of Suvorin and his Judeophobia. However, it is entirely possible that Chekhov realized the ambiguity of the image he described. He might have known of the Jewish interpretation that labels Christians as Edomites (he could have read of it, for instance, in the Russian translation of *Meir Ezofowicz*, or in Krestovsky's *Egyptian Darkness*).

The variety of the role models offered by Jacob and Esau parallels the multifarious possibilities engendered by an attempt to situate the biblical story against the narrative tradition making Jews into traffickers in flesh. In the first section, Esau, exhausted from hunting, sells his birthright to his brother in exchange for lentil stew (Gen. 25:29–34). The scene can be seen as an archetype of exploitative commerce, with Jacob playing the part of the deceptive merchant or evil capitalist, Esau that of both the innocent cus-tomer and the abused worker, forced by a monopolistic system into paying an extortionist's rates for food. Given the regnant understanding of the Jew's role in the money economy, so strongly articulated in Marx's essay, it could stand for Judeophobic arguments about the danger Jews pose to gentiles. However, as with the story of Susanna and the elders, the evocation of the biblical scene in Chekhov's tale inspires contradictory interpretations; rather than representing the capitalist's innocent customer, Esau could be seen as the ultimate capitalist, happily trading in his very identity—his birthright. He, as the seller of identity, and Jacob, as the buyer of identity, might be linked respectively to assimilated Jews and to the Russians they imitated. In any case, a close reading of the biblical story reveals its appropriateness as a metaphor for a situation in which some people, like Susanna Moiseevna, have assumed what appear to be false identities, but it is hard to determine who is to blame for the ensuing confusion.

The similarities between Susanna and a prostitute, though they appear to make her a victimizer, also contribute to the difficulty of assigning her such a role. She fits the broadest definition of a prostitute, in that she takes the two heroes' money—the twenty-three hundred rubles that her father owed Kriukov—and then has sex with them. She explains her own actions by distinguishing between her morality (her "own opinion" [*sobstvennyi vzgliad*]) and that of "so-called decent" women (p. 364), whom she despises. After Kriukov returns home from his night with Susanna, he coyly refers to the money she took as the price both cousins paid her for sex: "As for the IOU. . . . Write that it's gone. We're both terrible sinners. We're equally to blame. I'm not holding you responsible for the whole 2,300, but half of it" (p. 374). Susanna's home contributes to her association with prostitution; like the brothels in "A Nervous Breakdown," it reveals its owner's "tastelessness" [*bezvkusitsa*] (p. 366 in "The Mire" and p. 204 in "A Nervous Breakdown"). The overpowering scent of jasmine in Susanna's bedroom recalls the strong-smelling flowers that fill the dressing room of Zola's courtesan Nana.[54] Her seduction of the younger cousin, then the older one, also evokes Nana, who makes love first to the young Georges Hugon, then to his elder brother Philippe, whom she ruins financially. (The parallel is yet more apparent in Russian, since Kriukov is frequently referred to not as Sokol'sky's elder "cousin [*dvoiurodnyi brat*]" but simply as his "brother [*brat*].")

If Susanna Moiseevna is, as these details hint, a kind of prostitute, then she seems to have more in common with the victimizer described by Tarnovsky and Zola than the victim who appears in the works of Kuprin and Dostoevsky. She does not passively acquiesce to a man's offer of money for sex. Instead, as Tarnovsky asserts, she deliberately and repeatedly chooses her role, actively taking the two men's money and then offering them sex in exchange. Again in confirmation of Tarnovsky's views, Susanna's unconventional morality accompanies a tendency toward disease. Her house, she tells Sokol'sky, smells not of garlic but of medicine (p. 367); her bed curtain looks like a funeral canopy (p. 363); her skin and especially her gums are as pale as those of a corpse (p. 366).[55] She imagines Sokol'sky referring to her as a "scabby Yid [*parkhataia zhidovka*]" (p. 365), suffering from a skin ailment associated with Jews, but he sees her disease as mental, dismissing her as "some kind of psychopath" (p. 365).[56] As Tarnovsky would have seen it, Susanna poses a danger to the men with whom she has sex. Her laughter is "infectious" [*zarazitel'nyi*] (p. 368), and her immoral behavior is even more so.[57] Sokol'sky and Kriukov are startled by their own response to her and by the ease with which they forget their fiancée and wife, respectively. Their shock suggests that they, like the men Nana sleeps with, are innocent citizens who have been infected, if not with syphilis, then with a disease that is as much moral as physical, as manifested in the body and the actions of the woman who carries it.

Susanna's moral inadequacy leads her to enjoy the perverse. Sokol'sky's first encounter with her begins when she speaks to him: "the lieutenant heard a rich feminine voice, not unpleasantly gutturally pronouncing [*kartavia*] the letter R" (p. 363). In nineteenth- and twentieth-century Russia, people who pronounce a guttural *r* (as one does in French and German) rather than rolling it (as in Spanish) are often assumed to be Jews, foreigners, aristocrats, or those with aristocratic pretensions. By displaying her inability to speak "pure" Russian, Susanna embraces her own unconventionality, her distortion of the expected sounds of Russian. Eventually, her enthusiasm about herself (remember that she "loves herself very much") begins to act on Sokol'sky. In principle, he is not attracted to non-Russians, and indeed feels "prejudice against non-Russian faces" (p. 366). Nonetheless, he and Susanna speak about her own accent, he notes her guttural *r*, and then he thinks, "My God, she's magnificent!" (p. 368). Similarly, the heavy smell of jasmine in Susanna's room at first makes Sokol'sky feel ill (p. 365); after his return to his cousin's, though, the same smell—which remains in his clothing even after it is washed—makes him think of Susanna and draws him to her (p. 376). His urge to reexperience the sensation that had once made him sick indicates that he, like Susanna, finds pleasure in the perverse rather than the "pure" and healthy. Sokol'sky's reactions demonstrate what one critic calls the "negative effect" of sensory experience in Chekhov's stories of this period. Smell, touch, sight, hearing, and taste all awaken a tormenting sexual desire.[58] This pessimistic view of human sexuality, reminiscent of Tolstoy's, associated sex and sensuality with violence and disease.

How should Susanna's Jewishness be interpreted in light of her disturbing sensuality? Her ability to tempt Sokol'sky and Kriukov with her perverse charms evokes not only the literary tradition of Nana-like prostitutes but also the vision of the Jew in the 1880s associated with *Novoe vremia*: a dangerous person whose surface appeal conceals a threat to Russians. Like Tarnovsky's prostitutes, she deliberately "infects" her innocent sexual partners with her own moral disease. Critics in Chekhov's time and since have seen the story as an attack on the favorite targets of *Novoe vremia*: Jews, assimilated or not, and the "Jew-loving" intellectuals who defend them. Sokol'sky and Kriukov thus become two more in a series of trusting Russians, duped by a Jewish prostitute whose charms are deceiving and whose loyalty to Russian culture is only superficial.

Chekhov's liberal friends hinted that they were troubled by the Judeo-phobic implications of "The Mire," but they hesitated to state their objections explicitly.[59] The most famous response of this type came from Maria Kiseleva, a writer of children's stories. She excoriates Chekhov for concentrating on a "pile of manure" rather than the "pearl" that he might have found in it, and she cannot resist "cursing [him] and [his] vile [*merzkikh*] editors, who so calmly spoil [his] talent."[60] The veiled reference to Suvorin suggests that Kiseleva, like many of Chekhov's friends, was disturbed by his professional and personal reliance on the conservative editor, and that the story upset her because it suggested that he shared Suvorin's views on the Jewish question. In response to Kiseleva, Chekhov wrote a lengthy letter, often cited in discussions of his art. He refuses to avoid unattractive topics or characters, pointing out, "For chemists nothing on earth is impure. A writer should be as objective as a chemist. . . . piles of manure play a very respectable role in the landscape, and evil passions are just as appropriate [*prisushchi*] in life as good ones."[61] Tolstaia, who sees "The Mire" as a concealed attack on Dunya Efros, dismisses Chekhov's fine words about the role of art in this letter as an elegant feint when she asserts that his one sincere line is the admission that "I must confess, I speak sharply with my conscience when I write."[62]

One might also point out another phrase in the letter. In considering whether literature can be corrupting, Chekhov observes that "everything in this world is relative and approximate [*otnositel'no i priblizitel'no*]" (p. 11). A similar sentence appears in a letter written a year earlier, in which Chekhov informs Bilibin that he will not marry Efros: "I am still not married. I broke *definitively* with my fiancée. That is, she broke with me. But I haven't bought a gun yet, and I'm not writing a diary. Everything in the world is mutable, permutable, approximate, and relative [*prevratno, kolovratno, priblizitel'no i otnositel'no*]."[63] Both literary and real romances between Jewish women and Russian men make Chekhov say that everything in the world is relative and approximate, as well as mutable and permutable. His hesitation to assign unquestionable meaning suggests that we should not be too quick to give his fictional representations real-life significance. Susanna Moiseevna, then, may not equal Dunya Efros. She is, after all, fundamentally unlike Efros in that she has apparently converted to Russian Orthodoxy, making her potentially available to a non-Jewish suitor in a way that Efros, it seems, refused to be, and she is promiscuous and insincere precisely when compared to Efros.

The differences between the two women suggest that Chekhov, like so many of his contemporaries, was intrigued by the possibility that conversion offered Jews to change their identity officially. He may not have been in complete agreement with Suvorin about the Jewish question, regardless of his contemporaries' reading of "The Mire." The dual implications of Susanna's biblical name suggest that this Jewish woman, like Jewish women in general, was not the evil temptress she seemed. Rather than adhering to an exegesis of the Jacob and Esau story that would make one player the capitalist oppressor and the other his victim, Chekhov allows for an interpretation showing both characters as equally implicated by their transaction in birthrights.

Where Suvorin's editorialists viewed Jews in familiar patterns, leading to confrontation between nationalities, the characters in "The Mire" are going nowhere. Just as Kriukov's IOUs from Susanna will never mature, so his cousin, it seems, will never attack Susanna or leave her. Time in the story is not organized into idyllic past, transitional present, and apocalyptic future. Instead, it is empty of meaning, full, instead, of pointless, repeated actions. Like Chekhov's skepticism about Tarnovsky's views of prostitutes' congenital criminality, the story gives reason to doubt that he agreed with Suvorin that Jews are as "innately" duplicitous (or "innately" anything else). While Susanna does take Sokol'sky and Kriukov's money, she may be no more criminal than the prostitutes Chekhov discussed with such equanimity. Indeed, though the Shylock paradigm casts the Jew as moneylender, Susanna is in Antonio's position instead: she owes money, and she pays with her flesh. As in "A Gentleman Friend," the inconstancy associated with conversion and prostitution here taints Russian and Jew alike; rather than infecting Russian men with her immorality, acting the victimizer to their victim, Susanna responds to desires that she shares with them, to an attraction to inconstancy that can characterize not only Jews but other inhabitants of the empire as well.

"The Tumbleweed"

In 1887, a year after "The Mire," Chekhov published "The Tumbleweed" [Perekati-pole], another story of a Jewish convert, in *Novoe vremia*. Like the earlier story, this one, which describes the two days the narrator spends at a monastery in Sviatye Gory, engages and unsettles one of the negative Jewish literary types that Suvorin circulated. The narrator shares his room with Aleksandr Ivanych, a recent convert from Judaism and a touching, pathetic young man who tells the narrator his life story. The story consists of descriptions of the monastery, crowded with pilgrims for the festivals of John the Evangelist and Nikolai the Miracle Worker (May 8 and 9); the narrator's conversation with his roommate; and the former's thoughts. It concludes when the narrator gives the convert a pair of shoes before continuing on his journey. The tale was based on Chekhov's visit to the monastery in May 1887, when he returned to the south and to his home town, Taganrog, in order to prepare to write "The Steppe," and contains many of the same details as a letter to his family from that time.[64] Other aspects of the story, including the gift of shoes, are confirmed by the memoirs of A. Surat, who claimed to be the convert Chekhov met.[65]

The story's narrator, revealing the same concerns as Leskov, tries to discover why his companion converted to Russian Orthodoxy, but concedes, "No matter how pushy and clever I was, the reasons remained impenetrable to me (p. 261)."[66] The narrator considers the possibility that, like Judas, Aleksandr Ivanych is a false convert whose seeming change in faith is based on an urge for gain. However, he insists that the convert could not have made his decision for practical reasons: "it was equally impossible to presume that he had changed his faith for material gain: his cheap, worn clothing, subsistence on the monastery's bread, and unclear future bore little resemblance to material gain" (p. 261). It is possible that the narrator's refusal to believe in conversion for material gain is intended to demonstrate his naïveté.[67] The words of a reviewer for *Novoe vremia* exemplify this view: he states that Chekhov's story is realistic because the "young Jewboy [*evreichik*] with equal ease changes his residence, occupation, and religion."[68] In this reading, regardless of the narrator's denials, the story conforms to the Judas mastertext: the convert's inconstancy makes him exemplify the assimilated Jew who is willing to adapt to any new culture, and his conversion stems from a tendency toward betrayal, a flightiness fundamental to Jews.

Contemporaneous critics who were better disposed than Suvorin toward Jews also set Chekhov's story in the Judas tradition, agreeing that the Jew converted in order to improve his standard of living. Observing that the real person Surat, after converting to Orthodoxy, was in fact able to attain a post as a schoolteacher, T. Ardov insists that Surat converted precisely—and realistically—for "material gain," and explains that Surat's unwillingness clearly to communicate the reasons for his conversion to Chekhov resulted from his embarrassment: "Such a naked, selfish explanation would have been terribly awkward, violently rude. . . . So he told Chekhov a 'yarn' [*brekhal*], as he said in his southern way."[69] Chekhov's inability to grasp the reason for the conversion resulted, Ardov argues, not from naïveté but from the "pure" artistry that motivated his story and made him incapable of introducing crass reality into it.[70] The poet Semyon Frug, writing in the Jewish journal *Voskhod*, seconds Ardov, asserting that Chekhov could not understand the material gain that will result from the young man's conversion because he did not comprehend the severity of the situation that the convert is fleeing, that is, the poverty of the Jews in the Pale of Settlement. Chekhov did not grasp the vast improvement represented by the prospect of life as a country schoolteacher.[71]

The details of the narrator's discussion about religion with the convert support the critics' turn to the Judas prototype and reveal the convert's lack of originality or, apparently, sincerity. When the narrator tries to convince the convert to explain what led him to Christianity, he answers with set phrases [*shablony*]. The convert even tells his own biography in hackneyed terms: "'From my earliest childhood I felt a love for learning,' he began in such a tone that it seemed he was speaking not about himself, but about some great man who had died" (p. 257). His description of his decision to convert seems lifted from a religious tract:

> In my opinion, only one religion is possible for the thinking person, and that is Christianity. If you don't believe in Christ, then there isn't anything else to believe in. . . . Isn't that so? Judaism has outlived itself and survives only due to the peculiarities of the Jewish tribe. Once civilization touches the Jews, then no trace of Judaism will remain. You notice that all the young Jews are already atheists. The New Testament is the natural continuation of the Old. Isn't that so? (p. 257)

This speech is a pastiche of arguments used by missionaries from the Christian churches to the Jews.[72] The speaker's choppy style, the short sentences lacking transitions, and his interpolated requests for confirmation ("Isn't that so?") make him appear to be repeating a lesson learned by rote. The narrator is frustrated by his inability to get past these commonplaces: "I began to probe into the reasons that had led him toward a step as serious and bold as religious conversion, but he kept stating the same thing, that 'The New Testament is the natural continuation of the Old,' clearly someone else's sentence, which he had memorized and which did not answer the question at all" (p. 261). What frustrates the narrator is the convert's lack of conviction. No matter how hard he tries, the narrator cannot discover any feeling motivating the convert's ritual repetition of rationales.

The narrator's refusal to accept this well-rehearsed conversion narrative as authentic reveals the similarities in Chekhov's and Leskov's tales about converts, in that both writers inquired first of all into the new Christian's sincerity. In addition, Chekhov's story indicates the distance separating the religious worldview of intellectuals like himself from that endorsed by the Orthodox Church. Although he is frequently portrayed as a relatively anticlerical modern who turned his back on his authoritarian father's piety, Chekhov, like Tolstoy and Leskov, may have rejected not Christianity as a whole but only the potential hypocrisy in current Orthodox practice.[73] This attitude could lie behind his insistence that only an original narrative could tell of a genuine conversion. In fact, converts to Orthodoxy were not encouraged to develop original approaches to their faith. Instead, they were expected to be able to produce a doctrinally acceptable account of their behavior. They knew that Church representatives might check up on them, and therefore they had their narratives prepared. Indeed, Chekhov's real-life roommate at the monastery probably suspected that the writer was precisely such a spy and for that reason inquired into the motivations behind his conversion.[74] In any event, Chekhov's narrator's desire to hear a "sincere" conversion story indicates the similarity of Chekhov's and Leskov's literary approaches to Jewish acculturation. While Leskov uses Jewish converts to illustrate both sincere and insincere Christians, Chekhov appears to be interested in only half the picture. His "tumbleweed" convert, like Leskov's substitute recruit, chooses baptism without any real religious conviction.

Even though many points link Chekhov's Aleksandr Ivanych to the archetypal false convert, this character differs from the model in significant ways, as the narrator's skepticism suggests. Having eliminated a true change in faith or a desire for material gain as reasons, the narrator decides that the conversion resulted from a lack of conviction, a helpless urge to wander. Aleksandr Ivanych journeys from the province of Mogilev (one of the western provinces, today in Belarus) to Smolensk, Shklov, Starodub, Gomel', Kiev, Belaia Tserkov', Uman', Balta, Bendery, Odessa, and eventually the monastery at Sviatye Gory; he attempts to enter a technical institute, a veterinary school, and then a mining institute; he wants to be a doctor, a foreman miner, and finally a schoolteacher. This wandering shows that he cannot settle on a single residence, educational institution, or career: "There remained only to accept the thought that my roommate had been inspired to change his religion by that very same restless spirit that tossed him like a chip of wood from one city to another and which, using the common banality, he termed a striving for education" (p. 261).

What distinguishes "The Tumbleweed" from other depictions of Jewish converts is the extension of the convert's mutability beyond Jewishness. Marx and others saw Jews as imposing their own inconstancy on others by supporting an economic system in which goods and values were interchangeable; and Suvorin also blamed Jews for threatening Russians through their inconstancy. Chekhov, though, depicts a spread of mutability that is not the Jews' fault: rather than infecting non-Jews with inconstancy, the convert, and Jews in general, simply display a mutability that affects other groups in the Russian Empire. In the narrator's descriptions of the monastery and its visitors, many things and people are in flux, often disturbingly or unhappily so. The first paragraph compares the yard at the monastery in the evening to "a living kasha, full of movement, sounds, and the most original disorder." The dim light and the constant motion make things seem to change shape: "all of this in the thick twilight took on the most queer, whimsical forms: now the raised wagon shafts reached to the heavens, now fiery eyes appeared on the horse's head, now the novice grew black wings" (p. 253). Forms of the word "motion" [*dvizhenie, dvizhushchiesia*] appear three times in the first two pages.

The narrator understands his roommate as an example of a larger phenomenon that affects many, both inside and outside of the monastery:

No farther than a yard [*arshin*] from me lay the wanderer. Beyond the walls, in the rooms and the yard, by the wagons, among the worshipers, more than a hundred of the same kind of wanderers waited for the morning. Yet farther, if one could imagine the whole Russian land, what a multitude of the same kind of tumbleweeds [*perekati-pole*], seeking a better place, were walking the highways and byways or, waiting for sunrise, drowsing in coaching inns, taverns, hotels, on the grass under the sky. . . . Falling asleep, I imagined how all these people would be astonished and, perhaps, even overjoyed if they could find a logic and a language that could show them that their life is as little in need of justification as any other. (p. 263)

This passage transfers the inconstancy of the convert to people in general and inhabitants of the "Russian land [*russkaia zemlia*]" in specific. The phrase widens the scope of the description. The convert, as Chekhov's readers would have realized from the list of cities he names, confined his wanderings to places within the Pale of Settlement (except Smolensk). By associating "walking the highways and byways" with the whole terrain of the empire rather than confining it to the region where the Jews lived, the narrator suggests that the convert represents the empire's non-Jews as well as its Jews.

For Chekhov's readers, the wanderer [*skitalets*] in this passage might recall an episode of literary politics that had occurred seven years earlier. In 1880, Dostoevsky gave an acclaimed and tremendously influential speech defining Aleksandr Pushkin as a kind of Russian prophet, the bearer of a "powerful, profound, purely Russian idea." This idea, he said, finds expression in the "type" of Aleko, the hero of the long poem *Tsygane* [The Gypsies]:

[Aleko is] an unhappy wanderer [*skitalets*] in his native land, that age-old Russian sufferer, whose appearance in our society, cut off from the people [*narod*], was so historically inevitable. . . . That type is true and is captured correctly. . . . These homeless Russian wanderers [*skital'tsy*] continue their wanderings to this day and it seems that they will not disappear for a long time.[75]

By using the same word as Dostoevsky did to describe a class of restless, dissatisfied wanderers, who have left the place and the people who once defined them, Chekhov identifies his Jewish convert as a Russian "type"—which Dostoevsky associated with the "type" of the alienated Russian intellectual—accentuating the relationship between the "tumbleweed" and the non-Jews who surround him.

Another passage, echoing Dostoevsky's concerns, relates the convert's constant traveling and his dissatisfaction to the disappearance of a connection between location and identity. The narrator describes the visitors to the monastery by explaining where they came from: "Ukrainians from the nearby districts . . . Greek farmers from Mariupol', strong, steady, and gentle people . . . people from the Don river, with red trouser-stripes [identifying them as Cossacks], and Tauridians, who had left the Tauride province." In this picture, geographical origin conditions ethnic origin, and both together create identity, including dress, body type, and even character. Once the narrator knows where people are from and what their ethnicity is, he can "place" them and, he suggests, they can "place" themselves, which seemingly makes them happier than the convert. Ironically, Surat mentions in his memoirs that it was precisely the lack of an official identity that forced him to seek refuge in the monastery. Having recently converted to Christianity, he had given up his Jewish passport, but had not yet acquired a new one. Passportless, he feared the police.[76]

Alhough he may be the only one literally missing identification documentation, the convert, as the narrator points out, is not the only person in the story in an uncertain situation: "There were many worshipers here of an undefinable type, like my Aleksandr Ivanych. What kind of people they were and from where could not be understood from their faces, clothing, or speech" (p. 264). The narrator might be hinting that all these "undefinable" people were, like Aleksandr Ivanych, Jewish converts. However, it is more likely that they were simply people of mixed origins, rather like Chekhov himself, who, coming as he did by 1887 from both Taganrog and Moscow, probably could not be easily "placed." Indeed, Chekhov hints at a deeper similarity between the narrator and the convert at the end of the story, when the former gives the latter his boots. In this setting, where clothing and body type are clues to identity, the transferal of footwear contradicts expectations by showing that the two men can have not only the same shoes but also the same shoe size. The incident indicates that the disintegration of traditional identities affects both Jew and Russian.

The religious emptiness of the "tumbleweed's" baptism adds irony to his favorite phrase, "The New Testament is the natural continuation of the Old." The statement implies a teleology in which the outdated is punctually replaced by the modern and everything proceeds "naturally" forward. The convert himself, however, belies this logic. The narrator reiterates that his roommate seems unnaturally childish; he has "a round face, a sweet look, and dark childish eyes" (p. 255), "childish, affectionate eyes" (p. 256). Like a child, he is "excessively open" (p. 260), fears the dark (p. 262), and calls his parents "Mommy" and "Daddy" [*mamasha, papasha*] (p. 260). In the final scene, the narrator observes that the convert, "like a child" (p. 266), is enchanted with the new boots, and our final view of the roommate is of his "childish eyes" (p. 267). One of the few seemingly sincere moments in Aleksandr Ivanych's narration of his own life is a childish one. Distantly echoing the Haskalah literary tradition, he details his yearning for access to Western culture, his family's poverty, his parents' lack of sympathy for his dreams, and the tedium of traditional Jewish schooling. The one unpredictable moment occurs after he, like the heroes of so many narratives of assimilation, finds a scrap of paper with words in an unknown alphabet. Solomon Maimon had seized a similar moment to teach himself the Latin letters (from letters he found marking the signatures in Hebrew books), so as to struggle through secular books on his own. Chekhov's convert is less enterprising: "Once, when I found a Russian newspaper and brought it home to make a kite, I was beaten for it, although I couldn't read Russian" (p. 258). This admission accentuates the convert's immaturity and the insincerity of his earlier statements about his thirst for knowledge. Unlike Bogrov's hero, who sneaks Russian books into the house in order to read them on the sly, Chekhov's convert is only interested in childish games.

Rather than progressing "naturally" from one stage to the next, the convert suffers from retarded development, a condition that prefigures that of characters in the author's later works. A pessimistic reading of him and other characters in Chekhov who desire change but cannot enact it would see the author as a cynic who believes that no change is possible, that humans can only feebly protest against their circumstances by yearning, like the heroines of *The Three Sisters*, for Moscows they will never reach. This is the view that Leon Shestov takes, condemning Chekhov as the "poet of human hopelessness" who "expressed disgust for every kind of conception and idea."[77] However, one might instead see the theme of expressed but unrealized desire in the same light as Chekhov's theology. Just as, it would seem, Chekhov opposed not religion per se but the meaningless religion manifested in the repetition of set formulas, so he mocked not so much people's urge to change their lives as their restricting their aspirations to empty phrases.

The stagnancy of the convert's life marks the difference between Chekhov's story and the Judas tale. Chekhov's convert has no goal or purpose in life; he affects no one else; he is no one's oppressor and no one's victim. Instead, he is simply inconstant; he changes his place of residence and his legal identity, the narrator realizes, for no particular reason—and so do many other people in Russia. In thus describing his convert, Chekhov refuses to accept Suvorin's adaptation of the Judas image to assimilated Jews in Russia. Ultimately, the narrator's concern with the motivation for the Jew's conversion functions only as a distraction from the real focus of story, which is the inconstancy that affects both Jews and non-Jews.

Ivanov

Like "The Mire" and "The Tumbleweed," *Ivanov* describes a relationship between a Russian and a Jewish convert. Another way this play is similar to "The Mire" is that it evokes the narrative tradition associated with *The Merchant of Venice. Ivanov* opens on the estate of Nikolai Alekseevich Ivanov, an impoverished landowner, and his wife, Anna Petrovna, a Jewish convert formerly named Sarah Abramson. When Anna and Ivanov were married five years earlier, she had been required to convert to Russian Orthodoxy. As a result, she and her parents, like Jessica and Shylock, have severed their relationship with each other. At the start of the play, the viewer learns that Ivanov has fallen out of love with Anna and out of sorts in general. Anna, who has tuberculosis, is upset that Ivanov leaves her every evening to visit their neighbors, the Lebedevs, who have an attractive twenty-year-old daughter, Sasha. In the second act, she follows Ivanov to the Lebedevs' and surprises him kissing Sasha, who is in love with him. The local doctor, L'vov, constantly reminds Ivanov of his dishonorable behavior and blames him for Anna's poor health. By the end of the third act, Anna's imprecations, added to L'vov's, drive Ivanov to lash out at her, calling her a "Yid" [*zhidovka*] and telling her the secret that L'vov had kept from her: Anna will die soon. The fourth act begins a year later, after Anna's death, on the day when Ivanov and Sasha plan to marry. After failing to convince Sasha that the marriage should be called off, Ivanov shoots himself.

Chekhov wrote the play first in 1887 and edited it substantially after a disappointing run in Moscow, the second version premiering at the Aleksandrinsky Theater in St. Petersburg in 1889. (I consider both texts, but unless noted otherwise, references are to the 1889 play.) Chekhov's biographers agree that the play might be read as a conciliatory message directed toward Dunya Efros or toward Russian Jews in general.[78] Indeed, while literary prototypes associated with prostitutes and Jews emerge in the play as well as in the stories, they have evolved in this play well beyond the predictable distinctions between the Jew and the prostitute as oppressor and the Jew and the prostitute as victim. The story of Susanna Moiseevna goes some distance toward challenging this dichotomy, and that of the convert at the monastery goes further. Anna's role in the play undermines it completely. The obsolescence of traditional epistemologies is reflected in the characters' statements about honor and truth: if identity is mutable, then truth becomes harder to grasp.

Late-nineteenth-century Russian viewers struggled to locate moral lessons in *Ivanov*. Raised on Aleksandr Ostrovsky's denunciatory melodramas, they expected actors to demonstrate the folly of pride, greed, despotism, or hypocrisy. Imperial censorship, which applied stricter standards to plays than to prose, seemingly agreed that drama is inherently didactic and assumed that lessons proclaimed from the stage and to a collective audience would have greater effect than those in published texts. Perhaps the difference results from the less mediated quality of a staged performance. Nothing stands between an Ostrovsky play and the audience—not a narrator who takes over the viewer's obligation to interpret, nor a printed text that must be deciphered in real time, nor the obligation to transform written descriptions into mental pictures. The medium's directness can give viewers a sense of shared experience and even shared responsibility.

Chekhov is famous for having challenged theatrical tradition, inaugurating a new age of experimentation. *Ivanov* is frequently seen as a transitional piece, part way between the realism of Ostrovsky and the modernism of *The Seagull*. As Chekhov wrote about *Ivanov*, he did not give in to stage convention requiring easily identifiable types and clear distinctions between heroes and villains:

> Modern playwrights stuff their plays exclusively with angels, scoundrels, and jesters—but just try to find such characters in all of Russia! You will find them, but not in the extreme forms that playwrights need. . . . I wanted to be original: I didn't include a single scoundrel or a single angel (although I couldn't resist the jesters), I didn't blame anyone, and I didn't excuse anyone.[79]

Chekhov's critics and his friends reacted to his originality by seeking out the play's "real" hero. Many wanted to see it as a political statement about the intelligentsia's attitude toward the Jewish question. Writers for liberal journals attacked Ivanov and defended Anna or Jewish wives in general, whom one called "natural idealists."[80] Some said they were following Chekhov, who had intended to make Ivanov a despicable figure and thus mock his midlife conservatism. Others criticized what they saw as Chekhov's positive portrayal of the title character and his hostility to the Jewish wife.

The conservative Suvorin, in his reaction to the play, paused at Ivanov's rueful statement to L'vov that one should not marry "Jews, psychopaths, or bluestockings" (act 1, scene 5). In Suvorin's words, "every viewer will find a part of himself" in Ivanov, and every viewer should, he implies, agree that it is wiser to "live simply, like everyone else."[81] The recommendation that idealistic Russians avoid relationships with Jewish converts is consistent with Suvorin's politics. Indeed, writers for *Novoe vremia* had argued that marriages between converted Jews and Russians were dangerous for the Russians.[82] By taking Ivanov's suggestions to L'vov as Chekhov's advice to the audience, Suvorin assumed that the writer agreed with his belief that the title character, like any Russian involved with a Jewish convert, if not an angel, then at least deserved excusing.

One viewer who liked the play pointed out precisely its lack of coherence, the fact that it could not offer a clear message, political or otherwise. The Symbolist poet Andrei Bely admired the 1904 production at the Moscow Art Theater for conveying "the fantastic nightmare of life. . . . The whole play caught fire here with the light of other realities, and we saw that all these gray people, neurasthenics, alcoholics, misers, are the wondrous handiworks of dream."[83] Like Gogol's *Inspector General* and *Dead Souls*, both of which it refers to, *Ivanov* can be seen as a comedy that is more absurd than educational, where the oddity of the characters is so exaggerated that it compels the viewer more than any moral could.[84] Rather then depicting a world like Ostrovsky's, in which evil and good are easily recognizable as such, unhappy situations are caused by the bad actions of bad people, and the viewer as well as the characters can imagine a solution, Chekhov indicates that no one may be to blame. Both suffering and guilt are diffused among all the characters. The many references to card games—some characters say practically nothing except the names of cards—suggest the randomness of fate. Ivanov is stuck, as Bely perceived, in a "fantastic nightmare," which drama can do nothing to organize.

Ivanov's inability to solve his problems mirrors the crisis of the student in "A Nervous Breakdown" who is so tormented by his visit to a brothel that he collapses emotionally and ends up in a psychiatrist's office. Indeed, a reviewer noted the tie between Vasil'ev's case and Ivanov's, stating that both men break down when they confront the untreatable illnesses of society.[85] The parallel between these two characters suggests that prostitution and the debates associated with it in Chekhov's time provide an analogy for the situation in the play. Other references in the play also evoke the exchange of sex for money. The Lebedevs, their guests, L'vov, and ultimately Anna herself come to believe that Ivanov married her for her dowry and was disappointed when her parents, following her conversion, disinherited her. After Anna's death, Sasha's mother and others accuse Ivanov of planning his marriage with Sasha in order to acquire her dowry and avoid repaying the nine thousand rubles he owes her family. Meanwhile, in an absurd doubling of this plot, Borkin, Ivanov's knavish manager, tries to arrange a marriage between Ivanov's uncle Shabel'sky and a wealthy widow, Marfa Babakina. It is clear that Shabel'sky, if he is interested at all, wants only her money, while she is attracted only by his aristocratic title. The connection of sex and money in *Ivanov*, as well as the relationship between a Russian man and a female Jewish convert, recalls the illicit sexuality explored in "The Mire." The exact amount of money that Sokol'sky and Kriukov end up paying Susanna for sex, twenty-three hundred rubles, is a leitmotif in *Ivanov*: Borkin periodically tries to borrow this sum from Ivanov and other characters (2.2 and 2.12).

A superficial reading of the play, then, would place it in the genre that casts both Jew and prostitute as victim.[86] However, such an analysis would be as limited as one insisting that Susanna Moiseevna in "The Mire" is only and entirely a victimizer. While "The Mire" questions the literary tradition portraying prostitutes as opportunists, *Ivanov* subverts depictions of prostitutes as victims. Anna, like the stereotypical heroine of such a story, fell in love with Ivanov once and forever, which she demonstrated by her willingness to give up everything—wealth, family, and religion—in order to be with him. Now that he has ceased to love her, Anna, like the women in the brothel Kuprin describes, can never go home again. Ivanov indulges in self-accusatory outbursts, insisting that she is his victim. However, Chekhov's unwillingness to write a play with traditional villains and heroes makes it impossible for the reader to agree with Ivanov's assessment of himself. Unlike Kuprin's evil Gorizont, he did not marry with the intent of selling his wife.

Chekhov signals his rejection of the paradigm of the Jew as victim or victimizer by assigning different stereotypically Jewish traits to various characters in the play. When Jews are portrayed as oppressors, they are assigned certain stereotypical features: accented speech, miserliness, hypocrisy, and an obsession with shady moneymaking schemes (often described with a Russian Yiddishism, *geshefty*). Susanna appears to fit this model, with her guttural *r*, her refusal to return the money she owes, and the difference between her pronouncements and her behavior; Anna, in contrast, differs from the people around her precisely in her lack of these features. Shabel'sky affects a Jewish accent several times (*zhvinite, pozhalusta* ["excuse me, please," with hushing sounds in place of sibilants]) (1.4; 1.7) to tease Anna, but she speaks with an accent only when she decides to tease him back by repeating his words (1.7). The classic description of a prostitute as an opportunist who sees sex as a means of making money fits a number of the figures in *Ivanov*, but unlike Zinaida Lebedeva, who resents the dowry she will have to give at her daughter's marriage, Anna is not interested in money—as she demonstrates when she relinquishes her inheritance to marry a non-Jew. Not only are many of the characters more hypocritical than Anna, but Borkin is equated with the prototypical Jewish hypocrite when Lebedev asks Ivanov, "Why don't you throw this Judas out?" (he asks this twice in 2.5). Borkin, constantly brimming over with *geshefty*, plans to make money in many underhanded ways—poisoning livestock in order to collect the insurance or threatening to build a dam in order to extort payments from downstream neighbors—and frequently asks for loans to finance his schemes. All the stereotypically negative "Jewish" characteristics, rather than adhering to the one Jew in the play, are diffused throughout the characters.

When contrasted to Ostrovsky's orderly world, this moral wilderness might well appear as unpredictable as a nightmare—but Chekhov's medical model, in which any kind of person can transmit or receive contagion, corresponds to his new dramatic form, in which all characters have the potential to be equally "Jewish," equally mercenary in their attitude toward sex, equally to blame, and equally victimized. By diffusing the indications of villainy throughout the cast, Chekhov accomplishes the goal he stated to his brother: to prevent the audience from identifying individuals as scoundrels or angels, simply guilty or simply innocent.

In the dreamlike world of Chekhov's play, stock dramatic characters are not the only elements to mutate strangely. By rejecting Ostrovsky's dramatic formula, in which the presentation of a problem leads toward the audience's realization of its solution, Chekhov casts doubt on the notion that art should inculcate useful moral lessons or that one person could inspire others. The efforts of the humorless doctor L'vov to teach others are particularly ineffective: he refers so frequently to his own honor that Anna mocks him, pointing out that unlike him, her husband never says, "I am honorable! I am suffocating in this atmosphere!" (2.10). Sasha agrees that L'vov's persistent references to his honor are ridiculous: "He can't ask for water or smoke a cigarette without demonstrating his unusual sense of honor" (2.5). By the end, when L'vov's constant imprecations have driven Ivanov to despair, Sasha delivers a speech decrying the doctor's self-righteous persecution in the name of a meaningless notion of honor:

> What can you say? That you're an honorable person? The whole world knows that! . . . You came here as a honorable person and insulted him terribly. . . . you were certain . . . that you are an honorable person. You . . . slandered and judged him . . . sent me anonymous letters, and the whole time thought that you were an honorable person. Believing that it was honorable, you, a doctor, did not even take pity on his sick wife. . . . No matter what cruel mean trick [*podlost'*] you play, you think that you are an unusually honorable and progressive person!" (4.11)

By reiterating the word "honorable" [*chestno* and *chestnyi*] five times, Sasha is making fun of it, orally enacting its loss of meaning. Influenced by the mocking rhythm of Sasha's final speech, the viewer finds it easy to agree that this kind of honor has no real value.

In depicting the inadequacy of L'vov's sense of honor, Chekhov, like Bogrov, located his work in relation to the Russian Romantic tradition, contrasting outdated, aristocratic, Romantic values to the honesty represented in a clear-eyed description of the real world, poverty, dirt, vice, and all. In his letter to Kiseleva about "The Mire," the writer appealed to this appreciation of plainspeak: "We call literature an art because it shows us life as it actually is. Its goal is unconditional and honorable truth. . . . A writer is not a candy-maker, a beautician, or an entertainer: he is a person under an obligation, under contract to his duty and his conscience."[87] This frequently quoted passage enshrines truth and truth telling as the function of real literature. It defines "The Mire" as a good story, worth the reader's time, not because is it elegant or provocative, but because it is in some way true. In *Ivanov*, though, Chekhov casts doubt on this facile idealization of truth in art. The characters' uncertainty about what truth is and whether or not it should be told indicates that all is not as simple as the letter to Kiseleva pretends.

The scene at the end of the third act features a number of truths. After Anna had surprised Ivanov and Sasha kissing, Ivanov does not visit the Lebedevs for two weeks. Sasha, concerned about him, comes to his estate, and L'vov tells Anna that he saw her enter. The scene begins when Anna comes to Ivanov and asks him why Sasha had been there. He refuses to answer, saying, "I am deeply guilty. . . . don't ask. I don't have the strength to talk" (3.9). She then repeats the accusations that other characters have voiced throughout the play—that he is a liar who married her only for her money, and now he plans to marry Sasha soon for the same reason. He tells her that he never lied and asks her to be quiet, because he fears that he will offend her. When she continues, he says, "Shut up, you Yid!" [*Zamolchi, zhidovka!*], but she refuses to be silent. Then he says, "The doctor told me that you will die soon," at which point she sits down and asks quietly, "When did he say that?" Ivanov's response is to sob, moaning, "God, how guilty I am!"

The original audience found this scene fascinating and powerful. Modest Tchaikovsky (the composer's brother) wrote to Chekhov of his impressions: "[The actress Strepetova] pronounced the sentence, "When, when did he say that?" clearly and with a moan that, it seemed, would make anything except a stone cry. I was touched to the depths of my soul. The whole hall began to call out for you in a single voice. . . . In the foyer there were terrible arguments, rumors, and shouting."[88] Other viewers and critics, writing for both right-wing and left-wing publications, agreed with this evaluation of the scene and the audience's response.[89] The actress Pelagaia Strepetova (Figure 5), who was famous for her depictions of strong emotion on the stage (her best role was Katerina, the suicidal heroine of Ostrovsky's *The Storm* [Groza]), was a natural choice for the role of Anna. Years after her performance, watching another actress play the part, Suvorin's wife told Chekhov that she could not measure up to Strepetova because she could not inspire the same emotion in the audience: viewers felt pity for Strepetova's Anna, she said, not only when Ivanov insulted her, but even "when she sat on the steps near the house and listened to the siskin singing in the coachhouse."[90] (Ironically, even though Strepetova so successfully aroused the compassion of the audience for her assimilated Jewish character, the actress herself was not very sympathetic to assimilated Jews; she later argued for limitations on the number of Jewish actors permitted to perform in Russian theaters.)[91]

FIGURE 5. Il'ia Repin, portrait of P. A. Strepetova, 1882. Reproduced from *Il'ia Repin*, ed. Grigorii Sternin and Elena Kirillina (St. Petersburg: Avrora, 1996), p. 51.

The power of the famous scene, at any rate, resulted not only from Strepetova's ability to convey her shock and her pathos but also from the simultaneous rupture of two taboos. In Chekhov's Russia, liberal intellectuals like Ivanov avoided the terms *zhid* and *zhidovka* [Yid], especially when in the company of Jews, preferring the less marked word *evrei* [Jew].[92] Furthermore, there was a medical consensus that while doctors could tell the relatives of their patients that an illness would be fatal, the patients themselves should not be informed.[93] In this one speech, Ivanov broke these two rules and provoked the "arguments, rumors, and shouting" that Tchaikovsky witnessed. One might analyze the effect of this scene in light of the letter to Kiseleva, seeing it as an indication of Chekhov's dedication to an art that forces him to tell the truth, regardless of convention.

However, one might instead more closely examine the "truths" that Ivanov reveals. The characterization of Jews and the Jewish religion as having outlived their time and as condemned by history to extinction was a commonplace of both Christian apologetics and Romantic historiography since Hegel. The Russian Judeophobes of the 1880s could see Ivanov's outburst as containing two welcome truths: that Anna, regardless of her conversion and assimilation, remained a "Yid," a representative of a people hostile to Russians, and that she, like the "Yids" as a whole, would soon die. It may be for that reason that reviewers for the two farthest right-wing newspapers, *Novoe vremia* and *Grazhdanin*, were among those who praised that scene, and that a reviewer at one left-wing journal hinted angrily that the play's success in St. Petersburg in 1889 was the result of their support.[94]

But the right-wing reading of the scene and of the play as a whole cannot encompass all the possible meanings. Just as the belief that the Jews would soon die out was accompanied in late-nineteenth-century Judeophobic rhetoric by its opposite—the assertion that the Jews were increasing at a dangerous rate—so other elements in the play belie Ivanov's statements to Anna. As we saw, "Jewish" features characterize other figures rather than Anna herself; in addition, other characters, especially Ivanov himself, are also condemned to die, his abrupt death (caused by a heart attack in the 1887 version and by suicide in the 1889 one) at the end of the fourth act paralleling the discussion of Anna's death at the end of the third. Since she dies offstage during the year that separates the last two acts, her death seems as inevitable a conclusion to the third act as his is to the fourth: she seems to die as soon as she finds out that her illness is fatal.

Chekhov's biography also indicates that he would not have associated death from tuberculosis with Jews alone. By the late 1880s, his brother Nikolai and his brother Aleksandr's first wife, as well as other friends and acquaintances, had died of it. The writer knew that he too was dying of the disease. Although nineteenth-century science depicted Jews as afflicted by an assortment of illnesses, Chekhov, in a letter to Suvorin, associates disease yet more strongly with the play's Russian title character. "Ivanov" is the prototypical Russian last name, and Chekhov describes his Ivanov as typical of Russian intellectuals: no matter how energetic and idealistic they were in their youth, they begin to feel "exhaustion and boredom" at thirty or thirty-five. Chekhov diagnoses these symptoms as the result of a kind of character flaw: "Disappointment, apathy, nervous instability and exhaustion are the inevitable result of excessive excitability," an excitability, he notes in a post-script, that is a "purely Russian" quality.[95] As the play's title indicates, it is "about" the Russian character and his decline more than the Jewish woman's death. Thus, rather than reading it as the critics from *Novoe vremia* and *Grazhdanin* did and seeing it as a bold statement of the "truth" of the illness of Jews, one could see it as a more hesitant admission of a similar "truth" about the illness of Russians, a truth that becomes evident precisely when Russians are juxtaposed with Jews and seen through their eyes.

The characters' attitudes toward truth telling reveal a range of perspectives on the feasibility of these sorts of pronouncements in literary works. Two fig-ures make programmatic statements about their propensity to tell the truth. L'vov assures Ivanov that he is dedicated to telling the entire truth: "I am used to calling things by their real names" (3.6). His zeal, by his society's standards, comes into conflict with his professional obligations when it leads him to provoke Ivanov into telling Anna of her impending death. Shabel'sky, in con-trast, is proud of his tact: "I never called thieves thieves to their face, and I never mentioned rope in the house of a hanged man. I was educated" (2.4). Meanwhile, Shabel'sky, unlike the other characters, regularly refers to Anna as Sarah and calls her *zhidovka* to her face, neither of which seems to bother her. While Shabel'sky's behavior indicates that he is willing to condition his truth-telling according to the requirements of specific situations and interlocutors, L'vov's presents truth as an invariable value that takes precedence over all oth-ers. When he tells Anna that she will die, Ivanov not only repeats L'vov's words but also reveals the influence of L'vov's attitude toward truth. Just as Ivanov's words seem to lead to Anna's death, so L'vov's words, uttered in a similar spirit, provoke Ivanov's suicide in the next act. The parallel suggests the similarity between Ivanov and L'vov, both of whom can tell truths, but neither of whom can thereby solve problems. The sequence of events demon-strates that L'vov's conviction that one should "call things by their real names" and tell the truth at every possible moment can have fatal consequences.

Other aspects of the play question the very concept of "truth." As Che-khov indicated in his letter to his brother, he had no interest in writing a work in which moral lessons would be as unquestionable as in the dramas of Ostrovsky. Not only his revolutionary dramatic form but also his manipulations of literary types suggest the obsolescence of old "truths." Chekhov challenged representational patterns by creating a society in which every member partakes to some degree of the stereotypes associated with two marginal groups, Jews and prostitutes. The disappearance of "truth" as a value parallels the disappearance of consistent identities, which, whether in response to the marketplace or not, are no longer so distinct. Chekhov's hesitation to identify a single character with the negative images associated with Jews and prostitutes reveals the distance separating *Ivanov* from "The Mire." Whereas in the earlier work he, at least at first glance, created a Jewish character that conformed to the clichés of *Novoe vremia*, and he then justified his choices by evoking a writer's "obligation" to "life as it actually is," by the later one he had seemingly come to doubt both Suvorin's conservative doctrine and "truth telling" as a humane or even a feasible goal for art.

Truth telling in art is bound up with literary type. For Suvorin, "true" stories about assimilated Jews revealed their hidden hatred of non-Jews, especially Russians; similarly, for Tarnovsky, "true" stories about prostitutes told of the danger they posed to society. Their liberal counterparts told stories that contained the opposite "truth": that both Jews and prostitutes should and will make progress not toward confrontation but toward assimilation and reconciliation with Christians and respectable society. In *Ivanov*, though, none of the characters follow any of these itineraries. The Russians have not been "Judaized" or infected with inconstancy; the mutability of their identities has nothing to do with their contacts with Jews. The deaths of the two main characters at the conclusions of the two final acts reinforce a sense of stasis that is even stronger here than in "The Mire" or "The Tumbleweed." As Bely noticed, this is a new kind of art. Rather than, like Ostrovsky, depicting stable characters, moving through a plot in a way that generates meaning, Chekhov shows mutable characters who, literally and figuratively, are not going anywhere. His theatrical innovation conforms to a refusal to search for solutions to the "Jewish problem."[96]

In the world Chekhov shows in *Ivanov*, Jews and Russians pose no particular danger to each other. Even words such as *zhid* and *zhidovka*, while they may shock some people, are not dangerous. A distinction between the use of the kind of frank ethnic vocabulary that filled Chekhov's letters and other actions emerges as well in Suvorin's son's summary of a letter from Chekhov (the letter itself has never been found). The writer had offered to submit an article explaining his views on the controversy surrounding the choice of the design of a Jewish sculptor, Mark Antokol'sky, for a new statue of Catherine the Great. In the younger Suvorin's words, Chekhov proposed "remembering that the Yid is a Yid and treating him as one would any other Russian citizen [*otnosit'sia k nemu tak zhe, kak i ko vsiakomu drugomu russkomu grazhdaninu*]," a solution that, Suvorin responded, indicated a lack of understanding of "the difficulties of the Jewish question."[97] The term "citizen" [*grazhdanin*], as we remember, signals Chekhov's liberalism, his willingness to imagine a kind of Russian citizenship that would have room for Jews. Suvorin's dismissal of this possibility indicates that he, instead, sees Russian citizenship as identical to Russian national identity, and both as static and predetermined. Unlike Suvorin, Chekhov appears aware of the challenges that ethnic difference poses to unitary national identity and to the narratives that sustain it.

The experience of living in a multinational state, it seems, requires both minority and majority groups to adapt by questioning the narrative traditions they had used to explain their own identities. Russian writers had borrowed English literary types for the story of the Jew, telling of a miserly father and his rebellious daughter; in the second half of the nineteenth century, they adapted this model to the demands of stories about Jewish pimps and prostitutes. One might read Chekhov's works on assimilated Jews as an exemplification of this tradition, as yet more depictions of Jews who are either victimizers or victims of a system in which things such as human bodies and identities are for sale. Chekhov's Soviet critics, who saw the writer's works as lamentations for the precapitalist order of things in the Russian Empire, might agree, although a Marxist explanation of the novelty of Chekhov's works is as reductionist as an entirely biographical explanation. The biographers are undoubtedly correct when they assert that one impetus for Chekhov's Jewish stories was his involvement with Dunya Efros and the money-related anxieties that she produced in him. However, over the four years during which his writings reflected these emotions, the Jewish converts in Chekhov's work took on new meaning, becoming associated with his creation of a new kind of art.

Like other great Realist writers, Chekhov was innovative enough to go beyond familiar archetypes, to use them but at the same time to show their inadequacy. His depictions of Jews dispute not just the stereotypes but the entire notion of literary types, as his generation of Russian writers had inherited it from the radical critics. Pisarev and Chernyshevsky had defined literary types as means of inspiring self-reform by showing the reader the contrast between negative characters who represent the past and positive ones who exemplify the future. More and more from 1886 to 1889, Chekhov presents the self-creation of the Jew as one aspect of just such a self-transformation, undertaken by the Russians with whom the assimilating Jew comes into contact. In a letter to Suvorin, explaining *Ivanov*, Chekhov depicts his hero as an unsuccessful self-reformer: "Barely having arisen from the school bench, a man immediately assumes a burden beyond his strength. . . . he gives speeches, writes to the ministry, fights against evil, applauds good, falls in love not simply and anyhow, but necessarily with bluestockings, or psychopaths, or Yids, or even prostitutes that he saves, and so on and so forth."[98] With this list of activities, Chekhov satirizes idealistic youths who want to become active, to mobilize themselves and struggle for some better future, but who have not put much thought into what that better future could involve. He does not tell Suvorin what people like Ivanov give speeches and write letters about, because, it seems, they themselves do not know. Such people's love life reflects their political efforts: it is earnest and energetic, but it suffers from an excess of ideology and a deficit of content. In this analysis, Ivanov marries Anna not in spite of but because of her Jewishness, because by marrying a Jew (granted, one who had converted to Russian Orthodoxy), he can define himself—to his own satisfaction—as a new kind of person.

Suvorin probably understood Chekhov's explanation to mean that the play displayed the foolishness of the radical ideology of self-reform as well as the project of Jewish assimilation: both appear unrealistic and ill conceived. For him, perhaps, bluestockings, psychopaths, "Yids," and prostitutes belonged logically to the same category, because not only are they not ordinary wives for Russian landowners, but these four sorts of women are linked by their association with the dangerous changes of modernity—an association that accounts for the danger they pose to vulnerable Russian idealists. The play would then suggest that upper-class Russian men like Ivanov should not try to re-create their loves along ideological lines, they should not marry reformed prostitutes, and they should not get involved with Jewish women. This reading, though, would make Chekhov's play more proscriptive than he himself had indicated. While Pisarev had praised literature that featured "knights of the past" and "knights of the future," Chekhov deliberately avoided creating "scoundrels" and "angels." Rather than urging Russian men to avoid Jewish women, perhaps the playwright simply meant to acknowledge the limitations of deliberate self-re-creation, for Russians as well as Jews. It is unlikely that Chekhov truly disagreed with the goals of the idealistic youth he describes in his letter; he certainly worked hard to reform Russian life and to bring about a better future. He criticizes not Ivanov's ideals but only the headlong way he went about achieving them. None of Chekhov's characters, neither Jews nor Russians, are capable of the kind of deliberate and complete self-transformation that the radicals imagined—and Chekhov's portrayals indicate that he had no intention of motivating his own readers to implement such change.

Over the ideal of deliberate change, Chekhov endorsed—in these stories and elsewhere—the ideal of inconstancy, of recognizing and even enjoying two seemingly mutually exclusive conditions or identities at the same time. As Shabel'sky understood, the heroine of *Ivanov* is Sarah in addition to (not instead of) Anna, and Ivanov himself is and is not in love with her. Chekhov's letters admit the same kind of inconstancy—personal and professional—in himself, a quality that, rather than regretting, he embraced, seeing in it a source of pleasure and inspiration. Recall his often-cited line from an 1888 letter: "Medicine is my legal wife, and literature my mistress. When I get sick of the one, I spend the night at the other's. This may be indecent of me, but it's not so boring, and for that matter, clearly neither loses anything from my faithlessness."[99] This passage associates literature with inconstancy and both literature and inconstancy with pleasure: stability not only endangers creative work but prevents it altogether. Faithlessness is no vice but a virtue that benefits everyone involved.

The image of Chekhov himself that has, I hope, emerged in this chapter is an unfamiliar one. Unlike the "good doctor" of so many biographies, this Chekhov is more promiscuous, cold, and anxious to preserve his own freedom. With his elusive refusal to describe life as a set of problems that permit neat solutions and nice divisions between healthy and ill, moral and immoral, victim and victimizer, reformed and unreformed, own and other, he defines both his ethics and his modern aesthetics. I have focused in this study on stories about Jewish acculturation not only in order to learn about what Chekhov and other authors thought of the Jews and the "Jewish question," but also—indeed, primarily—to understand what these works can tell us about the relationship between narrative and changing concepts of national identity. Just as the English turned to *The Merchant of Venice* and other texts about Jews in order to confront questions about Englishness, so Chekhov's use of the archetype of the Jewish usurer reveals some of his answers—or his lack of answers—to questions about Russianness.[100] The first three chapters of this book examined authors who believed in a "Jewish problem" that might admit a solution. Chekhov's presentation of Jews, Russians, and prostitutes indicates not only that moral and medical diseases do not correspond to genetics, but also that neither kind of illness can be described in terms that define a single "solution" as "true." Chekhov's rejection of such solutions implies a denial of the very existence of a "Jewish problem." More than any of his contemporaries, he represents Jewish and non-Jewish identities in the Russian Empire as equally mutable, permutable, approximate, and relative.

CONCLUSION

BOGROV, ORZESZKOWA, Leskov, and Chekhov were born in four different parts of the Russian Empire and represent three ethnicities, religions, and native languages. However, they were linked not only by their common literary interest in Jewish acculturation between 1870 and 1890. In addition, they were all new kinds of writers, whose works would have been much less likely to appear earlier in the nineteenth century. Bogrov was in the vanguard of the acculturated Jews who moved to the Russian capitals and tried to blend with the Russian educated classes; his semiautobiographical book testifies to this aspect of his generation's experience. Orzeszkowa both justified and typified the Positivist female writer, who by her existence as well as her work challenged older, male, Romantic models for Polish patriotism and literary creativity. Both Leskov and Chekhov were *raznochintsy*, self-made men of nonaristocratic class origin, a type that emerged on the Russian social and literary scene in the 1860s. All of these authors matured in two locations, one provincial, the other cosmopolitan. Bogrov wrote of his childhood in Poltava while he lived as a writer and businessman in St. Petersburg; Orzeszkowa preached the ideals of liberal Warsaw society even after she returned to her home near Grodno; Leskov, more than other Petersburg litterateurs, prided himself on the firsthand knowledge of life in the provinces that he had gleaned from his childhood in Orel, his youth in Kiev, and his extensive travels; and the Taganrog from which Chekhov escaped into Moscow resurfaced throughout his writings. For each of these writers, the big city held possibilities that provincial life could not; they each displayed a provincial expertise while remaking themselves in the image of the urban literary establishment. The permutability of the Jewish characters they describe may reflect the demands of the metropolitan modernity in which the authors tried—sometimes painfully—to relocate themselves.

Although these four writers would have been unlikely to meet—especially as equals—in the provinces, they were more likely to do so in the city. With the exception of Leskov and Chekhov, whose friendship is well documented, they apparently did not meet in person—but they did, as we saw, read each other's works: Bogrov reviewed a story in which Leskov drew on descriptions of shtetl life produced in Russian by Bogrov and his fellow maskilim; Orzeszkowa subscribed to a Russian Jewish journal, *Evreiskaia biblioteka*, in which Bogrov frequently published; Chekhov referred to Orzeszkowa's works in his letters; and Leskov cited *Meir Ezofowicz* with admiration.[1]

These writers inhabited a shared intellectual environment, and the same editors and publishers accepted or rejected their works. The 1860s liberals Nekrasov and Shchedrin, who made Bogrov's reputation when they published his autobiography in *Otechestvennye zapiski*, first supported but later attacked Leskov. Rostislav Sementkovsky, a liberal of a later school and one of Leskov's posthumous editors whom we know as the author of *Jews and Yids*, published a collection of Polish fiction in Russian translation that highlighted Orzeszkowa's Jewish stories, and edited some of Chekhov's stories for the journal *Niva*. Leskov and Chekhov had similar relationships with the conservative publisher Suvorin: both appreciated the power of his patronage and were personally attached to him at least for a time, but both increasingly avoided his periodicals in favor of more mainstream outlets, such as Sergei Khudekov's *Peterburgskaia gazeta* and the publishing house of Adolf Marks.[2]

A set of shared political concerns united these authors, their texts, and their publishers. The journals that paid these writers, and their editorial staffs, each spoke for a set of positions on the "Jewish question" that grew out of their perspectives on other debates touching on national and personal identity. Broadly speaking, they were located along a single spectrum of ideas. At one end, liberals portrayed Jews as victims of the regime, decried Judeophobia, and argued for a reformed state, inhabited by reformed individuals, all of whom—peasants, Jews, even women—would be citizens with equal rights.³ At the other end, conservatives supported Judeophobia and other ideologies that could reinforce the estate system and the regime that relied on it. The former camp saw the personal transformation and the social change represented by Jewish acculturation as possible and advisable; the latter group both condemned such metamorphoses in principle and doubted their effectiveness in actual social life.

In historical accounts of the Russian nineteenth century, these positions are often linked to a philosophical controversy between Westernizers who argued for change that would bring Russia closer to European ideals, and Slavophiles who rejected the West and looked instead to peasant cultural models. The facileness of this neat taxonomy reveals its fraudulence: Russian liberal and conservative ideologies, especially when identified with the Westernizer/Slavophile dyad, betray a dependence on the same inconsistent notions of the nation.⁴ Nonetheless, these two poles can usefully be associated with the dichotomy between the conviction that, given the right education, any person can be transformed into material for a better society, and nationalisms that are based on the immutability of blood. These worldviews give rise to conflicting narratives of acculturation, which they present—respectively—as unproblematic and as impossible.

The reality—that the acculturation of Jews was possible, but problematic—forced writers who examined it closely to seek new ways of describing it, creating, in the process, new, hybrid literary types, situated between and beyond existing ones. Bogrov's autobiography shifts between the narrative of education and the adventure story or romance, thereby defining life in a new, less consistent way; Orzeszkowa's novel fits into the Enlightenment tradition and also contains the threads of Romantic nationalism that her translator exploited; Leskov's stories of Jews who redefine themselves through their original readings of sacred text rewrite the acculturation narrative as a parable of literary interpretation; while Bely's vision of Chekhov's staging of a Jew's life among Russians offers the even more modernist metaphor of a dream in which the shape of the story has become entirely unpredictable.

I began this study by contemplating the role of the Jew in definitions of European nationalisms. As the obligatory Other, the indigestibly foreign element, Jews have defined everything that Europeans, at various times and places, have felt that they are not. They have played this role effectively because they have been able to represent two opposites simultaneously: progress and tradition, revolution and capital, West and East, licentiousness and patriarchy. This system relies on the Jew as an empty sign, the single unpredictable and negative factor in an otherwise stable universe.

The world that the authors I have examined portray, however, is neither so simple nor so static. In the texts I read, the identity of the acculturating Jew is not anomalous but rather typical of the population at large. By deliberately taking on the cultural attributes of the Russian or Polish intelligentsia—dress, language, religion, professional aspirations, ideals—Jews could subvert the idea of the innateness of identity, whether religious, national, or personal. The acculturating Jews of the late-nineteenth-century Russian Empire offer a kind of epistemological challenge. That is, the stories of those Jews in the Russian Empire who learned Russian or Polish, acted like non-Jews, and sometimes even changed their own legal status through baptism, question the regnant paradigms of identity, simultaneously questioning the ideology that makes literature an instigator of self-transformation.

Because the Russian Jewish intelligentsia cherished such passion for Pisarev and Chernyshevsky, it is not surprising that they used the vocabulary of the radical critics to tell the story of Jewish acculturation. Bogrov brought that story into Russian literature but included with it a critique of the ideology making the positive literary hero into a means and a model for an effective recreation of the self. Orzeszkowa, Leskov, and Chekhov, in their variations on Bogrov's theme, extend his critique, probing the limitations of the radical notion of the positive type. Primary among those limitations is the impossibility of ensuring that the individual in transit will attain an unquestionably desirable goal and transform into the "right" kind of person. Bogrov's narrator ironically records an attraction to the type of the false assimilator who prefers trashy romances to serious literature; Orzeszkowa more seriously denounces the false patriot; Leskov warns of the spiritual danger of the false convert (whether Jewish or not); and Chekhov depicts the false lover who emerges from an abortive attempt at self-reform. Even while some of these writers treat the archetypal figure of the perfidious Jew with distance and doubt, they recognize it as a powerful counterargument to the optimism of the radicals.

Each of the authors I consider, in the way he or she pushes the limits of narrative prototypes, asks questions about identity; Bogrov, for example, in his "autobiography" wonders whether a Jew can deliberately and self-consciously rewrite his own life story. Are our lives, as Solomon Maimon wanted, subject to our will, guided by our intellect, or are they, as Lermontov feared, governed by forces beyond our control? This is a philosophical question posed by Jews attempting to remake themselves into Russians or Poles; it might also be asked by Russians or Poles debating the reform of their societies—or their personalities—according to borrowed literary models.

Orzeszkowa was troubled by another aspect of the attempt to re-create the self: is there any guarantee that a person who begins to remodel personal and cultural loyalties will not go too far or proceed in the wrong direction? For Maimon, the equation of the "civilization" that attracted the maskilim to Europe in general and to Berlin in particular was uncomplicated and self-evident. For Orzeszkowa, though, Jews who learned Russian instead of Polish, and thus demonstrated that they had chosen the wrong culture as their goal, are false assimilators. She portrays Jews like Eli Witebski as unreliable citizens, far too willing to redefine their loyalties. The image of Witebski brings larger issues of national identity into question: by too easily casting off their traditions, Jews could invoke the specter of the breakdown of other national categories. In Orzeszkowa's worldview, the false assimilator might stand in for the Russifying Poles in the borderlands. Her Russian translator, by reproducing the depiction of the false assimilator while cutting out Orzeszkowa's suggestions that Meir might become a true assimilator, subverts her contention that good citizens can be self-made. The translator's interpretation, like Krestovsky's *Egyptian Darkness*, undermines the Enlightenment belief in the power of civil education. The acculturating Jews in the original and in the translation of *Meir Ezofowicz* complicate the political question of how to create or define a sincerely and perpetually loyal citizen.

Leskov's descriptions of Jewish acculturation are more concerned with religious than political loyalty, though the two concepts were closely connected in a state that made baptism a means to change one's status legally. While Orzeszkowa distinguished between a sincere and an insincere attachment to Polish culture, Leskov, like his New Testament narrative prototypes, differentiated between a sincere and an insincere decision to accept baptism. His insistence on the true convert's ability to read the Bible and understand it independently challenges the legal assumption that the outward sign of a baptismal certificate could signify a real change in faith, for both Jews and Russians. In posing a religious question about the genuineness of Jewish conversion, Leskov suggests that the outward Orthodoxy of many Russians might bear reexamination.

While Leskov subjected the sincerity of Christians to careful examination,

Chekhov, in his portrayals of acculturating Jews, looked at the fidelity of lovers and spouses. Shakespeare's Jessica abandons her miserly Jewish father, Shylock, to cleave to her Christian husband, Lorenzo, but Chekhov's couples are less reliable: neither the Jewish convert Susanna Moiseevna nor the Russian Christian Ivanov proves a faithful lover. These texts ask questions about the sexual loyalties of Jews and non-Jews, and in the process confront larger dilemmas about identity and morality. While late-nineteenth-century Russians associated Jews with prostitutes and pimps, willing to trade anything in the capitalist marketplace, Chekhov shows a world in which everything is for sale; neither Russians nor Jews can be counted on to remain faithful to their lovers, their ideals, or the people they once were.

Like those of Bogrov, Orzeszkowa, and Leskov, Chekhov's tales of Jewish acculturation engage fundamental problems of human identity: How can we define ourselves or others and be sure that our definitions will remain valid? Can—or should—people change? Of course, these questions were asked before the nineteenth century, in places other than the Russian Empire, and they have been asked since. In considering the articulation of these questions in the works of a few writers who described Jewish acculturation and conversion in the Russian Empire between 1870 and 1890, I am not alleging that these concerns were unique to their time and place. However, because of the rise in Jewish acculturation and the tremendous interest in it in the 1870s and 1880s, discussion of this one question could become a way to talk about other matters, philosophical and political, religious and emotional. In engaging various prototypes for tales of Jewish education and conversion, the texts I have read strive to reproduce the experiences of what were seen as unprecedented human beings. No matter how successful they are in that effort, though, these authors cannot resolve the larger questions they address. They cannot say whether our identities are multiple or singular, whether a reformed, rewritten self will always be plagued by the residues of former selves, or whether any of our loyalties will last.

What I have read as the skepticism of late-nineteenth-century Russian literature about the project of Jewish self-reform produced varied repercussions for the generation of Russian Jewish writers and literary critics that came of age in the first decades of the twentieth century. Jabotinsky wrote an essay in

1909 on the "Jewish question" as reflected in Gogol's "Taras Bulba," Pushkin's *Covetous Knight*, Turgenev's "The Yid," a poem by Nekrasov, the novels of Dostoevsky, and an array of works by Chekhov, including "The Mire," "The Tumbleweed," and *Ivanov*. He concluded that Chekhov displayed the same anti-Jewish feelings as his literary predecessors and that Russian artists were consistently unsympathetic to Jews: "never did a single one of the great [Russian] writers raise his voice to defend that truth that was pounded into our backs."[5] According to Jabotinsky, once Russian Jews understand this fundamental hostility, they should be able to turn their back on Russian literature and culture, abandoning the hopeless project of self-reform once and forever. In this essay, Jabotinsky adopts the tone of a person made wiser by experience: although he, like his implied reader, once believed in Russian literature as an infallible moral standard, according to which he might redesign his own life, he now knows better. Jabotinsky chose publically to reject Russian literature and to define his statement as a critical act in the drama of return to the Jewish people and Jewish culture.[6]

Other Russian Jewish writers who did not reject Russian literature also addressed the problem of self-reform. Among them was Isaac Babel. In a short story from the 1920s, "Moi pervyi gonorar" [My First Fee], he speaks in the voice of a young man in Tbilisi who is consumed with passion for a prostitute. When he is finally alone with her, he tells her a touching and entirely fictional tale about his life as a male prostitute. She calls him "my little sister" [*sestrichka moia*] and makes love to him, then refuses his payment: the money she returns becomes his "first fee" as an author.[7] Babel's narrator does not trouble to make his story realistic, knowing that "a well-designed story has no reason to be like real life; life tries as hard as it can to be like a well-designed story."[8] One could read this line as a kind of response to Jabotinsky's scorn for Jews who attempt to rewrite themselves according to Russian literary models. Babel's hero does not regret his inability to take on one literary role and make it "stick"; instead, he cheerfully acknowledges and even celebrates the fluidity of his identity. The narrator delights in his ability to rewrite his own life at will, and the prostitute—along with the reader—delights in hearing his tales.

Against this background, I want to return to Moisei Maimon's account of the artillery general Arnoldi, who agreed to pose for the artist as a Marrano patriarch facing the Inquisition, and only later revealed his own Jewish roots. Maimon told Arnoldi's story in a solemn tone, making it clear that though the general and those like him might dream that Russian society would accept them, they will all eventually be unmasked by Inquisitors of one sort or another. One might instead imagine this man's life in a different light. Perhaps he did not experience his identity as either/or (Russian or Jewish, assimilated or not), but both/and (Russian and Jewish, retired general and Marrano patriarch). Perhaps in agreeing to pose for Maimon's painting, he experienced the same glee as Babel's narrator. Like any storyteller, he may have enjoyed his own ability to switch from one role to another.

REFERENCE MATTER

NOTES

BOOK EPIGRAPH: Isaak Babel', "Moi pervyi gonorar," in *Sochineniia v 2 tomakh* (Moscow: Terra, 1996), vol. 2, p. 280.

INTRODUCTION

1. Moisei Maimon, "Istoriia odnoi kartiny," *Evreiskaia letopis'*, vol. 1 (1923), p. 109. On Maimon and this picture, see [D. Maggid], "Maimon, Moisei L'vovich," *Evreiskaia entsiklopediia* (St. Petersburg: Brokgauz-Efron, c. 1910; facs. ed., Moscow: Terra, 1991), vol. 10, pp. 526–27. The engraving made from the painting is reproduced in the same volume on pp. 657–58. On cantonism, see Michael Stanislawski, *Tsar Nicholas I and the Jews: The Transformation of Jewish Society in Russia, 1825–1855* (Philadelphia: Jewish Publication Society, 1983). Also see Chapter 3 on literary depictions of cantonism.

2. For a summary of these historiographic changes, see Jonathan Frankel, "Assimilation and the Jews in Nineteenth-Century Europe: Towards a New Historiography?" and Eli Lederhendler, "Modernity Without Emancipation or Assimilation? The Case of the Russian Jews," both in *Assimilation and Community: The Jews in Nineteenth-Century Europe*, ed. Jonathan Frankel and Steven Zipperstein (Cambridge: Cambridge University Press, 1992).

3. For a discussion of these words and related ones in Russian and English and their meanings in the imperial period, see John Doyle Klier, *Imperial Russia's Jewish Question, 1855–1881* (Cambridge: Cambridge University Press, 1995), pp. 66–83. For a study of the difference between these concepts in practice, see Steven J. Zipperstein, *The Jews of Odessa: A Cultural History, 1794–1881* (Stanford, Calif.: Stanford University Press, 1986).

4. For a host of similar examples, see Eli Weinerman, "Racism, Racial Prejudice, and Jews in Late Imperial Russia," *Ethnic and Racial Studies*, vol. 17, nos. 3–4 (July–October 1994). For a contemporaneous analysis, see the (untitled and anonymous) lead article in *Nedel'naia khronika Voskhoda*, 1888, no. 42.

5. I am grateful to Ellen Chances for sharing memories of her grandparents, highly educated and acculturated Jews from Odessa, who identified exclusively with Russian high culture. In addition, Vera Bogrova describes her husband and his brothers as Jews of this sort (Memoirs of V. Bogrova, Manuscript Archives, Columbia University Library).

6. Estimates of the Jewish population in Russia have varied wildly over time and are notoriously inaccurate. See John Doyle Klier, *Russia Gathers Her Jews: The Origins of the Jewish Question in Russia, 1772–1825* (Dekalb: Northern Illinois University Press, 1985), p. 19, and [Ia. Shabad], "Naselenie," *Evreiskaia entsiklopediia*, vol. 11, p. 536.

7. S. M. Dubnow, *History of the Jews in Russia and Poland from the Earliest Times Until the Present Day* (New York: Ktav, 1975), p. 285. For more detail on the pogroms, see I. Michael Aronson, *Troubled Waters: The Origins of the 1881 Anti-Jewish Pogroms in Russia* (Pittsburgh, Pa.: University of Pittsburgh Press, 1990). For a discussion of the views of the tsars' officials, see "Russian Ministers and the Jewish Question," in Hans Rogger, *Jewish Policies and Right-Wing Politics in Imperial Russia* (Oxford: Macmillan, 1986).

8. Simon Kuznets, "Immigration of Russian Jews to the United States: Background and Structure," *Perspectives in American History*, vol. 9 (1975).

9. See [I. Cherikover], "Obrashchenie v khristianstvo," *Evreiskaia entsiklopediia*, vol. 11, p. 894, for these statistics and some analysis. For more analysis, see Michael Stanislawski, "Jewish Apostasy in Russia: A Tentative Typology," in *Jewish Apostasy in the Modern World*, ed. Todd Endelman (New York: Holmes and Meier, 1987). Cf. Mikhail Agursky, "Conversions of Jews to Christianity in Russia," *Soviet Jewish Affairs*, vol. 20, nos. 2–3 (Autumn–Winter 1990), and Todd M. Endelman, "Jewish Converts in Nineteenth-Century Warsaw: A Quantitative Analysis," *Jewish Social Studies*, vol. 4, no. 1 (Fall 1997). While historians of Western Jewries have shown that upper-class converted Jews tended to maintain a group identity, socializing and living in close proximity, no such studies have yet been done on converts in Russia. Cf. Marsha L. Rozenblit, *The Jews of Vienna, 1867–1914: Assimilation and Identity* (Albany: State University of New York Press, 1983).

10. By 1900, 20 percent of Jewish children were getting some instruction in Russian, and by 1910, 30 percent (Steven G. Rappaport, *Jewish Education and Jewish Culture in the Russian Empire, 1880–1914*, Ph.D. diss., Stanford University, 2000). For an argument that such acculturation did not necessarily result from "assimilationism," see Steven J. Zipperstein, "'Assimilation,' *Haskalah* and Odessa Jewry," in *The Great Transition: The Recovery of the Lost Centers of Modern Hebrew Literature*, ed. Glenda Abramson and Tudor Parfitt (New Jersey: Rowman and Allenheld, 1985).

11. Savelii Dudakov, *Istoriia odnogo mifa: Ocherki russkoi literatury XIX–XX vv.* (Moscow: Nauka, 1993).

12. S. Ettinger, *Anti-Semitism in the Soviet Union: Its Roots and Consequences* (Jerusalem: The Hebrew University of Jerusalem, 1983), p. v.

13. John D. Klier, "The Concept of 'Jewish Emancipation' in a Russian Context," in *Civil Rights in Imperial Russia*, ed. Olga Crisp and Linda Edmundson (Oxford: Clarendon Press, 1989), pp. 124, 132. Cf. Rogger, *Jewish Policies and Right-Wing Politics*, pp. 26–27.

14. Klier, "The Concept of 'Jewish Emancipation,'" pp. 124–25. For a discussion of the term *pravoslavnyi* in imperial Russia and the development of the concept of *russkii* (Russian) in the Soviet Union, see Gregory Freidin, "Romans into Italians: Russian National Identity in Transition," in *Russian Culture in Transition*, ed. Gregory Freidin (Stanford, Calif.: Stanford Slavic Studies, 1993).

15. Mikhail Chekhov, *Zakony o evreiakh: Spravochnaia knizhka dlia evreev i dlia uchrezhdenii, vedaiushchikh dela o evreiakh* (Yaroslavl: E. G. Fal'k, 1899), pp. 56–57.

16. "Ustav o pasportakh [Regulations on Passports] (1903)," chap. 4, art. 74, note [*primechanie*], *Svod zakonov Rossiiskoi imperii, Izdanie neoffitsial'noe* (St. Petersburg: Russkoe knizhnoe tovarishchestvo Deiatel', 1912), vol. 14, p. 10. Earlier laws cited: 1824 July 29 (30004) and 1833 July 4 (6304), art. 4. Cf. Andrew M. Verner, "What's in a Name? Of Dog-Killers, Jews, and Rasputin," *Slavic Review* (Winter 1994), pp. 1058–61.

17. On the 1903 code, its creators, and its fate, see Laura Engelstein, *The Keys to Happiness: Sex and the Search for Modernity in Fin-de-Siècle Russia* (Ithaca, N.Y.: Cornell University Press, 1992), pp. 22–24.

18. A. N., *Ugolovnoe ulozhenie, Vysochaishe utverzhdennoe 22 marta 1903 g., Izdanie neoffitsial'noe* (St. Petersburg: Gos. tip., 1903), art. 272, p. 104.

19. St. Petersburg city governor Peter Gresser (1882–92) insisted that Jewish shopkeepers display their names—in the most likely Yiddish form written on their passports—on their signs. See Benjamin Ira Nathans, *Beyond the Pale: The Jewish Encounter with Russia, 1840–1900* (Ph.D. diss., University of California at Berkeley, 1995), p. 112.

20. "Ustav o preduprezhdenii i presechenii prestuplenii [Regulations on Preventing and Stopping Crimes] (1890)," chap. 3, art. 43, *Svod zakonov* (1912), p. 102. Earlier laws cited: 1831 February 14; 1894 June 3; 1902 June 10.

21. Ibid., art. 42, p. 102. Earlier laws cited: 1770 August 2; 1802 November.

22. Cf. Rozenblit. Rates of conversion even in those years were low compared to the period after 1905: see Yehuda Slutsky, *Ha-itonut ha-yehudit-rusit bemeah ha-esrim* (Jerusalem: Bet ha-sefer limudei ha-yahadut, 1978), p. 16.

23. [Anon.], "Iz obshchestvennoi khroniki," *Vestnik Evropy* (October 1889), p. 869.

24. Rogger, *Jewish Policies and Right-Wing Politics*, pp. 35–36.

25. Weinerman, "Racism, Racial Prejudice, and Jews," pp. 444–45.

26. Slutsky, *Ha-itonut ha-yehudit-rusit bemeah ha-esrim*, p. 16.

27. Vladimir Dal', *Tolkovyi slovar' zhivogo velikorusskogo iazyka* (St. Petersburg: M. O. Vol'f, 1903), vol. 1, p. 1345.

28. Jeffrey Brooks, *When Russia Learned to Read: Literacy and Popular Literature, 1861–1917* (Princeton, N.J.: Princeton University Press, 1985), p. 218.

29. See paragraphs 1–4 of the commentary on "O otvlechenii i ostuplenii ot very [On Leading Astray from or Abandoning Faith]," art. 185, N. S. Tagantsev, *Ulozhenie o nakazaniiakh ugolovnykh i ispravitel'nykh 1885 goda* (St. Petersburg, 1901), p. 214.

30. The similarities between the conversion of Jews to Orthodoxy in the Russian Empire and that of Muslims are intriguing. See Paul W. Werth, "Baptism, Authority, and the Problem of Zakonnost' in Orenberg Diocese: The Induction of over 800 'Pagans' into the Christian Faith," *Slavic Review*, vol. 56, no. 3 (Fall 1997). Thanks to Robert Crews for discussing this question with me.

31. See John D. Klier, "*The Times of London*: The Russian Press and the Pogroms of 1881–1882," *The Carl Beck Papers in Russian and East European Studies*, ed. William Chase and Ronald Linden (Pittsburgh, Pa.: Russian and East European Studies Program, University of Pittsburgh, 1984), paper no. 308.

32. Klier, *Imperial Russia's Jewish Question*, p. xiv.

33. Austin Lee Jersild, "From Savagery to Citizenship: Caucasian Mountaineers and Muslims in the Russian Empire," in *Russia's Orient: Imperial Borderlands and Peoples, 1700–1917*, ed. Daniel R. Brower and Edward J. Lazzerini (Bloomington: Indiana University Press, 1997), p. 101. He cites Dov Yaroshevski, "Empire and Citizenship," in the same volume. For a discussion of the Jews within the estate system, see Nathans, *Beyond the Pale*, esp. pp. 20 ff.

34. N. A. Nekrasov, *Polnoe sobranie sochinenii i pisem v 15 tomakh* (Leningrad: Nauka, 1981), vol. 2, p. 10. Cf. Gregory Freidin, "Authorship and Citizenship: A Problem for Modern Russian Literature," *Stanford Slavic Studies*, vol. 1 (1987).

35. I. G. Orshanskii, "Obrusenie evreev," in *Evrei v Rossii. Ocherki ekonomicheskogo i obshchestvennogo byta russkikh evreev* (St. Petersburg: O. I. Baksta, 1877), p. 179. Cf. a discussion of Jewish lawyers' descriptions of themselves as "Russian Jews" [*russkie evrei*] in Nathans, *Beyond the Pale*, pp. 290–97. Nathans dates this article to 1870 (p. 54).

36. Nathans, *Beyond the Pale*, p. 296.

37. I. G. Orshanskii, *Russkoe zakonodatel'stvo o evreiakh. Ocherki i issledovaniia* (St. Petersburg: A. E. Landau, 1877), p. 3.

38. See Michael Jerry Ochs, *St. Petersburg and the Jews of Russian Poland, 1862–1905* (Ph.D. diss., Harvard University, 1986; Witold Rodkiewicz, *Russian Nationality Policy in the Western Provinces of the Empire During the Reign of Nicholas II, 1894–1905 (Lithuania, Belorussia, Ukraine, Poland)* (Ph.D. diss., Harvard University, 1996); Theodore R. Weeks, *Nation and State in Late Imperial Russia: Nationalism and Russification on the Western Frontier, 1863–1914* (DeKalb: Northern Illinois University Press, 1996); Eli Weinerman, *Russification in Imperial Russia: The Search for Homo-*

geneity in the Multinational State (Ph.D. diss., Indiana University, 1996). Benedict Anderson puts Russification in a broader context in *Imagined Communities: Reflections on the Origin and Spread of Nationalism* (New York: Verso, 1983), pp. 86–88.

39. While some historians insist that the government deliberately encouraged the Russification of the Jews after 1863, others assert that it made no such effort. John Klier discusses the support in the press for the Russification of the Jews, the attempts to implement it, and the aftermath. Klier, *Imperial Russia's Jewish Question*, pp. 152 ff. Löwe agrees that "this emphasis on Russification was strengthened during the Polish uprising and afterwards," Heinz-Dietrich Löwe, *The Tsars and the Jews: Reform, Reaction, and Anti-Semitism in Imperial Russia, 1772–1917* (New York: Harwood Academic Publishers, 1993), p. 44. In contrast, Ochs notes that "St. Petersburg never tried to make allies of the Polish Jews by Russifying them" (Ochs, *St. Petersburg and the Jews of Russian Poland*, abstr.), and Rogger writes that "if any systematic policy of Russification did exist, the Jews were not subjected to it" (Rogger, *Jewish Policies and Right-Wing Politics*, p. 26).

40. On the conversion of the non-Orthodox, see Peter Waldron, "Religious Toleration in Late Imperial Russia," in *Civil Rights in Imperial Russia*. Weinerman sees an intensification of conversion efforts after 1881. See *Russification in Imperial Russia*, pp. 91 ff.

41. Weinerman, *Russification in Imperial Russia*, p. 8.

42. This is the thesis of John W. Slocum, "Who, and When, Were the *Inorodtsy*? The Evolution of the Category of 'Aliens' in Imperial Russia," *Russian Review*, vol. 57, no. 2 (April 1998); Raymond Pearson, "Privileges, Rights, and Russification," in *Civil Rights in Imperial Russia*, p. 97.

43. Alexander Blok, "Vozmezdie," in *Sobranie sochinenii v 8 tomakh* (Moscow: Khud. lit., 1960), vol. 5, p. 339.

44. See Emanuel Etkes, "Immanent Factors and External Influences in the Development of the Haskalah Movement in Russia," and Israel Bartal, "'The Heavenly City of Germany' and Absolutism à la Mode d'Autriche: The Rise of the Haskalah in Galicia," both in *Toward Modernity: The European Jewish Model*, ed. Jacob Katz (New Brunswick, N.J.: Transaction Books, 1987).

45. See Joshua Kunitz, *Russian Literature and the Jew: A Sociological Inquiry into the Nature and Origin of Literary Patterns* (New York: Columbia University Press, 1929), and Shmuel Ettinger, *Ben polin le-rusiya* (Jerusalem: Mosad Bialik, 1994), pp. 385, 426. Kunitz stresses the economic roots of the writers' enmity with the Jews, while Ettinger focuses on the vehemence of the hostility to Jews that he elsewhere calls an "integral part of Russia's religious and cultural heritage." *Anti-Semitism in the Soviet Union*, pp. iii, iv.

46. On the history of Michał Landy, see Magdalena Opalski and Israel Bartal, *Poles and Jews: A Failed Brotherhood* (Hanover, Mass.: Brandeis University Press, 1992), pp. 44–45.

47. That literary-critical norm was formed by four works from the 1920s. D. Za-slavskii, "Evrei v russkoi literature," *Evreiskaia letopis'*, vol. 1 (1923), pp. 59–86, was apparently the model for Joshua Kunitz, *Russian Literature and the Jew*. Cf. B. Gorev, "Russian Literature and the Jews," published as the introduction to V. L'vov-Rogachevsky, *A History of Russian-Jewish Literature* (1922), ed. and trans. Arthur Levin (Ann Arbor, Mich.: Ardis, 1979); this edition includes some extremely informative essays by Levin. In the 1980s and 1990s, a remarkable amount of new material has come out. On the prerevolutionary period in Russian literature, see Felix Dreizin, *The Russian Soul and the Jew: Essays in Literary Ethnocriticism* (Washington, D.C.: University Press of America, 1990); David Goldstein, *Dostoevsky and the Jews* (Austin: University of Texas Press, 1981); the first chapters of Alice Stone Nakhimovsky, *Russian-Jewish Literature and Identity* (Baltimore: The Johns Hopkins University Press, 1992); Savelii Dudakov, *Istoriia odnogo mifa*; Elena Tolstaia, *Poetika razdrazheniia* (Moscow: Radiks, 1994); Shimon Markish, "Russko-evreiskaia literatura: Predmet, podkhody, otsenki," *Novoe literaturnoe obozrenie*, no. 15 (1995); Anne-Marie Pontis, *Antisémitisme et sexualité* (Paris: Le lion, 1996). Valuable primary sources have been recently reprinted, such as Vsevolod Krestovskii, *T'ma egipetskaia* (St. Petersburg: Sovremennik, 1995), and V. V. Shul'gin, *"Chto NAM v nikh ne nravitsia": Ob antisemitizme v Rossii* (St. Petersburg: Khors, 1992); and the papers and correspondences of Russian and Jewish intellectuals have been published, as in M. S. Al'tman, *Razgovory s Viacheslavom Ivanovym* (St. Petersburg: Inapress, 1995), and "Perepiska V. V. Rozanova i M. O. Gershenzona, 1909–1918," ed. V. Proskurina, *Novyi mir*, March 1991. On Polish literature, see Opalski and Bartal, *Poles and Jews: A Failed Brotherhood*; Eugenia Prokop-Janiec, *Międzywojenna literatura polsko-żydowska jako zjawisko kulturowe i artystyczne* (Cracow: Universitas, 1992); Chone Shmeruk, *The Esterke Story in Yiddish and Polish Literature: A Case Study in the Mutual Relations of Two Cultural Traditions* (Jerusalem: The Zalman Shazar Center, 1985). Exceptions to the tendency to focus either on literature by non-Jews or literature by Jews are Shmeruk, Tolstaia, and Opalski and Bartal.

48. Compare Benedict Anderson, *Imagined Communities*, and Ernest Gellner, *Nations and Nationalism* (Oxford: Basil Blackwell, 1983), to Anthony Smith, *The Ethnic Orgins of Nations* (Oxford: Basil Blackwell, 1986), and John Armstrong, *Nations Before Nationalism* (Chapel Hill: University of North Carolina Press, 1982).

49. E. J. Hobsbawm, *Nations and Nationalism Since 1780: Programme, Myth, Reality* (Cambridge: Cambridge University Press, 1990), p. 105; Etienne Balibar and Immanuel Wallerstein, *Race, Nation, Class: Ambiguous Identities*, trans. Chris Turner (New York: Verso, 1991), p. 52.

50. Linda Nochlin, "Starting with the Self: Jewish Identity and Its Representation," in *The Jew in the Text: Modernity and the Construction of Identity*, ed. Linda Nochlin and Tamar Garb (London: Thames and Hudson, 1995), p. 11.

51. Liah Greenfeld, *Nationalism: Five Roads to Modernity* (Cambridge: Harvard University Press, 1992), esp. pp. 227–35; Hans Rogger, *National Consciousness in*

Eighteenth-Century Russia (Cambridge: Harvard University Press, 1960). Czesław Miłosz touches on the orientations of Polish Romantic nationalism toward both Western Europe and the Slavic world in *The History of Polish Literature* (London: Macmillan, 1969), pp. 201, 226. In each case, a focus on one side of the equation implied a rejection of the other.

52. Nikolai Berdiaev, *The Russian Idea*, trans. R. M. French (Hudson, N.Y.: Lindisfarme Press, 1992), p. 20.

53. Nikolai Berdiaev, "Khristianstvo i antisemitism: Religioznaia sud'ba evreistva" (1938), in *Taina Izrailia: "Evreiskii vopros" v russkoi religioznoi mysli kontsa XIX–pervoi poloviny XX v.v.*, ed. V. F. Boikov (St. Petersburg: Sofiia, 1993), p. 328. This is a fascinating collection of essays on Judaism by nineteenth- and twentieth-century Russian religious thinkers.

54. Drawing on this connection, Gregory Freidin relates the family of the Russian-Jewish poet Osip Mandelstam to Russia itself: "Not unlike this 'assimilated' European country . . . [they] were neither quite Jewish nor quite Russian—two slates waiting to be erased and reinscribed." Freidin, *A Coat of Many Colors: Osip Mandelstam and His Mythologies of Self-Presentation* (Berkeley and Los Angeles: University of California Press, 1987), p. 22.

55. Perhaps this is what Homi Bhabha means when he refers to "the ambivalence of the 'nation' as a narrative strategy," which produces "a continual slippage of categories." Homi K. Bhabha, "Dissemination: Time, Narrative, and the Margins of the Modern Nation," in *The Location of Culture* (New York: Routledge, 1994), p. 140.

56. For a discussion of type in this period, see Charles A. Moser, *Esthetics as Nightmare: Russian Literary Theory, 1855–1870* (Princeton, N.J.: Princeton University Press, 1989), pp. 245–50.

57. Pavel Vasilevich Annenkov, "The Literary Type of the Weak Man (Apropos of Turgenev's Story 'Asya')," trans. Tatiana Goerner, *Ulbandus Review*, vol. 1, nos. 1–2 (Fall 1977–Spring 1978), p. 95. On Annenkov and his relation to the radical critics, see Moser, esp. p. 24.

58. N. G. Chernyshevsky, "Russkii chelovek na rendez-vous: Razmyshleniia po prochtenii povesti g. Turgeneva 'Asia,'" in *Estetika i literaturnaia kritika* (Moscow: Khud. Lit., 1951), p. 468.

59. P. N. Medvedev/M. M. Bakhtin, *The Formal Method in Literary Scholarship: A Critical Introduction to Sociological Poetics*, trans. Albert J. Wehrle (Baltimore: The Johns Hopkins University Press, 1978), p. 134.

60. Dmitry Pisarev, "Pushkin and Belinsky: *Eugene Onegin*," in *Russian Views of Pushkin's* Eugene Onegin, ed. and trans. Sona Hoisington (Bloomington: Indiana University Press, 1988), p. 52. Mitrofan Prostakov is the hero of Denis Fonvizin's play *The Minor* [Nedorosl']; Beltov the hero of Aleksandr Herzen's novel *Who Is to Blame?* [Kto vinovat?]; Chatsky the hero of Aleksandr Griboedov's play *Woe from Wit* [Gore ot uma]; and Rudin the hero of Turgenev's novel *Rudin*.

61. Ibid., p. 53.

62. Semen An-skii, *Sobranie sochinenii* (St. Petersburg: Prosviashcheniia, 1913), vol. 2, p. 23. Cf. Nakhimovsky, p. 17.

63. Eliezer Ben-Yehuda, *A Dream Come True*, trans. T. Muraoka, ed. George Mandel (Boulder, Colo.: Westview Press, 1993), p. 25.

64. Cited in Steven Cassedy, *To the Other Shore: The Russian Jewish Intellectuals Who Came to America* (Princeton, N.J.: Princeton University Press, 1997), pp. 19, 26.

65. Rostislav I. Sementkovskii, *Sochineniia* (St. Petersburg: A. F. Marks, 1905), vol. 3, p. 611.

66. See Irina Paperno, *Chernyshevsky and the Age of Realism: A Study in the Semiotics of Behavior* (Stanford, Calif.: Stanford University Press, 1988).

67. Annenkov, vol. 1, p. 101.

68. Ibid., pp. 95–96.

69. Rufus W. Mathewson Jr., in *The Positive Hero in Russian Literature* (Stanford, Calif.: Stanford University Press, 1958), examines this paradox in Russian literary theory from Vissarion Belinskii through the Soviets. Cf. Andrzej Walicki, *A History of Russian Thought from the Enlightenment to Marxism*, trans. Hilda Andrews Rusiecka (Stanford, Calif.: Stanford University Press, 1974), p. 194.

70. This is not unlike what the American critic Harry Levin calls the "literary technique of systematic disillusionment." *The Gates of Horn: A Study of Five French Realists* (New York: Oxford University Press, 1963), p. 48. On Belinskii, see Mathewson, p. 32.

71. Jurij Tynjanov, "On Literary Evolution," in *Readings in Russian Poetics: Formalist and Structuralist Views*, ed. Ladislaw Matejka and Krystyna Pomorska (Ann Arbor: Michigan Slavic Contributions, 1978).

CHAPTER 1 GRIGORY BOGROV

EPIGRAPH: M. M. Bakhtin, "The *Bildungsroman* and Its Significance in the History of Realism (Toward a Historical Typology of the Novel)," in *Speech Genres and Other Late Essays*, trans. Vern W. McGee, ed. Caryl Emerson and Michael Holquist (Austin: University of Texas Press, 1986), p. 23.

1. Grigorii Isaakovich Bogrov, *Sobranie sochinenii* (Odessa: Sherman, 1912–13).

2. G. Bogrov, letter to N. A. Nekrasov, 5 February 1871, in *Literaturnoe nasledstvo*, vols. 51–52 (1949), p. 163.

3. N. Shigarin, "Russkie evreiskie gazety (po evreiskomu voprosu)," *Biblioteka Zapadnoi polosy Rossii*, vol. 2 (St. Petersburg, 1879), p. 6.

4. L'vov-Rogachevsky, p. 96.

5. "Nekrolog," *Istoricheskii vestnik*, no. 7 (June 1885), p. 220; *Nov'*, no. 15 (1885), p. 182.

6. I. Turgenev, letter to G. Bogrov, 14/26 March 1882, in I. S. Turgenev, *Dokumenty po istorii literatury i obshchestvennosti* (Moscow: Gosizdat, 1923), p. 67.

7. For example, Vsevolod Vladimirovich Krestovskii cites *Notes of a Jew* frequently in his trilogy *Zhid idet* [The Jew Is Coming], and a collection of Judeophobic Russian works in German translation published in 1928 includes (at least parts of) *Notes of a Jew* as well as Brafman's *Book of the Kahal. Das Buch vom Kahal, auf Grund einer neuen Verdeutschung des russischen Originals,* trans. Siegfried Passarge (Leipzig: Hammer-Verlag, 1928). For discussions of Krestovskii and Brafman, see Chapter 2.

8. Nevskii kritik, "Zhurnal'naia i bibliograficheskaia letopis'," review of Bogrov, *Zapiski evreia, Vestnik russkikh evreev,* no. 16 (18 April 1871).

9. [Saul Chernikhovskii], "Russko-evreiskaia khudozhestvennaia literatura," *Evreiskaia entsiklopediia,* vol. 8, p. 642.

10. S. E. Lur'e, letters to F. M. Dostoevskii, 27 September 1876 and 13 February 1877, in "Neizdannye pis'ma k Dostoevskomu," ed. S. Ipatova, *Dostoevskii: Materialy i issledovaniia* (St. Petersburg: Akademiia nauk, 1996), vol. 12, pp. 209, 211. The editor notes that an 1874 edition of Bogrov's book appears in Dostoevskii's library.

11. Memoirs of V. Bogrova, chap. 9, p. 3.

12. Sholom Aleichem [Sholem Rabinovich], *From the Fair,* trans. Curt Leviant (New York: Penguin, 1985), p. 231. Rabinovich also writes that he believed Bogrov to be "one of God's angels," pp. 257–58.

13. Mordecai ben-Hillel Ha-Cohen, *Me-erev ad erev: Ne'esaf min ha-maamarim ha-yeshanim u-min ha-hadashim* (Vilna: Bi-defus P. Gerber, 1904), vol. 1, pp. 184, 182.

14. Supin, "Staraia insinuatsiia ili novaia bessmyslitsa?" *Den',* no. 15 (1871). On this journal and the views of its editors, see Alexander Orbach, *New Voices of Russian Jewry: A Study of the Russian-Jewish Press of Odessa in the Era of the Great Reforms, 1860–1871* (Leiden: J. Brill, 1980), pp. 182–95.

15. Page numbers refer to G. Bogrov, *Zapiski evreia v dvukh chastiakh* (St. Petersburg: V. Tushnova, 1874).

16. Kugel symbolized Jewishness not only for Bogrov. Consider the Yiddish saying "Der kugel ligt im afn ponim" [Kugel is on his face], said of a person who looks Jewish. Ignaz Bernstein, *Yidishe shprikhverter un rednsartn* (New York: Brider Kaminsky, 1908), p. 232.

17. Is Bogrov like Brafman? Sander Gilman's theory of Jewish self-hatred presents apostates such as the sixteenth-century Johann Josef Pfefferkorn, who, after converting to Christianity, publicly attacked Judaism, and *maskilim* such as Moses Mendelssohn into manifestations of a single phenomenon. Both, he argues, have internalized non-Jewish society's disdain for Jews and Jewish culture, which spurs them publicly to distinguish between themselves—the "good Jews"—and all the other "bad" Jews. Sander Gilman, *Jewish Self-Hatred: Anti-Semitism and the Hidden Language of the Jews* (Baltimore: The Johns Hopkins University Press, 1986). Bogrov's formulation, in my opinion, provides a useful corrective to Gilman's assertions. Unlike Brafman, he wanted to enlighten all his fellow citizens, gentile as well as Jewish. Rather than simply idealizing Russian society of his time, "kvas patriotism" and all,

he suggested that enlightened Jews and enlightened Russians could some day participate in an ideal civilization together. The conclusions of Israel Bartal, who points
out the disjuncture between European nationalisms and the universalism of the Haskalah, indicate that in this Bogrov was a typical maskil. Bartal, "'The Heavenly City
of Germany' and Absolutism à la Mode d'Autriche."

18. Lur'e, letter to Dostoevskii, 13 February 1877, p. 211.

19. M. Lazarev, "Literaturnaia letopis': Zadachi i znachenie russko-evreiskoi bel-
letristiki (Kriticheskii eskiz)," *Voskhod* (May 1885), pp. 35, 36.

20. Lazarev, *Voskhod* (June 1885), p. 38.

21. [S. Tsinberg], "Bogrov," *Evreiskaia entsiklopediia* (1913), vol. 4, p. 733.

22. L'vov-Rogachevsky, p. 96; Ha-Cohen, vol. 2, p. 134.

23. Cf. Ha-Cohen, vol. 1, pp. 80, 184.

24. Ibid., pp. 183–84.

25. G. Bogrov, "Man'iak: Nebyvalyi sluchai iz zhizni molodogo psikhiatra," *Voskhod*, nos. 1–5 (1884).

26. Ha-Cohen, vol. 2, pp. 137, 139. Yehuda Slutsky, an Israeli historian, also seems
shocked by this story. Slutsky, *Ha-itonut ha-yehudit-rusit bemeah ha-tsha-esreh* (Jerusalem: Bialik Institute, 1970), p. 186.

27. N. A. Bukhbinder, *Literaturnye etiudy* (Leningrad: Nauka i shkola, 1927), p. 61;
The New Standard Jewish Encyclopedia, ed. Geoffrey Wigoder (New York: Facts on
File, 1992), p. 164. A similar work published a century earlier reveals another personal
reason for the Russian Jewish intelligentsia's hostility to Bogrov: "[*Zapiski evreia*] is
considered a valuable contribution to Russian literature, yet the author's undignified
revelations of his family affairs called forth severe criticism." [H.R.], "Bogrov, Grig-
ori Isaacovich," *The Jewish Encyclopedia* (New York: Funk and Wagnells, 1901), vol. 5,
p. 286.

28. Meyer Waxman, *A History of Jewish Literature* (New York: Thomas Yoseloff,
1960), vol. 4, p. 610.

29. Markish, "Russko-evreiskaia literatura," pp. 228–29.

30. Olga Litvak, *The Literary Response to Conscription: Individuality and Autonomy in the Russian Jewish Enlightenment* (Ph.D. diss., Columbia University, 1999),
pp. 171–72.

31. [Anon.], "Russkaia literatura," *Syn otechestva*, no. 159 (14 July 1873), p. 1.

32. Shigarin, *Russkie evreiskie gazety*, p. 6.

33. [Tsinberg], "Bogrov," p. 733.

34. G. Bogrov, letter to L. Levanda, 14 August 1878, *Evreiskaia biblioteka*, vol. 10
(1903), p. 16.

35. V. Bogrova, certificate of G. Bogrov's acceptance to the bar, Memoirs, chap. 4,
p. 7; 2nd section, p. 5; chap. 3, p. 3. Also see V. Bogrov, *Dmitrii Bogrov i ubiistvo Stolypina* (Berlin: Strela, 1931), esp. pp. 46–47.

36. See Jonathan Frankel, "Assimilation and the Jews in Nineteenth-Century Eu-

rope." As an example of the view that the Russian Haskalah simply imported and re-cycled the ideas of the Berlin maskilim, he cites S. Ettinger, "The Modern Period," in H. H. Ben-Sasson, ed., *A History of the Jewish People* (Cambridge: Harvard University Press, 1976), p. 841.

37. On more religious supporters of secular knowledge, see David E. Fishman, *Russia's First Modern Jews: The Jews of Shklov* (New York: New York University Press, 1995), and Etkes, "Immanent Factors." On the advocates of reform, see Stanislawski, *Tsar Nicholas I and the Jews*, pp. 49–96.

38. David E. Fishman looks at some eighteenth-century "proto-maskilim" in *Russia's First Modern Jews*, and Emanuel Etkes examines a number of Eastern European figures whose radicalism owes as much to medieval Jewish philosophy as to the Berlin Haskalah in "Immanent Factors," pp. 16 ff.

39. Israel Bartal draws a distinction between the situations in Berlin and in abso-lutist states such as the Russian Empire. He also notes that the Enlightenment uni-versalism that the Berlin maskilim expressed as an allegiance to European civilization as a whole became increasingly difficult to sustain amid the developing nationalisms of the second half of the nineteenth century. Bartal, "'The Heavenly City of Ger-many,'" pp. 36, 38–39. Eli Lederhendler, building on Bartal's conclusions, states that by the 1870s, many Russian maskilim adopted views that were entirely foreign to the Berlin maskilim, rejecting *shtadlanut*—the concept of certain educated Jews inter-ceding to the government for the Jewish community—for a new emphasis on the rights and the will of the Jewish "people." Eli Lederhendler, *The Road to Modern Jew-ish Politics: Political Tradition and Political Reconstruction in the Jewish Community of Tsarist Russia* (New York: Oxford University Press, 1989), p. 134.

40. Ahad ha-Am, "Imitation and Assimilation," in *Modern Hebrew Literature*, ed. Robert Alter (New York: Behrman House, 1975), p. 95. Cf. Ezra Mendelsohn, *On Modern Jewish Politics* (New York: Oxford University Press, 1993), p. 16; Lederhendler, *The Road to Modern Jewish Politics*, p. 86; and Zipperstein, "'Assimilation,' *haskalah* and Odessa Jewry."

41. Michael Stanislawski asserts that though generations of readers have seen Gordon as calling for them to limit their expression of Jewishness to the home and to suppress it in public, the poet in fact spoke for the integration of Jewish and reli-gious identities: the famous line "advocated being both a full-fledged man—a free, modern, enlightened Russian-speaking *Mensch*—and a Jew at home in the creative spirit of the Hebrew heritage." *For Whom Do I Toil? Judah Leib Gordon and the Crisis of Russian Jewry* (New York: Oxford University Press, 1988), p. 52.

42. Etkes, p. 28. Bartal investigates the continuity of other literary images in nineteenth-century Hebrew and Yiddish literature, such as depictions of encounters between Jews and non-Jews. Israel Bartal, *Ha-loyehudim ve-hevratam besifrut ivrit veyidish bemizrah eropah ben ha-shanim 1856–1914* (Ph.D. diss., Hebrew University, 1980), p. xiii.

43. Bartal, "'The Heavenly City of Germany,'" p. 38; Lederhendler, *The Road to Modern Jewish Politics*, p. 100.

44. The novels of Mapu demonstrate the difficulty of turning the biblical language into a modern literary one, in that they suffer from stylistic problems that make them both unattractive to contemporary Hebrew readers and difficult to translate. For a plot summary of *The Hypocrite* and a brief excerpt in translation, see David Patterson, *Abraham Mapu: The Creator of the Modern Hebrew Novel* (London: Horovitz, 1964), pp. 146–67. On Mapu's attitude toward learning, especially languages, see p. 90. Also see David Patterson, *A Phoenix in Fetters: Studies in Nineteenth and Early Twentieth Century Hebrew Fiction* (Savage, Md.: Rowman and Littlefield, 1988), pp. 11–12; Simon Halkin, *Modern Hebrew Literature from the Enlightenment to the Birth of the State of Israel: Trends and Values* (New York: Schocken, 1970), p. 52. For a similar Hebrew work that has recently become available in translation in entirety, see Joseph Perl, *Joseph Perl's Revealer of Secrets: The First Hebrew Novel*, ed. and trans. Dov Taylor (Boulder, Colo.: Westview Press, 1997). This epistolary novel, written in Galicia and published in Vienna in 1819, spoofs the attempt of some Hasidim to find and destroy a German book that details their flaws.

45. Maimon too blamed the "backwardness" of the Jews on Hasidism. This Jewish sect arose in Poland after the Cossack invasions led by Bogdan Chmelnitsky in 1648 and the ensuing decimation of the Jews. The Hasidim [adherents of Hasidism] stress purity of heart over intensive study of the Talmud. Communities of Hasidim are each led by a "tzaddik," seen as an intermediary between the Jews and God. The movement of Mitnagged [in Hebrew, "opponent"], centered in Lithuania, attacked Hasidim and defended the intellectual traditions of Judaism. Many maskilim carried on the interest of Mitnagged in systematic study of Hebrew grammar, as well as retaining its fierce animus for the Hasidim. On the attitude to the Hasidim expressed in Hebrew literature, see Patterson, *A Phoenix in Fetters*, pp. 66–92. For an English translation of Aksenfeld's novella, see Yisroel Aksenfeld, "The Headband," in *The Shtetl*, ed. and trans. Joachim Neugroschel (Woodstock, N.Y.: Overlook Press, 1989). On Aksenfeld as a reformist, see Dan Miron, *A Traveler Disguised: The Rise of Modern Yiddish Fiction in the Nineteenth Century* (New York: Schocken, 1973), pp. 53–55. For some Yiddish works of the period with similar themes that are available in English, see Isaac Joel Linetski, *The Polish Lad*, trans. Moshe Spiegel (Philadelphia: Jewish Publication Society, 1975), and S. Y. Abramovich (Mendele Moykher Sforim), "Fishke the Lame," in *Tales of Mendele the Book Peddler*, ed. Dan Miron and Ken Frieden, trans. Ted Gorelick and Hillel Halkin (New York: Schocken, 1996).

46. Aksenfeld, p. 107.

47. Nevakhovich published *Vopl' dshcheri iudeiskoi* first in Russian in 1803, then in Hebrew. For a description and analysis, see Fishman, pp. 94–100.

48. See the list of Russian Jewish periodicals, 1860–1914, in V. L'vov-Rogachevsky, pp. 206–7.

49. Shimon Markish summarizes the achievements of the first Jews to write in Russian in "Russko-evreiskaia literatura." Also see his articles on Levanda and Rabinovich: "Osip Rabinovich," *Vestnik evreiskogo universiteta v Moskve*, nos. 1(5) and 2(6) (1994); "Stoit li perechityvat' L'va Levanda?" *Vestnik evreiskogo universiteta v Moskve*, nos. 3(10) and 4(11) (1995).

50. Fishman, pp. 94–100; Markish, "Russko-evreiskaia literatura," p. 225.

51. Alan Mintz, *"Banished from Their Father's Table": Loss of Faith and Hebrew Autobiography* (Bloomington: Indiana University Press, 1989), p. 5.

52. *Salomon Maimons Lebensgeschichte, von ihm selbst geschrieben* (Berlin: Karl Philipp Moritz, 1792–93). My citations refer to the most complete English translation, *The Autobiography of Solomon Maimon*, trans. J. Clark Murray (London: East and West Library, 1954), which is based not on the original German edition but on a later one, Salomon Maimon, *Geschichte des eigenen Lebens* (Berlin: Schocken, 1935), which (as explained in it on p. 215) omits several chapters on philosophy.

53. See Mintz, p. 10. On Rousseau's influence on Jewish autobiographers, including Maimon, see Marcus Moseley, *Jewish Autobiography in Eastern Europe: The Pre-History of a Literary Genre* (Ph.D. diss., Oxford University, 1990).

54. Solomon Maimon, "Iz avtobiografii Salomona Maimona, Glavy I–XVIII," *Evreiskaia biblioteka*, vol. 1 (1871).

55. For a useful discussion of autobiography and the theory that has developed around it, see Michael Sheringham, *French Autobiography, Devices and Desires: Rousseau to Perec* (Oxford: Clarendon Press, 1993), esp. chap. 1.

56. Even by the national census of 1897, only 42.9 percent of adult Jewish males and 22.5 percent of adult Jewish females were literate in Russian, while the majority of Jewish males learned the Hebrew/Yiddish alphabet in *heder* and many Jewish women knew it as well. See [Ia. Shabad], "Gramotnost' evreev v Rossii," *Evreiskaia entsiklopediia*, vol. 6, pp. 756–59.

57. Maimon wrote an entire chapter on the evils of Hasidism. See Maimon, *Autobiography*, pp. 166–79.

58. Lazarev, "Literaturnaia letopis'" (June), p. 36.

59. For a Modern English summary, see Eugen Kölbing, *The Romance of Sir Beues of Hamtoun* (London: N. Trübner, 1885), pp. xxi–xxxiv. The English version was based on a thirteenth-century French romance, *Beuves d'Hanstone*, by Pierre du Ries. On the source of the story, see Brooks, p. 75. On its diffusion in Russia, see Victor Terras, *A History of Russian Literature* (New Haven, Conn.: Yale University Press, 1991), p. 111.

60. Dieter Mehl, *The Middle English Romance of the Thirteenth and Fourteenth Centuries* (New York: Barnes and Noble, 1969), p. 220. For more on the story of Sir Beves and its formulaic plot, see Susan Wittig, *Stylistic and Narrative Structures in the Middle English Romances* (Austin: University of Texas Press, 1978).

61. Miron, pp. 2, 3, 150.

62. The creators of early Hebrew literature, for that matter, had some of the same tastes as Yiddish writers. One of the first Hebrew "best-sellers" was an 1858 adaptation of Eugène Sue's *The Mysteries of Paris*, featuring eight hundred pages of princes in disguise, redeemed prostitutes with hearts of gold, vicious criminals, and absurd coincidences, though with a healthy dose of social commentary thrown in.

63. Brooks, p. 75.

64. *Komu na Rusi zhit' khorosho?* in N. A. Nekrasov, vol. 5, p. 35, ll. 1175, 1180–83.

65. Aleksandr Il'in-Tomich, "Vot i vse, chto ostaetsia . . . ," intro. to Vasilii A. Vonliarliarskii, *Bol'shaia barynia: Roman, povest', rasskazy* (Moscow: Sovremennik, 1987).

66. Vonliarliarskii, p. 107. According to Russian folk beliefs, during *sviatki*, the two weeks between Christmas and the Orthodox festival of the Baptism of Christ, one could predict one's future in various ways, including this one.

67. Ibid., p. 97.

68. Mikhail Bakhtin, "Forms of Time and of the Chronotope in the Novel," in *The Dialogic Imagination: Four Essays by M. M. Bakhtin*, ed. Michael Holquist, trans. Michael Holquist and Caryl Emerson (Austin: University of Texas Press, 1981), p. 100. Lotman uses similar terms to describe the heroes of high Russian Romanticism, who understand that their lives are governed by "unknown factors." Iu. M. Lotman, "'Pikovaia dama' i tema kart i kartochnoi igry v russkoi literature nachala XIX veka," in *Pushkin* (St. Petersburg: Isskustvo-SPB, 1995), p. 794.

69. M. Iu. Lermontov, *Sobranie sochinenii v 4 tomakh* (Leningrad: Nauka, 1981), vol. 4, p. 290. Bogrov clearly read Lermontov as well as Vonliarliarskii: see the mentions of *Hero of Our Time* in the discussion of Bogrov's review of "Rakushanskii melamed" in the final section of this chapter.

70. Ibid., 309–10.

71. For instance, beautiful Polish blondes are featured in Nikolai Gogol's "Taras Bulba" and Alexandr Pushkin's "Bakhchisaraiskii fontan."

72. In fact, love affairs between Jews and gentiles that ended in marriage were a rarity even in Haskalah literature. Opalski and Bartal identify only one: P. Smoleskin's *Gmul yesharim* (1905), in which the Polish woman converts to Judaism. See Opalski and Bartal, pp. 93–97.

73. Litvak, pp. 186–87.

74. This early play appears in Lessing's collected works: G. E. Lessing, *Gesammelte Werke* (Leipzig, 1858), vol. 1, pp. 215–62. For an English summary and a partial translation, see "Lessing: *Die Juden*," trans. Ernest Bell, in *The Enlightenment: A Comprehensive Anthology*, ed. Peter Gay (New York: Simon and Schuster, 1973), pp. 746–65.

75. "Lessing: *Die Juden*," p. 764.

76. Patterson, *A Phoenix in Fetters*, p. 14.

77. David Biale, "Eros and Enlightenment: Love Against Marriage in the East European Jewish Enlightenment," *Polin*, vol. 1 (1986).

78. Dreizin, pp. 3–6. For a fascinating analysis of the Jewish tavern keeper's devil-

ish shiftiness in Polish literature, see Magdalena Opalski, *The Jewish Tavern-Keeper and His Tavern in Nineteenth-Century Polish Literature* (Jerusalem: The Zalman Shazar Center, 1986).

79. Anne-Marie Pontis asserts that these are the only Jewish bandits in nineteenth-century classic Russian literature. See her *Antisémitisme et sexualité*, p. 111.

80. G. Bogrov, letter to L. Levanda, 25 September 1878, *Evreiskaia biblioteka*, vol. 10, pp. 17–18.

81. In translating the story's title I follow Hugh McLean, who discovered that "Rakushan" is an obscure Slavic name for "Austria." Hugh McLean, *Nikolai Leskov: The Man and His Art* (Cambridge: Harvard University Press, 1977), p. 755. The story originally appeared as N. S. Leskov, "Rakushanskii melamed: Rasskaz na bivuake," *Russkii vestnik*, no. 3 (March 1878). Citations refer to N. S. Leskov, *Sobranie sochinenii v 12 tomakh* (Moscow: Pravda, 1989), vol. 5.

82. G. Bogrov, "Talmud i Kabbala po 'Russkomu Vestniku,'" *Russkii evrei*, no. 16 (1879).

83. Ibid., no. 11, p. 402.

84. Ibid., no. 16, p. 607.

85. N. S. Leskov, letter to A. S. Suvorin (Winter 1877–78), Rukopisnyi otdel Instituta russkoi literatury i iskusstva, St. Petersburg, f. 268, ed. khr. 131, l. 24. Suvorin apparently rejected the story, since it eventually appeared in Mikhail Katkov's *Russkii vestnik*.

86. In fact, Leskov based most of his claims about Judaism on a single book, published fifty years earlier in his hometown of Orel. [Anon.], *Obriady evreiskie, ili opisanie tseremonii i obyknovenii, nabliudaemykh Evreiami kak vne khrama, tak ravno i vo vse torzhestvennye dni, pri obrezanii, pri svad'bakh, rodinakh, smerti, pogrebeniiakh i proch.* (Orel: I. Sytina, 1830). See Gabriella Safran, "Ethnography, Judaism, and the Art of Nikolai Leskov," *Russian Review* vol. 59 (April 2000).

87. G. Bogrov, "Talmud i Kabbala po 'Russkomu Vestniku,'" no. 9, p. 322.

88. Ibid., no. 11, pp. 401–2.

89. Ibid., no. 13, pp. 489–90.

90. Ibid., no. 13, p. 490.

91. Ibid., no. 16, p. 606.

92. Ibid., no. 9, p. 322.

93. Ibid., no. 13, p. 488, and no. 16, p. 606.

94. Note the irony of Bogrov's exploitation of the genre of the military tale to signify his own assimilation. Military service has often been associated with the acculturation of minority populations in Europe and in the United States. The history of the Jewish draft in imperial Russia is more checkered; it has been more strongly associated with a forced Russification than with the extension of civil rights. In this context, it is amusing that Bogrov uses a genre associated with the military to represent himself as a fully Russified Jewish writer, one who is at home with Russian cul-

ture and who, no less than Leskov, possesses the right—as well as the necessary knowledge—to criticize the behavior of border populations and to point out how they too must strive for greater Russianness.

95. Lermontov, p. 235.

96. Bartal, *Ha-loyehudim ve-hevratam*, English abstract, p. ix.

97. Others observe the growth in the 1870s of resentment among Jewish writers of the availability of emancipation for assimilated Jewish elites and its denial to most others. Lederhendler relates Bartal's work on Mendele's stories of the early 1870s to a growing consciousness among educated Jews that government officials were not necessarily their allies in the project of Jewish emancipation (*The Road to Modern Jewish Politics*, pp. 144–45). Also see Nathans, p. 167. By 1878, in "Masoes Benyomin hashlishi" [The Travels of Benjamin III], Mendele would move from his earlier focus on the education of the masses to an interest in the fate of the Jewish nation as a whole. Dan Miron and Anita Norich, "The Politics of Benjamin III: Intellectual Significance and Its Formal Correlatives in Sh. Y. Abramovitsh's *Masoes Benyomin Hashlishi*," in *The Field of Yiddish: Studies in Language, Folklore, and Literature* (Philadelphia: Institute for the Study of Human Values, 1980), pp. 10–11. Indeed, Ruth Wisse points out that this story travels the full distance from Enlightenment to Romantic outlooks, "from the satire that exposes, attacks, and pleads for reform, to irony which is more tolerant if less optimistic." Ruth R. Wisse, *The Schlemiel as Modern Hero* (Chicago: University of Chicago Press, 1971), p. 39.

98. See his barbed comments about Russians who opposed eliminating the Pale of Settlement in "Zhit' ili ne zhit' evreiam povsemestno v Rossii?" *Slovo*, 1878, no. 2, pp. 12–20.

99. Jonathan Frankel, *Prophecy and Politics: Socialism, Nationalism, and the Russian Jews, 1862–1917* (Cambridge: Cambridge University Press, 1981), p. 60. He cites Ben-Rabbi [Bogrov], "Chto Delat'?," *Russkii evrei*, no. 34 (19 August 1881), pp. 1326–31, and "Pis'mo v redaktsiiu," *Russkii evrei*, no. 36 (3 September 1881), pp. 1408–9. Other scholars agree that Bogrov's hostility to Jews and Jewish culture seemed to diminish in the late 1870s. Ha-Cohen, vol. 1, p. 181; Slutsky, *Ha-itonut ha-yehudit-rusit bemeah ha-tsha-esreh*, p. 97.

100. G. Bogrov, editorials in *Russkii evrei*, nos. 3, 4, 5, 8, 10, 13, 14 (1883).

101. *Ispoved' prestupnika: Iumoristicheskii rasskaz iz zhizni peterburgskikh evreev* (St. Petersburg, 1881); "Prestupniki," *Voskhod*, no. 4 (1881), p. 161. Cited in Nathans, pp. 159–60.

CHAPTER 2   ELIZA ORZESZKOWA

1. L. L-a, "Bibliografiia: O Żydach i kwestii żydowskiej . . . (Vilno, 1882)," *Russkii evrei*, no. 24 (1882), pp. 927; no. 41 (1882), p. 1521.

2. Adolf J. Cohn, "Przegląd literacki," *Izraelita*, vol. 2, no. 4 (1878), p. 30.

3. S. Mstislavskaia [Sofiia Dubnova-Erlikh], "Eliza Ozheshko," *Evreiskoe obozrenie*, no. 2 (3 June 1910), p. 14.

4. Vladimir (Zeev) Zhabotinskii, "Chetyre stat'i o 'chirikovskom intsidente,'" *Izbrannoe* (Israel: Biblioteka-Aliia, 1978), p. 90.

5. M. E. Saltykov-Shchedrin, *Sobranie sochinenii* (Moscow: Khud. lit., 1973), vol. 15, bk. 2, p. 235.

6. N. S. Leskov, "Religioznye obriady evreev, Mezhdu Paskhoiu i Piatidesiatnitseiu." *Peterburgskaia gazeta*, 17 January 1881, p. 2.

7. Eliza Orzeszko, *Meer Ezofovich: Povest' iz evreiskogo byta. Biblioteka Zapadnoi polosy Rossii*, vol. 1 (1879), vol. 2 (1879), and vol. 1 (1880) (the first two were published in St. Petersburg, the third in Kiev), but then publication of the novel broke off; El. Orzheszkova, *Meer Ezofovich: Povest' iz byta zhidov. Gazeta Gattsuka* (supplement), no. 6 (1880), and *Meer Ezofovich: Povest' iz byta zhidov* (Moscow: Gazeta A. Gattsuka, 1881). (The translation appeared first as a supplement to the newspaper, then as a separate edition.) E. Orzeszko, *Meir Ezofovich*. Novel supplement to *Svet*, vol. 9, 1882.

8. See A. F. Koni, "Avtorskoe pravo" [Copyright Law], in *Novyi entsiklopedicheskii slovar'* (St. Petersburg: Brokgauz-Efron, 1911–16), vol. 1, pp. 332–34.

9. N. D. Shigarin, "Ot redaktsii," in *Biblioteka Zapadnoi polosy Rossii*, vol. 1, p. 2, and N. Shigarin, "Russkie evreiskie gazety (po evreiskomu voprosu)," *Biblioteka Zapadnoi polosy Rossii*, vol. 2, p. 8. On Orzeszkowa's encounters with Shigarin, an unusual and somewhat difficult person, see Joyce Story Kolodziej, *Eliza Orzeszkowa's Feminist and Jewish Works in Polish and Russian Criticism* (Ph.D. diss., Indiana University, 1975), p. 432.

10. [Anon.], "Ot perevodchika," in El. Orzeszkova, *Meer Ezofovich: Povest' iz byta zhidov* (Moscow: Gazeta A. Gattsuka, 1881). On the tendencies of *Gazeta A. Gattsuka*, "an illustrated periodical of dubious moral principles," and on A. Gattsuk himself, see Klier, *Imperial Russia's Jewish Question*, pp. 422, 434, 498n40.

11. Jacob Katz, *From Prejudice to Destruction: Anti-Semitism, 1700–1933* (Cambridge: Harvard University Press, 1980).

12. "In a nationalist age, societies worship themselves brazenly and openly." Gellner, p. 56.

13. Anderson, pp. 12–15.

14. Katz, pp. 17, 39–40, 74–91, 303–17.

15. Ibid., p. 17.

16. David Patterson details the maskilic critique of Hasidism, including the Hasidic approach to various parts of the Jewish textual tradition, in *A Phoenix in Fetters*, pp. 66–78. For an example, see the meticulously documented and footnoted attacks on Hasidic tales and hagiographies in Perl, *Joseph Perl's Revealer of Secrets*.

17. On the universalism of the maskilim and its conflict with nineteenth-century nationalisms, see Israel Bartal, "'The Heavenly City of Germany,'" pp. 36, 38–39.

18. I will use the imperial designation, the "western provinces," for the nine *gu-*

bernii [provinces administered by a "gubernator," a governor] of Kovno, Vilna, Vitebsk, Grodno, Minsk, Mogilev, Volhynia, Kiev, and Podolia. Poles frequently refer to the region as the *kresy* [borderlands].

19. For more details on imperial policy toward Poland, see Weeks, pp. 92–109. Although both the legal status and the name of this area changed after 1863, Poles continued to refer to it as the "Polish Kingdom," the "Congress Kingdom," the "Kingdom," or "Poland" [Polska], until the Russian Revolution. I will follow the first of these usages.

20. Nathans (p. 51) notes that "the right to reside in the Russian interior" was consistently the "cornerstone of Jewish appeals" to the imperial government.

21. Weeks, pp. 117–19.

22. Cited in Artur Eisenbach, *The Emancipation of the Jews in Poland, 1780–1870* (Oxford: Basil Blackwell in association with the Institute for Polish-Jewish Studies, 1991), p. 478.

23. According to the 1897 census, the Jews constituted 17.4 percent of the population of Grodno Province, while Catholics were 24.1 percent, of whom Poles (as opposed to Lithuanian and Belorussian Catholics) were only 6.2 percent. Jews owned 18.77 percent of the land in the province, a figure undoubtedly increased by the presence of the large and primarily Jewish city of Białystok (Weeks, pp. 85, 86, 88).

24. Letter to Malwina Blumberg, 28 January 1887, ms. no. 287 in the Archiwum Orzeszkowej in Grodno. Cited in Jan Detko, "Narodowy aspekt kwestii żydowskiej u Elizy Orzeszkowej," *Biuletyn Żydowskiego Instytutu Historycznego w Polsce*, no. 40 (1961), p. 50.

25. Eliza Orzeszkowa, Letter to Adolf Cohn, 9/21 January 1877, in "Pis'ma Elizy Orzeszko (1876–1883 g.)," *Evreiskaia starina*, vol. 7 (1914), p. 50.

26. Orzeszkowa voiced her distrust of all forms of Jewish separatism and nationalism in "O Żydach i kwestii żydowskiej." Toward the end of her life she made her point yet more strongly in an unfinished article, published after her death. See "Orzeszkowa o nacjonaliźmie żydowskim," *Kurier Warszawski*, 24, 25, and 26 September 1911.

27. "Positivism," in Roger Scruton, *A Dictionary of Political Thought* (New York: Harper and Row, 1982), p. 364.

28. In seventeenth- and eighteenth-century Poland, the nobility exercised power over the country by means of a parliament, the Sejm, whose decisions could be vetoed by a single member.

29. See the section on Positivism in Miłosz, *The History of Polish Literature*. For a more thorough exposition of the philosophy that inspired the literary movement, see Leszek Kolakowski, *The Alienation of Reason: A History of Positivist Thought*, trans. Norbert Guterman (Garden City, N.J.: Anchor Books, 1969).

30. Aleksander Hertz, *The Jews in Polish Culture*, trans. Richard Lourie (Evanston, Ill.: Northwestern University Press, 1988), p. 69.

31. On Positivism and the Jews, see Henryk Grynberg, "The Jewish Theme in Polish Positivism," *The Polish Review*, vol. 25, nos. 3–4 (1980); Stanislaw Blejwas, "Polish Positivism and the Jews," *Jewish Social Studies*, vol. 46, no. 1 (Winter 1984); and the tremendously informative Alina Cała, *Asymilacja Żydów w Królestwie Polskim (1864–1897): Postawy, konflikty, stereotypy* (Warsaw: Państwowy Instytut Wydawniczy, 1989).

32. Magdalena Opalski observes that "*Meir Ezofowicz*'s indebtedness to Niemcewicz's *Lejbe i Sióra* was a matter of course for most contemporary critics" ("The Concept of Jewish Assimilation in Polish Literature of the Positivist Period," *The Polish Review*, vol. 32, no. 4 [1987], p. 377). She cites W. Marrené-Morzkowska, "Kwestia żydowska w powieści współczesnej," *Tygodnik Ilustrowany*, no. 19 (1879).

33. Julian Ursyn Niemcewicz, "Do czytelnika," in *Lejbe i Sióra* (Cracow: Towarzystwo Miłośników Książki, 1931), p. xii. Also see the summary of the novel and the translated excerpts from it in Harold B. Segel, ed., *Stranger in Our Midst: Images of the Jew in Polish Literature* (Ithaca, N.Y.: Cornell University Press, 1996), pp. 43–60.

34. Magdalena Opalski, "Jewish Reformers of Polish Society and Their Programs in Nineteenth-Century Polish Fiction," in *Proceedings of the Conference on Poles and Jews: Myth and Reality in the Historical Context* (New York: Columbia University, 1986).

35. For descriptions and analyses of these folkloric images, see Hertz, *The Jews in Polish Culture*, and Alina Cała, *The Image of the Jew in Polish Folk Culture* (Jerusalem: Magnes Press, 1995), esp. chap. 1.

36. Weeks, p. 99.

37. The first letter is quoted in Edmund Jankowski, *Eliza Orzeszkowa* (Warsaw: Państwowy Instytut Wydawniczy, 1973), p. 181, the second in Kolodziej, p. 432.

38. Jankowski, p. 85.

39. Ibid., p. 73.

40. Ibid., pp. 124, 178 ff.

41. Letter to Jan Karlowicz, cited in ibid., p. 184.

42. Cała, *Asymilacja*, p. 373. She cites A. Zalewski, *Towarzystwo Warszawskie: Listy do Przyjaciółki przez baronową XYZ* (Cracow, 1888), pp. 262–73.

43. An edited selection of these letters fills an entire volume of her correspondence. Eliza Orzeszkowa, *Listy zebrane*, ed. Edmund Jankowski (Wrocław: Zakład Imienia Ossolińskich, Wydawnictwo Polskiej Akademii Nauk, 1955), vol. 2.

44. Cała, *Asymilacja*, p. 97. See Orzeszkowa's letters to him in vol. 1 of *Listy Zebrane*.

45. Cała, *Asymilacja*, p. 91. Orzeszkowa's letters to him appear in vol. 3 of *Listy Zebrane*.

46. Cała, *Asymilacja*, p. 217.

47. Orzeszkowa's letters to Cohn, translated into Russian, appear in "Pis'ma Elizy Orzeszko (1876–1883 g.)."

48. Cited in Irena Butkiewiczówna, *Powieści i nowele żydowskie Elizy Orzeszkowej* (Lublin: Towarzystwo naukowe Katolickiego uniwersytetu lubelskiego, 1937), p. 2.

49. Specifically, she read Kraszewski's novel *Żyd* [The Jew] (Poznań, 1866).

50. See Heinrich Hirsch Graetz, *History of the Jews* (1853–75) (Philadelphia: Jewish Publication Society, 1898).

51. For a somewhat later edition, see J. Brafman, *Żydzi i kahały* (Warsaw: Drukarnia synów St. Niemiry, 1914); I. I. Shershevskii, *O Knige kagala* (St. Petersburg: Tip. Skriatina, 1872). Orzeszkowa mentions her readings in various letters to Cohn, published in "Pis'ma Elizy Orzeszko," pp. 47, 51, 52, 46, 48; and in a letter to Aleksander Kraushar, 2 October 1881, *Listy zebrane*, vol. 8, p. 104.

52. In one of her stories, she suggests that the Polish language can be the first and best means to rectify all that she finds objectionable about Jewish life. A Jewish child who had been taught two Polish words—*daj kwiatek* ["give me a flower"]—remembers them and associates them with an angelic Polish lady. When a rabbi tells him a Jewish legend about an angel, he responds with these words. Orzeszkowa here hints that even the smallest exposure to Polish can demonstrate the virtues of the Polish culture and of Poles themselves, thereby making future fellowship possible. "Daj kwiatek," in Eliza Orzeszkowa, *Pisma Zebrane*, ed. Julian Krzyżanowski (Warsaw: Wiedza, 1948), vol. 18.

53. Cała, *Asymilacja*, pp. 267, 242. See A. Noemi, "Eliza Orzheshko," *Rassvet*, no. 20 (16 May 1910).

54. Letter to Peltyn, 2 October 1870, cited in Butkiewiczówna, p. 3.

55. J. J. K. [Kotarbiński], "Przegląd literacki: Meir Ezofowicz, powieść z życia Żydów, przez Elizę Orzeszkową," *Przegląd Tygodniowy*, no. 2 (31 January 1879), p. 22.

56. J. J. K., "Sprawa żydowska w powieściach i pismach Orzeszkowej," *Kraj*, no. 50 (13/25 December 1891).

57. Butkiewiczówna, p. 132.

58. The Karaites are a sect within Judaism that does not recognize the Oral Law, that is, the Talmud and its traditional interpretations. Of the traditional Jewish texts they respect only the Bible, of which they have their own interpretations. After the Russian annexation of Poland-Lithuania in the late eighteenth century, the Karaites were able to persuade the government of Catherine the Great that they were not real Jews and thus should not be subject to restrictive legislation affecting other Jews (who, to distinguish them from the Karaites, were called "Rabbinites"). Throughout the nineteenth century, Karaite spokesmen argued for this distinction. They asserted (incorrectly) that their ancestors had split off from Judaism before the Crucifixion and thus did not share in the "guilt" of contemporary Jews for the death of Jesus. In addition, they escaped the hostility non-Jews directed at the Talmud, suggesting that they held to a better form of Judaism, "purer" because free of Talmudic influences. The legal distinction that the imperial authorities made between Rabbinites and Karaites was continued by the Nazis, who did not kill Karaites. It is undoubtedly due to their different treatment by the authorities that relations between Karaites and Rabbinites were worse in Poland-Lithuania in the nineteenth and twentieth centuries

than at most other points in Jewish history. See Nathan Schur, *History of the Karaites* (Frankfurt am Main: Peter Lang, 1992), esp. pp. 112 ff. For a study that continues the tradition of emphasizing the distinction between Karaites and Rabbinites, cf. Simon Szyszman, *Les Karaïtes d'Europe* (Uppsala, Sweden: University of Uppsala, 1989).

59. Letter to Lewental, 12 March 1884, *Listy zebrane*, p. 132.

60. Butkiewiczówna, p. 75. See also Moshe Altbauer, "Aspects of the Life of Abraham Ezofowicz, Treasury Minister of the Grand Duchy of Lithuania in the Days of Zygmunt I Jagiełło,—a Historical-Philological Sketch" (in Hebrew), *Gal-Ed*, no. 12 (1991).

61. On the Jewish legislation considered by the Four Years Diet, see Eisenbach, pp. 106–12.

62. Graetz, vol. 3, pp. 524–25.

63. Page numbers refer to Eliza Orzeszkowa, *Meir Ezofowicz* (Warsaw: Spółdzielna Wydawnicza "Czytelnik," 1988).

64. Cała, *Asymilacja*, p. 266. For an example of such a young person, see Orzeszkowa's two letters to Bronisława Fajwelson, *Listy zebrane*, vol. 7, pp. 54–61. Also see [S. Dubnova (Erlikh)], "Orzheshko, Eliza," *Evreiskaia entsiklopediia*, vol. 12, p. 132.

65. Although Orzeszkowa did not mention Maimon's book in any of her correspondence regarding her Judaica reading, she did read Niemcewicz, whose *Lejbe i Sióra* was clearly influenced by the *Autobiography*. See Mieczysław Inglot, "The Image of the Jew in Polish Narrative Prose of the Romantic Period," *Polin*, vol. 2 (1987) p. 203. For a discussion of the connections between the Berlin Haskalah of the late eighteenth century and that of Eastern Europe in the nineteenth century, see Chapter 1.

66. Letter to Cohn, 9/21 January 1877, "Pis'ma Elizy Orzeszko," p. 51.

67. Graetz, vol. 2, p. 355.

68. Ibid., vol. 5, p. 183.

69. While traditional Jews in Polish shtetlach spoke primarily Yiddish, the Karaite community in the area spoke a Turkic dialect, reflecting its Crimean origins. See Schur, pp. 113–17.

70. J. I. Kraszewski, "Listy z zakątka," *Biesiada Literacka*, no. 173 (1879), p. 263.

71. Roman Nałęcz, "Przegląd literacki," *Przegląd Polski*, vol. 55 (1879), p. 314. I would like to thank Michael Steinlauf for pointing out that this insistence on the division between Poles and Jews, whose world the author has "discovered" and reveals for the first time, itself became a topos that would characterize Polish literature on the subject through the 1930s.

72. For some of Andriolli's other Jewish pictures, see an 1876 woodcut of "A Jew at prayer," reproduced in Michael C. Steinlauf, *Bondage to the Dead: Poland and the Memory of the Holocaust* (Syracuse, N.Y.: Syracuse University Press, 1997), and an illustration of Adam Mickiewicz's most famous Jewish character, Jankiel the musician in "Pan Tadeusz," which is reproduced on the cover of Hertz.

73. Nałęcz, p. 317.

74. Mstislavskaia, p. 14.

75. The historian Andrzej Walicki acknowledges this possibility in a different context: he analyzes the mixture of a Positivist commitment to "organic labor" and a Romantic vision of the nation in Orzeszkowa's 1880 brochure *Patriotism and Cosmopolitanism*. See Walicki, *Philosophy and Romantic Nationalism: The Case of Poland* (Oxford: Clarendon Press, 1982), pp. 342–43.

76. Edom was a Canaanite kingdom mentioned in the Bible; its inhabitants were believed to descend from Esau. Since the Middle Ages, European Jews sometimes referred to Christians as "Edomites." Edomites are condemned in Obadiah.

77. Letter to Bronisława Fajwelson, 8/20 March 1881, *Listy zebrane*, vol. 7, p. 54.

78. Mark Baker, "The Reassessment of *Haskala* Ideology in the Aftermath of the 1863 Polish Revolt," *Polin*, vol. 5 (1990); Mendelsohn, pp. 40–41.

79. Letter to Adolf Cohn, 9/21 January 1877, "Pis'ma Elizy Orzeszko," p. 50.

80. Julian Ursyn Niemcewicz, *Rok 3333 czyli sen niesłychany* (Warsaw: Biblioteka im. Jana Jelieńskiego, 1911). Also see the translated excerpts in Segel, *Stranger in Our Midst*. This pamphlet was written after *Lejbe i Sióra* and first published in 1858, after the author's death. It was issued as a separate volume in the early twentieth century.

81. N. S. Leskov, "Iz odnogo dorozhnogo dnevnika" [From a travel diary], *Polnoe sobranie sochinenii* (Moscow: Terra, 1996), vol. 3, p. 17. As Hugh McLean notes, Leskov's selection of representative Polish writers is idiosyncratic but does confirm his own familiarity with the subject (*Leskov*, pp. 86, 657).

82. N. D. Shigarin, "Ot redaktsii," p. 1.

83. *Pol'skaia biblioteka*, ed. and trans. R. I. Sementkovskii (St. Petersburg, 1882) (mentioned in Kolodziej, p. 451).

84. "Ot perevodchika," in *Meir Ezofovich*, p. 1.

85. On the discrediting and elimination of the *kahal*, see [Iu. Gessen], "Kagal v Rossii," *Evreiskaia entsiklopediia*, vol. 9, pp. 87–94. Cf. Michael Stanislawski's discussion of the kahal's role in furnishing recruits in *Tsar Nicholas I and the Jews*, pp. 127–33.

86. "Ot perevodchika," p. 5.

87. See Aleksander Żyga, "Wymienne nazwy Żydów w piśmiennictwie polskim w latach 1794–1863 na tle głównych orientacji społeczno-politycznych i wyznaniowych żydowstwa polskiego: Rekonesans," in *Literackie portrety Żydów*, ed. Eugenia Łoch (Lublin: Wydawnictwo Uniwersytetu Marie Curie-Skłodowskiej, 1996), pp. 320–29.

88. See Hertz, p. 253n5, for a discussion of *parch*.

89. Fishman, p. 80.

90. As early as the "Illiustratsiia affair" in 1858, Russian intellectuals decried the use of *zhid*. See Klier, *Imperial Russia's Jewish Question*, pp. 51ff. In 1879, Nikolai Leskov asked his publisher, Aleksandr Suvorin, to change the title of a series of articles from "Zhidovskaia vera" [Yids' Beliefs] to "Nabozhnye evrei" [Pious Jews] because the former was, he felt, *grubo* [rude]. N. S. Leskov, letter to A. S. Suvorin, 25 December 1879, *Sobranie sochinenii v 11 tomakh* (Moscow: Khud. lit., 1958), vol. 10, p. 468. Also note Vladimir Dal's definition of *zhid, zhidovin, zhidiuk* as *skupoi,*

skriaga, korystnyi skupets [a miser, a penny-pincher, an avaricious miser] in the original edition of *Tolkovyi slovar' zhivogo velikorusskogo iazyka* (St. Petersburg: M. O. Vol'f, 1903), vol. 1, p. 1315. Dal' did not include an entry for *evrei* at all.

91. Compare the Hebrew (and modern Russian) word for the Hebrew language, *ivrit*. See Max Vasmer, *Russisches etymologisches Wörterbuch* (Heidelberg: Karl Winter, 1953), pp. 389, 423, 492.

92. The translator for *Biblioteka Zapadnoi polosy Rossii* uses *evrei* in place of both Polish terms. The *Svet* translator sometimes uses *zhid* and *izraelit*, but at other points chooses *evrei* instead.

93. Fedor M. Dostoevskii, "Evreiskii vopros," in *Dnevnik pisatelia, Polnoe sobranie sochinenii v 30 tomakh* (Leningrad: Nauka, 1983), vol. 25, p. 75.

94. I. A. Brafman, *Kniga kagala* (Vilna: Pechatnia gubernskogo pravleniia, 1869). For an excellent summary of Brafman's ideas in this and other publications, their evolution, and the controversy surrounding them, see the chapter on "A state within a state," in Klier, pp. 263–83.

95. This chapter from a novel by Goedsche, a German who wrote under the pseudonym of Sir John Retcliffe, provided the skeleton for the *Protocols*. See Herman Bernstein, *The History of a Lie: "The Protocols of the Wise Men of Zion," a Study* (New York: Ogilvie, 1921); Mikhail Zolotonosov, *"Master i Margarita" kak putevoditel' po subkul'ture russkogo antisemitizma (SRA)* (St. Petersburg: Inapress, 1995), p. 8. Even while he insists that Bulgakov was not an anti-Semite, Zolotonosov argues that *Master and Margarita* relies on a set of images associated with the "subculture of Russian anti-Semitism."

96. Dudakov, p. 8.

97. Ibid., p. 134.

98. On the publication history of Krestovskii's novel, see Dudakov, p. 126; cf. Witold Kowalczyk, "Stereotyp Żyda w twórczości Wsiewołoda Kriestowskiego (na przykładzie trylogii Żyd)," in *Literackie portrety Żydów*, ed. Eugenia Łoch (Lublin: Wydawnictwo Uniwersytetu Marii Curie-Skłodowskiej), 1996. The trilogy appears in Vsevolod Vladimirovich Krestovskii, *Sobranie sochinenii*, vol. 8. Krestovskii published the beginning of the first volume, *T'ma egipetskaia* [Egyptian Darkness] in Katkov's *Russkii vestnik* in 1881, but it was broken off after a few chapters, perhaps in connection with the beginning of the pogroms, perhaps due to Katkov's evident dislike of the work. See Iu. Elets, "Biografiia Vsevoloda Vladimirovicha Krestovskogo," in Krestovskii, *Sobranie sochinenii*, vol. 1, pp. xxxvi–xl. It continued only in 1889, after a new editor took over at *Russkii vestnik*. The second volume, *Tamara Ben-David*, was published in 1892, and the third, *Torzhestvo Baala* [The Victory of Baal], left unfinished at the author's death in 1895, was published by his coworker Iu. Elets in 1899.

99. See Dudakov, pp. 118–30, for an account of Krestovskii's life that mentions his Polonophobia, his Germanophobia, and his none-too-warm sentiments about most other non-Russian groups.

100. Klier, *Imperial Russia's Jewish Question*, pp. 436–37.

101. Krestovskii, vol. 8, p. 485. Krestovskii's fascination with blood demonstrates the similarity between his ideology and that of the Western European racializing anti-Semitism that arose in the 1880s. Nevertheless, one should heed the many scholars who warn of the distinctions between Russian and German anti-Semitism in both the nineteenth and the twentieth centuries. The concept of race was differently valenced in the Russian Empire and in Europe. Even while Krestovskii and his ilk used German-sounding "blood-language," both the tsars' anti-Jewish policies and the population's hostility to Jews stemmed from economic and political causes that existed before the idea of race. Eli Weinerman reviews the historical literature on the evolution of anti-Semitism in the Russian Empire, in "Racism, Racial Prejudice, and Jews in Late Imperial Russia." Cf. Heinz-Dietrich Löwe, *The Tsars and the Jews*, esp. pp. 1–12.

102. Krestovskii, letter to N. A. Liubimov, 1 September 1879, cited in Iu. Elets, p. xxxvii.

103. Krestovskii, vol. 8, pp. 91, 92, 102, 139, 140, 142, 156. On his study of Judaism, see Elets, p. xxxix.

104. Krestovskii, letter to Iu. Elets, no date, cited in Elets, p. xlvii.

105. See [E. Orzheshko], "Tormozy sliianiia evreev s korennym nasileniem," *Voskhod*, no. 11 (1881), p. 63.

106. Stanisław Tarnowski, in "Z najnowszych powieści polskich" (*Niwa*, no. 20 [1881]), imagines a young, innocent Polish reader of *Meir Ezofowicz* who first simply questions his stereotypes about Jews, considering Orzeszkowa's argument that one must see them in their historical context and blame persecutions such as those that occurred during the Inquisition for their isolationism. Next, having begun to think about the Inquisition, he starts to compare Catholic fanaticism to Jewish fanaticism. Finally, he decides (in reference to one of the most important doctrinal differences separating Catholicism from Eastern Orthodoxy) that it may be completely unimportant "whether the Holy Spirit proceeds from the Father and the Son or from the Son alone" (p. 371).

107. Krestovskii, vol. 8, p. 16.

108. Ibid., p. 19. Rabbi Ionafan's assertion that it is "even permitted . . . in an extreme case" for Jews insincerely to convert to another religion is incorrect. According to traditional interpretations of Jewish law, one should allow oneself to die a martyr rather than consent to commit idolatry (both Christianity and Islam are usually defined in this context as idolatry). The question of the correct attitude toward forced converts is, however, somewhat controversial. For a discussion of Maimonides' opinions about the legal status of unwilling apostates, see Haym Soloveitchik, "Maimonides' *'Iggeret Ha-Shemad*: Law and Rhetoric," in *Rabbi Joseph H. Lookstein Memorial Volume*, ed. Leo Landman (New York: Ktav, 1980).

109. Jean-Paul Sartre, *Anti-Semite and Jew: An Exploration of the Etiology of Hate*, trans. George J. Becker (New York: Schocken, 1995), p. 19.

110. Weeks, pp. 96–103. Also see the discussion of legislative attempts to regulate the shifting national identities of individuals in the western provinces in Witold Rodkiewicz, "Telling Poles from Russians: The Tsarist Administration and Its Attempts to Define Polish and Russian Nationality in the Western Borderlands of the Russian Empire, 1863–1914," paper delivered at the American Historical Association, New York, January 1997.

111. The repression after 1863 indeed caused some people who might have identified themselves as Polish to "decide" that they were Russian. D. S. Mirsky sees the family of the Russian writer Vladimir Galaktionovich Korolenko as an example: "In his childhood Korolenko did not know very well to which nationality he belonged, and learned to read Polish before he did Russian. Only after the Revolt of 1863 did the family have definitely to 'choose' its nationality, and they became Russian." *A History of Russian Literature: From Its Beginnings to 1900* (New York: Vintage, 1958), p. 355.

112. See Detko; Cała, p. 224.

113. In Lev Anninsky's words, "it was the historic task of empire (and its concomitant values of universality and of sympathy with and understanding for all) that brought Russians into being as a nation in the first place." Lev Anninsky, "In a Somersaulting Spaceship," trans. Helen Burlingame, *Common Knowledge* (Spring 1995), p. 75.

114. For a few examples of relatively recent scholarly work that comes to this conclusion, see the dissertations by Rodkiewicz (1996) and Weinerman (1996), Weeks (1996), and Edward C. Thaden, ed., *Russification in the Baltic Provinces and Finland, 1855–1914* (Princeton, N.J.: Princeton University Press, 1981).

115. Katkov's comment is quoted in N. A. Liubimov, letter to Krestovskii, n.d., cited in Elets, p. xxxix.

116. N. S. Leskov, "Religioznye obriady evreev, Mezhdu Paskhoiu i Piatidesiatnitseiu." *Peterburgskaia gazeta*, 17 January 1881, p. 2; J. I. Kraszewski, "Listy z zakątka," p. 263; Roman Nałęcz, "Przegląd literacki," *Przegląd Polski*, vol. 55 (1879), p. 314.

117. Mstislavskaia, p. 14.

CHAPTER 3   NIKOLAI LESKOV

1. "Vladychnyi sud. Byl' (Iz nedavnikh vospominanii)," *Strannik*, vol. 1 (1877), nos. 1–2; "Rakushanskii melamed: Rasskaz na bivuake," *Russkii vestnik*, no. 3 (March 1878); "Zhidovskaia kuvyrkollegiia. Povest'. Ob odnom Kromchanine i o trekh zhidovinakh," *Gazeta A. Gattsuka*, no. 33 (14 August 1882), no. 34 (21 August 1882), no. 35 (28 August 1882), no. 36 (4 September 1882); "Rasskazy kstati: Novozavetnye evrei," *Nov'*, vol. 1, no. 1 (November 1884); "Rasskazy kstati: Ukha bez ryby," *Nov'*, vol. 8, no. 7 (February 1886); "Skazanie o Fedore-khristianine i o druge ego Abrame-zhidovine," *Russkaia mysl'*, no. 12 (20 December 1886). In translating the titles, I follow Hugh McLean in *Nikolai Leskov*. For a discussion of "Rakushanskii melamed," see Chapter 1.

2. These ethnographic articles are listed in the Bibliography.

3. *Evrei v Rossii* (St. Petersburg: 1884); reissued as *Evrei* [singular] *v Rossii*, with an introduction by Iulii Gessen (Petrograd, 1919). For an English translation, see Nikolai S. Leskov, *The Jews in Russia: Some Notes on the Jewish Question*, ed. and trans. Harold Klassel Schefski (Princeton, N.J.: Kingston Press, 1986). Although there is no proof that Leskov was paid to produce this book, it is unlikely that he wrote it for free.

4. See [V. Vodovozov], "Leskov, Nikolai Semenovich," in *Evreiskaia entsiklopediia*, vol. 10, pp. 415–18; [William B. Edgerton], "Leskov, Nikolay Semyonovich," in *Encyclopedia Judaica* (Jerusalem: Ketzer, 1971), vol. 11, pp. 45–46; Iulii Gessen's introduction to the postrevolutionary edition of *Evrei v Rossii*; Noé Gruss, "N. S. Leskov et les Juifs de Russie," *AMIF* (1974); Hugh McLean, "Theodore the Christian Looks at Abraham the Hebrew: Leskov and the Jews," *California Slavic Studies* 7 (1973), and "Abraham the Hebrew," in *Nikolai Leskov*; Harold Klassel Schefski, introduction to Nikolai S. Leskov, *The Jews in Russia*; and A. A. Gorelov, *N. S. Leskov i narodnaia kul'tura* (Leningrad: Nauka, 1988), p. 167n12.

5. N. S. Leskov, letter to K. A. Grehwe, 5 December 1888, *Sobranie sochinenii v 11 tomakh* (Moscow: Khud. lit., 1958), vol. 11, p. 404.

6. A. I. Faresov, *Protiv techenii* (St. Petersburg: M. Merkushev, 1904), p. 301.

7. Ibid., p. 293.

8. See the discussion of conversion from Judaism in the Introduction. Cf. the history of conversion to Orthodoxy in seventeenth- and eighteenth-century Russia in Michael Khodarkovsky, "'Not by Word Alone': Missionary Policies and Religious Conversion in Early Modern Russia," *Comparative Studies in Society and History: An International Quarterly*, vol. 38, no. 2 (April 1996).

9. This was the opinion of Prince Meshcherskii, the publisher of the journal *Grazhdanin*. See *Nedel'naia khronika Voskhoda*, 1 November 1887, p. 1099; cf. a series of articles in *Novorossiiskii telegraf*: "Po povodu perekhoda evreev v pravoslavie," no. 4184 (10 September 1888), "Po povodu perekhoda evreev v pravoslavie," no. 4200 (26 September 1888), "O perekhode evreev v pravoslavie," no. 4588 (7 November 1888). Many thanks to Ben Nathans for these articles!

10. "Iz obshchestvennoi khroniki," p. 869.

11. *The Confessions of St. Augustine*, trans. John K. Ryan (New York: Image Books, 1960), p. 202.

12. On the conversion tale, see Bakhtin, "Forms of Time and Chronotope in the Novel," pp. 115, 116, 118, 120.

13. For discussion of the splitting of the image of the Jewish convert into the "real" and the "false," see Gilman, *Jewish Self-Hatred*, pp. 22–67.

14. Erich Auerbach, "Figura," in *Scenes from the Drama of European Literature* (Minneapolis: University of Minnesota Press, 1984), p. 29.

15. Ibid., p. 58.

16. For some typical stories of good converts, see Father Ioann Verzhekovskii, letter to the editor, *Kievlianin*, no. 124 (17 October 1867); an autobiographical account in

Aleksandr Alekseev, *Obshchestvennaia zhizn' evreev, ikh nravy, obychai, i predrassudki, s prilozheniem biografii avtora* (Novgorod, 1868); and fictional depictions in Vl. Levinskii, *Perekreshchenets iz evreiskogo byta* (Moscow, 1870), and Krestovskii, *Sobranie sochinenii*, vol 8. For more on Krestovskii, see Chapter 2.

17. [Anon.], "Novozavetnye evrei," *Peterburgskaia gazeta*, no. 4 (5 January 1885). This is not the story I discuss later, but a newspaper article with the same title. Inès Müller de Morogues, in *L'oeuvre journalistique et littéraire de N. S. Leskov: Bibliographie* (New York: Peter Lang, 1984), identifies the author as Leskov. On New Israel, see [I. Cherikover], "Novyi Izrail'," *Evreiskaia entsiklopediia*, vol. 11, pp. 769–71. On the leader of the movement, see Steven J. Zipperstein, "Heresy, Apostasy, and the Transformation of Joseph Rabinovich," in *Jewish Apostasy in the Modern World*, ed. Todd M. Endelman (New York: Holmes and Meier, 1987).

18. A. F. Pisemskii, *Polnoe sobranie sochinenii* (St. Petersburg: M. O. Vol'f, 1896), vol. 23.

19. M. E. Saltykov-Shchedrin, *Sobranie sochinenii* (Moscow: Khud. lit., 1973), vol. 15, pt. 1, p. 255.

20. N. S. Leskov, "Russkie deiateli v ostzeiskom krae," *Istoricheskii vestnik* (November 1883), p. 242.

21. Karl Marx, "*On the Jewish Question*, by Bruno Bauer," in *Selected Writings*, ed. David McLellan (Oxford: Oxford University Press, 1990), p. 59.

22. Stanislawski, *Tsar Nicholas I and the Jews*, p. 15; Shaul Ginzburg, *Historishe verk*, vol. 2, pp. 7–8.

23. Page numbers refer to N. S. Leskov, "Vladychnyi sud," *Sobranie sochinenii v 11 tomakh* (Moscow: Khud lit., 1957), vol. 6.

24. Stanislawski, p. 25; he cites N. Samter, *Judentaufen im 19ten Jahrhundert* (Berlin, 1906), p. 42.

25. Stanislawski, pp. 25–29.

26. Aleksandr I. Gertsen, *Byloe i dumy* (Moscow: Khud. lit., 1958), vol. 1, p. 209.

27. For a tremendously informative history of literary depictions of cantonists in Russian, Hebrew, and Yiddish, see Olga Litvak, *The Literary Response to Conscription*.

28. Stanislawski, p. 184.

29. He wrote *O raskol'nikakh goroda Rigi, preimushchestvenno v otnoshenii k shkolam* (1863); "S liud'mi drevlego blagochestiia," (1863) *Biblioteka dlia chteniia*, vol. 153, no. 11 (November 1863); "Iskanie shkol staroobriadtsami" (a series of feuilleton articles, 1869, in *Birzhevye vedomosti*); and many other articles in *Birzhevye vedomosti*, *Istoricheskii vestnik*, and other newspapers and journals, 1863–86.

30. *O raskol'nikakh goroda Rigi*, p. 33; "Iskanie shkol staroobriadtsami," 30 January 1869; "Irodova rabota," *Istoricheskii vestnik*, (April 1882), p. 191. In selecting this biblical verse to signify the mourning of the righteous oppressed, Leskov echoed one of his era's most popular books, in Russia as elsewhere: Harriet Beecher Stowe used the same line as the epigraph to vol. 1, chap. 12, of *Uncle Tom's Cabin*. In 1881, Dosto-

evskii would have Father Zosima quote the same line in *The Brothers Karamazov* (Dostoevskii, *Polnoe sobranie sochinenii,* vol. 14, p. 46).

31. "Iskanie shkol staroobriadtsami," 7 February 1869.

32. "Irodova rabota," p. 197.

33. See Gregory L. Freeze, *The Parish Clergy in Nineteeth-Century Russia: Crisis, Reform, Counter-Reform* (Princeton, N.J.: Princeton University Press, 1983).

34. I. S. Bellyustin, *Description of the Clergy in Rural Russia,* trans. Gregory L. Freeze (Ithaca, N.Y.: Cornell University Press, 1985).

35. Freeze, *The Parish Clergy,* p. 220.

36. Nikolai S. Leskov, *Velikosvetskii raskol* (St. Petersburg: V. Tushnova, 1877); N. S. Leskov, *Schism in High Society: Lord Radstock and His Followers,* trans. James Y. Muckle (Nottingham, England: Bramcote Press, 1995).

37. Vladimir Solov'ev, "Evreistvo i khristianskii vopros," in *Taina Izrailia: "Evreiskii vopros" v russkoi religioznoi mysli kontsa XIX–pervoi poloviny XX v.v.,* ed. V. F. Boikov. (St. Petersburg: Sofiia, 1993), p. 31.

38. Judith Deutsch Kornblatt, "Vladimir Solov'ev on Spiritual Nationhood, Russia, and the Jews," *Russian Review,* vol. 56, no. 2 (April 1997), p. 158.

39. See "Novye knigi," *Delo,* no. 9 (1879); "Bibliograficheskie izvestiia," *Pravoslavnyi sobednik* (April 1887); *Tserkovno-obshchestvennyi vestnik,* no. 54 (18 May 1877), p. 3; McLean, *Nikolai Leskov,* p. 311.

40. I would like to thank Inès Müller de Morogues for pointing out to me that one might make a similar observation about another story that Leskov wrote in 1877, "Nekreshchennyi pop" [The Unbaptized Priest].

41. Dmitrii S. Likhachev, *Literatura—real'nost'—literatura* (Leningrad: Sovetskii pisatel', 1984), p. 132.

42. This would be consistent with the reaction of the anonymous reviewer in *Otechestvennye zapiski,* no. 8 (August 1877), who rejects the substitute recruit as a representative of the morals of Jews in general: "In no place and at no time has it been possible to make judgments about the religiosity of a people based on the rabble of that people, for that matter the most base rabble" (p. 271).

43. McLean, *Nikolai Leskov,* p. 311.

44. N. S. Leskov, letter to A. S. Suvorin (Winter 1877–78), Rukopisnyi otdel Instituta russkoi literatury i iskusstva, St. Petersburg, f. 268, ed. khr. 131, l. 24.

45. Approximation of V. V. Kapnist epigram (Leskov, Sobranie, vol. 6, p. 632).

46. *Otechestvennye zapiski,* no. 8 (August 1877), p. 271.

47. *Nash vek,* no. 20 (March 1877), p. 3.

48. "K biografii N. S. Leskova (+21 fevralia 1895 g.)," *Russkaia starina* (December 1895), p. 206.

49. Andrei Leskov, *Zhizn' Nikolaia Leskova po ego lichnym, semeinym i nesemeinym zapisiam i pamiatiam, v dvukh tomakh* (Moscow: Khud. lit., 1984), vol. 1, p. 106; see also vol. 2, p. 27.

50. See James Y. Muckle, *Nikolai Leskov and the "Spirit of Protestantism"* (Birmingham, England: Birmingham Slavonic Monographs, no. 4 [1978]), pp. 113–25.

51. N. S. Leskov, "Rasskazy kstati: Novozavetnye evrei," *Nov'* (1 November 1884), pp. 71–84.

52. The movement begun by Edward Irving is known today as the Catholic Apostolic Church. Leskov referred to it in several stories; see Muckle, pp. 83–85.

53. Such a rendition appears in Russian in the biography of "James Adler," the son of a rabbi in the Pale of Settlement, who reads the New Testament, becomes a Protestant over the protests of his parents and community, leaves for England, becomes a missionary, and in that capacity returns to Russia in 1887. A. S. Ardov, *Evrei-evangelisty* (Moscow: N. L. Kazetskogo, 1914), p. 40. Also see the mentions of narratives of this sort in English literature in Michael Ragussis, *Figures of Conversion: "The Jewish Question" and English National Identity* (Durham, N.C.: Duke University Press, 1995). He cites, for example, a work called *The Russo-Polish Jew: A Narrative of Conversion* (p. 45). For a discussion of the motivations of the Jews in the Russian Empire who became Protestants, see Endelman, "Jewish Converts in Nineteenth-Century Warsaw."

54. N. S. Leskov, *Schism in High Society*, p. 73.

55. *Nedel'naia khronika Voskhoda*, vol. 8, no. 45 (11 November 1884), p. 1284.

56. Dostoevskii, vol. 25, pp. 74–92.

57. Moshe Barash, *Icon: Studies in the History of an Idea* (New York: New York University Press, 1992), p. 202. Leskov's narrator in "Zapechatlennyi angel" [The Sealed Angel] repeats Gregory's argument.

58. Ibid., pp. 204–18.

59. Pavel Florensky, *Iconostasis*, trans. Donald Sheehan and Olga Andreev (Crestwood, N.Y.: St. Vladimir's Seminary Press, 1996), pp. 52, 62.

60. Indeed, Florensky, the modern iconodule, shared with the Symbolists an opposition to rational knowledge as such. See Richard F. Gustafson, introduction to Pavel Florensky, *The Pillar and Ground of the Truth*, trans. Boris Jakim (Princeton, N.Y.: Princeton University Press, 1997), pp. xv–xvii.

61. Goldstein, pp. 159, 140.

62. Joseph Frank, foreword to Goldstein, *Dostoyevsky and the Jews*.

63. Gary Saul Morson, "Dostoevsky's Anti-Semitism and the Critics: A Review Article," *Slavic and East European Journal*, vol. 27. no. 3 (Fall 1983).

64. Dreizin, pp. 65, 113.

65. Gary Rosenshield, "Dostoevskii's 'The Funeral of the Universal Man' and 'An Isolated Case' and Chekhov's 'Rothschild's Fiddle': The Jewish Question," *Russian Review*, no. 56 (October 1997), p. 487.

66. According to the notes to the Academy edition of Dostoevskii, this passage paraphrases a number of points in M. I. Grinevich, *O tletvornom vliianii evreev na ekonomicheskii byt Rossii i o sisteme evreiskoi ekspluatatsii* (St. Petersburg, 1876). In

fact, a number of "translations" and "interpretations" of the Talmud in specific and Judaism in general, some more reliable than others, could have been available to Dostoevskii and might have inspired this passage.

67. Nikolai Danilevskii (1822–85) articulated his nationalist political philosophy in *Rossiia i Evropa* (1871), a book that Dostoevskii discussed in his correspondence with Sofiia Lur'e.

68. Leskov borrowed much of his information from a single source, a book on Jewish ritual published in Orel in 1830: *Obriady evreiskie, ili opisanie tseremonii i obyknovenii, nabliudaemykh evreiami kak vne khrama, tak ravno i vo vse torzhestvennye dni, pri obrezanii, pri svad'bakh, rodinakh, smerti, pogrebeniiakh i proch. s 4–mia kartinami* [Jewish Rites, Or a Description of the Ceremonies and Customs Observed by the Jews Both Outside of the Temple and on All the Holy Days, During Circumcisions, Weddings, Births, Deaths, Burials, and So On. With Four Pictures]. While it criticizes Jewish ritual, this book contains only minor inaccuracies in its descriptions and does not mention the blood libel. It seems to be a translation, most likely from German or Latin; the translator sometimes inserts footnotes expanding on items described in the text or pointing out the errors of the original author. For a detailed analysis of Leskov's use of his source, see Safran, "Ethnography, Judaism, and the Art of Nikolai Leskov."

69. N. S. Leskov, "Religioznye obriady evreev: Shabash, ili prazdnik sedmits," *Peterburgskaia gazeta*, no. 252 (20 December 1880). In fact, the Midrashic legend about the dead drinking at dusk (Midrash Tekhillim, Ps. 11) most likely derives from ancient Near Eastern tradition; it was also known in Sumer. While one might on these grounds suggest that Ukrainian peasants borrowed this belief from the Jews, it is more likely that such beliefs among Ukrainians stem from the Slavic folkloric conception of water as a liminal space between the worlds of the living and the dead.

70. N. S. Leskov, "Religioznye obriady evreev: Prazdnik trub (ili Novogo Goda)," *Peterburgskaia gazeta*, no. 38 (14 February 1881).

71. Johann Pfefferkorn (1469–1521) was a Jew who converted to Christianity in Cologne and then wrote a number of works critical of Judaism.

72. N. S. Leskov, "Obriady i sueveriia evreev: Den' ochishcheniia," *Peterburgskaia gazeta*, no. 68 (21 March 1881).

73. Goldstein, p. 163.

74. Walter Benjamin, "The Storyteller: Reflections on the Works of Nikolai Leskov," in *Illuminations*, ed. Hannah Arendt, trans. Harry Zohn (New York: Schocken, 1969), pp. 88, 89.

75. E. K. Romodanovskaia, *Russkaia literatura na poroge novogo vremeni* (Novosibirsk: VO Nauka, 1994), p. 112.

76. McLean, *Nikolai Leskov*, p. 434.

77. Isaiah Berlin, "Herder and the Enlightenment," in *Vico and Herder: Two Studies in the History of Ideas* (London: Hogarth Press, 1976), p. 153. My presentation of

Herder relies on Berlin's summary of his views. As recent scholarship has made clear, Herder's views on the "Jewish question" were not entirely in accord with the principles of the value of folk cultures and their incommensurability. I became aware of this after reading Liliane Weissberg, "Jews or Hebrews? Religious and Political Conversion in Herder," a seminar paper presented at a faculty seminar at the University of Pennsylvania, "The West in Global Perspective," 28 February 1997.

78. Maksim Gor'kii, *Sobranie sochinenii v 30 tomakh* (Moscow: Khud. lit., 1953), vol. 24, pp. 237, 228.

79. See Kathleen Parthé, "The Righteous Brothers (and Sisters) of Contemporary Russian Literature," *World Literature Today: A Literary Quarterly of the University of Oklahoma* (Winter 1993), pp. 94, 95.

80. William Edgerton, in "Leskov and Russia's Slavic Brethren," *American Contributions to the Fourth International Congress of Slavicists, Moscow, September 1958* (The Hague: Mouton, 1958), concludes that Leskov was especially internationalist during the final, Tolstoian period of his life, in the 1880s and 1890s; T. S. Sal'nikova, in "Ideia bratstva narodov v putevykh ocherkakh N. S. Leskova," *Voprosy russkoi literatury*, vol. 27, no. 1 (1976), argues that these views were already apparent in a series of travel sketches he wrote in 1862.

81. Inès Müller de Morogues, "Le patriotisme de Leskov," *Schweizerische Beiträge zum X. internationalen Slavistenkongress in Sofia 1988* (Bern: Peter Lang, 1988), p. 282. Cf. an examination of the roles of non-Russian ethnicities in the creation of Leskov's "prosaics": Knut Andreas Grimstad, "Nikolai Leskov and the Problem of Polyethnicity," in *Celebrating Creativity: Essays in Honor of Jostein Børtnes*, ed. Knut Andreas Grimstad and Ingunn Lunde (Bergen, Norway: University of Bergen, 1997).

CHAPTER 4   ANTON CHEKHOV

1. See the letters to V. V. Bilibin of 18 January 1886, 1 February 1886, 14 February 1886, and 28 February 1886, and the letter to M. P. Chekhov of 6 May 1886, in Anton P. Chekhov, *Polnoe sobranie sochinenii i pisem v 30 tomakh* (Moscow: Nauka, 1974), *Pis'ma*, vol. 1, pp. 183, 190, 197, 205, 241. In future references, the eighteen volumes of prose in this edition will be listed as *PSS*, with the volume number, and the twelve volumes of letters will be listed as *Pis'ma*, with the volume number.

2. Letter to V. V. Bilibin, 11 March 1886; ibid., p. 213.

3. Ibid., 4 April 1886, p. 226.

4. Letter to M. V. Kiselova, 21 September 1886; ibid., p. 262.

5. Ibid., 29 October 1886, p. 271.

6. *Perekati-pole*, literally "baby's-breath," figuratively means a person who is constantly on the move. The story's title is often translated as "The Rolling Stone," but I prefer "The Tumbleweed," which retains the plant imagery as well as the metaphor.

7. For a brief treatment of the available evidence, see Carolina de Maegd-Soëp,

Chekhov and Women: Women in the Life and Work of Chekhov (Columbus, Ohio: Slavica, 1987), pp. 102–7. For a longer analysis, see Elena Tolstaia, *Poetika razdrazheniia: Chekhov v kontse 1880–kh—nachale 1890–kh godov* (Moscow: Radiks, 1994), chap. 1. The same material appears as Elena Tolstaia, "'Tsenzura ne propuskaet . . . ': Chekhov i Dunia Efros," *Novoe literaturnoe obozrenie*, no. 8 (1994), pp. 221–49. In the following references, I will cite the book version.

8. Ragussis, pp. 58, 60.

9. *Moscow Herald*, 1828, cited in David Magarshak, *Gogol: A Life* (New York: Grove Press, 1969), p. 123, itself cited in Dreizin, p. 10.

10. Kunitz, pp. 18, 29. Kunitz gives examples of avaricious Jewish men and their sexy daughters in Pushkin's play "Skupoi rytsar'" [The Covetous Knight] and his mock-biblical epic, "Gavriiliada" (the Jewish father is in the former and the daughter in the latter), Lermontov's long poem "Sashka," and N. V. Kukol'nik's play *Kniaz' Vasil'evich Kholmsky* [Prince Vasil'evich Kholmsky].

11. See Edward J. Bristow, *Prostitution and Prejudice: The Jewish Fight Against White Slavery, 1870–1939* (New York: Schocken, 1982); Laura Engelstein, *The Keys to Happiness*, esp. chap. 8; Laurie Bernstein, *Sonia's Daughters: Prostitutes and Their Regulation in Imperial Russia* (Berkeley: University of California Press, 1995), esp. pp. 161–66; Donna J. Guy, *Sex and Danger in Buenos Aires: Prostitution, Family, and Nation in Argentina* (Lincoln: University of Nebraska Press, 1991), esp. chap. 1; and Sander Gilman, *The Jew's Body* (New York: Routledge, 1991), esp. chap. 4.

12. Zhabotinskii, p. 88. Cf. Betty Valdman, "Turgenev, Jews, and the Russian-Jewish Press," *Shvut*, vol. 6, no. 22 (1997). She argues that although Turgenev's narrator in "The Yid" is hostile to Jews, the writer was not, as demonstrated in his other writings, especially in the 1869 novella *Neschastnaia* [The Unhappy Girl].

13. Karl Marx, "*On the Jewish Question*." Cf. Marx, "The Communist Manifesto" (1848), in *Selected Writings*, pp. 223, 224, and Friedrich Engels's association of marriage and prostitution in "The Origin of the Family, Private Property, and the State," in *The Marx-Engels Reader*, ed. Robert Tucker (New York: W. W. Norton, 1978), p. 742.

14. Löwe, p. 8. I discuss literary examples of wealthy Jews who exploit non-Jews in the introduction to this study.

15. On Ignat'ev and Pobedonostsev, see Rogger, *Jewish Policies and Right-Wing Politics in Imperial Russia*, pp. 61, 67.

16. Kunitz, pp. 104–67. For examples, see note 33 in the current chapter. Historical presentations of Jews killed in the Inquisition reinforced the image of the Jew as victim rather than victimizer, an image that reached its strongest and most controversial form with the identification of Jews with Jesus (implied in the literary debate on whether Jesus should be identified as a Jew). See the discussion of Jesus' Jewishness in Zolotonosov, pp. 51 ff. Zolotonosov cites a poetic debate on the question between E. Gollerbakh and Zinaida Gippius that took place in 1917.

17. Leo N. Tolstoi, *Sobranie sochinenii v 20 tomakh* (Moscow: Khud. lit., 1964),

vol. 12, p. 153. English translation quoted from Leo Tolstoi, *The Death of Ivan Ilych and Other Stories*, Trans. Aylmer Maude (New York: New American Library, 1960), p. 178.

18. Bristow, pp. 48–50. Engelstein points out that because Jews and prostitutes were both overwhelmingly urban, the statistics showing a preponderance of Jewish prostitutes are misleading (Engelstein, p. 307). Nonetheless, Laurie Bernstein points out, the involvement of Jews in prostitution was "disproportionate" (L. Bernstein, p. 164).

19. L. Bernstein, p. 164.

20. Ibid., pp. 163, 165; Guy, pp. 10 ff.

21. L. Bernstein, p. 38.

22. Veniamin M. Tarnovskii, *Prostitutsiia i abolitsionizm: Doklad Russkomu sifili-dologicheskomu i dermatologicheskomu obshchestvu* (St. Petersburg: Karla Rikkera, 1888), pp. 133, 135, 160, 172. Engelstein notes that Tarnovskii was alone among the Russian followers of the Italian criminologist Cesare Lombroso in insisting on both prostitutes' responsibility for their actions and their lack of free will. Others proceeded from the belief in a biological cause for criminality to the necessity of medical intervention (Engelstein, p. 137). However, Tarnovskii remained an influential and not entirely anomalous figure, who embodied one pole of the prostitution debate.

23. L. Bernstein, pp. 266–95.

24. For a thorough discussion of prostitution in Russian literature, see A. K. Zholkovskii, "Prilozhenie 1: Topos prostitutsii v literature," in *Babel'/Babel*, by A. K. Zholskovskii and M. B. Iampol'skii (Moscow: Carte Blanche, 1994).

25. A. I. Kuprin, *Iama*, in *Sobranie sochinenii v 6 tomakh* (Moscow: Khud. lit., 1994), vol. 4, p. 266.

26. In her discussion of beliefs regarding the spread of syphilis, Engelstein explains that the refusal to admit that peasants engaged in illicit or commercial sexual relations led to the insistence than syphilis in the countryside was nongenitally transmitted. See Engelstein, chap. 5.

27. See Dreizin, p. 3.

28. Tarnovskii, pp. 171–72.

29. Engelstein, pp. 132 ff.

30. Sander Gilman, who focuses on early-twentieth-century Germany rather than late imperial Russia, offers some provocative speculation about the belief that Jews were infected with syphilis, the prototypical disease of prostitutes. He links the perception of syphilis and hysteria to each other, to modernity, and to a racializing conception of Jews as the prototypically genetically flawed group: "The Jew is predisposed to hysteria both by heredity and consanguinity . . . and, as we shall see, by the trauma of civilization as represented by the Jews' predisposition to the somatic diseases linked to hysteria—such as syphilis. . . . The merging of various forms of illness, from syphilis to hysteria, is through the model of inherited characteristics. The

'real' disease is the degeneracy of the parent and its manifestation in specific 'illness' can vary from individual to individual. Thus syphilis and hysteria are truly forms of the same pattern of illness." Gilman, pp. 79, 84: Cf. Stephen Jay Gould's summary of the methods of nineteenth-century criminal anthropology in *The Mismeasure of Man* (New York: W. W. Norton, 1996), pp. 151–72.

31. *Narody Rossii: etnograficheskie ocherki* (St. Petersburg: Obshchestvennaia pol'za, 1878–80), vol. 1, pp. 391–92.

32. It is intriguing that Tarnovskii's opinions about prostitutes apparently extended to Jews as well. Engelstein notes that Cesare Lombroso, himself an Italian Jew (and a vigorous assimilationist), was disturbed by what he saw as Tarnovskii's anti-Semitism (Engelstein, p. 308). See C. Lombroso, *Der Antisemitismus und die Juden* (Leipzig: Georg H. Wigands Verlag, 1894).

33. After 1881, Jews in Russia "acquired the symbolic meaning of victims" (Dreizin, p. 1). In addition, although much of his discussion of the image of the Jew in Russian literature is so uncompromisingly Marxist as to distort the picture, Joshua Kunitz's analysis of the postpogrom literature is valuable. His argument that authors began to see Jews as oppressed by the government and the class system is probably most true for writers such as Uspenskii, Gor'kii, Korolenko, and the contributors to *The Shield*, a 1916 anthology of stories touching on the Jewish question; see Kunitz, pp. 104–38. Recent scholarship on the pogroms challenges the notion that the tsarist authorities were primarily to blame for the violence. See John D. Klier and Shlomo Lambroza, eds., *Pogroms: Anti-Jewish Violence in Modern Russian History* (Cambridge: Cambridge University Press, 1993).

34. See L. Bernstein, pp. 189–218.

35. Page numbers refer to "Pripadok," in Chekhov, *PSS*, vol. 7.

36. L. Bernstein, pp. 66–67.

37. Donald Rayfield, *Chekhov: A Life* (London: HarperCollins, 1997), p. 183; A. Chekhov, *Anton Chekhov's Life and Thought: Selected Letters and Commentary*, trans. Michael Henry Heim, ed. Simon Karlinsky (Berkeley: University of California Press, 1973), pp. 203–5.

38. Engelstein, p. 144.

39. Letter to Elena Shavrova-Iust, 28 February 1895, *Pis'ma*, vol. 6, pp. 26–31.

40. For a discussion of the debates associated with this piece, see Klier, *Imperial Russia's Jewish Question*, pp. 403–7.

41. Chekhov, diary entry, February 1897, *PSS*, vol. 17, p. 224; Chekhov, letter to O. Knipper, 7 April 1902, *Pis'ma*, vol. 10, p. 214. See Tolstaia, pp. 350 ff.

42. Viktoriia Levitina, *Russkii teatr i evrei* (Israel: Biblioteka-Aliia, 1988), vol. 1, pp. 75–109; A. Lavretskii, "Chekhov i evrei," *Novyi put'*, no. 28 (31 July 1916), p. 34.

43. Zhabotinskii, p. 77.

44. Ibid., p. 92.

45. Tolstaia, pp. 20, 33, 34, 40.

46. Chekhov, *Anton Chekhov's Life and Thought*, ed. Karlinsky, pp. xiii, 315–20.

47. Julie de Sherbinin, *Chekhov and Russian Religious Culture: The Poetics of the Marian Paradigm* (Evanston, Ill.: Northwestern University Press, 1997), p. 5.

48. De Maegd-Soëp addresses Chekhov's views of marriage throughout her work; see esp. pp. 82–100. The comment about "boredom" appears in a letter to A. S. Suvorin, 18 October 1892, *Pis'ma*, vol. 5, p. 117. Chekhov's remarks on prostitution and on sex in general are usually omitted in Soviet biographies and editions of his letters, but they are all restored in Rayfield, *Chekhov: A Life*.

49. Page numbers refer to "Tina," in Chekhov, *PSS*, vol. 5.

50. See Robert Louis Jackson, "'If I Forget Thee, O Jerusalem': An Essay on Chekhov's 'Rothschild's Fiddle'," *Slavica Hierosolymitana: Slavic Studies of the Hebrew University*, vol. 3 (1978), pp. 62 ff.

51. The Hermitage acquired a 1721 version of de Troy's *Susanna and the Elders* between 1766 and 1768. The Pushkin Museum possesses a 1715 version. Inna S. Nemilova, *The Hermitage Catalogue of Western European Painting: French Painting, Eighteenth Century* (Florence: Giunti Barbèra Martello; Moscow: Iskusstvo, 1986), p. 345.

52. Savelii Senderovich, "O chekhovskoi glubine, ili iudofobskii rasskaz Chekhova v svete iudaisticheskoi ekzegezy," in *Avtor i tekst: Sbornik statei*, ed. V. M. Markovich and Vol'f Shmid (St. Petersburg: S-Peterburgskogo universiteta, 1996), pp. 334–35. Senderovich mentions a number of renditions of *Susanna and the Elders* that Chekhov could have seen. In the context of desirable Jews who were off-limits, one might recall Sarah Bernhardt, the French actress of Jewish origin. Like Susanna, she was dark, slim, and associated with illness: in *La dame aux camélias*, her most famous role, she played a tubercular heroine. Sander Gilman sees her as "the essential *belle juive*," who is "as dangerous as she is seductive." Gilman, "Salome, Syphilis, Sarah Bernhardt, and the Modern Jewess," *The Jew in the Text: Modernity and the Construction of Identity*, ed. Linda Nochlin and Tamar Garb (London: Thames and Hudson, 1995), p. 113. Chekhov saw Bernhardt perform in Moscow in 1881 and wrote two reviews, in which he mocked the European and American public for their adoration of the actress, whose success, he said, owed more to hard work than to talent. However, there are no striking similarities between his description of Bernhardt and that of Susanna. See "Sara Bernar" and "Opiat' o Sare Bernar," *PSS*, vol. 1.

53. Senderovich, "O chekhovskoi glubine," pp. 320–21.

54. Nana's primary victim, the Count Muffat, falls "into turmoil" when surrounded by "that strong sweet perfume" (Emile Zola, *Nana* [New York: Modern Library, 1929], pp. 60, 166).

55. See Tolstaia, p. 28.

56. "There had been a long tradition in Europe which held that the skin of the Jew is marked by a disease, the '*Judenkratze*' or '*parech*,' as a sign of divine displeasure." Gilman, *The Jew's Body*, p. 100.

57. Although *zarazitel'nyi* is often used for metaphorical infection, such as with

happiness, and *zaraznyi* for literal contagion, the former can indicate a transfer of disease as well.

58. Joseph L. Conrad, "Sensuality in Cexov's Prose," *Slavic and East European Journal*, vol. 24, no. 2 (Summer 1980), p. 113.

59. Senderovich, "O chekhovskoi glubine," p. 306.

60. M. Kiseleva, letter to Anton Chekhov, December 1886, cited in *PSS*, vol. 5, p. 660.

61. Letter to M. V. Kiseleva, 14 January 1887, *Pis'ma*, vol. 2, p. 12.

62. Tolstaia, p. 38.

63. Letter to V. V. Bilibin, 28 February 1886, *Pis'ma*, vol. 1, p. 205.

64. Letter to the Chekhovs, 11 May 1887, *Pis'ma*, vol. 2, pp. 80–84.

65. See the notes to "Perekati-pole," *PSS*, vol. 6, pp. 675–76. Also see T. Ardov, "Zhivoi original 'Perekati-Polia,'" in *Otrazheniia lichnosti* (Moscow: Sfinks, 1909).

66. Page numbers refer to Chekhov, "Perekati-pole," in *PSS*, vol. 6.

67. Such an attitude would be confirmed by Chekhov's apparent conviction that the man with whom he shared his room at Sviatye Gory was a spy, presumably sent by the government. Chekhov reported this belief to his sister, who mentioned it in a memoir. M. P. Chekhov, *Anton Chekhov i ego siuzhety* (Moscow, 1923), p. 23, cited in Chekhov, *Pis'ma*, vol. 2, p. 382. It is difficult to imagine that a tsarist administrator would have felt the need to keep careful track of a young writer best known for the comic sketches he published in the pro-regime *Novoe vremia* and other newspapers. Indeed, Kornei Chukovskii, citing people who had known Surat, denied that he could have been a government agent (K. I. Chukovskii, "Liapsusy," *Literatura i zhizn'*, 17 January 1960, p. 3, cited in Chekhov, *PSS*, vol. 6, p. 676).

68. "Bibliograficheskie novosti. Anton Chekhov. Rasskazy," *Novoe vremia*, no. 4420 (20 June 1888), no page.

69. Ardov, p. 229.

70. Ibid., p. 228.

71. S. G. [Semen Frug], "Literaturnaia letopis': V korchme i v buduare," *Voskhod* (October 1889), p. 36.

72. For some examples of these arguments, see Aleksandr Alekseev, *Obshchestvennaia zhizn' evreev*.

73. A. Chudakov, in "'Mezhdu "Est' Bog" i "Net Boga" lezhit tseloe gromadnoe pole': Chekhov i vera," *Novyi mir*, no. 9 (1996), addresses the recent explosion of scholarship on Chekhov's religiosity. For some examples of it, see de Sherbinin, *Chekhov and Russian Religious Culture*; Senderovich, *Chekhov—s glazu na glaz*; Maxim D. Shreyer, "Conflation of Christmas and Paschal Motifs in Cexhov's 'V rozdestvenskuiu noch,'" *Russian Literature* (15 February 1994); Willa Chamberlain Axelrod, *Russian Orthodoxy in the Life and Fiction of A. P. Chekhov* (Ph.D. diss., Yale University, 1991); Mark Stanley Swift, *Biblical Subtexts and Religious Themes in Works of Anton Chekhov* (Ph.D. diss., Bryn Mawr, 1996).

74. On the mechanics of conversion to Russian Orthodoxy in the late imperial period, see Nicholas B. Breyfogle, *Heretics and Colonizers: Colonization of Transcaucasia, 1830–1890* (Ph.D. diss., University of Pennsylvania, 1998), chap. 5.

75. Dostoevskii, vol. 26, p. 137.

76. Cited in V. P. Konovalova, "Osobennosti putevogo nabroska A. P. Chekhova 'Perekati-pole,'" *Stat'i o Chekhove* (Rostov-na-Donu: Rostovskii-na-Donu gosudarstvennyi pedagogicheskii institut, 1972), p. 47.

77. Leon Shestov locates the break in Chekhov's career between his earlier humorous stories and his later more pessimistic ones with *Ivanov*. "Anton Tchekhov (Creation from the Void)," in *Chekhov and Other Essays,* intro. Sidney Monas (Ann Arbor: University of Michigan Press, 1966), pp. 4, 7, 12.

78. Elena Tolstaia, who sees the description of Susanna Moiseevna as a kind of revenge against Efros, analyzes *Ivanov* as a later, more conciliatory response to their brief engagement (Tolstaia, chap. 1); Aimée Alexandre, who assumes that Chekhov had wanted to marry Efros only for her money, argues that *Ivanov* expresses his horror at his own cynicism and the anti-Semitism he had trouble controlling in himself (Aimée Alexandre, *A la recherche de Tchékhov: Essai de biographie intérieure* [Paris: Editions Buchet/Chastel, 1971], pp. 69–71); and Simon Karlinsky reads "The Mire" and *Ivanov* as equally sympathetic to the Jewish woman who is misunderstood by Russians, calling them "works ... which examined ... the reactions of sensitive Russian Jews to the discrimination and repression with which they had to live ... depicted with remarkable understanding" (in Chekhov, *Anton Chekhov's Life and Thought,* p. 55).

79. Letter to A. P. Chekhov, 24 October 1887, *Pis'ma*, vol. 2, p. 138.

80. B-ch, "Literaturnye ocherki: Fel'eton," *Saratovskii dnevnik*, no. 75 (6 April 1889), p. 1. For more examples of this approach, see Ph., *Russkii kurier*, 1887, no. 325, p. 1, in Iurii Sobolev, ed., *Anton Chekhov: Neizdannye stranitsy* (Moscow: Severnye dni, 1916), p. 83; K-ii, "Pis'mo iz Peterburga," *Moskovskie vedomosti*, no. 36 (5 February 1889), p. 4.

81. A. S-in, "Teatr i muzyka," *Novoe vremia*, no. 7744 (18/30 September 1897), p. 4; Suvorin (1889), in Sobolev, p. 89.

82. Cited in a summary of the views of various publications on mixed marriage ("Otgoloski pechati," *Nedel'naia khronika Voskhoda*, no. 37 [18 September 1883], p. 505). Intriguingly, the year before, *Novoe vremia* had published a piece by Bogrov arguing that obstacles to marriages between Jews and Christians should be eliminated (Bogrov, *Novoe vremia*, no. 2134 [5 February 1882], cited in Klier, *Imperial Russia's Jewish Question,* p. 403).

83. Andrei Belyi, "'Ivanov' na stsene Khudozhestvennogo teatra" (1904), in *Arabeski: Kniga statei* (Moscow: Musaget, 1911), p. 407.

84. See the citation of references to *Revizor* and *Mertvye dushi* in the notes to the 1887 text, *PSS*, vol. 11, pp. 424–25. Those in 1.4, 2.4, and 4.4 remain in the 1889 version.

85. Sozertsatel', "Obo vsem (kriticheskie zametki): 'Ivanov', drama A. Chekhova," *Russkoe bogatstvo*, no. 3 (March 1889), p. 200. Cf. Walter Smyrniw, "Chekov's Depiction of Human Stress: The Case of Nikolai Ivanov," *Canadian Slavonic Papers* (December 1992).

86. Cynthia Ozick agrees that Chekhov has "made use, consciously or otherwise, of a culturally embedded myth" [about wealthy, exploitative Jews], but she also points out that Chekhov has "twelve points of view about everyone and everything." Ozick, "Twelve Points of View: Cynthia Ozick on *Ivanov*," *The New Theater Review: A Lincoln Center Publication*, no. 17 (Fall 1997), p. 10.

87. Letter to M. V. Kiseleva, 14 January 1887, *Pis'ma*, vol. 2, p. 12.

88. M. I. Chaikovskii, letter to A. P. Chekhov, 7 February 1889, in *Gosudarstvennaia biblioteka SSSR im. Lenina. Zapiski otdela rukopisi. vyp. 8. A. P. Chekhov* (Moscow: Gospolitizdat, 1941), p. 72.

89. On the right, see Kol'tsov, *Grazhdanin*, no. 54 (23 February 1889), p. 3; S-in, p. 4. On the left, cf. K-ii, p. 4.

90. *Pis'ma*, vol. 7, p. 471. Chekhov responded to Suvorina's letter on 10 November 1897.

91. Levitina, *Russkii teatr*, vol. 1, pp. 190–91.

92. See Chapter 2 for an explanation of the difference between the two words and their histories.

93. For this reason, Anton Chekhov and his family persistently lied to his older brother Nikolai, informing him that he (Nikolai) had only typhoid, when in fact he was dying of tuberculosis. See Rayfield, p. 196.

94. "It seems that certain influential newspapers, for which Mr. Chekhov works and which have loyal readers and supporters, helped him in Petersburg more than a little" (Sozertsatel', p. 210).

95. Letter to A. S. Suvorin, 30 December 1888, *Pis'ma*, vol. 3, pp. 110, 111, 115.

96. For a reading of "Rothschild's Fiddle" as another story in which Chekhov "does not envision the solution of the Jewish question," see Rosenshield, p. 503.

97. A. A. Suvorin, letter to A. P. Chekhov, 6 September 1888, *Pis'ma*, vol. 2, p. 530.

98. Letter to A. S. Suvorin, 30 December 1888, *Pis'ma*, vol. 3, pp. 109–10.

99. Ibid., 11 September 1888, vol. 2, p. 326.

100. James Shapiro, *Shakespeare and the Jews* (New York: Columbia University Press, 1996), p. 1.

CONCLUSION

1. See the references to Orzeszkowa's works listed in A. P. Chekhov, *Polnoe sobranie sochinenii*, p. 197.

2. On Leskov, Suvorin, and the "Jewish question," see Safran, "Ethnography, Judaism, and the Art of Nikolai Leskov."

3. With the exception of *Golos* [The Voice], liberal Russian publications before 1881 maintained a consensus "that the Jews were remediable, that the Pale must be abolished and that the negative features of Jewish life must be combated with education" (Klier, *Imperial Russia's Jewish Question*, p. 373).

4. See, for instance, the chapter "The Slavophiles and Nationalism" in Martin Malia, *Alexander Herzen and the Birth of Russian Socialism, 1812–1855* (Cambridge: Harvard University Press, 1961).

5. Zhabotinskii, pp. 88–90.

6. See Nakhimovsky, esp. pp. 44–53.

7. Babel', p. 282. The story cannot be dated precisely; it was not published during the author's lifetime.

8. Ibid., p. 280.

BIBLIOGRAPHY

Abramovich, S. Y. [Mendele Moykher Sforim]. *Tales of Mendele the Book Peddler.* Ed. Dan Miron and Ken Frieden. Trans. Ted Gorelick and Hillel Halkin. New York: Schocken, 1996.

Agursky, Mikhail. "Conversions of Jews to Christianity in Russia." *Soviet Jewish Affairs,* vol. 20, nos. 2–3 (Autumn–Winter 1990).

Ahad ha-Am. "Imitation and Assimilation." In *Modern Hebrew Literature,* ed. Robert Alter. New York: Behrman House, 1975.

Aksenfeld, Yisroel. "The Headband." In *The Shtetl,* ed. and trans. Joachim Neugroschel. Woodstock, N.Y.: Overlook Press, 1989.

Alekseev, Aleksandr. *Obshchestvennaia zhizn' evreev, ikh nravy, obychai, i predrassudki, s prilozheniem biografii avtora.* Novgorod, 1868.

Alexandre, Aimée. *A la recherche de Tchékhov: Essai de biographie intérieure.* Paris: Editions Buchet/Chastel, 1971.

Altbauer, Moshe. "Aspects of the Life of Abraham Ezofowicz, Treasury Minister of the Grand Duchy of Lithuania in the Days of Zygmunt I Jagiełło—a Historical-Philological Sketch (in Hebrew)." *Gal-Ed,* no. 12 (1991).

Al'tman, M. S. *Razgovory s Viacheslavom Ivanovym.* St. Petersburg: Inapress, 1995.

Anderson, Benedict. *Imagined Communities: Reflections on the Origin and Spread of Nationalism.* London: Verso, 1983.

Annenkov, Pavel Vasilevich. "The Literary Type of the Weak Man (Apropos of Turgenev's Story 'Asya')." Trans. Tatiana Goerner. *Ulbandus Review,* vol. 1, nos. 1–2 (Fall 1977–Spring 1978).

Anninsky, Lev. "In a Somersaulting Spaceship." Trans. Helen Burlingame. *Common Knowledge* (Spring 1995).

An-skii, Semen. *Sobranie sochinenii.* St. Petersburg: Prosviashcheniia, 1913.

Ardov, A. S. *Evrei-evangelisty.* Moscow: N. L. Kazetskogo, 1914.

Ardov, T. "Zhivoi original 'Perekati-Polia.'" In *Otrazheniia lichnosti.* Moscow: Sfinks, 1909.

Armstrong, John. *Nations Before Nationalism.* Chapel Hill: University of North Carolina Press, 1982.

Aronson, I. Michael. *Troubled Waters: The Origins of the 1881 Anti-Jewish Pogroms in Russia.* Pittsburgh, Pa.: University of Pittsburgh Press, 1990.

Auerbach, Erich. "Figura." In *Scenes from the Drama of European Literature.* Minneapolis: University of Minnesota Press, 1984.

Augustine. *The Confessions of St. Augustine.* Trans. John K. Ryan. New York: Image Books, 1960.

Axelrod, Willa Chamberlain. *Russian Orthodoxy in the Life and Fiction of A. P. Chekhov.* Ph.D. diss., Yale University, 1991.

Babel', Isaak. *Sochineniia v 2 tomakh.* Moscow: Terra, 1996.

Baker, Mark. "The Reassessment of *Haskala* Ideology in the Aftermath of the 1863 Polish Revolt." *Polin,* vol. 5 (1990).

Bakhtin, M. M. "The *Bildungsroman* and Its Significance in the History of Realism (Toward a Historical Typology of the Novel)." In *Speech Genres and Other Late Essays,* trans. Vern W. McGee, ed. Caryl Emerson and Michael Holquist. Austin: University of Texas Press, 1986.

———. "Forms of Time and of the Chronotope in the Novel." In *The Dialogic Imagination: Four Essays by M. M. Bakhtin,* ed. Michael Holquist, trans. Michael Holquist and Caryl Emerson. Austin: University of Texas Press, 1981.

Balibar, Etienne, and Immanuel Wallerstein. *Race, Nation, Class: Ambiguous Identities.* Trans. Chris Turner. London: Verso, 1991.

Barash, Moshe. *Icon: Studies in the History of an Idea.* New York: New York University Press, 1992.

Bartal, Israel. *Ha-loyehudim ve-hevratam besifrut ivrit veyidish bemizrah eropah ben ha-shanim 1856–1914.* Ph.D. diss., Hebrew University, 1980.

———. "'The Heavenly City of Germany' and Absolutism à la Mode d'Autriche: The Rise of the Haskala in Galicia." In *Toward Modernity: The European Jewish Model,* ed. Jacob Katz. New Brunswick, N.J.: Transaction Books, 1987.

B-ch. "Literaturnye ocherki: Fel'eton." Review of Chekhov, *Ivanov. Saratovskii dnevnik,* no. 75 (6 April 1889).

Bellyustin, I. S. *Description of the Clergy in Rural Russia.* Trans. Gregory L. Freeze. Ithaca, N.Y.: Cornell University Press, 1985.

Belyi, Andrei. "'Ivanov' na stsene Khudozhestvennogo teatra" (1904). In *Arabeski: Kniga statei.* Moscow: Musaget, 1911.

Benjamin, Walter. "The Storyteller: Reflections on the Works of Nikolai Leskov." In *Illuminations*, ed. Hannah Arendt, trans. Harry Zohn. New York: Schocken, 1969.

Ben-Yehuda, Eliezer. *A Dream Come True*. Trans. T. Muraoka. Ed. George Mandel. Boulder, Colo.: Westview Press, 1993.

Berdiaev, Nikolai A. "Khristianstvo i antisemitizm: Religioznaia sud'ba evreistva." In *Taina Izrailia: "Evreiskii vopros" v russkoi religioznoi mysli kontsa XIX–pervoi poloviny XX vv.*, ed. V. F. Boikov. St. Petersburg: Sofiia, 1993.

———. *The Russian Idea*. Trans. R. M. French. Hudson, N.Y.: Lindisfarme Press, 1992.

Berlin, Isaiah. "Herder and the Enlightenment." In *Vico and Herder: Two Studies in the History of Ideas*. London: Hogarth Press, 1976.

———. "The Romantic Revolution: A Crisis in the History of Modern Thought." In *The Sense of Reality: Studies in Ideas and Their History*. London: Chatto and Windus, 1996.

Bernstein, Herman. *The History of a Lie: "The Protocols of the Wise Men of Zion," a Study*. New York: Ogilvie, 1921.

Bernstein, Ignaz. *Yidishe shprikhverter un rednsartn*. New York: Brider Kaminsky, 1908.

Bernstein, Laurie. *Sonia's Daughters: Prostitutes and Their Regulation in Imperial Russia*. Berkeley: University of California Press, 1995.

Bhabha, Homi K. *The Location of Culture*. New York: Routledge, 1994.

Biale, David. "Eros and Enlightenment: Love Against Marriage in the East European Jewish Enlightenment." *Polin*, vol. 1 (1986).

"Bibliograficheskie izvestiia." Review of Leskov, "Vladychnyi sud." *Pravoslavnyi sobesednik* (April 1887).

"Bibliograficheskie novosti. Anton Chekhov. Rasskazy." Review of Chekhov, "Perekati-pole." *Novoe vremia*, no. 4420 (20 June 1888).

Blejwas, Stanislaw. "Polish Positivism and the Jews." *Jewish Social Studies*, vol. 46, no. 1 (Winter 1984).

Blok, Alexander. *Sobranie sochinenii v 8 tomakh*. Moscow: Khud. lit., 1960.

Bogrov, Grigorii Isaakovich. Editorials in *Russkii evrei*, nos. 3, 4, 5, 8, 10, 13, 14 (1883).

———. Letters to L. Levanda, 1880s. In "Iz perepiski L. O. Levandy," ed. A. E. Landau. *Evreiskaia biblioteka*, vol. 10 (1903).

———. Letter to N. A. Nekrasov, 5 February 1871. In *Literaturnoe nasledstvo*, vols. 51–52 (1949).

———. "Man'iak: Nebyvalyi sluchai iz zhizni molodogo psikhiatra." *Voskhod*, nos. 1–5 (1884).

———. "Poimannik." *Evreiskaia biblioteka* (1874).

———. *Sobranie sochinenii*. Odessa: Sherman, 1912–13.

———. "Talmud i Kabbala po 'Russkomu Vestniku.'" *Russkii evrei*, nos. 9, 11, 13, 16 (1879).

———. *Zapiski evreia v dvukh chastiakh.* St. Petersburg: V. Tushnova, 1874.

———. "Zhit' ili ne zhit' evreiam povsemestno v Rossii?" *Slovo*, no. 2 (1878).

Bogrov, V. *Dmitrii Bogrov i ubiistvo Stolypina.* Berlin: Strela, 1931.

Bogrova, Vera. Memoirs of V. Bogrova. Gen. Ms. Coll. Bogrova, Manuscript Archives, Columbia University Library.

Brafman, I. A. *Das Buch vom Kahal, auf Grund einer neuen Verdeitschung des russischen Originals.* Trans. Siegfried Passarge. Leipzig: Hammer-Verlag, 1928.

———. *Kniga kagala.* Vilna: Pechatnia gubernskogo pravleniia,1869.

———. *Żydzi i kahały.* Warsaw: Drukarnia synów St. Niemiry, 1914.

Breyfogle, Nicholas B. *Heretics and Colonizers: Colonization of Transcaucasia, 1830–1890.* Ph.D. diss., University of Pennsylvania, 1998.

Bristow, Edward J. *Prostitution and Prejudice: The Jewish Fight Against White Slavery, 1870–1939.* New York: Schocken, 1982.

Brooks, Jeffrey. *When Russia Learned to Read: Literacy and Popular Literature, 1861–1917.* Princeton, N.J.: Princeton University Press, 1985.

Bukhbinder, N. A. *Literaturnye etiudy.* Leningrad: Nauka i shkola, 1927.

Bulgarin, Faddei Venediktovich. *Ivan Ivanovich Vyzhigin.* Moscow: Itogi, 1993.

Butkiewiczówna, Irena. *Powieści i nowele żydowskie Elizy Orzeszkowej.* Lublin: Towarzystwo naukowe Katolickiego uniwersytetu lubelskiego, 1937.

Cała, Alina. *Asymilacja Żydów w Królestwie Polskim (1864–1897): Postawy, konflikty, stereotypy.* Warsaw: Państwowy Instytut Wydawniczy, 1989.

———. *The Image of the Jew in Polish Folk Culture.* Jerusalem: Magnes Press, 1995.

Cassedy, Steven. *To the Other Shore: The Russian Jewish Intellectuals Who Came to America.* Princeton, N.J.: Princeton University Press, 1997.

Chaikovskii, M. I. Letter to A. P. Chekhov, 7 February 1889. In *Gosudarstvennaia biblioteka SSSR im. Lenina. Zapiski otdela rukopisi. vyp. 8. A. P. Chekhov.* Moscow: Gospolitizdat, 1941.

Chekhov, Anton P. *Anton Chekhov's Life and Thought: Selected Letters and Commentary.* Trans. Michael Henry Heim. Ed. Simon Karlinsky. Berkeley: University of California Press, 1973.

———. *Polnoe sobranie sochinenii i pisem v 30 tomakh.* Moscow: Nauka, 1974.

Chekhov, Mikhail. *Zakony o evreiakh: Spravochnaia knizhka dlia evreev i dlia uchrezhdenii, vedaiushchikh dela o evreiakh.* Yaroslavl: E. G. Fal'k, 1899.

Chekhov, M. P. *Anton Chekhov i ego siuzhety.* Moscow: n.p., 1923.

Chernyshevskii, N. G. *Estetika i literaturnaia kritika.* Moscow: Khud. lit., 1951.

Chudakov, A. "'Mezhdu "Est' Bog" i "Net Boga" lezhit tseloe gromadnoe pole': Chekhov i vera." *Novyi mir*, no. 9 (1996).

Cohn, Adolf J. "Przegląd literacki." Review of Orzeszkowa, *Meir Ezofowicz. Izraelita*, vol. 2, no. 4 (1878).

Conrad, Joseph L. "Sensuality in Cexov's Prose." *Slavic and East European Journal,* vol. 24, no. 2 (Summer 1980).

Dal', Vladimir. *Tolkovyi slovar' zhivogo velikorusskogo iazyka.* St. Petersburg: M. O. Vol'f, 1903.

de Maegd-Soëp, Carolina. *Chekhov and Women: Women in the Life and Work of Chekhov.* Columbus, Ohio: Slavica, 1987.

de Sherbinin, Julie. *Chekhov and Russian Religious Culture: The Poetics of the Marian Paradigm.* Evanston, Ill.: Northwestern University Press, 1997.

Detko, Jan. "Narodowy aspekt kwestii żydowskiej u Elizy Orzeszkowej." *Biuletyn Żydowskiego Instytutu Historycznego w Polsce,* no. 40 (1961).

Dostoevskii, Fedor M. *Polnoe sobranie sochinenii v 30 tomakh.* Leningrad: Nauka, 1983.

Dreizin, Felix. *The Russian Soul and the Jew: Essays in Literary Ethnocriticism.* Washington, D.C.: University Press of America, 1990.

Dubnow, S. M. *History of the Jews in Russia and Poland from the Earliest Times Until the Present Day.* New York: Ktav, 1975.

Dudakov, Savelii. *Istoriia odnogo mifa: Ocherki russkoi literatury XIX–XX vv.* Moscow: Nauka, 1993.

[Edgerton, William B]. "Leskov, Nikolay Semyonovich." In *Encyclopedia Judaica,* vol. 11. Jerusalem: Ketzer, 1971.

———. "Leskov and Russia's Slavic Brethren." *American Contributions to the Fourth International Congress of Slavicists, Moscow, September 1958.* The Hague: Mouton, 1958.

Eisenbach, Artur. *The Emancipation of the Jews in Poland, 1780–1870.* Oxford: Basil Blackwell in Association with the Institute for Polish-Jewish Studies, 1991.

Elets, Iu. "Biografiia Vsevoloda Vladimirovicha Krestovskogo." In Vsevolod Vladimirovich Krestovskii, *Sobranie sochinenii,* vol. 1. St. Petersburg: Obshchestvennaia pol'za, 1899.

Endelman, Todd M. "Jewish Converts in Nineteenth-Century Warsaw: A Quantitative Analysis." *Jewish Social Studies,* vol. 4, no. 1 (Fall 1997).

Engels, Friedrich. "The Origin of the Family, Private Property, and the State." In *The Marx-Engels Reader,* ed. Robert Tucker. New York: W. W. Norton, 1978.

Engelstein, Laura. *The Keys to Happiness: Sex and the Search for Modernity in Fin-de-Siècle Russia.* Ithaca, N.Y.: Cornell University Press, 1992.

Etkes, Emanuel. "Immanent Factors and External Influences in the Development of the Haskalah Movement in Russia." In *Toward Modernity: The European Jewish Model,* ed. Jacob Katz. New Brunswick, N.J.: Transaction Books, 1987.

Ettinger, S. *Anti-Semitism in the Soviet Union: Its Roots and Consequences.* Jerusalem: The Hebrew University of Jerusalem, 1983.

———. *Ben polin le-rusiya.* Jerusalem: Mosad Bialik, 1994.

———. "The Modern Period." In *A History of the Jewish People*, ed. H. H. Ben-Sasson. Cambridge: Harvard University Press, 1976.

Evreiskaia entsiklopediia. St. Petersburg: Brokgauz-Efron, n.d. (c. 1910). Facs. ed., Moscow: Terra, 1991.

Faresov, A. I. *Protiv techenii*. St. Petersburg: M. Merkushev, 1904.

Fishman, David E. *Russia's First Modern Jews: The Jews of Shklov*. New York: New York University Press, 1995.

Florensky, Pavel. *Iconostasis*. Trans. Donald Sheehan and Olga Andreev. Crestwood, N.Y.: St. Vladimir's Seminary Press, 1996.

———. *The Pillar and Ground of the Truth*. Trans. Boris Jakim. Princeton, N.J.: Princeton University Press, 1997.

Frank, Joseph. Foreword to David Goldstein, *Dostoyevsky and the Jews*. Austin: University of Texas Press, 1981.

Frankel, Jonathan. "Assimilation and the Jews in Nineteenth-Century Europe: Towards a New Historiography?" In *Assimilation and Community: The Jews in Nineteenth-Century Europe*, ed. Jonathan Frankel and Steven Zipperstein. Cambridge: Cambridge University Press, 1992.

———. *Prophecy and Politics: Socialism, Nationalism, and the Russian Jews, 1862–1917*. Cambridge: Cambridge University Press, 1981.

Freeze, Gregory L. *The Parish Clergy in Nineteeth-Century Russia: Crisis, Reform, Counter-Reform*. Princeton, N.J.: Princeton University Press, 1983.

Freidin, Gregory. "Authorship and Citizenship: A Problem for Modern Russian Literature." *Stanford Slavic Studies*, vol. 1 (1987).

———. *A Coat of Many Colors: Osip Mandelstam and His Mythologies of Self-Presentation*. Berkeley and Los Angeles: University of California Press, 1987.

———. "Romans into Italians: Russian National Identity in Transition." In *Russian Culture in Transition*. Stanford, Calif.: Stanford Slavic Studies, 1993.

Gellner, Ernest. *Nations and Nationalism*. Oxford: Basil Blackwell, 1983.

Gertsen, Aleksandr I. *Byloe i dumy*. Moscow: Khud. lit., 1958.

———. *Sochineniia v 9 tomakh*. Moscow: Khud. lit., 1958.

Gilman, Sander L. *Jewish Self-Hatred: Anti-Semitism and the Hidden Language of the Jews*. Baltimore: The Johns Hopkins University Press, 1986.

———. *The Jew's Body*. New York: Routledge, 1991.

———. "Salome, Syphilis, Sarah Bernhardt, and the Modern Jewess." In *The Jew in the Text: Modernity and the Construction of Identity*, ed. Linda Nochlin and Tamar Garb. London: Thames and Hudson, 1995.

Ginzburg, Shaul. *Historishe verk*. 3 vols. New York: S. M. Ginzburg Testimonial Committee, 1937.

———. *Meshumodim in tsarishn rusland*. New York: Bicher-ferlag, 1946.

Gogol, N. V. *Sobranie sochinenii v 6 tomakh*. Moscow: Khud. lit., 1959.

Goldstein, David. *Dostoyevsky and the Jews*. Austin: University of Texas Press, 1981.

Gorelov, A. A. *N. S. Leskov i narodnaia kul'tura*. Leningrad: Nauka, 1988.

Gor'kii, Maksim. *Sobranie sochinenii v 30 tomakh*. Moscow: Khud. lit., 1953.

Gould, Stephen Jay. *The Mismeasure of Man*. New York: W. W. Norton, 1996.

Graetz, Heinrich Hirsch. *History of the Jews* (1853–75). Philadelphia: Jewish Publication Society, 1898.

Greenfeld, Liah. *Nationalism: Five Roads to Modernity*. Cambridge: Harvard University Press, 1992.

——. "Transcending the Nation's Worth." *The Proceedings of the American Academy of Arts and Sciences: Reconstructing Nations and States*, vol. 122, no. 3.

Grimstad, Knut Andreas. "Nikolai Leskov and the Problem of Polyethnicity." In *Celebrating Creativity: Essays in Honor of Jostein Børtnes*, ed. Knut Andreas Grimstad and Ingunn Lunde. Bergen, Norway: University of Bergen, 1997.

Gruss, Noé. "N. S. Leskov et les Juifs de Russie." *AMIF* (revue de l'association des médecins israélites de France) (1974).

Grynberg, Henryk. "The Jewish Theme in Polish Positivism." *The Polish Review*, vol. 25, nos. 3–4 (1980).

Gustafson, Richard F. Introduction to Pavel Florensky, *The Pillar and Ground of the Truth*, trans. Boris Jakim. Princeton, N.J.: Princeton University Press, 1997.

Guy, Donna J. *Sex and Danger in Buenos Aires: Prostitution, Family, and Nation in Argentina*. Lincoln: University of Nebraska Press, 1991.

Ha-Cohen, Mordecai ben-Hillel. *Me-erev ad erev: Ne'esaf min ha-maamarim ha-yeshanim u-min ha-hadashim*. Vilna: Bi-defus P. Gerber, 1904.

Halkin, Simon. *Modern Hebrew Literature from the Enlightenment to the Birth of the State of Israel: Trends and Values*. New York: Schocken, 1970.

Hegel, Georg W. F. *The Philosophy of History*. Trans. J. Sibree. Buffalo, N.Y.: Prometheus Books, 1991.

Hertz, Aleksander. *The Jews in Polish Culture*. Trans. Richard Lourie. Evanston, Ill.: Northwestern University Press, 1988.

Hobsbawm, E. J. *Nations and Nationalism Since 1780: Programme, Myth, Reality*. Cambridge: Cambridge University Press, 1990.

Il'ia Repin. Ed. Grigorii Sternin and Elena Kirillina. St. Petersburg: Avrora, 1996.

Inglot, Mieczysław. "The Image of the Jew in Polish Narrative Prose of the Romantic Period." *Polin*, vol. 2 (1987).

"Iz obshchestvennoi khroniki." *Vestnik Evropy* (October 1889).

Jabotinsky. *See* Zhabotinskii.

Jackson, Robert Louis. "'If I Forget Thee, O Jerusalem': An Essay on Chekhov's 'Rothschild's Fiddle.'" *Slavica Hierosolymitana: Slavic Studies of the Hebrew University*, vol. 3 (1978).

Jankowski, Edmund. *Eliza Orzeszkowa*. Warsaw: Państwowy Instytut Wydawniczy, 1973.

Jersild, Austin Lee. "From Savagery to Citizenship: Caucasian Mountaineers and Muslims in the Russian Empire." In *Russia's Orient: Imperial Borderlands and Peoples, 1700–1917,* ed. Daniel R. Brower and Edward J. Lazzerini. Bloomington: Indiana University Press, 1997.

The Jewish Encyclopedia. New York: Funk and Wagnalls, 1901.

J. J. K. [Kotarbiński]. "Przegląd literacki: Meir Ezofowicz, powieść z życia Żydów, przez Elizę Orzeszkową." *Przegląd Tygodniowy,* no. 2 (31 January 1879).

———. "Sprawa żydowska w powieściach i pismach Orzeszkowej." *Kraj,* no. 50 (13/25 December 1891).

Katz, Jacob. *From Prejudice to Destruction: Anti-Semitism, 1700–1933.* Cambridge: Harvard University Press, 1980.

"K biografii N. S. Leskova (+21 fevralia 1895 g.)." *Russkaia starina* (December 1895).

Khodarkovsky, Michael. "'Not by Word Alone': Missionary Policies and Religious Conversion in Early Modern Russia." *Comparative Studies in Society and History: An International Quarterly,* vol. 38, no. 2 (April 1996).

K-ii. "Pis'mo iz Peterburga." *Moskovskie vedomosti,* no. 36 (5 February 1889).

Klier, John D. "The Concept of 'Jewish Emancipation' in a Russian Context." In *Civil Rights in Imperial Russia,* ed. Olga Crisp and Linda Edmundson. Oxford: Clarendon Press, 1989.

———. *Imperial Russia's Jewish Question, 1855–1881.* Cambridge: Cambridge University Press, 1995.

———. *Russia Gathers Her Jews: The Origins of the Jewish Question in Russia, 1772–1825.* Dekalb: Northern Illinois University Press, 1985.

———. "*The Times of London*: The Russian Press and the Pogroms of 1881–1882." Paper no. 308 in *The Carl Beck Papers in Russian and East European Studies,* ed. William Chase and Ronald Linden. Pittsburgh, Pa.: Russian and East European Studies Program, University of Pittsburgh, 1984.

Klier, John D., and Shlomo Lambroza, eds. *Pogroms: Anti-Jewish Violence in Modern Russian History.* Cambridge: Cambridge University Press, 1993.

Kolakowski, Leszek. *The Alienation of Reason: A History of Positivist Thought.* Trans. Norbert Guterman. Garden City, N.J.: Anchor Books, 1969.

Kölbing, Eugen. *The Romance of Sir Beues of Hamtoun.* London: N. Trübner, 1885.

Kolodziej, Joyce Story. *Eliza Orzeszkowa's Feminist and Jewish Works in Polish and Russian Criticism.* Ph.D. diss., Indiana University, 1975.

Kol'tsov. Review of Chekhov, *Ivanov. Grazhdanin,* no. 54 (23 February 1889).

Koni, A. F. "Avtorskoe pravo." In *Novyi entsiklopedicheskii slovar',* vol. 1. St. Petersburg: Brokgauz-Efron, 1911–16.

Konovalova, V. P. "Osobennosti putevogo nabroska A. P. Chekhova 'Perekati-pole.'" *Stat'i o Chekhove.* Rostov-na-Donu: Rostovskii-na-Donu gosudarstvennyi pedagogicheskii institut, 1972.

Kornblatt, Judith Deutsch. "Vladimir Solov'ev on Spiritual Nationhood, Russia, and the Jews." *Russian Review*, vol. 56, no. 2 (April 1997).

Kowalczyk, Witold. "Stereotyp Żyda w twórczości Wsiewołoda Kriestowskiego (na przykładzie trylogii *Żyd*)." In *Literackie portrety Żydów*. Ed. Eugenia Łoch. Lublin: Wydawnictwo Uniwersytetu Marii Curie-Skłodowskiej, 1996.

Kraszewski, J. I. "Listy z zakątka." Review of Orzeszkowa, *Meir Ezofowicz*. *Biesiada Literacka*, no. 173 (1879).

Krestovskii, Vsevolod Vladimirovich. *Sobranie sochinenii*. St. Petersburg: Ob-shchestvennaia pol'za, 1899.

———. *T'ma egipetskaia*. St. Petersburg: Sovremennik, 1995.

Kunitz, Joshua. *Russian Literature and the Jew: A Sociological Inquiry into the Nature and Origin of Literary Patterns*. New York: Columbia University Press, 1929.

Kuprin, A. I. *Sobranie sochinenii v 6 tomakh*. Moscow: Khud. lit., 1994.

Kuznets, Simon. "Immigration of Russian Jews to the United States: Background and Structure." *Perspectives in American History*, vol. 9 (1975).

L-a, L. [Lev Levanda]. "Bibliografiia: O Żydach i kwestii żydowskiej . . . (Vilno, 1882)." *Russkii evrei*, no. 24 (1882) and no. 41 (1882).

Lavretskii, A. "Chekhov i evrei." *Novyi put'*, no. 28 (31 July 1916).

Lazarev, M. "Literaturnaia letopis': Zadachi i znachenie russko-evreiskoi belletritiki (Kriticheskii eskiz)." *Voskhod* (May–June 1885).

Lederhendler, Eli. "Modernity Without Emancipation or Assimilation? The Case of the Russian Jews." In *Assimilation and Community: The Jews in Nineteenth-Century Europe*, ed. Jonathan Frankel and Steven Zipperstein. Cambridge: Cambridge University Press, 1992.

———. *The Road to Modern Jewish Politics: Political Tradition and Political Reconstruction in the Jewish Community of Tsarist Russia*. New York: Oxford University Press, 1989.

Lermontov, M. Iu. *Sobranie sochinenii v 4 tomakh*. Leningrad: Nauka, 1981.

Leskov, Andrei. *Zhizn' Nikolaia Leskova po ego lichnym, semeinym i nesemeinym zapisiam i pamiatiam, v dvukh tomakh*. Moscow: Khud. lit., 1984.

Leskov, Nikolai Semenovich. Articles on Jewish rituals, published in *Peterburgskaia gazeta*: "Religioznye obriady evreev." no. 244 (11 December 1880); "Religioznye obriady evreev," no. 245 (12 December 1880); "Religioznye obriady evreev: Shabash, ili prazdnik sedmits," no. 252 (20 December 1880); "Religioznye obriady evreev. Shabash, ili prazdnik sedmits," no. 254 (23 December 1880); "Religioznye obriady evreev: Novomesiachiia," no. 255 (24 December 1880); "Religioznye obriady evreev: Prigotovlenie opresnokov," no. 1 (1 January 1881); "Religioznye obriady evreev: Paskha," no. 8 (10 January 1881); "Religioznye obriady evreev: Mezhdu Paskhoiu i Piatidesiatnitseiu," no. 14 (17 January 1881); "Religioznye obriady evreev," no. 20 (24 January 1881); "Religioznye obriady evreev: Plach o razorenii Ierusalima," no. 26 (31 January 1881); "Religioznye obriady evreev:

Prazdnik trub (ili Novogo Goda)," no. 38 (14 February 1881); "Obriady i sueveriia evreev: Den' ochishcheniia," no. 68 (21 March 1881).

————. [pseud. ***]. Articles on Jewish rituals, published in *Ezhenedel'noe novoe vremia*: "Evreiskaia nabozhnost' (Religioznye obriady i obychai u evreev)," no. 53 (3 January 1880); "Evreiskoe blagochestie v nachale dnia," no. 55 (17 January 1880); "Evreiskaia nabozhnost'. III," no. 57 (31 January 1880); "Evreiskaia nabozhnost': Vecher i noch' v evreiskom dome. IV," no. 59 (14 February 1880).

[————]. Articles on Jewish rituals, published in *Peterburgskaia gazeta*: "Kuchki (Zavtrashnii prazdnik u evreev)," no. 260 (21 September 1884); "Evreiskaia gratsiia (Verbnyi den' u evreev)," no. 265 (26 September 1884); "Radostnyi den' u evreev (Poslednii prazdnik oseni)," no. 268 (29 September 1884); "Religioznye illiuminatsii u evreev," no. 348 (18 December 1884).

[————]. "Evrei i khristianskaia krov'." *Peterburgskaia gazeta*, no. 20 (21 January 1892).

————. [pseud. N. L.]. "Evrei i obiazannosti khristian (Retsenziia)." *Istoricheskii vestnik*, no. 5 (May 1882).

[————]. *Evrei v Rossii* (St. Petersburg, 1884); reissued, with an introduction by Iulii Gessen. Petrograd, 1919 [cover 1920].

[————]. "Evreiskie 'khedery' i 'melamedy.'" *Peterburgskaia gazeta*, no. 11 (12 January 1885).

————. "Irodova rabota." *Istoricheskii vestnik* (April 1882).

————. "Iskanie shkol staroobriadtsami." *Birzhevye vedomosti*, nos. 28, 30, 37, 43, 44, 48, 65, 71, 89, 102, 134 (1869).

————. *The Jews in Russia: Some Notes on the Jewish Question.* Ed. and trans. Harold Klassel Schefski. Princeton, N.J.: Kingston Press, 1986.

[————]. "Kniga kagala (retsenziia)." *Novoe vremia*, no. 2186 (1 April 1882).

————. Letters to A. S. Suvorin. Rukopisnyi otdel Instituta russkoi literatury i iskusstva, St. Petersburg, f. 268.

[————]. "Novozavetnye evrei." *Peterburgskaia gazeta*, no. 4 (5 January 1885).

————. *O raskol'nikakh goroda Rigi, preimushchestvenno v otnoshenii k shkolam.* St. Petersburg, 1863.

————. *Polnoe sobranie sochinenii.* Moscow: Terra, 1996.

————. "Rakushanskii melamed: Rasskaz na bivuake." *Russkii vestnik*, no. 3 (March 1878).

————. "Rasskazy kstati: Novozavetnye evrei." *Nov'*, vol. 1, no. 1 (November 1884).

————. "Rasskazy kstati: Ukha bez ryby." *Nov'*, vol. 8, no. 7 (February 1886).

————. "Russkie deiateli v ostzeiskom krae." *Istoricheskii vestnik* (November 1883).

————. *Schism in High Society: Lord Radstock and His Followers.* Trans. James Y. Muckle. Nottingham, England: Bramcote Press, 1995.

————. "Skazanie o Fedore-khristianine i o druge ego Abrame-zhidovine." *Russkaia mysl'*, no. 12 (20 December 1886).

———. "S liud'mi drevlego blagochestiia." *Biblioteka dlia chteniia*, vol. 153, no. 11 (November 1863).

———. *Sobranie sochinenii v 11 tomakh*. Moscow: Khud. lit., 1958.

———. *Sobranie sochinenii v 12 tomakh*. Moscow: Pravda, 1989.

———. "U evreev." *Peterburgskaia gazeta*, no. 251 (12 September 1884).

———. *Velikosvetskii raskol*. St. Petersburg: V. Tushnova, 1877.

[———] "Vladychnyi sud. Byl' (Iz nedavnikh vospominanii)." *Strannik*, vol. 1, nos. 1–2 (1877).

———. "Zhidovskaia kuvyrkollegiia. Povest'. Ob odnom Kromchanine i o trekh zhidovinakh." *Gazeta A. Gattsuka*, no. 33 (14 August 1882), no. 34 (21 August 1882), no. 35 (28 August 1882), no. 36 (4 September 1882).

Lessing, G. E. *Gesammelte Werke*. Leipzig, 1858.

———. "Lessing: *Die Juden*." Trans. Ernest Bell. In *The Enlightenment: A Comprehensive Anthology*, ed. Peter Gay. New York: Simon and Schuster, 1973.

Levin, Harry. *The Gates of Horn: A Study of Five French Realists*. New York: Oxford University Press, 1963.

Levinskii, Vl. *Perekreshchenets iz evreiskogo byta*. Moscow, 1870.

Levitina, Viktoriia. *Russkii teatr i evrei*. Israel: Biblioteka-Aliia, 1988.

Likhachev, Dmitrii S. *Literatura—real'nost'—literatura*. Leningrad: Sovetskii pisatel', 1984.

Linetski, Isaac Joel. *The Polish Lad*. Trans. Moshe Spiegel. Philadelphia: Jewish Publication Society, 1975.

Litvak, Olga. *The Literary Response to Conscription: Individuality and Autonomy in the Russian Jewish Enlightenment*. Ph. D. diss., Columbia University, 1999.

Lombroso, C. *Der Antisemitismus und die Juden*. Leipzig: Georg H. Wigands Verlag, 1894.

Lotman, Iu. M. "'Pikovaia dama' i tema kart i kartochnoi igry v russkoi literature nachala XIX veka." In *Pushkin*. St. Petersburg: Isskustvo-SPB, 1995.

Löwe, Heinz-Dietrich. *The Tsars and the Jews: Reform, Reaction, and Anti-Semitism in Imperial Russia, 1772–1917*. New York: Harwood Academic Publishers, 1993.

Lur'e, S. E. Letters to F. M. Dostoevskii. In "Neizdannye pis'ma k Dostoevskomu," ed. S. Ipatova. *Dostoevskii: Materialy i issledovaniia*, vol. 12. St. Petersburg: Akademiia nauk, 1996.

L'vov-Rogachevsky, V. *A History of Russian-Jewish Literature* (1922). Ed. and trans. Arthur Levin. Ann Arbor, Mich.: Ardis, 1979.

Maimon, M. "Istoriia odnoi kartiny." *Evreiskaia letopis'*, vol. 1 (1923).

Maimon, Solomon. *The Autobiography of Solomon Maimon*. Trans. J. Clark Murray. London: East and West Library, 1954.

———. *Geschichte des eigenen Lebens*. Berlin: Schocken, 1935.

———. "Iz avtobiografii Salomona Maimona, Glavy I–XVIII." *Evreiskaia biblioteka*, vol. 1 (1871).

———. *Salomon Maimons Lebensgeschichte, von ihm selbst geschrieben.* Berlin: Karl Philipp Moritz, 1792–93.

Malia, Martin. *Alexander Herzen and the Birth of Russian Socialism, 1812–1855.* Cambridge: Harvard University Press, 1961.

Markish, Shimon. "Osip Rabinovich." *Vestnik evreiskogo universiteta v Moskve,* nos. 1(5) and 2(6) (1994).

———. "Russko-evreiskaia literatura: Predmet, podkhody, otsenki." *Novoe literaturnoe obozrenie,* no. 15 (1995).

———. "Stoit li perechityvat' L'va Levanda?" *Vestnik evreiskogo universiteta v Moskve,* nos. 3(10) and 4(11) (1995).

Marx, Karl. "The Communist Manifesto" (1848). In *Selected Writings,* ed. David McLellan. New York: Oxford University Press, 1990.

———. "*On the Jewish Question,* by Bruno Bauer" (1843). In *Selected Writings,* ed. David McLellan. Oxford: Oxford University Press, 1990.

Mathewson, Rufus W., Jr. *The Positive Hero in Russian Literature.* Stanford, Calif.: Stanford University Press, 1958.

McLean, Hugh. *Nikolai Leskov: The Man and His Art.* Cambridge: Harvard University Press, 1977.

———. "Theodore the Christian Looks at Abraham the Hebrew: Leskov and the Jews." *California Slavic Studies,* vol. 7 (1973).

Medvedev, P. N./M. M. Bakhtin. *The Formal Method in Literary Scholarship: A Critical Introduction to Sociological Poetics.* Trans. Albert J. Wehrle. Baltimore: The Johns Hopkins University Press, 1978.

Mehl, Dieter. *The Middle English Romance of the Thirteenth and Fourteenth Centuries.* New York: Barnes and Noble, 1969.

Mendelsohn, Ezra. *On Modern Jewish Politics.* New York: Oxford University Press, 1993.

Merezhkovskii, D. S. "Evreiskii vopros kak russkii" (1915). In *Taina Izrailia: "Evreiskii vopros" v russkoi religioznoi mysli kontsa XIX–pervoi poloviny XX vv.,* ed. V. F. Boikov. St. Petersburg: Sofiia, 1993.

Miłosz, Czesław. *The History of Polish Literature.* London: Macmillan, 1969.

Mintz, Alan. "*Banished from Their Father's Table": Loss of Faith and Hebrew Autobiography.* Bloomington: Indiana University Press, 1989.

Miron, Dan. *A Traveler Disguised: The Rise of Modern Yiddish Fiction in the Nineteenth Century.* New York: Schocken, 1973.

Miron, Dan, and Anita Norich. "The Politics of Benjamin III: Intellectual Significance and Its Formal Correlatives in Sh. Y. Abramovitsh's *Masoes Benyomin Hashlishi.*" In *The Field of Yiddish: Studies in Language, Folklore, and Literature.* Philadelphia: Institute for the Study of Human Values, 1980.

Mirsky, D. S. *A History of Russian Literature: From Its Beginnings to 1900.* New York: Vintage, 1958.

Morson, Gary Saul. *The Boundaries of Genre: Dostoevsky's* Diary of a Writer *and the Traditions of Literary Utopia.* Evanston, Ill.: Northwestern University Press, 1981.

———. "Dostoevsky's Anti-Semitism and the Critics: A Review Article." *Slavic and East European Journal,* vol. 27. no. 3 (Fall 1983).

Moseley, Marcus. *Jewish Autobiography in Eastern Europe: The Pre-History of a Literary Genre.* Ph.D. diss., Oxford University, 1990.

Moser, Charles A.. *Esthetics as Nightmare: Russian Literary Theory, 1855–1870.* Princeton, N.J.: Princeton University Press, 1989.

Mstislavskaia, S. [Sofiia Dubnova-Erlikh]. "Eliza Ozheshko." *Evreiskoe obozrenie,* no. 2 (3 June 1910).

Muckle, James Y. *Nikolai Leskov and the "Spirit of Protestantism."* Birmingham, England: Birmingham Slavonic Monographs, no. 4 (1978).

Müller de Morogues, Inès. *L'oeuvre journalistique et littéraire de N. S. Leskov: Bibliographie.* New York: Peter Lang, 1984.

———. "Le patriotisme de Leskov." *Schweizerische Beiträge zum X. internationalen Slavistenkongress in Sofia 1988.* Bern: Peter Lang, 1988.

Nakhimovsky, Alice Stone. *Russian-Jewish Literature and Identity.* Baltimore: The Johns Hopkins University Press, 1992.

Nałęcz, Roman. "Przegląd literacki." Review of *Meir Ezofowicz. Przegląd Polski,* vol. 55 (1879).

Nathans, Benjamin Ira. *Beyond the Pale: The Jewish Encounter with Russia, 1840–1900.* Ph.D. diss., University of California at Berkeley, 1995.

Nedel'naia khronika Voskhoda, vol. 8, no. 45 (1884), p. 1284; no. 44 (1887), p. 1099; and no. 42 (1888), pp. 1–2.

Nekrasov, Nikolai Alekseevich. *Polnoe sobranie sochinenii i pisem v 15 tomakh.* Leningrad: Nauka, 1981.

"Nekrolog." Obituaries of G. Bogrov. *Istoricheskii vestnik,* no. 7 (June 1885); and *Nov',* no. 15 (1885).

Nemilova, Inna S. *The Hermitage Catalogue of Western European Painting: French Painting, Eighteenth Century.* Florence: Giunti Barbèra Martello; Moscow: Iskusstvo, 1986.

Nevskii kritik. "Zhurnal'naia i bibliograficheskaia letopis'." Review of Bogrov, *Zapiski evreia. Vestnik russkikh evreev,* no. 16 (18 April 1871).

The New Standard Jewish Encyclopedia. Ed. Geoffrey Wigoder. New York: Facts on File, 1992.

Niemcewicz, Julian Ursyn. *Lejbe i Sióra.* Cracow: Towarzystwo Miłośników Książki, 1931.

———. *Rok 3333 czyli sen niesłychany.* Warsaw: Biblioteka im. Jana Jelieńskiego, 1911.

Nochlin, Linda. "Starting with the Self: Jewish Identity and Its Representation." In

The Jew in the Text: Modernity and the Construction of Identity, ed. Linda Nochlin and Tamar Garb. London: Thames and Hudson, 1995.

Noemi, A. "Eliza Orzheshko." *Rassvet*, no. 20 (16 May 1910).

"Novye knigi." Review of Leskov, "Vladychnyi sud." *Delo*, no. 9 (1879).

Obriady evreiskie, ili opisanie tseremonii i obyknovenii, nabliudaemykh evreiami kak vne khrama, tak ravno i vo vse torzhestvennye dni, pri obrezanii, pri svad'bakh, rodinakh, smerti, pogrebeniiakh i proch. Orel: I. Sytina, 1830.

Ochs, Michael Jerry. *St. Petersburg and the Jews of Russian Poland, 1862–1905.* Ph.D. diss., Harvard University, 1986.

Opalski, Magdalena. "The Concept of Jewish Assimilation in Polish Literature of the Positivist Period." *The Polish Review*, vol. 32, no. 4 (1987).

———. "Jewish Reformers of Polish Society and Their Programs in Nineteenth-Century Polish Fiction." *Proceedings of the Conference on Poles and Jews: Myth and Reality in the Historical Context.* New York: Columbia University, 1986.

———. *The Jewish Tavern-Keeper and His Tavern in Nineteenth-Century Polish Literature.* Jerusalem: The Zalman Shazar Center, 1986.

Opalski, Magdalena, and Israel Bartal. *Poles and Jews: A Failed Brotherhood.* Hanover, Mass.: Brandeis University Press, 1992.

Orbach, Alexander. *New Voices of Russian Jewry: A Study of the Russian-Jewish Press of Odessa in the Era of the Great Reforms, 1860–1871.* Leiden: J. Brill, 1980.

Orshanskii, I. G. *Evrei v Rossii. Ocherki ekonomicheskogo i obshchestvennogo byta russkikh evreev.* St. Petersburg: O. I. Baksta, 1877.

———. *Russkoe zakonodatel'stvo o evreiakh. Ocherki i issledovaniia.* St. Petersburg: A. E. Landau, 1877.

Orzeszkowa, Eliza. *Listy Zebrane.* Ed. Edmund Jankowski. Wrocław: Zakład Imienia Ossolińskich, Wydawnictwo Polskiej Akademii Nauk, 1955.

———. [E. Orzheshko.] *Meir Ezofovich.* Novel Supplement to *Svet*, vol. 9, 1882.

———. *Meer Ezofowicz* (1878). Warsaw: Spółdzielna Wydawnicza "Czytelnik," 1988.

———. [Orzheshkova, El.] *Meer Ezofovich: Povest' iz byta zhidov.* Moscow: Gazeta A. Gattsuka, 1881. Originally pub. as novel supplement to *Gazeta A. Gattsuka*, no. 6 (1880).

———. [Orzheshko, Eliza.] *Meer Ezofovich: Povest' iz evreiskogo byta.* Biblioteka Zapadnoi polosy Rossii, vol. 1 (1879), vol. 2 (1879), and vol. 1 (1880).

———. "Orzeszkowa o nacjonaliźmie żydowskim." *Kurier Warszawski*, 24, 25, and 26 September 1911.

———. "O Żydach i kwestii żydowskiej." Vilna, 1882.

———. "Pis'ma Elizy Orzeszko (1876–1883 g.)." *Evreiskaia starina*, vol. 7 (1914).

———. *Pisma zebrane.* Ed. Julian Krzyżanowski. Warsaw: Wiedza, 1948.

———. [Orzheshko, E.] "Tormozy sliianiia evreev s korennym nasileniem." *Voskhod*, no. 11 (1881).

"O perekhode evreev v pravoslavie." *Novorossiiskii telegraf*, no. 4588 (7 November 1888).

"Otgoloski pechati." *Nedel'naia khronika Voskhoda*, no. 37 (18 September 1883).

"Ot perevodchika." In *Meir Ezofovich: Povest' iz byta zhidov*, by Eliza Orzeszkowa. Moscow: Gattsuk, 1881.

Ozick, Cynthia. "Twelve Points of View: Cynthia Ozick on *Ivanov*." *New Theater Review: A Lincoln Center Publication*, no. 17 (Fall 1997).

Paperno, Irina. *Chernyshevsky and the Age of Realism: A Study in the Semiotics of Behavior*. Stanford, Calif.: Stanford University Press, 1988.

Parthé, Kathleen. "The Righteous Brothers (and Sisters) of Contemporary Russian Literature." *World Literature Today: A Literary Quarterly of the University of Oklahoma* (Winter 1993).

Patterson, David. *Abraham Mapu: The Creator of the Modern Hebrew Novel*. London: Horovitz, 1964.

———. *A Phoenix in Fetters: Studies in Nineteenth and Early Twentieth Century Hebrew Fiction*. Savage, Md.: Rowman and Littlefield, 1988.

Pearson, Raymond. "Privileges, Rights, and Russification." In *Civil Rights in Imperial Russia*, ed. Olga Crisp and Linda Edmundson. Oxford: Clarendon Press, 1989.

"Perepiska V. V. Rozanova i M. O. Gershenzona, 1909–1918." Ed. V. Proskurina. *Novyi mir*, March 1991.

Perl, Joseph. *Joseph Perl's Revealer of Secrets: The First Hebrew Novel*. Ed. and trans. Dov Taylor. Boulder, Colo.: Westview Press, 1997.

"Petersburgskaia letopis'." *Nedel'naia khronika Voskhoda*, no. 45 (1884).

Pisarev, Dmitry. "Pushkin and Belinsky: *Eugene Onegin*." In *Russian Views of Pushkin's* Eugene Onegin, ed. and trans. Sona Hoisington. Bloomington: Indiana University Press, 1988.

Pisemskii, A. F. *Polnoe sobranie sochinenii*. St. Petersburg: M. O. Vol'f, 1896.

Pontis, Anne-Marie. *Antisémitisme et sexualité*. Paris: Le Lion, 1996.

"Po povodu perekhoda evreev v pravoslavie." *Novorossiiskii telegraf*, no. 4184 (10 September 1888); and no. 4200 (26 September 1888).

Prokop-Janiec, Eugenia. *Międzywojenna literatura polsko-żydowska jako zjawisko kulturowe i artystyczne*. Cracow: Universitas, 1992.

Prus, Boleslaw. *Lalka*. Ed. Józef Bachórz. Wrocław: Zakład Narodowy im. Ossolińskich, 1991.

Pushkin, Aleksandr Sergeevich. *Polnoe sobranie sochinenii*. Leningrad: Akademiia nauk, 1946.

Ragussis, Michael. *Figures of Conversion: "The Jewish Question" and English National Identity*. Durham, N.C.: Duke University Press, 1995.

Rappaport, Steven G. *Jewish Education and Jewish Culture in the Russian Empire, 1880–1914*. Ph. D. diss., Stanford University, 2000.

Rayfield, Donald. *Chekhov: A Life*. London: HarperCollins, 1997.

Renan, Ernest. "What Is a Nation?" In *Nation and Narration*, ed. Homi K. Bhabha. New York: Routledge, 1990.

Reviews of Leskov, "Vladychnyi sud." *Nash vek*, no. 20 (March 1877); *Tserkovno-obshchestvennyi vestnik*, no. 54 (18 May 1877); and *Otechestvennye zapiski*, no. 8 (August 1877).

Rodkiewicz, Witold. *Russian Nationality Policy in the Western Provinces of the Empire During the Reign of Nicholas II, 1894–1905 (Lithuania, Belorussia, Ukraine, Poland).* Ph.D. diss., Harvard University, 1996.

———. "Telling Poles from Russians: The Tsarist Administration and Its Attempts to Define Polish and Russian Nationality in the Western Borderlands of the Russian Empire, 1863–1914." Paper delivered at the American Historical Association, New York, January 1997.

Rogger, Hans. *Jewish Policies and Right-Wing Politics in Imperial Russia.* Oxford: Macmillan, 1986.

———. *National Consciousness in Eighteenth-Century Russia.* Cambridge: Harvard University Press, 1960.

Romodanovskaia, E. K. *Russkaia literatura na poroge novogo vremeni.* Novosibirsk: VO Nauka, 1994.

Rosenshield, Gary. "Dostoevskii's 'The Funeral of the Universal Man' and 'An Isolated Case' and Chekhov's 'Rothschild's Fiddle': The Jewish Question." *Russian Review*, no. 56 (October 1997).

Rozenblit, Marsha L. *The Jews of Vienna, 1867–1914: Assimilation and Identity.* Albany: State University of New York Press, 1983.

"Russkaia literatura." Review of Bogrov, *Zapiski evreia. Syn otechestva*, no. 159 (14 July 1873).

Safran, Gabriella. "Ethnography, Judaism, and the Art of Nikolai Leskov." *Russian Review*, vol. 59 (April 2000).

Said, Edward W. *Orientalism.* New York: Vintage, 1978.

Sal'nikova, T. S. "Ideia bratstva narodov v putevykh ocherkakh N. S. Leskova." *Voprosy russkoi literatury*, vol. 27, no. 1 (1976).

Saltykov-Shchedrin, Mikhail Evgrafovich. *Sobranie sochinenii.* Moscow: Khud. lit., 1965–77.

Sartre, Jean-Paul. *Anti-Semite and Jew: An Exploration of the Etiology of Hate.* Trans. George J. Becker. New York: Schocken, 1995.

Schefski, Harold Klassel. Introduction to *The Jews in Russia: Some Notes on the Jewish Question*, by Nikolai S. Leskov, ed. and trans. Harold Klassel Schefski. Princeton, N.J.: Kingston Press, 1986.

Schur, Nathan. *History of the Karaites.* Frankfurt am Main: Peter Lang, 1992.

Scruton, Roger. *A Dictionary of Political Thought.* New York: Harper and Row, 1982.

Segel, Harold B., ed. *Stranger in Our Midst: Images of the Jew in Polish Literature.* Ithaca, N.Y.: Cornell University Press, 1996.

Sementkovskii, Rostislav I. *Sochineniia.* St. Petersburg: A. F. Marks, 1905.

Senderovich, Savelii. *Chekhov—s glazu na glaz. Istoriia odnoi oderzhimosti A. P. Chekhova.* St. Petersburg: Dmitry Bulanin, 1994.

———. "O chekhovskoi glubine, ili iudofobskii rasskaz Chekhova v svete iudaisticheskoi ekzegezy." In *Avtor i tekst: Sbornik statei*, ed. V. M. Markovich and
Vol'f Shmid. St. Petersburg: S.-Peterburgskogo universiteta, 1996.

S. G. [Semen Frug]. "Literaturnaia letopis': V korchme i v buduare." Review of
Chekhov, "Tina." *Voskhod* (October 1889).

Shapiro, James. *Shakespeare and the Jews.* New York: Columbia University Press,
1996.

Sheringham, Michael. *French Autobiography, Devices and Desires: Rousseau to Perec.*
Oxford: Clarendon Press, 1993.

Shershevskii, I. I. *O Knige kagala.* St. Petersburg: Tip. Skriatina, 1872.

Shestov, Leon. "Anton Tchekhov (Creation from the Void)." In *Chekhov and Other
Essays.* Intro. Sidney Monas. Ann Arbor: University of Michigan Press, 1966.

Shigarin, N. D. "Ot redaktsii." In *Biblioteka Zapadnoi polosy Rossii*, vol. 1. St. Petersburg, 1879.

———. "Russkie evreiskie gazety (po evreiskomu voprosu)." *Biblioteka Zapadnoi
polosy Rossii.* Vol. 2. St. Petersburg, 1879.

Shmeruk, Chone. *The Esterke Story in Yiddish and Polish Literature: A Case Study in
the Mutual Relations of Two Cultural Traditions.* Jerusalem: The Zalman Shazar
Center, 1985.

Sholom Aleichem. *From the Fair.* Trans. Curt Leviant. New York: Penguin, 1985.

Shreyer, Maxim D. "Conflation of Christmas and Paschal Motifs in Cekhov's 'V
rozdestvenskuiu noch.'" *Russian Literature* (15 February 1994).

Shul'gin, V. V. *"Chto NAM v nikh ne nravitsia": Ob antisemitizme v Rossii.* St. Petersburg: Khors, 1992.

S-in, A. "Teatr i muzyka." Review of Chekhov, *Ivanov. Novoe vremia*, no. 7744
(18/30 September 1897).

Slocum, John W. "Who, and When, Were the *Inorodtsy*? The Evolution of the
Category of 'Aliens' in Imperial Russia." *Russian Review*, vol. 57, no. 2 (April
1998).

Slutsky, Yehuda. *Ha-itonut ha-yehudit-rusit bemeah ha-esrim.* Jerusalem: Bet
ha-sefer limudei ha-yahadut, 1978.

———. *Ha-itonut ha-yehudit-rusit bemeah ha-tsha-esreh.* Jerusalem: Bialik
Institute, 1970.

Smith, Anthony. *The Ethnic Orgins of Nations.* Oxford: Basil Blackwell, 1986.

Smyrniw, Walter. "Chekov's Depiction of Human Stress: The Case of Nikolai
Ivanov." *Canadian Slavonic Papers* (December 1992).

Sobolev, Iurii. Review of Chekhov, *Ivanov.* In *Anton Chekhov: Neizdannye stranitsy.*
Moscow: Severnye dni, 1916.

Soboleva. "Evrei." In *Narody Rossii: Etnograficheskie ocherki*, vol. 1. St. Petersburg,
1878–80.

Soloveitchik, Haym. "Maimonides' *'Iggeret Ha-Shemad*: Law and Rhetoric." In *Rabbi
Joseph H. Lookstein Memorial Volume*, ed. Leo Landman. New York: Ktav, 1980.

Solov'ev, Vladimir. "Evreistvo i khristianskii vopros." In *Taina Izrailia: "Evreiskii vopros" v russkoi religioznoi mysli kontsa XIX–pervoi poloviny XX v.v.*, ed. V. F. Boikov. St. Petersburg: Sofiia, 1993.

Sozertsatel'. "Obo vsem (kriticheskie zametki): 'Ivanov,' drama A. Chekhova." *Russkoe bogatstvo*, no. 3 (March 1889).

Stanislawski, Michael. *For Whom Do I Toil? Judah Leib Gordon and the Crisis of Russian Jewry*. New York: Oxford University Press, 1988.

————. "Jewish Apostasy in Russia: A Tentative Typology." In *Jewish Apostasy in the Modern World*, ed. Todd Endelman. New York: Holmes and Meier, 1987.

————. *Tsar Nicholas I and the Jews: The Transformation of Jewish Society in Russia, 1825–1855*. Philadelphia: Jewish Publication Society, 1983.

Steinlauf, Michael C. *Bondage to the Dead: Poland and the Memory of the Holocaust*. Syracuse, N.Y.: Syracuse University Press, 1997.

Stowe, Harriet Beecher. *Uncle Tom's Cabin*. Ed. Elizabeth Ammons. New York: W. W. Norton, 1994.

Supin. "Staraia insinuatsiia ili novaia bessmyslitsa?" Review of Bogrov, *Zapiski evreia. Den'*, no. 15 (1871).

Suvorin, Aleksei S. *Dnevnik*. Moscow: Novosti, 1992.

Svod zakonov Rossiiskoi imperii, Izdanie neoffitsial'noe. St. Petersburg: Russkoe knizhnoe tovarishchestvo Deiatel', 1912.

Swift, Mark Stanley. *Biblical Subtexts and Religious Themes in Works of Anton Chekhov*. Ph.D. diss., Bryn Mawr, 1996.

Szyszman, Simon. *Les Karaïtes d'Europe*. Uppsala, Sweden: University of Uppsala, 1989.

Tagantsev, N. S. *Ulozhenie o nakazaniiakh ugolovnykh i ispravitel'nykh 1885 goda*. St. Petersburg, 1901.

Tarnovskii, Veniamin M. *Prostitutsiia i abolitsionizm: Doklad Russkomu Sifilidologicheskomu i Dermatologicheskomu Obshchestvu*. St. Petersburg: Karla Rikkera, 1888.

Tarnowski, Stanisław. "Z najnowszych powieści polskich." Review of Orzeszkowa, *Meir Ezofowicz. Niwa*, no. 20 (1881).

Tchaikovsky. *See* Chaikovskii.

Terras, Victor. *A History of Russian Literature*. New Haven, Conn.: Yale University Press, 1991.

Thaden, Edward C., ed. *Russification in the Baltic Provinces and Finland, 1855–1914*. Princeton, N.J.: Princeton University Press, 1981.

Tolstaia, Elena. *Poetika razdrazheniia: Chekhov v kontse 1880–kh—nachale 1890–kh godov*. Moscow: Radiks, 1994.

————. "'Tsenzura ne propuskaet . . .': Chekhov i Dunia Efros." *Novoe literaturnoe obozrenie*, no. 8 (1994).

Tolstoi. Leo. *The Death of Ivan Ilych and Other Stories*. Trans. Aylmer Maude. New York: New American Library, 1960.

————. *Sobranie sochinenii v dvadtsati tomakh.* Moscow: Khud. lit., 1964.

Turgenev, I. Letter to G. Bogrov, 14/26 March 1882. In *Dokumenty po istorii literatury i obshchestvennosti.* Moscow: Gosizdat, 1923.

————. *Polnoe sobranie sochinenii i pisem v 28 tomakh.* Moscow: Akademiia nauk, 1963.

Tynjanov, Jurij. "On Literary Evolution." In *Readings in Russian Poetics: Formalist and Structuralist Views,* ed. Ladislaw Matejka and Krystyna Pomorska. Ann Arbor: Michigan Slavic Contributions, 1978.

Ugolovnoe ulozhenie, Vysochaishe utverzhdennoe 22 marta 1903 g., Izdanie neoffitsial'- noe. St. Petersburg: Gos. tip., 1903.

Valdman, Betty. "Turgenev, Jews, and the Russian-Jewish Press." *Shvut,* vol. 6, no. 22 (1997).

Vasmer, Max. *Russisches etymologisches Wörterbuch.* Heidelberg: Karl Winter, 1953.

Verner, Andrew M. "What's in a Name? Of Dog-Killers, Jews, and Rasputin." *Slavic Review* (Winter 1994).

Verzhekovskii, Father Ioann. Letter to the editor. *Kievlianin,* no. 124 (17 October 1867).

Vonliarliarskii, Vasilii A. *Bol'shaia barynia: Roman, povest', rasskazy.* Ed. A. A. Il'in-Tomich. Moscow: Sovremennik, 1987.

Waldron, Peter. "Religious Toleration in Late Imperial Russia." In *Civil Rights in Imperial Russia,* ed. Olga Crisp and Linda Edmundson. Oxford: Clarendon Press, 1989.

Walicki, Andrzej. *A History of Russian Thought from the Enlightenment to Marxism.* Trans. Hilda Andrews Rusiecka. Stanford, Calif.: Stanford University Press, 1974.

————. *Philosophy and Romantic Nationalism: The Case of Poland.* Oxford: Clarendon Press, 1982.

Waxman, Meyer. *A History of Jewish Literature.* New York: Thomas Yoseloff, 1960.

Weeks, Theodore R. *Nation and State in Late Imperial Russia: Nationalism and Russification on the Western Frontier, 1863–1914.* DeKalb: Northern Illinois University Press, 1996.

Weinerman, Eli. "Racism, Racial Prejudice, and Jews in Late Imperial Russia." *Ethnic and Racial Studies,* vol. 17, nos. 3–4 (July–October 1994).

————. *Russification in Imperial Russia: The Search for Homogeneity in the Multi-national State.* Ph.D. diss., Indiana University, 1996.

Weissberg, Liliane. "Jews or Hebrews? Religious and Political Conversion in Herder." Paper presented at a faculty seminar at the University of Pennsylvania, The West in Global Perspective, 28 February 1997.

Werth, Paul W. "Baptism, Authority, and the Problem of Zakonnost' in Orenberg Diocese: The Induction of over 800 'Pagans' into the Christian Faith." *Slavic Review,* vol. 56, no. 3 (Fall 1997).

Wisse, Ruth R. *The Schlemiel as Modern Hero.* Chicago: University of Chicago Press, 1971.

Wittig, Susan. *Stylistic and Narrative Structures in the Middle English Romances.* Austin: University of Texas Press, 1978.

Yaroshevski, Dov. "Empire and Citizenship." In *Russia's Orient: Imperial Borderlands and Peoples, 1700–1917,* ed. Daniel R. Brower and Edward J. Lazzerini. Bloomington: Indiana University Press, 1997.

Zaslavskii, D. "Evrei v russkoi literature." *Evreiskaia letopis',* vol. 1 (1923).

Zhabotinskii, Vladimir (Zeev). "Chetyre stat'i o 'chirikovskom intsidente.'" *Izbrannoe.* Israel: Biblioteka-Aliia, 1978.

Zholkovskii, A. K., and M. B. Iampol'skii. *Babel'/Babel.* Moscow: Carte Blanche, 1994.

Zipperstein, Steven J. "Ahad Ha'am and the Politics of Assimilation." In *Assimilation and Community: The Jews in Nineteenth-Century Europe,* ed. Jonathan Frankel and Steven Zipperstein. Cambridge: Cambridge University Press, 1992.

———. "'Assimilation,' *Haskalah,* and Odessa Jewry." In *The Great Transition: The Recovery of the Lost Centers of Modern Hebrew Literature,* ed. Glenda Abramson and Tudor Parfitt. Totowa, N. J.: Rowman and Allenheld, 1985.

———. "Heresy, Apostasy, and the Transformation of Joseph Rabinovich." In *Jewish Apostasy in the Modern World,* ed. Todd M. Endelman. New York: Holmes and Meier, 1987.

———. *The Jews of Odessa: A Cultural History, 1794–1881.* Stanford, Calif.: Stanford University Press, 1986.

Zola, Emile. *Nana.* New York: Modern Library, 1929.

Zolotonosov, Mikhail. *"Master i Margarita" kak putevoditel' po subkul'ture russkogo antisemitizma (SRA).* St. Petersburg: Inapress, 1995.

Żyga, Aleksander. "Wymienne nazwy Żydów w piśmiennictwie polskim w latach 1794–1863 na tle głównych orientacji społeczno-politycznych i wyznaniowych żydowstwa polskiego: Rekonesans." In *Literackie portrety Żydów.* Ed. Eugenia Łoch. Lublin: Wydawnictwo Uniwersyteta Marie Curie-Skłodowskiej, 1996.

INDEX

References to illustrations are given in italic.

12–13, 14; definition of, 5; and Haskalah, 35, 174; and Jews as prostitutes, 151; and Krestovsky, 101, 103–4, 105, 106; and legal regulations, 9; and Leskov, 145–46; and literature, 20, 36; and Maimon, 1–2; and Marx, 113–14; and national identity, 2, 4, 18–19; and Orzeszkowa, 64, 77, 79–80, 83, 87–90, 95, 102–4, 194; and Poland, 71, 72, 103; and Polish Positivism, 17, 73; and racializing approach, 69; and Russian Empire, 18–19, 105; and Russian literature, 15, 16, 36; and Suvorin, 157, 171, 175; and terms for Jew, 92–93

Jewish canon: and Haskalah, 35, 68–69, 82; and non-Jews, 67–69; and Orzeszkowa, 81–87, 92, 101–2, 104

Jewish conversion: and Bogrov, 32, 33–34; and cantonism, 7, 11, 114–15, 119; and Chekhov, 148, 158, 159, 167–75, 177, 186, 187; and Christian Bible, 103, 111–12, 120–21, 125–26, 132, 134, 169–70, 173, 192, 194; and citizenship, 13; and Disraeli, 91; and geographical separation, 10; and Krestovsky, 99–100, 103–4, 224n108; and legal regulations, 6, 8, 9, 10, 110–11, 112, 113, 120, 122; and Leskov, 108, 110, 111–14, 117, 119–21, 131–35, 145–46, 168, 170; and Maimon, 1–2; and nationalism, 67; and Polish Positivism, 73; and racializing approach, 69; and Russian Empire, 6–7, 8, 171–72; and Russian literature, 112, 113; and sincere/false dichotomy, 5, 69, 104, 108, 111–14, 119–21, 123, 124, 133–34, 168–71, 193, 194; skepticism about, 11–12, 17, 110–11, 139, 157. *See also* Protestantism

Jewish folk culture, 142, 144

Jewish question: and Chekhov, 159, 167, 176, 185, 186, 188–89, 196; debate over, 4, 8, 12, 92, 191; and Dostoevsky, 91, 94, 135, 137–40, 142–43, 145, 196; and Jabotinsky, 195–96; and Leskov, 108, 109, 110, 144, 159; and literary type, 24–25; and Marx, 150–51; and non-Jews, 66–69; and Orzesz-kowa, 77–79, 90, 102, 159; and press, 7, 10, 12; and Saltykov-Shchedrin, 64

Jewish stereotypes: and Chekhov, 159, 161,

179, 187; and Christianity, 96, 131; and Jewish woman/Christian man, 149–50; and Leskov, 54–59, 63, 64, 109, 131; and narratives, 20; and Polish Positivism, 73, 75; and Russian Realism, 16, 17

Jews: as aliens, 8, 14; and Christianity, 25, 118, 162, 163, 183; and citizenship, 31; hetero-geneity of, 4; images of, 102, 149; and Jew-ish conversion, 112; legal regulation of, 6, 8–12, 34; and literary types, 168; and liter-ature, 15–18; and name changes, 9–10, 47; and national identity, 18–20, 66, 67, 68, 69, 86–87, 97–98, 104–6; non-Jews writing about, 58, 66–69, 121; and Poland, 70–80, 81, 83, 92–93, 104; and prostitution, 150–55, 195, 233n18; and Russian Empire, 6–18, 25, 71, 91, 94, 138–39, 149, 151; and Russian literature, 15–18, 53, 64–65, 155, 195–96, 234n33; Russification of, 11, 22, 62, 89, 104, 158, 205n39, 215n94; and syphilis, 154, 233–34n30; terms for Jew, 11, 77, 92–94, 111, 148, 158, 159, 182, 185–86, 222–23n90; as victims, 17, 117, 151, 155, 176, 178–79, 191, 232n16, 234n33

Jeż, Teodor Tomasz, 75

John of Damascus, 136

Judeophilia, *see* Philo-Semitism

Judeophobia: and Bogrov, 33, 49, 54–55, 56; and Chekhov, 157–59; and Dostoevsky, 138–41; and Leskov, 109–10, 135, 145, 222n90; and Poland, 90, 93; and Russia, 91–94, 97–101; and Solv'ev, 118. *See also* Anti-Semitism; Christian Hebraics

Kabbalah, 40–41, 67, 81, 82, 83, 101

Kahals, 91, 97–98

Karaites, 80, 81–82, 84, 220–21n58

Karlinsky, Simon, 159

Kasprowicz, Jan, 74

Katkov, Mikhail, 54, 105, 223n98

Katz, Jacob, 66, 67–68, 69, 102

Khudekov, Sergei, 191

Khvol'son, Daniel, 5

Kiseleva, Maria, 166

Kłosy [Ears of Grain], 65, 77

Knipper, Ol'ga, 159

Konopnicka, Maria, 16
Kornblatt, Judith, 118
Korolenko, Vladimir, 17, 225n111, 234n33
Kotarbinski, J., 79–80
Kovner, Abraham Uri, 137, 140, 142
Kraszewski, Józef Ignacy, 16, 74, 78, 85
Kraushar, Aleksander, 78
Krestovsky, Vsevolod, *The Yid is Coming*, 98–106, 148, 155, 157, 163, 194, 224nn101, 108
Krylov, Ivan, 57
Kryzhanovskaia, V. I., 98
Kugel, A. R., 158
Kukolnik, Nestor, 149
Kunitz, Joshua, 149
Kuprin, Aleksandr, 153–54

Lamarck, Jean-Baptiste-Pierre-Antoine de Monet de, 154
Landau, Adolf, 38
Landy, Michał, 17, 71
Lermontov, Mikhail, 45, 193–94; *Hero of Our Time*, 46, 49, 58–59; "The Criminal," 53
Leskov, Andrei, 130
Leskov, Nikolai: and Bogrov, 54–60; and cantonism, 114, 115–17, 118, 119, 120, 122–24, 130–31; and Chekhov, 158, 191; and Dostoevsky, 110, 135–46; "Episcopal Justice," 114, 118–31, 134, 139, 144, 145; and Jewish acculturation, 4, 170, 190, 194; and Jewish conversion, 108, 110, 111–14, 117, 119–21, 131–35, 145–46, 168, 170; and Jewish question, 108, 109, 110, 144, 159; and Jewish ritual, 108, 141–42, 230n68; and Jewish stereotypes, 54–59, 63, 64, 109, 131; *The Jews in Russia*, 109, 226n3; and literary types, 25, 54–59, 145, 193; "The Melamed of Österreich," 54–60, 64, 109; "New Testament Jews," 131–35, 145; "On the Edge of the World," 119–20; and Orzeszkowa, 64–65, 191; and parables, 128–29, 135, 136, 143–44; and Polish literature, 90; and Russian Orthodoxy, 117–18, 124, 128, 130, 131, 132, 134, 146, 168, 170, 194; "The Tale of Fedor the Christian and His Friend Abraham the Jew," 135, 144; and Western critics, 6

Lessing, Gotthold Ephraim, 50
Levanda, Lev, 16, 37, 54, 63
Levitan, Isaac, 147
Lewental, Franciszek Salezy, 77, 85
Lifshits, Gershon, 62
Likhachev, Dmitry, 122–23
Lilienblum, Moses Leib, 15
Linetski, Y. Y., 40
Literary types: and Bogrov, 37, 40, 43, 44, 46, 49, 50, 51–52, 53, 54, 60, 62, 106, 193; and Chekhov, 25, 148, 162, 175–76, 185, 187, 193; and Chernyshevsky, 20, 21, 22, 23, 24, 43, 51, 187; and Haskalah, 25, 34, 35–36, 37; and Leskov, 25, 54–59, 145, 193; and Orzeszkowa, 25, 66, 84–85, 87–90, 94–96, 106–7, 193; and Polish literature, 75; and Russian literature, 21, 22, 24, 53, 59, 149–50, 152–54, 186; and self-reform, 21, 22, 23–24, 187, 193
Litvak, Olga, 49
Lur'e, Sofia, 30, 31, 137

Maciejowski, Ignacy, 74
Maimon, Moisei, *The Marranos*, 1–2, 3, 4, 7, 196–97
Maimon, Solomon, 37–41, 46, 49, 51, 61, 83, 102, 174, 193
Maimonides, 81, 82, 83, 101
Mandelstam, Osip, 17, 132
Mapu, Abraham, 15, 22, 36
Markish, Shimon, 33
Marks, Adolf, 191
Marx, Karl, 113–14, 150–51, 163, 171, 186
Maskilim, *see* Haskalah
McLean, Hugh, 109, 123, 144
Medvedev, Pavel, 21
Meisels, Dov, 71
Mendele Moikher Sforim, 15–16, 42, 61, 216n97
Mendelssohn, Moses, 35, 36, 50
Méyet, Leopold, 77
Minei-chetii (collection of Russian saints' lives), 144
Mintz, Alan, 37
Morson, Gary Saul, 138
Mosalski, I. T., 74

Muckle, James, 132
Müller de Moroques, Inès, 145

and Kabbalah according to *Russkii vestnik*"

Russkoe bogatstvo [Russian Wealth], 183

Russo-Turkish War, 91

Saltykov-Shchedrin, Mikhail, 17, 29, 64, 78, 113, 191

Salvador, Joseph, 78

Sarecki, Zygmunt, 74

Sartre, Jean-Paul, 104

Schulz, Bruno, 17

Scott, Walter, *Ivanhoe*, 149, 150

Self-reform: and Babel, 196; and Bogrov, 43–44, 51, 52, 55, 60, 61, 62, 193; and Chekhov, 187, 193; and Haskalah, 15–16; and Jewish assimilation, 2, 195; and Jewish self-transformation, 4, 22, 23; and literary types, 21, 22, 23–24, 187, 193

Sementkovsky, Rostislav, 23, 90, 191

Senderovich, Savelii, 161–63, 235n52

Shabel'skaia, E. A., 98

Shakespeare, William, *The Merchant of Venice*, 25, 148, 149, 160, 162, 174, 189, 195

Shaykevich, N. M., 42

Sherbinin, Julie de, 159

Shershevsky, I. I., 78, 84

Shestov, Leon, 174

Shigarin, N. D., 90

Shliapkin, Il'ia, 130

Sholem Aleikhem, 5, 30, 61

Shteinberg, Iakov, 62

Sir Beves of Hamtoun, see The English Milord

Slavic folk beliefs, 25, 142

Socialism, 8, 72

Solov'ev, Vladimir, 118, 132

Stolypin, Peter, 34

Stowe, Harriet Beecher, *Uncle Tom's Cabin*, 227n30

Strepetova, Pelegaia, 181–82, *182*

Sue, Eugène, 99

Surat, A., 168–69, 173

Suvorin, Aleksei: and Chekhov, 160, 163, 183, 185, 186, 187, 191; and Jewish assimilation, 157, 171, 175; and Jewish conversion, 177;

and Jewish question, 166, 167; and Jewish stereotypes, 161; and Leskov, 56–57, 191; and literary types, 168

Svet [The World], 65, 223n92

Świętochowski, Aleksander, 16

Syn otechestva [Son of the Fatherland], 33, 61

Talmud, 38, 66, 67, 81, 82, 83, 101–2, 121, 126, 140

Tarnovsky, Veniamim, 153, 154, 155, 157, 164, 165, 185, 233n22, 234n32

Tchaikovsky, Modest, 181, 183

Tchernikhovsky, Saul, 30

Thomas Aquinas, Saint, 125

Tolstaia, Elena, 158, 166, 237n78

Tolstoy, Leo, 117, 165, 170; *The Kreutzer Sonata*, 151–52, 156

Traugutt, Romuald, 76

Troy, Jean-François de, 161

Turgenev, Ivan: "Asya," 21, 22, 23, 24, 107; and Bogrov, 29–30; *Fathers and Children*, 20; and Jews as prostitutes, 150; and literary types, 20, 21, 23, 24, 25, 43, 107; *Notes of a Hunter*, 28–29, 34; *On the Eve*, 23; "The Yid," 150, 196, 232n12

Ukrainian language, 127

United States, 8, 12, 19

Vestnik russkikh evreev* [Herald of the Russian Jews], 30

Vodovodov, V., 109

Voltaire, 67, 68, 73, 101

Volynsky, Akim, 158

Vonliarliarsky, Vasily, *The Great Lady*, 45–46, 47, 48, 49, 51, 60

Voskhod [The Sunrise], 31. *See also Nedel'naia khronika Voskhoda*

Wagner, N. P., 98

Weinerman, Eli, 11

Western provinces, 70–71, 75, 76, 77, 84, 88, 102, 104, 106

Wielopolski, Aleksander, 71

Women's rights, 77

Yiddishism, 72

Yiddish language: and Bogrov, 38, 41; and Haskalah, 15, 16, 35, 36, 37; and Polish Jews, 6, 77, 79; and Polish Positivism, 74

Yushkevich, Semyon, 62

Zapolska, Gabriela, 74

Zhabotinskii, *see* Jabotinsky

Zhitlovsky, Chaim, 22, 23

Zionist movement, 8, 61, 72

Zola, Emile, 153, 164

Zygmunt (king of Poland), 81

CONTRAVERSIONS

JEWS AND OTHER DIFFERENCES